Въ Субботу, 26-го Октября 1913 г.,

# 2-й АБОНЕМЕНТНЫЙ КОНЦЕРТЪ.

## ПРОГРАММА:

1. \*) Ботническая сюита . . . . . . . . . *Т. Куула.*

    Подъ управленіемъ **автора.**

2. Концертъ для ф.-п. съ оркестромъ . . . . *Грига.*

    **П. Гренджеръ.**

3. Испанская рапсодія . . . . . . . . . . *М. Равеля.*

4. 5 Gedichte для голоса съ оркестромъ. . . *Вагнера.*

    Солистка ЕГО ВЕЛИЧЕСТВА

    **Фелія Литвинъ.**

5. Вступленіе къ «Парсифалю». . . . . . . *Вагнера.*

Разовыя цѣны мѣстамъ—повышенныя (см. стр. 11).

---

\*) Въ 1-й разъ.

4

# Percy Grainger

# Percy Grainger

## JOHN BIRD

**Paul Elek**
London

for
J.B.P.
'My playmate beyond the hills'
in
friendship
and
admiration

First published 1976 by
Elek Books Limited
54-58 Caledonian Road    London    N1 9RN

Copyright © 1976 by John Bird

ISBN 0 236 40004 5

Printed in Great Britain by Unwin Brothers Limited
The Gresham Press, Old Woking, Surrey
A member of the Staples Printing Group

# Contents

# List of Illustrations

viii

# Prefatory Note
## by Benjamin Britten and Peter Pears

To have met Percy Grainger even as an old man is a cherished memory. His warmth, his originality, his charm were unforgettable, and his genial energy had already become a myth. The masterly folksong arrangements with their acutely beautiful feeling for sound were our first musical introduction, and later the preparation of a record of his music was an exciting and revealing experience. Repeated performances strengthened our respect for his work, and our few meetings confirmed our affection and admiration for the man.

It was hardly to be expected that the depths beneath the dazzling surface could be without some turbulence. In John Bird's sympathetic and tactful biography he has beautifully balanced the brilliance and turbulence of this unbalanced genius — we are grateful to him.

*Benjamin Britten*

*Peter Pears*

# Appreciation by Leopold Stokowski

My memories of Percy Grainger take me back to London before the First World War when he was already one of the finest pianists on the concert platform.

Later I had the pleasure of conducting for him in memorable performances of his own delightful works and of the Grieg concerto in Philadelphia and Hollywood.

The spontaneity and warmth in his playing and compositions made him a very special musician to work with.

# Author's Preface

No single work can hope to do justice to the life of George Percy Grainger. Perhaps no musician of any era has bequeathed such a large and bewildering collection of letters, manuscripts and documents to the world. The fruits of his teeming intellect and imagination present the student at times with glaring inconsistencies and infuriating questions, some of which must remain unanswered and perhaps unanswerable. His own relentless pursuit of what he felt was truth created many admirers and a few enemies. After much heart-searching I decided to deal in this book with a few aspects of his life which some urged me to leave untouched. Conscious as I was that it would be all too easy to make of him a monster or a buffoon, I have earnestly tried to cover these matters with compassion and with no eye to sensationalism. I firmly believe that to have omitted such areas of his life would have presented a picture not only incomplete and misleading but also incorrect and far removed from what Grainger himself would have wished.

To protect the innocent involvement of those still living, however, I have sometimes deliberately fallen short of as ruthless and thorough-going an investigation as I had originally intended. The onus for such a biography will fall on another generation of writers. The time for a complete and detailed assessment of his life and artistic output is perhaps not yet ripe. This work, then, may be regarded as a preliminary exercise.

It is implicit in much of Grainger's autobiographical writing that he believed there was a direct link between the man, the artist and his art. There are times when this bond is very hard to follow, yet the temptation remains very strong to read into Grainger's life a pattern of a Jungian character. I have tried to resist such an interpretation, but this book is in part an attempt to enquire into the truth as Grainger saw it by constant and carefully considered reference to his written legacy. Despite this there were times when I felt it necessary to draw a few subjective conclusions which I hope are not taken as an abuse of the biographer's privileged position.

Much has already been written about Grainger, yet with a few notable exceptions most of the writers have fallen into the traps which Grainger himself knowingly or otherwise set. He would often tell the most outrageous lies and present absurd ideas (especially to journalists) simply to provoke. His views on any particular subject could change drastically within a matter of days or he could present completely different views to different people on the same day. This is sometimes confusing especially when his feelings of friendship or enmity towards other people could be presented in differing lights on any one occasion. Grainger consistently presented a façade of childlike lightheartedness and jollity. It was his natural defence against what he felt was a hostile world. And though the childlike elements are reasonably consistent throughout all levels of his life, there was a rarely perceived level of tragedy and self-torture. I typed the last full stop in this book sad that I had not been able to explore every recess of Grainger's mind and life but happy that the last word on the subject had not been written.

I have made extensive use of Grainger's letters and other writings in the text. These are often written in what he chose to call 'Blue-eyed' or 'Nordic' English — a partly successful attempt to create for his own purposes and aims a form of the language purged of all words with Latin or Greek roots. Grainger's spelling and grammar, moreover, are often strange and unconventional. I have scrupulously avoided, however, any temptation to change this in any way with the exception of the few very obvious typing errors. It was Grainger's habit to follow a 'Blue-eyed' word with the conventional English word in either [square] or ((double)) brackets. In a handful of cases where Grainger has not provided the equivalent to an obscure linguistic creation of his own which might cause some difficulty, I have done so to facilitate the reader's comprehension. For the sake of uniformity I have changed all of Grainger's brackets to the double form, reserving the square brackets for my own use. On no occasion have I used the term '[sic]', believing this to indicate an un-necessary attitude of superiority and condescension on the part of the writer.

Every effort has been made to credit the sources of material and to obtain copyright clearance. I apologise for any unwitting infringements.

My researches have brought me into contact with many individuals throughout the world and I have gained many friends thereby. I list below all those to whom I owe a debt of gratitude. The list also contains the names of those individuals and organizations who have so kindly granted me permission to quote from books, letters, radio interviews and other documents. The help given by universities, libraries and museums was unforgettable. I must also record the monumental indifference and indeed hostility which came from a blessedly small number of indi-viduals, institutions and companies in reply to my enquiries. To spare them the embarrassment and myself the dubious pleasure I am refrain-ing from listing their names.

I owe Ella Grainger more than words can tell. Without her inspiration and continued interest, this book would never have been. I thank my parents and brother for their boundless generosity, patience and kindness. To Tony Wood, Leslie Howard, Lionel Carley and Patrick O'Shaughnessy I owe my profound acknowledgements for having nursed me with enormous skill and patience through every stage of the book's production. Together, they have unsplit more split infinitives, unmixed more mixed metaphors and demolished more clichés than Fowler ever knew existed (though through sheer cussedness I have kept a few). To my mother a special note of thanks for the sore fingers and two wrecked typewriters caused by copying so much research material.

There was also a small number of people whose personal kindness and generosity far outreached all my hopes and expectations and to indicate my special thanks I am mentioning their names at the head of the alphabetical list that follows.

Gordon, Evie and Robin Aldridge (Australia), Michael Aspinall (Italy), Gregor Benko (United States), Norman, Edith, James and Dorothy Bird (United Kingdom), Storm Bull (United States), Burnett Cross (United States), the late Kitty Eisdel (Australia), William Fitzwater (Australia), Eileen Joyce (United Kingdom/Australia), Stewart Manville (United States), Dr. Kaare K. Nygaard (United States), N. F. Sandby (Denmark), Michael R. Scott (United Kingdom), David Stanhope (Australia).

*New Zealand*
Frederick Page.

*Norway*
Dagny Petersen, S. Torsteinson ('Troldhaugen'—Hop).

*Singapore*
Miss Hee-Leng Tan.

*South Africa*
R. F. M. Immelman (University of Cape Town).

*United Kingdom*
John Amis (BBC), Amyn Bhagat, Stephen Banks, Michael Blayney, the late Sir Arthur Bliss, Alan Boon (Mills & Boon Limited), Sir Adrian Boult, Trevor Bray, Benjamin Britten, Ann Buckner, the late Basil Cameron, Douglas Copeland, H. P. Chadwyck-Healey, G. Chandler (Record Office—City of Liverpool), Shura Cherkassky, R. A. Clarke, A. B. Craven (Leeds City Libraries), Kathleen Dale, Frank Daunton (Schott & Co. Ltd), Prof. Basil Deane (University of Sheffield), T. H. Eckersley (BBC), Captain Jeremy Elwes, the late Philip Emanuel (the Delius Trust), Bryan Fairfax, R. J. E. Fellows, Eric Fenby (Royal Academy of

Music), R. L. E. Foreman, the late Rolf Gardiner, William E. R. Hallgarth, Bernard Herrmann, Imogen Holst, Frank Howes, Derek Hudson, the late Dom Anselm Hughes OSB, H. Montgomery Hyde, the late Lieut. Colonel C. H. Jaeger, Antony Jennings (BBC), Dr Maud Karpeles, Michael Kennedy, William Krasnik, Marion P. Linton (National Library of Scotland), A. L. Lloyd, Dr Brigitte Lohmeyer (Embassy of Federal Republic of Germany), Alastair Londonderry, Geoffrey Milne (The Decca Record Company Ltd), Donald Mitchell (Faber Music), Edward D. Myers (United States Information Service), Raymond Newport, Ates Orga, Richard Ormond (National Portrait Gallery), Peter Pagan (Bath Municipal Libraries and Victoria Art Gallery), Margaret Palmer (Oxford University Press), Michael Parkin (The Parkin Gallery), John Payne, Peter Pears, Mark Physick, K. Ploughman (Royal Danish Embassy), David Pogue, William Rathbone, Paul Ries, Routledge & Kegan Paul Ltd, Brian A. L. Rust, the late Cyril Scott, Marjorie Hartston Scott, Kaikhosru Shapurji Sorabji, Ronald Stevenson, Leopold Stokowski, Gerald Stonehill, Roger G. Tanner, John M. Thomson, Ursula Vaughan Williams, Prof. C. P. Wells, Dr Percy Young.

*Australia*
Beryl Armstrong, Martin Arnold, Ian Atkins, Vera Bradford, Alan Brown (ABC), Prof. Frank Callaway (University of Western Australia), Michael Cannon, Denis Condon, Roger Covell (University of New South Wales), A. G. W. Dent, George and Kay Dreyfus, Neville Drummond (History Section — Education Department of Victoria), Dr Werner Gallusser (Elder Music Library — University of Adelaide), Dr and the late Mrs A. J. S. Halkyard, Mrs N. A. Hill, Clifford Hocking, John Hopkins (ABC), Brefni and Thea Hosking, Keith Humble, Paggie and Grant Laver, Ivan Lund, Ann Mitchell, the late Max Oldaker, Michael Pharey, F. H. Rogan, Peter Sculthorpe, John Sinclair (the *Herald* — Melbourne), Milton Stevens (ABC), Douglas Stewart, Margaret Sutherland, Michael Tipper, Claude Trevelion, Robert Trumble (ABC), Frank Van Straten, Jan Whitehead (Royal Historical Society of Victoria), Bryan Yeates, the goodly 'Mrs W.'.

*Canada*
S. B. Frost (McGill University, Montreal), John Roberts (Société Radio-Canada).

*Denmark*
Hans Meyer Petersen.

*France*
Mme E. Lebeau (Bibliothèque Nationale — Paris).

*Federal Republic of Germany*
Breitkopf & Härtel (Wiesbaden), Carl Stoll (Staatliche Hochschule für Musik und Darstellende Kunst — Frankfurt-am-Main).

*Holland*
Robert Hyner, Johannes Röntgen.

*Italy*
Sylvia Harrison, Gaetano Torino.

*United States of America*
J. W. Aldrich, The Rt. Rev. F. H. Belden, Edith Borroff (Eastern Michigan University), Inez Brown (Parker), Luis Bueno (the *Miami Herald*), Athel C. Burnham, Allen D. Bushong (University of South Carolina), Hannah Busoni, Richard and John Contiguglia, E. T. Draper-Savage, Prof. Leon Edel, Edith Fairchild, Elsie Fardig (Music ' Library — University of Miami), S. Finkelstein (Vanguard Recording Society Inc.), Sylvia Grace, Lyell Gustin, Beatrice Hurwitz (Simon & Schuster Inc.), Edwyn H. Hames, Frances E. Henschel, Mark Hindsley (University of Illinois), Gloria Jahoda, William Lichtenwanger (Library of Congress), Harriet D. Luehrs (Chicago Public Library), Claus Magnusen, Hellen MacCollum, Brad McEwen (RCA Victor), David McKibbin (Library of Boston Athenaeum), John Mullane (Library of Cincinatti and Hamilton County), W. W. Norton & Company Inc., Evelyn Tennyson Openhymer, Dorine Pruce (Library of Los Angeles), Marguerite Reiners, Mrs Jean Reti-Forbes (University of Georgia), Wayne D. Shirley (Library of Congress), Robert Lewis Taylor, Constance D. Vulliamy (Park College, Parkville, Missouri), Eugene Weintraub (Music Sales Corporation), Robert Bray Wingate (Pennsylvania State Library), Herbert Winter, Prof. Joseph Yasser.

*Union of Soviet Socialist Republics*
Mme E. N. Alekseyeva (Glinka Musical Museum), Mme E. Shibrayevskaya (Moscow Conservatory of Music), Mr M. J. Llewellyn Smith (Cultural Attaché — British Embassy).

John Bird
Cambridge
January 12, 1976

Destroy nothing, forget nothing.
Remember all, say all.
Trust life, trust mankind.
As long as the picture of truth is placed
in the right form (art, science, history)
it will offend none!

*Percy Grainger*

November 13, 1936

# 1

## 'Bubbles'

The City of Melbourne in the early 1880s found itself riding high on the crest of one of the most startling bonanzas ever to hit any city or state anywhere in the world. A decade previously Melbourne, the capital city of the state of Victoria, had been unattractive and undeveloped. Unmetalled streets in and around the centre of the city within minutes of a downpour became oozing rivers of mud, churned up and rutted by the flow of the horse-drawn transport of the day. The stench from the huge open roadside sewers would make the warmer months almost unbearable. In the main streets they were so wide that footbridges had to be constructed to enable pedestrians to cross them unsullied.

The general aspect of the city had been one of a typical colonial community, having little more to show than the usual collection of state government offices, buildings of commerce and hotels interspersed with single-storey houses and shops of predominantly wooden construction. The only cultural life had been directly imported from Europe and displayed little or no awareness of the new and untamed world around it.

Then came the land boom of the 1880s, drawing into its whirlpool of frenzied activity every type of individual from the humble artisan to the man of wealth and property. The face of Melbourne changed almost overnight. The city itself became a bustling metropolis, throwing up mammoth stores, offices, hotels, churches and meeting halls, the neo-gothic splendour of which was to become the envy and amazement of the southern hemisphere. The tentacles of economic expansion were to reach far out into the surrounding districts, engulfing outlying townships and villages. Tens of thousands of acres of the pleasantly undulating countryside around Melbourne were opened up along the forward-looking lines of the grid-and-block system envisaged and laid down by the founders of the settlement more than fifty years before. Gas, water, sewerage and railway services were extended to these newly developed areas. Immigrants, anxious to take every advantage of the bountiful opportunities which Victoria offered, poured in from all parts of the globe. Many Australians from other states moved to Melbourne. The population of Brighton, for example, a small seaside township lying some seven miles south-east of Melbourne along the coast of Port Phillip

Bay, doubled from 5,000 to 10,000 between the years 1880 and 1890.

Around the 1880s a new breed of Australian artist and writer was beginning to make the individuality of its creative ideas felt. The artistic pioneers were shaking off the fetters of European cultural and social values and turning instead towards the healthy, rugged energy of Australian life and landscape for inspiration.

The economic bubble, however, was soon to burst and the early years of the 1890s ushered in all the horrors of a depression, the seriousness and extent of which can only be compared in modern history to that which ravaged Germany around 1923. After ten years of speculation, over-investment, double-dealing and the general misuse of finance, bank and other shares began to drop in value. Very soon the banks found it necessary to call in overdrafts and by 1893 there was virtually a total collapse of the banking system.

It was the profiteering activities of a handful of businessmen — mainly 'respectable', teetotal, church-going Scots — that had caused Melbourne and Victoria to nose-dive into the most fearful slump of their history, and some years were to pass before a recovery was made. During the desperate years of privation between 1891 and 1894 more than 60,000 people left Melbourne either to move to other colonies (many went to join the gold rush at Coolgardie, Western Australia) or to return disillusioned and penniless to Europe.[1]

It was into this Victoria that John Grainger brought his newly wedded bride Rosa late in 1880. Rosa Annie Aldridge (most frequently referred to as Rose) was a mere girl of nineteen when John Harry (also known as Henry) Grainger, then twenty-five, had married her at St Matthew's Church, Kensington Road, in Adelaide on October 1, 1880.

Rose Aldridge was born on July 3, 1861 in a block of buildings in King William Street, Adelaide, South Australia, known in those days as White's Rooms. She was the third daughter and eighth child of a family of nine. Her parents, Sarah Jane and George, were born in London, of Kentish stock, within three years of each other around 1820. Together with Sarah Jane's mother, Sarah Brown, they emigrated to Australia in 1847, married and settled in South Australia to raise what was in those days an average-sized family.

A son had been born out of wedlock in England (Sarah Jane was George's second wife) and the social problems which this event would have caused in England at the time almost certainly contributed to their decision to move to Australia and start a fresh life. George began work as a baker on the goldfields, making long treks on horse and camel to his place of work. He eventually returned to Adelaide to raise his family; there he earned his livelihood at various times as a baker, entrepreneur, storekeeper and hotel keeper. George's stern prejudices earned him some notoriety in Adelaide. If he discovered that a Jew or bookmaker had registered at his hotel without his knowledge, he would storm up to the room and take the unfortunate by the scruff of the neck and show him the door. His baggage would then be hurled down the stairs after him.

Rose was always considered the tomboy of the girls and would often remove her clean white pinafore and ribbon sash and, donning a scruffy tweed cap, would dash off to join her brothers and boy friends to climb trees and share in other boyish pranks in the nearby parks. Her doting mother, to whom the discipline of the girls had been delegated, was a slightly built, blue-eyed creature of a gentle, withdrawn and forgiving nature.

Like other members of the Aldridge clan, however, Rose's mother was a mixture of extremes and there were times when she displayed a curiously stern and hardy side to her personality. One such occasion was during a storm on the six-month outward trip from England to Australia when she insisted on having herself lashed to the mast so as to witness the ferocity of the elements.

Rose's father, who concerned himself almost exclusively with the upbringing of the boys, was hard-drinking, impulsive and quick-tempered. As a matter of course he would resort to corporal punishment of the most severe and brutal kind to bring back into line his erring male offspring. Every Sunday afternoon he would take his horse-fearing wife and children out driving to demonstrate before them his mastery of a mettlesome horse. Australia in these days was largely a rough and uncivilized country where the trouncing of men, horses and dogs by the lash of the whip was part of everyday experience.

Rose was fond of birds, animals and the countryside. She was always successful during her three years of schooling and became an avid reader whose particular predilections were Hans Christian Andersen, Greek mythology, Heine, Goethe, Byron and Dickens amongst others. The single unpleasant memory she kept of her schooldays was her nickname of 'Carrots', earned for her by the reddish tinge in her golden hair. She became remarkably proficient in her piano studies before the age of ten and though her preference was for vocal music (old English songs, Stephen Foster, Schubert and opera selections), she was to broaden her scope to cover the solo piano works of Beethoven, Grieg, Schumann and Chopin. In spite of her fondness for acting, dancing, music and reading, it was outdoor activities that occupied much of her time and energy. She would delight in driving a horse-drawn vehicle at such a speed that it would round corners on two wheels, terrifying all the neighbours. Riding to the hunt was also a favourite pastime.

John Grainger, who was fond of tracing his ancestry back to a misty, pure Celtic origin, was born on a train approaching London on November 30, 1855. He came from a Durham family and was educated mainly in Durham, at Westminster School and later in France. John claimed that in his London days he had served his apprenticeship as an architect and engineer on the construction of King's Cross Station.

This could hardly have been true, however, because King's Cross Station was completed in 1852—three years before he was born. (Some of John's tall stories are quite amusing. He would declare to anyone who cared to listen that he had lived in Paris during the siege of that city in the Franco-Prussian War. He was fond of boasting to any doctor who questioned his stamina that during his prime he would have thought nothing of taking on fourteen whores in one night.) John emigrated to Australia in 1877 where he took up the post of Assistant Architect and Engineer for the South Australian government in Adelaide. He held this post for three years, then moved to Melbourne in October 1880 to establish a private practice. Contacts with Adelaide, however, were not severed after this move, for he continued to make frequent trips to the South Australian capital thereafter.

When John was first invited into the Aldridge household by Rose's father he was in his early twenties, and though yet quite young had been the winner of a competition run in 1879 by the Melbourne Public Works Department for the design of the new Princes Bridge which was to lead across the River Yarra into the heart of the City of Melbourne.

As a young man John was kindly natured, of dignified bearing and cultural leanings and would spend many hours reading poetry to the Aldridge girls. He possessed considerable talents as a painter and had refined musical tastes. He was fond of singing and though he was unable to play a musical instrument he had started the first string quartet in Adelaide. (By a strange coincidence, in 1883 the same string quartet, which by then had formed itself into a club, took on as its honorary director a twenty-four-year-old English immigrant by the name of Cecil Sharp—who on his return to England was to have such a profound and stimulating influence on the first English folk-song revival in which Percy Grainger was to play an important part.) Having already established himself as an architect and civil engineer of some note and means, the young man was soon to gain a firm place in the affections and plans of George Aldridge.

With the death of her husband in December 1879 it became a matter of some urgency for Mrs Aldridge to settle Rose with a suitable spouse. Her late husband had sponsored John for this role and John had already declared his serious intentions to Rose. Rose and her mother, however, harboured doubts. The entire Aldridge family had certain physical characteristics in common. They were all fair-haired and blue-eyed. John was possessed of dark hair and brown eyes. The Aldridges had a concept of their own 'Nordicness' and to them it was a matter of utmost importance. It was part of the pseudo-psychological paraphernalia which made them such a well-knit unit and it played a large part in forming their attitudes towards outsiders.

Rose was never very keen on the idea of marrying John, but when the growing need of a husband presented itself, he seemed the obvious choice. Sarah wrestled with her daughter after the latter had found herself cornered into making John her intended husband. Sarah always warned her children never to have any dealings with dark-eyed folk since she claimed that all her troubles in life had come from such people. This concern with blue eyes was to become part of the legacy of bigotry passed down through Rose to her son.

Rose had already heard rumours concerning John's flirtatious character and at one time it was felt that he intended marrying her sister Clara. She also knew of his fondness for heavy drinking. A few weeks before the marriage she must have had these matters in mind when in a display of supremely self-centred indifference in reply to her mother's question 'Do you think you'll really be happy with Jack in the long run?' she had said 'If I'm happy with him for six months, that's all I care about.'[2]

Rose's feelings and experiences around this time concerning the marriage can be discerned from the following retrospective notes which she made in the spring of 1918: '[. . .] Cannot remember having any unpleasant experiences before marriage, no quarrel with any-one at all. Always had the feeling of being liked & loved, by men & women, children & animals [. . .] Married young. Impelled by some Fate to marry an Englishman whose physical attraction & mental outlook never appealed to me [. . .] Married life — unhappy — experiencing both physical & mental Cruelty [. . .]'[3]

And so it was, it seems, against her better judgement and in a moment of wanton impulse that she married her dark-eyed English suitor; her first disastrous experiment in human relationships.

For their honeymoon they travelled to Sydney and later explored the Blue Mountain region of New South Wales. A profound shock awaited Rose on their return to Adelaide, however, for a young girl had written to her from England telling how she had borne a child to John Grainger, to whom she was betrothed. The writer blamed Rose for keeping John in Australia and ended her letter by wishing that Rose might suffer all her life for the misery which her own predicament was causing her. The girl eventually committed suicide from grief.

Shortly after they were wed they moved to Melbourne so that John could be nearer his work, and it was a single-storey, eight-roomed brick house called 'Finchal' in New Street, North Brighton, which was to be their first home. During these Brighton years the Graingers were able to afford the services of three housemaids, and later, when their child was born, a nursemaid.

Despite Rose's foregone conclusion that the relationship would be unsuccessful, John entered into the institution of marriage in all good faith. He saw to it that the house was well and tastefully fitted out. The walls of the house were hung with reproductions of Rubens and Titian masterpieces and a selection of his own finely worked paintings. He bought a quantity of small reproductions of Greek sculpture. The combined book collections of John and Rose formed a well-stocked library, though John's tastes were far more conservative than those of his wife, not extending much beyond works on art, architecture, engineering, 'Empire building' and religion (for he was a devout, if non-practising, Christian). Rose, like her mother, was an atheist and neither the Bible nor organized religion in any form held any appeal for her.

As soon as it became clear that a child was expected, what little affection Rose had previously held for her husband was quickly stifled and she redirected all her thoughts, emotions and energies with an almost maniacal intensity towards her as yet unborn child. John had by now been removed to a separate bedroom and during the months of pregnancy Rose would indulge in the bizarre practice of having a statue of a Greek god facing her as she lay on her bed for her afternoon nap and before sleep at night, in the hope that her thoughts resting on the Hellenic beauty would invest the unborn child with similar godlike qualities. In times of stress, she would sometimes forget her atheism, and now she offered up fervent prayers that her child might be gifted with artistic talents.

On July 8, 1882 Rose gave birth to a son whose name was duly registered as George Percy Grainger. Dr Henry Michael O'Hara assisted at the birth, which was long and difficult, involving an operation. In the meantime John lounged around the house and explained his unconcerned mood to Dr O'Hara by boasting that this was not the first time he had fathered a child.


From the moment of his birth, Rose took a completely protective attitude towards Percy; protective against his father and against the world. In later years Percy often remarked that one of the strongest qualities in the relationship between him and his mother was the mutually held thought of 'Us two *against* the World' or 'Two Australians *against* the World'. Indeed Rose was to wield such power over the heart and mind of her son that it can be said that from the beginning he was created psychologically in her own image.

As a result of the constant and violent quarrels between his parents, home life for the abnormally impressionable Percy must have been quite a harrowing experience. John was rarely, if ever, deliberately cruel or bad-tempered to Rose or Percy, though he was often quick-tempered. From time to time he would ask his wife to play a solo piece he particularly liked on the upright Kapps piano which stood in the drawing room. If she refused — and she nearly always did, either out of pure stubbornness or because their musical tastes differed so much — he would fly into a rage and leave the house, slamming the door behind him. He would find refuge in the local hostelry and companionship with the barmaid who would always agree to play the piano pieces which his wife had refused. He invariably returned after a few days with his clothes covered in filth from lying drunk in the gutter. On his knees with tears streaming down his face he would beg forgiveness and swear to drink no more. Rose often took her personal problems to Dr O'Hara, who listened patiently to her tales of John's drinking and unfaithfulness. On one occasion when Dr O'Hara was between wives he even proposed that together with Percy they should leave Melbourne and begin a fresh life in San Francisco. Rose decided against the offer, however, for she obviously thought that John was not yet beyond redemption. Whenever John returned his personality would change dramatically and even Rose was forced to admit that at such times a more lovable and companionable man could not be found. John's letters to his father at this time were full of what a wonderful wife he had and how well she was bringing up her son. But the contrition rarely lasted long.

When John's drinking became worse, he would on many occasions threaten to tear the house down and the only way Rose could control him was with a horsewhip with which she chased him around and out of the house. Percy was to witness many such violent scenes. In the first few years he had been able to find comfort and solace in the arms of his beloved nurse Annie, but later there was nowhere to flee. The horsewhip was always to be seen in the front hall wherever they lived in Melbourne. Though John had a great affection for Percy, his efforts to show it were severely limited by Rose's neurotic guardianship of her son. Rose did everything in her power to alienate Percy from his father and she made her son promise never to touch alcohol or tobacco as long as he lived. He kept his promise.

Whilst Rose's attitude towards her son was always severely positive, his father was never known to subject him to corporal punishment or harsh verbal censure. The Graingers once lived in a neighbourhood where there had been several burglaries, and on returning home one evening they had seen a man leap over their garden fence. Percy went into the back part of the house which was in darkness and, overcome with sudden panic from fear of the dark, he ran screaming 'Thief! Thief!' into the lighted front room which acted as his father's studio. This caused his father to tip a bottle of Indian ink over his latest design, yet all he said to Percy was 'What a stoopid chump you are!'[4]

Rose often wondered whether John lied or was simply forgetful. She once found him crying and when asked the reason, he said 'My dear old Dad is dead', his voice heavy with remorse. A few days later he said 'Just got a splendid letter from the dear old Dad.'

Astonished by the revelation, Rose retorted 'I thought you said he had died a few days ago!'

'I never said anything of the kind. What stoopid rot!' was John's only reply.[5]

Rose's more unconventional attitudes, however, had the more marked impression on Percy. In later years he wrote: 'I grew up in an atmosphere of scorn. My mother was scornful of prosperity, law, Christianity and general rightness. She was always on the side of the lawbreakers, always on the side of those hunted down by the police and discriminated against by communities.'[6] Alongside these nonconformist views she felt it necessary to foster an outwardly conformist façade for herself and her son. She was fond of dressing him up in sailor suits or Eton collars and jackets and generally making a Little Lord Fauntleroy of him.

With John's somewhat theatrical drunkenness, however, Rose found it increasingly difficult to preserve the cloak of respectability she so much sought. Her efforts to lead a normal life were almost shattered shortly after Percy was born when she discovered that she had caught syphilis from her husband.

It was her fear of passing the disease on to her son that induced her to employ a nurse for his care soon after he was born. Annie was a giantess of an Irishwoman who loved Percy with a fierce Irish motherliness which encouraged him to love her dearly and which excited Rose's jealousy. If Annie saw Rose shouting at Percy, she would whisk him up in her arms and take him out of the room. Although Rose would scold Annie for spoiling young Percy, her fear of physical contact with her son rendered the nurse indispensable and for most of the time Annie's position was unassailable. Rose eventually overcame her fear of contagion, however, and one day, when the child was about five years old, sacked Annie to Percy's great grief.

Doubtless John had contracted syphilis as a result of his alcohol-induced promiscuity. When Dr O'Hara was consulted by Rose he said that it would have been kinder had John taken a pistol and shot her dead—knowing perhaps that there was no certain cure for the disease in those days. The sole treatment offered was for symptoms only and this treatment was known to be sometimes as dangerous as the disease itself. Dr O'Hara did send her for a 'cure' in Sydney, however, but Rose did not continue with the prescriptions and the fear of becoming insane as a consequence of the disease stayed with her always. Moreover she was gripped by the fear of giving birth to a child by John which might be born retarded, deformed or blind. Frequently, when her fears overcame her, she would seek the security and comfort of being with her family by dashing off to Adelaide—though the Aldridges were never offered a truthful explanation. John, of course, refused to admit to his wife that she had caught the disease from him.

When the Graingers left Brighton around the latter half of 1884, they moved for a short period to the Old England Hotel in Heidelberg, a very picturesque northern suburb of Melbourne. Indeed this move seems to have heralded a period during which they lived in various hotels throughout Melbourne and the outlying districts. One of the longest periods of residence took place in St Kilda on Port Phillip Bay at the

Esplanade Hotel. It was here, not far from Port Melbourne, that Percy began to nurture a lifelong love of ships and the sea. This period of hectic address-changing continued until 1887 when they moved to Glenferrie, an eastern suburb where they rented a house called 'Killalah', which in those days was number 36 Oxley Road. Although their domicile frequently changed whilst they were in Melbourne their mode of life did not. The feuds between John and Rose continued and Percy was drawn ever more towards his mother and away from his father. It would seem that John increased his drinking mainly as a result of the treatment which was meted out at home by his unloving wife. To everyone else who knew the Graingers, John was regarded as one of the most upstanding, gentle and kindly of men and he was much loved by all. Because of his alcoholism, his work and the family income began to suffer. As a result Rose decided to take in piano pupils. Later she took up teaching at nearby schools.

One of John's professional contacts and closest friends was a certain David Mitchell. Concerning this friendship there was one family legend which Percy was told by his father and which in turn Percy later related. John frequently claimed that it was he who 'discovered' what was perhaps the most beautiful voice of the age, namely that of David's daughter Nellie, later to be known as Melba. It is an indisputable fact that John was very close to the Mitchell family, who lived at that time in the Melbourne suburb of Richmond. As an architect and civil engineer John sometimes worked on the same projects with David Mitchell, who was a building contractor with a considerable reputation throughout Victoria. John was therefore a frequent visitor to the Mitchell household.

John did not come to Australia until 1877, and since he took up a post in Adelaide first it is difficult to imagine that he would have taken any extended trips to Melbourne before 1879 when he first became involved with the design of Princes Bridge. And by 1879 Melba already seems to have been taking singing lessons from her greatest teacher, Pietro Cecchi, in Melbourne. The part John played in Nellie's early career, therefore, may have been that he gave her strong and friendly encouragement; more important, there is every likelihood that he helped break down David Mitchell's determination that his daughter should not take up singing as a career.

On his visits to Richmond, John would often be asked to sing a song or two and the teenaged Nellie, by then a competent pianist, would be called upon to accompany him. Nellie always had a great affection for John and followed the career of his son very closely. Their early friendship was not forgotten for it was John who was asked to design 'Coombe Cottage', Melba's Australian house at Coldstream, Victoria, around 1912.

Aside from the discordant domestic scene, the Graingers led a full social life. As well as the Mitchells, they had as their close friends the

O'Haras and the Blacks of Brighton. Dr O'Hara was a keen music lover
and fine singer. They frequently had musical 'At-Homes' to which the
Graingers and their neighbours the Blacks were always invited. John
would arrive at the O'Hara home with his songs buttoned across his chest
and would be called upon to sing various songs. He had a fine tenor
voice and his Northumbrian accent would come out clearly in his
rendition of Edward German's *Three Jolly Sailor Boys*.

His parents at weekends often took Percy on the steamer to Portarling-
ton and on other occasions would take him to the Dandenong Ranges
which overlook Melbourne and which form the most southerly tip of
the Great Dividing Range. Here they would wander through the
magnificent hills and lush forests collecting flowers and mushrooms.
Frequently Rose would take Percy to Adelaide to meet his relatives.
Percy became fascinated by the Australian countryside and in particular
by certain parts through which the train would pass between Adelaide
and Melbourne. He would wake early in the bright summer mornings
and see the gently undulating sandy plains, clad with low bushy scrub,
roll past the windows. He was completely captivated by this scenery and
even at that early age he longed to walk through the 'Ninety Mile Desert',
as it was then known, which stretched between Cook's Plains and Border-
town in South Australia. Indeed it was in those early days that he also
developed a passion for energetic pursuits. He was fond of walking into
town and there indulging in tramcar hopping. As a special favour his
mother would allow him to go sailing or pony trekking with friends of
the family.

A section of the garden at 'Killalah' was given to Percy so that he could
plant and cultivate whatever he wanted. His parents gave him flower and
vegetable seeds to sow but he discarded their gifts. Instead he scoured
the vacant lots nearby and collected as many different kinds of weeds
and wild flowers as he could find. These he planted in his garden plot
and nurtured with great love and care. When his parents and relatives
remarked on his unconventional tastes in horticulture he would reply,
'What's the difference? I think the weeds are just as pretty as the other
flowers.'[7] In later years he regarded his folk-song collecting activities in
much the same light. His love of the musical weeds upon which other
professional musicians had often poured scorn came into play when
thinking of a title for his masterpiece for band. Being an arrangement of
his musical wild flowers and weeds from Lincolnshire, it recalled his
childhood experiences and he lighted on the name *Lincolnshire Posy*.

From the age of five Percy began taking piano lessons from his mother.
She sat by him at the piano for two or more hours every day and watched
over him with a mixture of discipline and encouragement. Her abilities
as a pianist were sufficient to provide Percy with a very adequate knowledge of keyboard technique and musical interpretation. She saw to it
that every moment of her son's day was gainfully filled and Percy worked

hard so as not to fall short of Rose's expectations. This involved long hours of solitary study and perhaps partly caused Percy to invent the imaginary friend whom he called 'Shot-a-tee' and with whom he would engage in deeply absorbed conversation. He would often introduce his 'friend' to visitors to the Grainger house.

From the time Percy was four or five years old a certain period each day was set aside for reading out aloud. The writings of Hans Christian Andersen were the first pieces of literature which he thus encountered. Later came the Icelandic Sagas of Njal and 'Grettir the Strong' and he was determined that one day he would learn a Scandinavian language so that he could read the Sagas in their original form. From the Sagas he turned to early English history with a strong emphasis on that period when the Nordic influence was greatest due to the Viking invasions. By the age of ten he had devoured a huge array of literature which included such material as Freeman's *History of the Norman Conquest* and the *Anglo-Saxon Chronicles*.

Percy's involvement with Nordic legend and pre-Norman England and the extent of the influence it was to have on him in later life was enormous. Years later he wrote:

The Icelandic 'Saga of Grettir the Strong' immediately became, & has always remained, the strongest single artistic influence in my life, providing me [. . .] with an ideal example of what Nordic art should be; shapely yet 'Formless', many-sided yet monotonous, rambling, multitudinous, drastic, tragic, stoical, ruthlessly truth-proclaiming. Out of the Freeman book the Battle of Hastings had become (& still is) an acute personal tragedy. My duty as a composer seemed clear: to turn back, in my music, the tide of the Hastings battle, by cele-brating all seemingly Old English (Anglo-Saxon) & Norse character-istics, by ignoring, as far as possible, all seemingly Norman traits & influences & those derived from the civilization of the Roman Empire. That is why I have called my quartets 'four-somes', have coined 'louden' & 'middle fiddle' to replace 'crescendo' & 'viola' & have refused to write in any form bearing Southern-European titles such as Sonata, Symphony, Concerto.[8]

At an early age Percy would write to his grandmother in Adelaide signing himself 'Grettir the Strong' after the hero who had impressed him so much. Such a degree of identification is extraordinary and verges on fanaticism.

Percy's childhood eating habits were carried into adulthood almost unchanged. One reason for his becoming a teetotaller was his mother's habit of adding a drop of brandy or whisky to his castor oil. Whenever anyone offered him strong drink in adulthood his nostrils were immedi-ately assailed with the unforgettable smell of castor oil. Boiled rice with milk and brown sugar or golden syrup was always his favourite food, closely followed by tinned California peaches, brown sugar sandwiches, bread and milk, bread and butter and bread and jam. (For reasons which always puzzled him he was never given bread and butter *and* jam.) Rose never forced him to eat what he refused, though he did need extra coaxing with the castor oil. Calling into account his manly hero-worship, she would say, 'What's the use of your admiring the Vikings and then not being able to swallow a spoonful of castor oil?'[9]

Percy was brought up by his mother according to a very strict black-and-white philosophy of reward and punishment. The rewards were the trips to the Dandenongs, pony rides, tramcar hopping, being allowed to go sailing or to make model boats (in which he especially delighted). The punishment was simply the whip. If he misbehaved or if he neglected his piano practice his mother would beat him severely. This form of corporal punishment continued until he was fifteen or sixteen. Perhaps the most curious aspect of this regime was not the nature or vehemence of the punishment, but the fact that whilst Percy did not have any particular liking for being at the receiving end, he never for one moment bore any resentment towards his mother for it. On the contrary, he came to love and worship her all the more.

He was a remarkably fluent speaker from a very early age and, with a wide vocabulary at his command, started writing letters when he was five years old. His early proficiency and interest in English were helped by the fact that his parents did not use 'baby talk' in his earliest years but purposefully used intelligible English from the first. Coupled with this was his parents' insistence that he should not be allowed to mix with other children of his own age. Instead he was kept occupied with other pursuits at home and his mother permitted him to mix with adults only.

This aspect of his abnormally 'hot-house' upbringing certainly produced deeply ingrained habits and attitudes which were always to be part of him. His passion for long hours of hard and frenzied work, his curious lack of guile and his unsophisticated humour, his yearnings for the things and places of his childhood (a childhood which, in the normal sense of the word, had never existed) and the fact that in so many ways he, like Peter Pan, never grew up, could all be traced back to his strange upbringing. In his own words, as Percy later wrote: 'Why my mother was able to make an artist of me (& I wasn't such good material. I mean, I never had much "talent" if there is such a thing) was because she didn't allow me to waste my time with other children, or in "play", but gave me the habit of almost continual work. When I was not working at music I was drawing hens or trees or portraits or still lifes & when I wasn't doing either drawing or music we were reading aloud to each other.'[10]

Certain shapes and sounds had a great influence on Percy. The gently rolling hills of South Australia formed pleasing lines which he adored. As a child he was often taken boating by his mother on the lake in Melbourne's Albert Park, known then as the Albert Park Lagoon. When leaning over the bows of the boat he became fascinated by the smooth lines of the waves as they lapped against the sides. He would listen to the sounds of the water as it was ploughed up by the movement of the boat. Sometimes he spent many hours listening to the formless and eerie sounds made by the wind howling down chimneys or through telegraph wires. He carried these sounds in his head till the day he died, for they were to play a vital part in his 'Free Music' experiments which he considered to be the culmination of his entire artistic life.

It is also significant to remember that Percy's earliest musical recollections were those of his mother singing him to sleep with the songs of Stephen Foster. Percy's particular favourite was *Camptown Races* and years later he was to embody this charming American ditty in his own composition *Tribute to Foster*. Yet another important and early musical experience was that of Chinese and Japanese music.

One legacy from Australia's gold rush days was a large Chinese population. Subsequently the Chinese were ruthlessly discriminated against, maltreated and sometimes murdered by the Europeans and largely driven out of Australia. For many years, however, each major city had its own 'Chinatown' and Melbourne was no exception in this respect. A section of Little Bourke Street was one of the most colourful districts of the City of Melbourne around this time and Percy would love to be taken to see the Chinese shops, houses and places of entertainment. The most lasting impression, however, was the music, to which he listened with great relish. He also held fond memories of a visit paid to Melbourne by a group of Japanese artists. On this occasion also he found the musical and painting displays unforgettable.

Of the many attitudes which Rose inculcated in her young son, an unswerving loyalty and devotion to relatives and friends was perhaps the most powerful. From a very early age Percy was obliged to attend to his regular duties of corresponding with the Adelaide branch of the Aldridge family and after a time these duties became a form of self-discipline. The collective idea of the blue-eyed, fair-haired Aldridges became one of the shrines at which he worshipped all his life.

From the age of five Percy developed a keen interest in drawing, lettering and painting. Much of his spare time was given over to this pursuit and he produced some fine pencil drawings of horses, ships and faces. He always painted his own Christmas and greetings cards and they depicted characters from Dickens, cartoons of pixies and toadstools and delightful self-portraits. Above all he loved making copies of his father's collection of nude paintings and the Greek statues which were to be found around the household. Indeed, there was a time when he showed such a sensitive talent for art that ideas of a musical career for him were almost shelved.

Percy's early artistic efforts were greatly encouraged by his father, who

tried to communicate many of his enthusiasms to his son. John Grainger
would refer to the young boy as 'Bubbles' because he so resembled the
child in the famous advertisement for Pear's soap. Percy was a healthy
child and this was reflected in his exquisitely proportioned facial
features, intense blue eyes, fair hair and skin. His elders quite naturally
doted on this 'Nordic' inheritance.

Despite John's shortcomings Percy derived much from his father's
love and solicitude. Following his father's example, he developed a
veritable passion for cricket, football and walking. It may also have
been a result of his father's influence that Percy evolved a considerable
talent for telling the occasional tall story. It has been recorded that on
the train journeys into the city of Melbourne, he would regularly keep
the entire carriage entertained with pranks, childish diatribes or even
singing. His early enthusiasm for the Icelandic Sagas inspired him to
engage in mock swordfighting with neighbourhood boys which was at
times so rough that it had to be halted by adult intervention.

Around 1888 John began to experience severe attacks of delirium
tremens. His sickness was complicated by nicotine poisoning — Rose
would roll cigarettes by the hundred for him. There were times when
Rose felt that her husband should not be left to himself and would go
with him to the office every day. He would then be so sensible and sober-
minded that Rose confessed that she could not possibly believe that he
would be weak again. So she would let him go alone to the City and in a
few days he would be back where he had been before — drunk, wretched
and irritable.

The attacks became so bad that Rose eventually felt forced to drag
him off to a hospital on the outskirts of Melbourne for a rest cure. Her
next problem was to find the necessary money to pay for the treatment.
As a civil engineer, one of John's specialities was rescuing buildings
built on the soft earth on the banks of the River Yarra which were
suffering from sinking foundations. At the time of this, his most serious
collapse of health, he was working for a Scottish businessman whose
factory was in the throes of such constructional problems. Rose went to
see him with the hope of borrowing some money. She felt that such an
approach would bear fruit, for the Scotsman had tried the services of
several other Melbourne architects and engineers without success and it
was not until he had tapped this specialist knowledge of John's that a
lasting solution had been found. Rose thought that his gratitude would
extend to some financial assistance in their present dire situation. But
her hopes were quickly dashed, for all the Scotsman did was question
whether she really was Rose Grainger or not. The interview was devas-
tatingly brief and on the stairway outside his office she began to cry. At
that moment an Irishman whom Rose knew only slightly saw her pathetic
condition and asked the cause of her sorrow. On hearing how matters
stood, he took £100 from his wallet and handed the sum to Rose, making

no mention of any need for its return.

The hospital treatment, however, was to no avail and shortly John returned home and took to his old habits. When it became obvious that precious little could be done for John's desperate condition their local doctor and friend, Robert Hamilton Russell, was called to give further advice. Russell had only been in Australia for a few months and at that time was living and practising in Glenferrie, where the Graingers also resided. His advice was unequivocal when he ordered complete rest for John. John would have nought of the good doctor's suggestion but instead decided to quit his work, pack up his belongings and take a trip to England. This impulsive decision was taken because not only did he usually respond favourably to sea voyages but he realized that it would give him the chance of fleeing the eccentricities of his wife at last. The idea was irresistible.

When Dr. Russell heard of his decision he helped him pack and even escorted him to the steamship *Oruba* to take him to England. On his return from Port Melbourne Dr Russell said to Rose, 'Jack will not live to see Colombo.'[11] But by the time he had reached Colombo he had recovered sufficiently to be taking part in the deck games.

He left Melbourne early in September 1890, but when he arrived in England his father refused to see him, doubtless because stories of John's drinking and womanizing had filtered back. John re-embarked on the same ship and was back in Adelaide on December 18 of the same year. From this time, he and Rose never lived together again, though they frequently wrote to each other and sometimes met.

# 2

## Doctors and Dustbin Lids

For a time Rose and Percy continued to live in Oxley Road, and the piano lessons which Rose gave to other people's children seem to have been lucrative enough for them to have retained one maid during this period — Martha was her name and Percy was devoted to her. From time to time they also took in a boarder whose rent helped them to survive.

One such boarder was the English botanical artist A.E. Aldis. Percy later wrote:

> Mr. Aldis was a most lovable friend & artist through & through & no doubt it was his delightful drawings of men, beasts & birds that led me to make endless drawings of our Killalah. But it was his recitings of Maori chants that constituted his greatest influence on me — & a life-long one. He would keep the marrow-curdling Maori rhythms hammering away by the hour or so it seemed to me. So that when I heard the Maori speech at Rotorua in 1909 it was like a home coming for me. I have always adored heroic sounding languages. When I composed 'Father and Daughter' (Faroe Islands) for five solo male voices, double mixed chorus & orchestra in 1908 & 1909, it was the heroic sonorities of A. E. Aldis that I was trying to re-enact.[1]

One of the most influential events in Percy's artistic life, however, had taken place a little earlier in 1889 when a group of painters had organized an important exhibition in Melbourne. It was in many senses a turning point in Australia's artistic history. The painters belonged to Australia's Impressionist period and the core of the Victorian group called themselves the 'Heidelberg School' because many of them lived and worked in the area so named outside Melbourne. At the exhibition, to which they took their son, the Graingers met and befriended Charles Conder and Arthur Streeton — two brilliant artists. They possibly met the equally famous Tom Roberts also. During the following year Percy was often taken to Streeton's studio, where he would sit for many hours watching the artist work.

In 1892 after John Grainger had left Melbourne, Rose's less fortunate financial circumstances forced her and her young son to move to more

modest accommodation at a house called 'Sofiero' at what was then 48
Rathmines Road in the neighbouring suburb of Auburn. They stayed
there for about eighteen months and in late 1893 they moved to a suburb
nearer the centre of Melbourne called South Yarra which formed part of
the City of Prahran. They were then living at 63 Caroline Street, where
they stayed until they left Australia.

The accommodation in Caroline Street, five minutes' walk from the
gentle banks of the River Yarra, probably consisted of unfurnished
rooms which they rented. Rose continued to watch over Percy's musical
progress and he was obliged to put in long hours at piano practice whilst
other children were out playing with their friends down by the River
Yarra or in the paddocks nearby.

Although Percy had a great love and respect for his mother's family he
was not blind to their inadequacies. His uncles, for example, he felt were
hard-headed, and the indifference shown by one of them to Percy's
musical career was brought home to him on one occasion when Rose had
taken him to stay with his uncle Jim at Richmond Park in Adelaide.
James Aldridge was the owner of a very prosperous stud farm and, like
his brothers, was fond of lecturing his musical nephew. Percy was about
ten at the time; Rose was his only provider and she found it difficult to
make ends meet. James said to Rose one day, 'I think Percy has a talent
for riding. He ought to have a horse and I'll be glad to give him one.'

Rose turned on her brother and said, 'But we're practically starving!
We have no place to graze a horse and certainly could not afford to buy it
food so what should we do with it? If you're so generous that you want to
give him a horse, why don't you give me a little money so that I can get
him a proper musical training?'

'Oh!' he said, 'I wouldn't do that. I don't believe in music.'[2]

During the South Yarra period Rose joined a local dramatic society
and made several appearances in their productions. She also performed
in public as a pianist at an end-of-the-year concert at a local school
where she taught piano. It was also during this period that Percy under-
went his only formal schooling. Although a Compulsory Education Act
had come into force in January 1873 and truant officers were working by
the end of the decade, Percy's entire schooling lasted no longer than
three months and probably took place at a state school in South Yarra in
1894. Percy hated school and would run home every day to avoid the
brawls which usually broke out after hours. He found the schoolchildren's habit of torturing chickens particularly distasteful, though at
times he himself was known to be cruel to cats. He did, however, enjoy
the sporting activities of school life, particularly football and cross-
country running. Having no faith in schoolroom education, Rose had
taken upon herself the task of educating the young Percy, which in her
hands meant concentrating almost exclusively on English and music with
small doses of history. At the age of seven or eight he had been sent to a

lady in Melbourne for private French tuition. This seems to have been the first of many languages he was to master. His French tutor and his mother were surprised by the ease and rapidity with which he had acquired more than a tolerable fluency in the language. But Rose was never concerned that Percy had not mastered elementary mathematics and that he was unable to count his change. She was, however, determined that her son should acquire the necessary talents to take him to a state of financial independence where he could be indifferent to whether he was given the correct change or not.

Around 1891 Percy came into contact with another English artist, Thomas A. Sisley, who was the first secretary of the Victorian Artists' Society. He was a singer, elocution teacher and amateur musician—in fact, a man of broad culture and interests and a type who was always to have a very special magnetism for Percy. John Grainger already knew him well and once remarked, 'His learning is good, extensive and solid, pure to a degree, and though a bit exacting in manner and temperament he is my "beau idéal" of a teacher to those who really wish to learn. Those who don't can stop away, and better for all they do so.'[3]

Sisley had established classes in elocution and painting in Melbourne and one of his pupils for a time was Percy, who recalled having been obliged to learn by heart and recite *Hiawatha* and playing Puck in a children's production of *A Midsummer Night's Dream* that Sisley had organized. He also recalled his own utter lack of talent for acting and his dislike of it. On the other hand Percy and Thomas Sisley struck up an immediate friendship and understanding where music was concerned and he held fond memories of Sisley's singing of *Es ist vollbracht* from Bach's *St. Matthew Passion* at a private concert of the music of Bach and Handel which Percy organized at their home in Caroline Street around 1894. It was probably Sisley who introduced Percy to George Webbe Dasent's translation of the Icelandic Sagas and other works such as Tennyson's translation of *The Battle of Brunanburh*—all of which were ideal fuel for Percy's already insatiable Nordic fervour.

The friendship which Percy had formed with Dr Russell in his Glenferrie days was always an influence of considerable importance. In 1889 Russell had emigrated from England where he had been surgical dresser and later house surgeon under the great Lord Lister, innovator of antiseptic surgery. He had moved to Australia because he was consumptive—a very common reason in those days, for it was felt that Australia's more clement weather might cure such a condition. Very soon he was charming all of his new friends with his fine piano playing, especially his interpretation of the music of Schumann.

In 1890, when Sir Charles Hallé, whom Percy later referred to as an 'Anglicized German stick-in-the-mud', was announced to tour Australia, Percy said to Dr Russell, 'I don't believe he plays any better than you.' Dr Russell replied with excessive modesty, 'You won't want to listen to

me when you've heard Sir Charles.' Percy, however, was singularly
unimpressed with the playing of Sir Charles, which he described at a
later date as 'soullessly pedantic'. After the recital Percy said to Dr
Russell, 'I guessed right, he is not nearly as good as you are.'[4] In such a
fashion did the eight-year-old Percy dismiss a man who had personally
heard and known Chopin and Liszt and had been the first pianist to play
the thirty-two Beethoven sonatas in public. Similarly when Percy was
about eight years old he was taken to have elementary harmony and
counterpoint lessons from a Melbourne conductor called Julius Hertz.
Percy dismissed this musician, referring to him as a 'complete and utter
idiot' after only a few lessons.

In fact, Percy was fearless and sometimes devastating in his criticisms
and it made no difference to him that his views were contrary to those
held by the majority. He himself remarked, 'In matters musical my
father was always judging between the quick & the dead. He would say:
The E flat isn't a patch on the Jupiter. This put me in the enviable position, even as a child, of feeling that there was nothing, not even the
greatest classics, that I might not sharply criticize.'[5]

A year or so after Percy had heard Sir Charles Hallé he was taken by
Dr Russell to meet the youthful Australian pianist Ernest Hutcheson,
who had freshly returned from his studies under Reinecke in Leipzig and
Stavenhagen—a legendary pupil of Liszt—in Weimar. Here, coinciden-
tally, his fellow students had included Percy Pitt (later to become first
conductor of the BBC Orchestra), Robin Legge (later music critic of the
*Daily Telegraph*) and the young 'Fritz' Delius. At the age of twelve Hutcheson had been a member of a concert party headed by Melba which
had toured Australia. At the turn of the century he moved to the United
States, where he later became Dean and President of the Juilliard School
of Music. Percy and Hutcheson became lifelong though not close friends
and in subsequent years Percy would often send his piano pupils on to
Hutcheson. The one thing they had in common was a profound love of
the music of Bach. Percy wrote in 1945 of this meeting: 'My memory of
the beauty, perfection & smoothness of his [Bach] playing has never
dimmed.'[6]

Percy had a profound, almost filial affection for Dr Russell and referred to him as 'the first exquisite pianist of my life'.[7] There is no doubt
that Russell—a lifelong bachelor—radiated an extraordinary personal
magnetism and there is no reason to suppose that Percy did not derive a
great deal, musically and otherwise, from this friendship. In his youth
and middle years Russell had been blessed with remarkable good
looks—silver-white hair, blue eyes and classically fine features—a certain
candidate for Percy's Nordic hero-worship.

By the age of ten Percy had progressed so well with his piano studies
that it was felt he had outgrown Rose's lessons. Dr O'Hara stepped in

with the suggestion that he be taken to see his friend Herr Louis Pabst, who was at that time the most respected piano teacher in Melbourne.

Pabst was born in Königsberg, Germany, on July 18, 1846, and was the son of a composer, Auguste Pabst, whose operas were sometimes performed in Königsberg and Dresden. His younger brother Paul (one of Rachmaninov's piano teachers) was also a pianist of some note in Germany and Russia towards the end of the nineteenth century and his paraphrase of the waltz from Tchaikovsky's *Eugene Onegin* was frequently programmed by the grand virtuosos of the day. Pabst's own musical credentials were impeccable. He had studied in his native Germany and later in St Petersburg under the formidable Russian pianist and pedagogue Anton Rubinstein. Very few of Rubinstein's pupils made names for themselves as concert pianists; of the four or five who did, Josef Hofmann, Ossip Gabrilowitsch and Louis Pabst were perhaps the most significant. It is said that Rubinstein did not attempt to impose his own style on pupils or create his own school, but encouraged them to develop in their own ways.

In 1884 Pabst had moved from Germany to Melbourne, where his fine piano playing soon became greatly admired by serious music lovers and he became in demand as a teacher. With his wife he had established a regular series of musical entertainments at their home in Hotham Street, South Melbourne, and later at the Masonic Hall, Collins Street, Melbourne (another building designed by John Grainger), which they called 'Risvegliato' concerts. Dr O'Hara was often invited to sing at these concerts. For the young Percy these were heady feasts of music and he remarked once:

> [. . .] I remember in particular a Concerto of Bach for two pianos & strings, the string part being played on a third piano, that struck me as a wonder of richness & complexity. Pabst was the first to reveal to me the glories of Bach, thereby opening the door to the only realm of music—the many-stranded melodies—that I have ever deeply loved [. . .] when at the age of ten I first got to know Bach through Louis Pabst & his pupils I felt that I was hearing the full art of music for the first time [. . .] & hearing his magnificent renderings of Bach gave me whatever is good in my Bach playing.[8]

Percy also took some harmony lessons from Pabst in 1893. Pabst it seems charged between ten and twelve guineas an hour for his piano lessons—a considerable fee for those days—but special terms were arranged for yearly pupils. Doubtless Pabst knew of the Graingers' dire financial situation and was very elastic when it came to Percy's tuition fees. He charged Mrs Grainger £1 11s 6d for three months' harmony lessons for her son which began on August 9th of that year.

The Pabsts took an almost parental interest in Percy, to the extent of expressing a desire to adopt him and take him back to Europe when they returned in 1894. Pabst wanted to make of his student a real virtuoso. To do this, he explained he would have to forbid him to compose at all until he was sixteen. By then, having concentrated on piano playing for four years, he would have acquired a first-rate technique on the piano. When Rose was faced with this proposition she answered, 'But if Percy is not to compose until he is sixteen it will be too late. I should rather he gave up music altogether than see him become a mere pianist. It doesn't seem to me worth all the bother.'[9]

The wisdom of his mother's reaction was, to say the least, questionable. The notion that it can ever be 'too late' to begin to compose perhaps reveals a fault in her thinking. In later years Percy always claimed that the peak of his musical creativity had been reached and passed by the time he was twenty-five. Whether this could have been delayed some years by a period of intense piano study with Pabst, or whether his creative spirit would have been stifled altogether, one can but wonder. But one can have no doubts as to the truth of his concluding statement concerning this episode: '[. . .] so I was not adopted by the Pabsts but became the passive vehicle of a mother's aesthetic will'.[10] It is certain, moreover, that it was at this juncture that the signs of a bitter conflict of loyalties made their first appearance. The conflict was to torture him for the rest of his life and consisted of a cruel tussle between the creative and the re-creative arts. Percy's indecisiveness only complicated matters.

Louis Pabst was almost as interested in Percy's talent as a painter as in his pianistic ability. He gave Percy great encouragement and frequently asked him to bring to the classes his latest artistic efforts so that they could be shown to his fellow students. Percy's own comments on this dual aspect of his studies were: 'I never had more talent for music than for painting. I did hundreds of portrait drawings as a child. I never had a good "ear", nor a good musical memory, nor any facility for a special musical instrument.'[11] This was typical of the naively modest and self-deprecatory attitude which he nearly always took when he discussed his own talents, for not only were his artistic feats well above average for a child of his age, but his piano playing was already widely talked about in Melbourne's musical circles.

After about a year's study with Louis Pabst, it was thought that Percy ought to make his debut before the public. This took place on the evening of Monday, July 9, 1894 at a 'Risvegliato' concert at Melbourne's Masonic Hall in the presence of a large audience. The following day the music critic of the Melbourne *Age* wrote:

> [. . .] the youngster has a touch so firm, a technique so nearly faultless, a musical perception so acute, and an aplomb so surprising — see him look calmly round as he plays without a trace either of nervousness or self-consciousness — that one would say that he cannot fail to

win for himself name and fame in the career that has been so carefully
mapped out for him; and yet the music he tackled yesterday—of
course without the aid of the book—is no child's play; the Gavotte &
Musette in G minor, the Prelude and Gigue from the Partita in B
flat—Master Grainger is partial to Sebastian Bach, and usually confines himself from choice to that composer—most emphatically wants
playing. But he acquitted himself in such works as these in a style that
many a finished pianist would have envied, and that at an age when
most boys are playing marbles or whipping tops. [. . .] This is a kind of
pupil of whom any teacher might well be proud, and young Australians may watch his future career with mingled pride & confidence.

With that prophetic criticism, the concert life of Percy Grainger had
begun.

Meanwhile, Percy continued his lessons with Pabst, but the latter
became a little troubled that the boy wanted to study only Bach. Pabst
gave him Grieg's *Norwegian Bridal Procession* and Chopin's 17th
Prelude in A flat to study, saying to his mother, 'We mustn't allow Percy
to grow narrow minded, must we?'[12] These two pieces struck Percy at the
time as being debased and maudlin respectively and he said to his
mother that he would never feel the same about Pabst again, for he had
no taste.

At the next concert in which Percy appeared, he was billed as the star.
It took place at another 'Risvegliato' concert at the Melbourne Masonic
Hall at 8 p.m. on Monday September 10 of the same year. As assisting
artists he was given his dear friend Henry O'Hara and a bass-baritone by
the name of Friedrich Moosbrugger. Percy performed the Allegro from
Sonata Opus 10 No.1 by Beethoven, a Prelude and Gigue by J.S. Bach,
*La Fileuse* by Raff, *Träumerei* by Schumann, a *Moment Musical* in F
minor by Schubert, the *Pastorale* by Scarlatti and Louis Pabst's own
transcription of the Minuet from Handel's *Samson*. The concert was
given under the patronage of a most distinguished array of colonial and
civic dignitaries which included the Governor of Victoria. The Melbourne press continued singing Percy's praises.

Shortly after this concert Louis Pabst returned permanently to
Europe. His pupils were mostly taken over by a Miss Adelaide Burkitt
who had also studied with Louis Pabst. Luckily, Percy had no difficulty
with the change of teachers, for he had known Miss Burkitt previously
and delighted in the lessons he took from her thereafter. During this
period she prepared Percy for a wider audience and the concerts which
were to take place in Melbourne's Exhibition Building.

Two of the most prominent men in Melbourne's musical and academic
life around this time were Professor Marshall Hall and Professor William
Adolphus Laver. Marshall Hall was a colourful, flamboyant and energetic person, William Laver a somewhat withdrawn, well-respected and

solid academic. Amongst the pupils of the latter could be numbered Adelaide Burkitt and William Murdoch—later to win international fame. Both Hall and Laver were to have an influence on Percy. Marshall Hall, who was then organizing a regular series of concerts which he called 'The People's Promenade Concerts' in Melbourne's Exhibition Building, was attracted by the acclaim that Percy was being accorded and saw to it that the prodigy made appearances at his Promenade Concerts. The three concerts in which Percy was to appear all took place during the month of October 1894. Practically the entire repertoire was a repeat of the 'Risvegliato' material, but with another item from Schumann's *Kinderszenen*, Schulhoff's transcription of the Minuet from Mozart's E flat Symphony and the Rondo from Beethoven's 'Pathétique' Sonata.

The performances in the Exhibition Building were to have a far-reaching effect on Percy's style of playing. In his subsequent career in Europe and America Percy was occasionally accused of having an insensitive 'touch' at the keyboard. He was aware of this inadequacy in his playing and often chose his repertoire to suit his pianism, having a certain preference for pieces that would throw into bold relief the declamatory, incisive and percussive qualities of the concert grand. One newspaper music critic of the 1940s went so far as to suggest that Percy's 'touch' was 'as hard as nails'. The critic must have been greatly surprised when he received a letter from Percy himself saying that he agreed with him entirely. Percy explained that this characteristic in his playing resulted from his childhood when he had played a series of concerts in Melbourne's Exhibition Building. He went on to write that the very size of the hall in which he had played as a lad of twelve had horrified him and in order to make himself heard in the place he had been forced to over-amplify everything he tackled. Melbourne's Exhibition Building was about as suitable for a piano recital as an aircraft hanger is for poetry reading. It is a vast construction built in 1880 and can hold 20,000 people. The interior is in the style of London's Crystal Palace and was conceived with a total disregard for the science of acoustics. Regrettably, Percy concluded, he always felt that the people at the back of the hall wherever he played in later years would not be able to hear him unless he added some degree of force to his playing. As a result of these childhood experiences he adopted highly individual mannerisms. But individual mannerisms are frequently the very stuff of which great playing is (or was) made.

All three performances were exceptionally well received by the Melbourne critics. The critic of the *Age* called Percy 'the flaxen haired phenomenon who plays like a master on the piano'.

Apart from a concert on October 30 at the Hibernian Hall in Swanston Street, Melbourne, and another at Prahran Town Hall on February 13, 1895 (both for church funds), Percy made no further public appearances until the following May. By this time Rose had decided to take her son to Frankfurt-am-Main, where he would continue his studies in the world-famous Hoch Conservatorium of Music. This decision must have been taken during the latter half of 1894, but almost certainly after the departure of Louis Pabst. Pabst would have been deeply hurt since he himself had offered to take the youngster to Europe to continue his piano studies under his personal tutelage. Percy himself claimed that the decision was taken after certain well-meaning friends had suggested various musical academies in Austria, France, Italy and Germany. He immediately opted for Germany because it was the country closest geographically and culturally to Iceland, with whose sagas he was still obsessed at that time.

Professor William Laver, head of the piano department at Melbourne's Conservatorium of Music, was also a keen concert-goer and had met the Graingers after one of Percy's recitals. He had studied at the Hoch Conservatorium, where he became the closest friend of a fellow pupil named Frederic Lamond.[13] Laver spoke to the Graingers of the Hoch Conservatorium in glowing terms and talked with pride of the successes which were being achieved by his former fellow students.

Very soon a group of friends decided to hold a benefit concert to give financial help to the Graingers, for they were still very poor. The committee formed to organize the concert, which succeeded in obtaining some very respectable patronage, consisted mainly of former members of the Pabst 'Risvegliato' circle of friends. The chairman of the committee was Professor Marshall Hall and a prominent member was Dr O'Hara.

The concert took place at the Melbourne Town Hall in Swanston Street on the evening of May 14, 1895, nearly two months before Percy's thirteenth birthday and the hall was packed with Melbourne's music lovers who had come to wish the boy well. Percy and his mother had decided to walk from their home in South Yarra to the Melbourne Town Hall and on the way Percy had found a rusty dustbin lid. Not wishing to upset her son, Rose allowed him to play with his splendid new toy and thought no more of it even when they arrived at the Town Hall. Here they separated, Percy entering by the side door and Rose going through the front foyer to take her seat in the auditorium. When Percy's turn came to perform, however, Rose was alarmed to witness her son march on to the platform holding the dustbin lid as a soldier would hold a shield. He propped the object up against the leg of the Blüthner concert grand and commenced to play. When he had played his last piece, he picked up his precious dustbin lid and marched off again, grinning with pride.[14]

Percy performed a selection of Bach pieces, the *Pastorale* by Scarlatti, the Allegro and Andante from Beethoven's Sonata in G major, Opus 14, and Pabst's arrangement of the Minuet from Handel's *Samson*. His performances were greeted with wild applause and he was given many bouquets of flowers.

The next week, on May 24, Percy gave a successful recital in the music rooms of S. Marshall & Sons in Adelaide. Immediately after the recital the Graingers returned to Melbourne, where they packed up their few belongings and on May 25 boarded the steamer SS *Gera* at Port Melbourne. Most of their friends came to see them off and their cabin was bedecked with flowers and farewell telegrams.

On Wednesday May 29, 1895 Rose and her son left Adelaide and Australia, and with fifty pounds between them, raised by the Melbourne Town Hall benefit concert, they headed for the Old World and a new life.

# 3

## 'Perks' joins the Frankfurt Gang

The SS *Gera* was a small and very comfortable ship and Percy found the voyage an exciting experience. It reinforced his already strong passion for ships and the sea. He joined in all the deck sports and spent some of his time teaching himself German. The Graingers disembarked at Genoa and made the remainder of their journey to Frankfurt-am-Main by train in order that they might see a little of Europe before Rose found it necessary to settle down and earn a living.

On arrival at Frankfurt Station they were met by a Frau Wertheim whose father-in-law was a former friend of theirs in Melbourne. Next morning they moved out to the Pension Pfaff in Blumenstrasse. Very soon Rose began giving private lessons in English to the sons and daughters of her new German contacts, charging the equivalent of sixpence an hour. After a short time the classes had grown so much that she felt it necessary to separate her students into Jewish and non-Jewish groups. Her new occupation not only provided a modest income for herself and her son but enabled them to enlarge their social circle. In the course of time the Graingers were receiving more social invitations than they could accept. Rose had always had a strong leaning towards German literature and music and the move to Frankfurt brought a sense of contentment and liberation which she had not previously experienced.

During these years of separation, John Grainger continued to correspond with his wife and son. He still felt a strong loyalty and affection for both and periodically sent sums of money ranging between £5 and £50 to help with expenses. Occasionally he held out the feeble hope of a possible reunion with his family and in 1895 he wrote to Percy: 'You must give Mother a good hug for me (she prefers my hugs by proxy) and whisper her in the ear that none loves her better than I do, if she only knew it. Perhaps one of these days she will discover how much really.'[1]

For his part, Percy remained very dutiful in his letter-writing to his father. He often sent examples of his drawing and painting for criticism and approval. Some years later when John had established himself in Perth and had become very much involved with the activities of the Perth Orchestral Society, Percy, who had by then started composing in earnest, sent him some of his pieces in the hope of their being performed. But

Perth lost its chance of being the first city to hear a public performance of his work. As John explained to his son shortly afterwards, his compositions had contained too many sharps, flats and difficult rhythms and the society members had found them beyond their comprehension and performing ability. John was also determined to fulfil his capacity as father and fount of all wisdom and he would freely lecture Percy on matters of etiquette, Christian morals and general behaviour.

Percy did not enrol at the Hoch Conservatorium until the autumn of that year, and during the months which preceded his intensive piano studies he passed his time gainfully by continuing his studies of the German language, in which he quickly became completely fluent. He soon developed a fondness for painting and sketching the beautiful old houses, castles and ruins which abounded in Frankfurt. Herr Wertheim paid for him to have weekly art lessons with a painter in Sachsenhausen and he numbered these amongst the happiest memories of what he otherwise considered a very unpleasant period of his life.

During the first year Rose saved most of her earnings and the only luxuries she seems to have allowed herself and Percy were two American bicycles on which they explored the surrounding countryside. Above all they loved to ride and walk in the Taunus Mountains near Frankfurt. They would encounter villages and small towns nestling in these hills and mountains which had hardly changed since mediaeval times. On such trips Percy always carried his drawing pad, paint box and pencils in order to capture on paper the many architectural and scenic beauties which they discovered. Once Rose had set herself on a firmer financial footing they began travelling further afield and boat trips down the Rhine to Heidelberg were some of their most memorable experiences.

Percy continued his piano practising, but this created certain problems. The Graingers were often asked to leave because the residents of the many pensions at which they stayed objected to so much music. After only two years in Frankfurt they had changed addresses three times. By the time they arrived in Germany, however, they had become so used to frequent moves that the Frankfurt experience did not bother them unduly.

The Hoch Conservatorium, under the directorship of the awesome and stern Dr Bernard Scholtz, was numbered amongst the four or five finest establishments of its kind in Europe. The teaching staff during the last decade of the nineteenth century included Clara Schumann (piano), James Kwast (piano), Hugo Becker (cello),[2] Hugo Heermann (violin),[3] Engelbert Humperdinck (composition) and Ivan Knorr (composition). Clara Schumann had given her last public performance in 1890 and with increasing deafness resigned her post as head of the piano department of the Conservatorium in 1892. This department had been under her firm control for fourteen years, and it carried its reputation of excellence well into the following century.

In the autumn of 1895 the thirteen-year-old Percy was enrolled at Dr Hoch's Conservatorium. His teacher in pianoforte was James Kwast.

Kwast was born in 1852 in Nijkerk, Holland, and after some preliminary studies in his native country moved to Germany, where he studied under Reinecke and Hans Richter at the Leipzig Conservatorium. After some further studies in Berlin his piano playing received a final polish from Gevaert and Louis Brassin[4] in Brussels. His first wife Antoine was the daughter of Ferdinand Hiller and from this union came a daughter Mimi, of whom more shall be said later. After a divorce from his first wife he married Frieda Hoddap, a former piano pupil who was also a contemporary of Percy.

Percy did not enjoy working with Kwast and in later years he always maintained that his studies in Melbourne with his mother, Louis Pabst and Adelaide Burkitt had been the most fruitful. 'When in Frankfurt, I learned practically nothing,' he would often say. Be that as it may, the German correspondent of the weekly American musical magazine *Musical Courier* was in Frankfurt for what seems to have been the Australian's first student concert in October 1896, and filed a report which suggests that despite Percy's feelings Kwast's tuition was having some effect:

The first Hoch Conservatory recital of the year on Friday brought many good things to light. Herr Professor Kwast allowed another prodigy to show himself in public, and he proved beyond doubt that the reports concerning his playing are true. His name is Grainger [. . .] and in appearance all you could wish for in a prodigy; blue eyes, golden hair (actually golden), ivory skin and delicate features. Melbourne was his home, but he comes here to be made a virtuoso; it certainly looks like a sure thing. Master Grainger played a Mozart concerto with Herr Professor Kwast at the second piano. He has a touch that any virtuoso might be proud of and a technic as sure as it is wide in its scope. His legato playing is worth coming across to hear.

Nevertheless, Percy was disillusioned with more than the piano tuition he was receiving at that time. In 1945 he recalled the first impressions his mother and he had received of German people and German musical life in the following words:

[. . .] her [Rose's] first impression of the Hoch Conservatorium of Frankfurt was that of amazement at Frankfurt's musical backwardness, slovenliness & ungiftedness. My piano teacher, the Dutchman, James Kwast advised my Mother & me to go to the Uebungsabende Vortragsabende of the Conservatorium at which concerts the students performed. After the first one, Kwast asked my Mother what she thought of it. She said the standard was much lower than in Melbourne, 'the only pianist I really liked was Balfour Gardiner'. This was our first contact with that heaven-gifted composer destined to be the good angel of the British composers of his generation. This was an unpopular remark as Gardiner was studying with Engesser a rival teacher, not liked by Kwast. As for myself, I went to Frankfurt ready to worship everything German [. . .] I was all agog to see the Kriegspiel that I had read took place between German boys in the streets of German towns. Instead I was amazed to find the German boys the greatest sissies I had ever seen. I went to Frankfurt expecting to find the German student gifted & innately musical, but I soon found that the English students in Frankfurt were the only ones with any talent at all. When Cyril Scott returned to Frankfurt around 1897, we were all enchanted with his euphonious & dexterous playing of Bach & Mozart, & with his own sparkling improvisation. I suppose his own playing of such things as his Piano Sonata Opus 66 & such trifles as 'Rainbow Trout', 'English Waltz' constituted the highest pinnacle of sheer giftedness & natural adroitness in pianism I had ever witnessed anywhere. When Ethel Liggins (later Ethel Leginska) turned up from Hull around 1898/9 she eclipsed us all with her girlishly winsome Mozart playing. She was about twelve or thirteen years old. But I must mention one exception to the ungiftedness of German pupils, Frieda Hoddap,[5] then about eighteen or nineteen & studying with Kwast. She was the most prodigious talent amongst women pianists I have ever encountered. She learned Chopin's B minor Sonata in a week, yet her renderings were never shallow, but always deeply expressive & human. But with the exception of Hoddap, the English held the whole field in Frankfurt. Cyril Scott outsoared all others in composition, but all the other gifted composers were English too, Norman O'Neill, Roger Quilter, Balfour Gardiner. One would hear the teachers talk of the English as unmusical, but the next moment they would mention Leonard Borwick as the only student at the Conservatorium who had played the Museumsgesellschaft (Orchestral Concerts) while still a student.[6]

During these years Percy met and heard two men who were destined to carve out for themselves the most brilliant careers as concert pianists, Eugen D'Albert and Frederic Lamond. Both were Glaswegians and had been very talented students of Liszt. Of these two, Percy went on to write:

D'Albert gave a piano recital soon after I got to Frankfurt, & I was enthralled by his slapdash English style [. . .] he played his own Piano Sonata with his feet & hands flying all over the place & wrong notes one or two to the dozen. Of course, D'Albert was full of un-English blood & un-English backgrounds, yet his overweaningness, his Cockney patter, his flirtuousness, his overpowering energy were all as truly English as his early influences & his early pianistic training. When I saw D'Albert swash around over the piano with the wrong notes flying to the left & right & the whole thing a welter of reckless-ness, I said to myself, 'That's the way I must play'. I'm afraid I learnt his propensity for wrong notes all too thoroughly. When I heard Fred-eric Lamond about 1898, I was less impressed with his playing, though very struck by his typically British sweetness, kindness & tenderness to me personally, when I, a miserably raw pianist, was stupid enough to play for him.[7]

Despite Percy's remarks, Lamond, a dour Scot of unquestionable genius, had a great admiration and affection for him and followed his subsequent career with considerable interest. Around this time the Aus-tralian was taken to hear D'Albert play Beethoven's G major Piano Con-certo and he was to number this as one of the most moving musical experiences of his life—a high compliment indeed coming from a life-long hater of the music of Beethoven. Another pianist whose Frankfurt concert he attended was Ossip Gabrilowitsch. The young Russian's play-ing impressed him with its charm and poetry and many years later he was to make a fine recording of one of Percy's most popular works, *Shep-herd's Hey*.

There is some evidence to show that around 1896 Rose and Percy may have become dissatisfied with the piano tuition he was receiving from Kwast—although only one undated letter has survived to substantiate such a theory. At least it is obvious that Rose had written to her old friend Nellie Melba in England for advice. Melba's reply is interesting:

> Fernley,
> Marlow Road,
> Maidenhead.
>
> August 6th.

My dear Mrs Grainger,
    Many thanks for your kind note, I am glad to hear Percy is getting on so well, it is very difficult to advise about a Master for him but I should think the Master Paderewski studied under would be the best, he is certainly having great success with his pupils his name is Leshetitzki[8] & he lives in Vienna—I would advise you to go & see him [. . .]. I would love to see Percy—he must be about 14 now Georgie[9] is 12—They are both growing up.
    With best wishes & with love to Percy
                                Yrs very Sincerely,
                                Nellie Melba
Would you like me to get a letter from Paderewski for Leshetitzki?

For reasons which are now obscure Rose did not take Melba's kindly and very sound advice, though it is tempting to speculate how the course of Percy's life and subsequent musical career might have differed had she done so.

The senior lecturer in composition and theory at the Hoch Conservatorium at that time was Ivan Knorr. Knorr was born in Mewe, West Prussia, in 1853 and studied under Richter and Reinecke in Leipzig. He later lived for many years in Russia, where he married a Russian woman and was able to count Tchaikovsky as one of his friends. His position at the Hoch Conservatorium was secured in 1883 on the personal recommendation of Brahms. He was a man of charm, wit and broad culture, all of which were belied by the somewhat alarming visual impact he had on those around him. A pork-pie hat perched on iron-grey hair cut in the fashion of a convict and baggy yellowish trousers seem to have been the most striking aspects of his appearance. Amongst his many talented students were Hans Pfitzner, Frederic Lamond, Herman Sandby, Carl Friedberg, Clemens von Franckenstein, Balfour Gardiner, Roger Quilter and Cyril Scott.

Percy and Ivan Knorr disliked each other from the beginning of their short association. Knorr's wit, it seems, often bore a sting of malice and on one occasion he played a particularly spiteful trick on Percy. The Australian was cycling with his mother in the woods around Frankfurt one day when they heard another cyclist whistling a simple tune. The melody fascinated Percy and he used it as the basis for a set of variations for string quartet which had been requested by Knorr. When Knorr saw the finished product he brought his sarcasm into play by telling him that it was a work of considerable importance and he should hear it performed. Knorr organized the players and an audience by persuading the entire staff of the Conservatorium to turn up for the feast of musical comedy. The work, of course, was rather juvenile and Knorr was merely taking unfair advantage of Percy's painful gullibility. The event became vividly etched in his mind, for he later recalled that the entire staff did turn up and that they 'simply squirmed with laughter'.

When Percy was enrolled in Knorr's classes he and Rose had already moved to rooms over a bakery near the Conservatorium. Here he spent much of his time reading about the poverty-stricken lives of the great composers and he vowed that such conditions would never afflict him. At that time his favourite literary food was Grove's *Dictionary of Music and Musicians*. Knorr always cycled to the Conservatorium and each day had to pass the house where the Graingers lived. Percy would wait for his teacher to pass and then follow him on his own bicycle and gently mock him with some extraordinary feats of trick riding. He was able to stand still and even cycle backwards—something that apparently angered Knorr.

It is not possible to ascertain with complete accuracy how long he studied with Knorr. In his book *The Philosophy of Modernism (in its connection with music)*[10] Cyril Scott suggests that apart from a certain grounding in harmony and counterpoint Percy never took Knorr's criticism in purely compositional matters. It would seem, moreover, that courses in harmony and counterpoint on the one hand and orchestration and instrumentation on the other were entirely separate, and the very first lesson which Percy received from Knorr in the latter is well documented. Percy himself related how he disliked Knorr because of his tendency to sway his pupils too much in the direction of his own personal tastes. At this first lesson, Knorr, who was naturally very keen on the music of Tchaikovsky, suggested that his charges take the Russian master as their model for orchestration. Percy, who for the most part disliked Tchaikovsky, approached Knorr privately after the lesson and asked if he could not take Bach as his example. Knorr was taken aback by the young Australian's request and indignantly retorted that what Bach wrote was not orchestration. But the main argument came about when Percy told Knorr that he was already using a whole-tone scale for his compositions. Knorr had no patience with such modern experiments.

Although Rose had paid for the entire course in advance Percy refused to attend any further lessons with Knorr. Rose, however, was by now taking large classes in English and through these contacts she was put in touch with a remarkable man by the name of Karl Klimsch who offered to take her son under his wing. It turned out that Klimsch, an amateur musician, was to become Percy's only true composition teacher whilst Percy became his only pupil. Their association was to become one of the most important in Grainger's early life. The Graingers soon moved to rooms in a boarding house called the Pension Schöne near where Klimsch lived.

Karl Klimsch was born around 1840 and was the son of a travelling lithographer. Karl's father, a Bohemian, had roamed from town to town with his lithographic kit, printing trade and visiting cards. Lithography was then a new luxury and proved very popular. When the time came for Karl to take over the family concern the young man set up a business in Frankfurt. During this period of his life he would spend his evenings drawing lithographic copy-book designs from which aspiring lithographers could learn their art. Klimsch's business soon became one of Europe's leading photographic, lithographic and three-colour process firms, and with it he became a millionaire in marks. When the Graingers became acquainted with the Klimsch family in the early part of 1896, Karl had just retired from his business, leaving it entirely in the hands of his son and son-in-law and throwing himself with the energy of a man half his years into riding, cycling, painting and music.

Klimsch had a snow-white beard and hair, and intense piercing blue eyes. Percy described him as having the nature of an angel expressed in the manners of a fiend. His family thought the world of him but insisted that living with him was mental torture. Almost everything anybody did was wrong in his eyes and though he was never physically violent he could be devastating with his tongue. Percy summed him up : 'The fact was that everything he did himself, everything he wanted to do was pure goodness, pure generosity, pure rightness, pure wisdom.'[11]

At last Percy had found one teacher for whom he could have an unqualified respect. Klimsch, however, was very critical of his piano playing and especially of his compositions — by this time he had composed a few piano pieces and one movement of a piano concerto. They were all very derivative and written in a sort of Bach/Handel/Mozart/Haydn pastiche. Klimsch was horrified by these pieces when Percy presented them to him and exclaimed, 'You are as florid as Mendelssohn. Do you really want to be a florid composer?'[12]

Percy related that Klimsch's theory of composition was this: 'If you have no theme or melody in your head, don't compose at all. If you have a theme or melody, start off with it right away and the moment your melodic inspiration runs out stop your piece. No prelude, no interlude, no postlude: just the pith of the music all the time.'[13] This was a piece of advice with which he tried to comply all his life — though he was not always successful.

Klimsch was an ardent Anglophile. He had an English governess for his children and spent each summer with his family in Scotland. It was Klimsch who revealed to Percy for the first time the beauties of English and Scottish folk-song some ten years before he was to meet Grieg and involve himself in the activities of the first English folk-song revival.

During his years in Frankfurt, Percy fell in with four English students at the Conservatorium: Roger Quilter, Cyril Scott, Balfour Gardiner and Norman O'Neill. They called their new Australian friend 'Perks' — a nickname they continued to use into adulthood. At various times they were referred to as the 'Frankfurt Five', the 'Frankfurt Group' or the 'Frankfurt Gang'. The bond of a common language naturally drew them close together and Percy found in three of them, Quilter, Gardiner and Scott, close lifelong friends.

Although O'Neill kept very close to Gardiner, Scott and Quilter throughout his life, Percy and he were never to form a truly close relationship. In fact Percy harboured a well-concealed dislike for O'Neill, describing him as being a 'tame cat' and despising the way he was, as he put it, 'with the crowd, against the genius'.[14]

War, pursuit of individual careers and sometimes petty differences were eventually to sunder the group, but Percy often maintained that had they continued to live and work together they would have been every bit as strong and respected as 'Les Six' or the Russian Nationalist Group. Such a dream was not to be, primarily, it would seem, because none of the constituent members believed that there was a strong enough artistic bond linking them. Even Percy once admitted that apart from a commonly held sensitivity to a certain harmonic idiom the only factor which united them was a unanimous hatred of the music of Beethoven and that it was misleading to think of them as a group of conformists. Each possessed highly individual personal characteristics and their artistic leanings were no less polarized.

Roger Quilter was born in Brighton in the year 1877. He was a man of extraordinary generosity and gentleness of nature and Percy had a very special affection for him. Quilter's youthful talents as a mimic and entertainer made him popular amongst his fellow students. But it was his budding talents as a composer that first attracted Percy. The Australian was walking along the corridors of the Conservatorium one day when he heard some music for violin, cello and piano emanating from the composition classroom. He recalled that it sounded like 'enriched Schumann' and he stood enraptured as the heart-warming sounds surged through him. He did not know who the composer was until a few minutes later when Quilter emerged from the room. Percy approached the older boy and immediately struck up a conversation. Their friendship soon became intense and they became regular visitors to each other's rooms in Frankfurt and frequently went on jaunts together through the Taunus Mountains.

Like Quilter, Balfour Gardiner came from a well-to-do family background and he too was born in 1877. He had a pronounced Oxford accent and a sophisticated sense of humour. The fact that he had large trusting blue eyes also must have been a special attraction for Percy. But with Gardiner his eyes were the mirrors of his soul—a characteristic which Percy was also quick to appreciate. His humanity and friendliness were of a high and rare order. Like Quilter he was essentially highly introspective and remained so all his life—though his bluff, no-nonsense façade often belied the fact to those who knew him only casually. One manifestation of his introspection was a hyper-critical attitude towards his own compositions and some years later he was to abandon his art altogether. He was, however, an opinionated young man, determined to have his own way where and whenever possible.

Having studied music for a brief period at New College, Oxford—a period which interrupted his Frankfurt training—Balfour Gardiner returned to Germany in the late 1890's utterly disillusioned as to the value of university education. Here his independence of spirit very soon made itself manifest in occasional confrontations with Dr Bernard Scholtz.

It was the Klimsch family who introduced Percy to Cyril Scott. When Percy had quit Knorr's composition classes, he would often hear the Klimsches sing the praises of their young English friend whom they had come to know a few years previously during his first period of study at the Hoch Conservatorium and who was about to return to Frankfurt. The Klimsches' daughter Butzie introduced the two one day, telling Scott:

'Percy has just written a piano concerto.' Scott then tossed the question over his shoulder, 'Do you know anything about musical form?' Percy's answer was negative. 'Then you can't call it a concerto', replied Scott.[15]

Their relationship had not begun well and Scott made matters worse by vainly trying to persuade him to return to Knorr's composition classes. The initial coolness quickly thawed, however, and in many ways Cyril Scott became a father substitute in Percy's mind in those Frankfurt days. To begin with, Scott was the elder by three years and this at an age when three years can make the difference between boyhood and manhood. At this time, Percy's works were the object of much scorn and derision among his fellows and mentors. Scott, however, quickly discovered that the boy had developed a style of his own by the age of sixteen. As Scott himself writes: 'At an age when Wagner was writing offensively like Meyerbeer, Grainger was already writing like himself. [. . .] Swerving away from his Handelian tendencies he began to show a harmonic modernism which was astounding in so young a boy, and at times excruciating to our pre-Debussian ears; and, strange to say, he began writing in a whole-tone scale without knowing of Debussy's existence.'[16] His early draft of a setting of *Love Verses from 'The Song of Solomon'* and his *Bush Music* and *Train Music* were works in which Scott felt that Percy was many years ahead of his time.

The two were excellent company for each other during these days, and not just on a purely musical level. As an escape from his work at Frankfurt, Scott would often go by train to a village called Cronberg in the Taunus Mountains about forty-five minutes from the city. Here he would take rooms at the 'Bathing Establishment'. Scott described his visits in *My Years of Indiscretion:*

> Cronberg is a beautiful, medieval-looking village, its cottages clustering round a highly perched ruin, reminding one of the feudal system to which it obviously owed its origin. In the vicinity were woods, orchards, sloping meadows with an abundance of wild flowers, streams fringed with forget-me-nots—in a word everything which delights the soul of a nature loving poet. [. . .]
>
> But in spite of the rural beauty I should have felt somewhat lonely, had not Grainger, who was almost a trick rider, bicycled to see me once or twice a week; and those hours we spent together on such occasions were magical hours indeed. I had the youthful pleasure (long since departed from me) of showing him my latest piece of work and of hearing his enthusiasms—unaccountable though it seems now. Often we used to go for long rambles, during which he would divest himself of his shoes and socks, and paddle in the streams, while I looked on; for I was less enthusiastic over that sort of sport than he. But then he had just discovered Walt Whitman,[17] and was imbued with the idea of living up to his, shall we say athletic philosophy; while I for my part

was a worshipper of that very different kind of poet, Ernest Dowson, and more inclined to dream of pale nuns and Horatian courtesans than of brawny sunburnt bodies. [. . .]

Perhaps the most astonishing feature in Grainger's make-up at the time was his capacity for eating cakes: I have seen him polish off ten Berlin pancakes for his tea alone, and without noticeably bad effects.[18]

It was Cyril Scott who introduced Percy to the music of Alexander Scriabin and César Franck — two of the few late Romantic composers for whom Percy was to develop a lasting admiration. Scott also played for him some of the latest works of Grieg and the less known works of Tchaikovsky. He also provided friendly support when the more eccentric of Percy's suggestions brought upon him the ridicule of friends and academic superiors. On one occasion Percy had intended entering a composition for the Mendelssohn Prize, which was competed for each year at the Hoch Conservatorium. When asked what he intended doing with the prize money in the event of winning he explained that he very much wanted to go to China and there make a study of its music. This only succeeded in drawing mirth and derision from those present. Cyril Scott, however, was most sympathetic when Percy explained the love he had developed in Melbourne for oriental music. This, of course, rang a concordant note with Scott, who had always been attracted by things oriental.

Scott, the first of the Frankfurt Group to have a major work publicly performed, listened with great patience to the youthful and revolutionary outpourings of Percy's artistic imagination. One of his ideas at this time was to dispense with the baton-waving conductor at public orchestral concerts. He wished to substitute for the conductor an 'orchestral supervisor' who would operate, by some form of remote control, mechanical music desks through which would pass the parts of the score written out in strip fashion. Apart from translating the supervisor's wishes regarding tempo more precisely, he no doubt felt that it would eliminate in some measure the human element in the performance of orchestral music. Percy liked mechanical contraptions and perhaps in the idea of the orchestral supervisor can be seen the embryonic stages of a desire totally to eliminate the human element from the performance of all kinds of music. In later years this led to the construction of machines for the creation of his Free Music.

Several other young men were loosely associated with the Frankfurt Group in those days. Baron Clemens von Franckenstein,[19] Carlo Fischer and Herman Sandby could be counted amongst these. Franckenstein, a precocious music student from Munich, was a close friend of O'Neill and Percy often met both in Frankfurt and, later, in London.

Carlo Fischer was an American cellist from Washington DC who had played in orchestras in St Petersburg, Kiev and Helsingfors before arriving in Frankfurt late in 1898 to study with Hugo Becker. He and Percy were to become close friends and before Fischer left for America in July 1899 he had become sufficiently impressed with Percy's powers as a pianist to suggest that they should make a concert tour of America together. Rose, however, found Fischer a tiresome and forward young man — he had made no efforts to conceal his amorous feelings towards her — and forbade Percy to entertain such ideas. When Fischer returned to America he became a cellist with the Minneapolis Symphony Orchestra and eventually its assistant general manager.

Herman Sandby, a Dane, was to become the closest of Percy's male friends. Like Fischer he had come to Frankfurt to study under Hugo Becker. Percy and Herman loved playing piano and cello works together and some years later they were to make concert tours of England and parts of Scandinavia. Sandby was the first person to take Percy's music seriously — some time before Scott. The young Australian would often perform his latest compositions for the 'Gang' and these intimate recitals were nearly always greeted with laughter and derision by Scott, O'Neill, Quilter and Gardiner. On one occasion Sandby stayed behind after the others had left and confided in Percy that he thought his music was not at all funny and that it was worthy of very serious consideration. At this, Percy broke into tears of joy and relief. He and Sandby became firm friends thereafter.

In the late spring of 1897 Rose suffered a minor breakdown in health due to neuralgia. She was ordered by her doctor to abandon her evening classes in English and all reading and writing. This was unfortunate because her evening classes provided the greater part of her income. She had saved enough money, however, to tide them over until she had recovered and they were even able to afford a holiday during the summer of the same year.

Meanwhile, Mimi, James Kwast's daughter by his first marriage, began to take a leading role in Percy's life around 1897. Just as Percy was a favourite with the Kwasts — he was referred to as 'their youngest son' — so was Mimi a favourite with the Graingers. Mimi was Rose's favourite pupil in her English classes at that time and Percy had become well acquainted with the girl, three years his senior. It never would have occurred to him, however, to take the association any further than that of a childhood friendship, for it was his mother who provided all the female company he desired and it was she who decided for him the beginning, termination, extent and nature of all outside friendships. This state of affairs was to last until her death.

In this fashion, therefore, it fell to the lot of Mimi to be chosen as Percy's first sweetheart. Rose's 'arrangement', moreover, was deemed agreeable by the Kwasts, for they wanted to find means of helping Mimi overcome her grief arising from her separation from her real 'amour' Hans Pfitzner.[20] Pfitzner was disapproved of by James Kwast as a suitor for his daughter.

Rose chose a suitably romantic evening in the spring of 1898 to set the affair in motion. She had taken Percy and Mimi to Cronberg and the three were walking back after a day's ramble in the surrounding countryside. It was a balmy evening with the fireflies sparkling in their myriads and Rose turned to her son, saying, 'Why don't you take Mimi's arm?'[21] Percy obeyed.

Unbeknown to Rose, however, the new relationship was to play havoc with her son's emotions. It unleashed in him a Niagara of pent-up affection and he directed it all upon a girl who was after all much more interested in someone else. For the moment Mimi responded with an equal degree of feeling and once went to the extent of suggesting that her sixteen-year-old Australian suitor should marry her forthwith. But when matters had come to this point Percy moderated the ardour of his feelings. Mimi became irked and scornfully suggested that he return to his mother as she was the only one he would ever love.

The affair continued amidst a few minor trials and tribulations. Then the gossip-mongers proceeded to do their worst and it was whispered to Rose one day that Mimi and Percy had been seen hand in hand in the city. Rose became a little concerned and went to see James Kwast about the situation — not telling her son of the minor scandal for the time being. Kwast was not in the least worried by the story with which Rose confronted him and merely said, 'Mimi is so much nicer since Percy and she have formed an affection for each other.'[22] This quelled Rose's anxieties for the present and Percy and Mimi were permitted to continue with their relationship.

Mimi had always loved Hans Pfitzner more than she had Percy and Pfitzner's jealousy and frustration came to a head sometime late in 1898. Percy returned to his rooms one evening to find an urgent note asking him to go to the home of the Cossmanns — friends of the Kwasts. They had received a telegram from Pfitzner, which simply stated that if Mimi did not join him at once in Berlin he would kill himself. Percy was not aware that Pfitzner's flame burned brighter in Mimi's heart than did his own, but not wishing to have a suicide on his conscience he spirited Mimi away from under the noses of her parents and took her to the Frankfurt railway station. Here he argued with Mimi that it would be better to go to Pfitzner to discuss matters and then decide whether she wanted to marry him or not. Mimi agreed and she was put on the first express for Berlin.

Percy presented the Kwasts with the *fait accompli* the following morning. It may have been this bombshell which eventually broke up James Kwast's first marriage. Pfitzner left Berlin and moved to Italy and eventually England, where he married Mimi the following year. But despite the Mimi affair, Percy continued to study under Kwast for the remainder of his time in Frankfurt. Shortly after his separation James Kwast remarried.

Not much is known about the personality of Mimi. Percy once wrote that she was 'not middle class' and 'not moved by commonplace stirs'[23] — whatever those negative descriptions may mean. When the subject of Mimi was brought up in correspondence some forty years later he described her, somewhat cruelly perhaps, as having been a 'lump' when he knew and loved her and a 'mountain' before she died. He went on 'I did not heroically "give her up" to another. I never dreamt she would not come back to me.'[24]

In December 1899 Rose suffered her first serious nervous breakdown, probably brought on by syphilis. When she was recovering, she and Percy received a visit from John Grainger who was on his way from Australia to France, where he had been engaged to build the Western Australian Court at the Paris Exhibition of 1900. They had not seen each other for almost five years. John's visit lasted only a few days and, though there were no arguments, the atmosphere generated by the reunion was distinctly cool. During his visit, Rose took him to meet Karl Klimsch one evening. John was always given to a certain degree of bombast that seems to have increased over the years and on this occasion he spent the whole evening talking about himself and said next to nothing about his wife and son. Klimsch was greatly offended by John's behaviour and later told Rose that she must never return to him.

John was also introduced to Cyril Scott at the West End Pension where Rose and Percy were then living. Scott played through his *Magnificat*, which was then nearing completion. When Scott had finished playing, John put down his cigarette, leered over his spectacles, and turning to the young English composer, said, 'Very reverent!' Scott and Percy found John's remark highly amusing and exploded in fits of laughter. When composing his *Magnificat* the last thing Scott had had in mind was reverence — any interest in religion Scott may have had at that time was purely academic.

Rose, however, was not yet completely recovered from her nervous breakdown and one day Karl Klimsch handed her an envelope containing a sum of money. 'Use this for a holiday in the South of France or anywhere you like. But I give it only on the condition that you never make an attempt to repay it and that you never mention the money again,' he said.[25]

Rose and Percy were thrilled with the gift and they used it during the spring and summer of 1900 to visit San Remo, Nice, Paris, Amsterdam, London and Glasgow. It was whilst travelling by train in southern France and Italy that Percy was suddenly struck by the rhythmical complexities of the sounds penetrating the railway carriage as it rattled over point systems. For Percy this single experience touched off a desire to make radical experiments with irregular rhythms in music.

In Paris they were reunited for a few days with John before going on to London, where they arrived on the night the news broke of the relief of Mafeking. Apart from seeing a few sights of London, the Graingers spent most of their time with Dr Fenner, the brother-in-law of Dr Hamilton Russell, in Surbiton. Percy liked Dr Fenner enormously for he possessed an Aeolian Orchestrelle (a reed organ mechanically operated by paper rolls). Then they moved on to Scotland, where they felt completely at home. The days spent in Glasgow gave Percy the opportunity of making a three-day tramp through the breathtaking mountains and lochs in the nearby countryside of West Argyllshire. The rich accents of the Scots, the stark shapes of the hills, the swirling tartans and the strident sounds of the bagpipes proved a great intoxicant. He later described this as the most important single artistic influence in his life. His two *Hill-Songs*, which can be numbered amongst his finest compositions, were commenced within a year of his return to Frankfurt, and bagpipe-like sonorities are easily discernible in these works.

Soon after their return to Frankfurt in the autumn of 1900 Percy resumed his studies with Kwast and Klimsch whilst his mother began giving English lessons once more. For their return they had moved into the house of Frau Outh where Roger Quilter lived. Later they moved to another boarding house called the English Pension. Catastrophe soon struck, however, when Rose suffered her second serious breakdown in health. She fell on an icy pavement and besides suffering physical injuries had a further nervous collapse. Since they had spent most of their savings on the European trip and the sole provider was now totally incapacitated, Percy was forced to act quickly. He decided to seek a livelihood by giving recitals, accompanying singers and holding private piano classes for local children. Rose meanwhile was desperately ill and was forced to lie on iced pipes for many months. She was nursed chiefly by her son, who sat by her bed for many hours often reading from her favourite books.

It was the circumstances surrounding Rose's illness and Percy's own enforced plunge into the life of a concert pianist that made him take a decisive turning in his life as a composer. He wrote of this period:

[. . .] my mother had become an invalid, constantly threatened with paralysis, & from then on my main anxiety was to be able to earn enough as a concert pianist (for I was not willing to degrade my compositional life by allowing any commercial considerations to enter into it) to secure for her a reasonable degree of comfort & security. With this end in mind I vowed not to publish or (conspicuously) perform the main body of my compositions until I was forty years old; for I feared that the radical nature of much of my music would stir up animosities against me that would undermine my earning power as a pianist.[26]

By the summer of 1901 Percy had learned under Kwast's tutelage a selection of solo piano items and a few piano concertos including those of Grieg, Schumann and Haydn. This list also contained a Mozart concerto, the Second and Fourth Concertos of Saint-Saëns, the Third and Fourth Concertos of Beethoven and the piano part of the same composer's *Choral Fantasy*, the D minor Concerto of Brahms, the first two concertos of Tchaikovsky and Liszt's *Hungarian Fantasia*. Once Percy had established himself in London, however, and had become associated with the interpretation of a few particular concertos, some of these were dropped from his repertoire.

During the spring of 1901 Rose had recovered sufficiently to leave her sickbed and was pushed around in a wheelchair for the several months of her convalescence. Percy had behind him one successful season as a mature concert pianist and stood poised on the very brink of his most active years as a composer and concert pianist in London. The thirteen years he was to spend in London were to bring fame and fortune, torment and tragedy.

In the summer of 1901 Rose and Percy sailed for England.

# 4

## Saint and Sinner

The years spent in Frankfurt saw the emergence of three marked developments in Percy Grainger's character and music. They were to become the nuclei around which the rest of his life and personality growth revolved and for this reason these years must be considered as the most crucial period of his life. In the order of importance given to them by Grainger himself, these three elements were: the development of distinctly abnormal sexual appetites, the evolution of a highly idiosyncratic personal philosophy based on the concept of 'racial charactology', and the maturing of an individual musical style.

In one of the many rambling autobiographical essays written in his adult years, Grainger remarked: '[. . .] so by sixteen or seventeen I was already sex-crazy'.[1] The psychological data lying behind this statement are not difficult to determine. The omniscient, omnipotent and omnipresent mother figure and the weak, downtrodden and eventually outcast father figure made for an overwhelming identification with his mother. Rose was for Percy the symbol of fertility, wisdom, beauty and all-provision. This was complicated by the fact that his childhood had been starved of the element of play and companions of his own age, which led to an excessive degree of introspection. If pure Freudian methodology were to be applied at this stage, all might have augured for an adulthood of homosexuality. And this element was, indeed, to be ever present in his psychological make-up.

Experiences of cruelty, harsh discipline and punishment in both physical and mental forms were also part of his childhood and these served as the main direction pointers for the eventual channelling of his sexual urges. Allied to this kind of experience was the literary diet of his childhood:

Between seven & ten I read a lot of Homer & phrases like 'The javelin crashed through the shield' were always on my lips. Later on when I was ten or twelve when I read the Icelandic Sagas the thought of the battleaxe hewing from the shoulder to the waist gave me the greatest mental delights. In the meantime, I had read in Dickens passages such as the one where Nicholas [Nickleby] strikes the schoolmaster on the cheek leaving a livid streak — & all sorts of stories — one about a boy leaving home to join the circus & being whipped by the circus manager. [. . .] These passions were quite unconscious & I had no idea what caused me to shake with delight when I read such descriptions [. . .] each person must have some subject that fires him to madness, whatever it is. To put up with less seems crazy.[2]

It is reasonable to conclude, therefore, that Grainger's 'home-ground' where sexual expression was concerned was to be flagellism. And by the age of sixteen he had already begun auto-erotic experiments in sado-masochism. The whip, then, was no longer simply an instrument of anger or punishment; instead it had become a means of expressing his innermost urges.

He went on to write:

Out of this World of violence, war, cruelhood & tragedy, my longing to compose arose. Many children are cruel to animals & many little boys harsh to little girls, but this fierceness wanes as they grow up. But I never grew up in this respect & fierceness is the keynote of my music. [. . .] What is all this unrelieved misery for? I haven't the faintest idea. Is it because our era (with its myriads of young men doomed to facing death in the sky & wholesale drownings in the sea) needs to have its injustices to the young brought home by art?[3]

And again:

The object of my music is not to entertain, but to agonize — to make mankind think of the agony of young men forced to kill each other against their will & all the other thwartments & torturings of the young.[4]

Art for Grainger, therefore, was partly a protest against the evil of the world,[5] and this artistic protest came to be born through a strange metamorphosis of his awareness of what he always admitted as being the cruelty and evil in his nature. But he was forever confusing symbol with reality and once during the Second World War he said to a news reporter, 'I am personally an example in music of everything I hate and decry. People like that ought to be burned at the stake. I can't help what I am.'[6] The completely dumbfounded reporter saw to it that every word of this curious interview was reproduced in the next day's edition.

There can be little doubt that the ethical content of his protest represented a fine and noble ideal, but the strangely tortuous lines of his thinking and the extraordinary acrobatics of logic and rationalization which he felt obliged to perform in order to arrive at his conclusions — many of which were very sound — almost defy analysis or understanding.

Flagellism was not the only sexual abnormality towards which he was inclined. He seems to have been broad enough of spirit to have pondered a multitude of deviations — even if it is probable that flagellism was the only one in which he habitually indulged. The element of homosexuality has already been mentioned, and though there is no proof that he was at any time a practising homosexual there are many pointers to indicate that he was at least a latent one. Moreover, many of his closest friends were homosexuals of varying degrees of overtness who might well have been attracted by his undeniably striking and somewhat effeminate looks.

In Australia the oft-encountered and utterly bogus concept of the athletic, fair-haired and bronzed 'Aussie' and the folk-philosophy of 'mateship' are as old and myth-encrusted as Ned Kelly himself. Herein has always existed ample scope for unconsciously sublimating any amount of homosexual urges. Where Australians are concerned, they have mostly hidden behind earnest desires to 'prove' their manliness. In this respect Grainger was Australian to the boot straps, and particular instances of his need to prove or demonstrate his manliness turn up at many points in his life. In Frankfurt, for example, he sometimes walked out on to the two-inch strip of moulding which connected windows on the outsides of buildings. He seems to have been fond of doing this on the third and fourth storeys, apparently with the intention of scaring the ladies of the neighbourhood. Having heard that German soldiers did route marches with packs weighing fifty pounds on their backs, he once decided to fill a pack with sixty pounds of sand and take a long walk through the surrounding hills to see if he was as good as they. In this respect he was. In the harsh German winters he sometimes flung open the windows of his room and spreadeagled himself stark naked on the lid of his grand piano. At other times he would walk into the surrounding woods, strip off and stand statue-like in the snow. His hair, however, always proved to be something of a problem when the outward signs of masculinity/femininity were at stake. It was his mother who decided that he should wear it long à la Paderewski, and Grainger was to receive many doubting remarks as to his sexual tendencies on account of this. Though in childhood the colour of his hair had been naturally fair, it had been kept 'Nordic' by his mother's liberal application of hydrogen peroxide when it began to grow darker. After his mother's death he continued with this treatment for some time.

Like his mother, Percy always had a razor-edged sensitivity to human physical beauty and this sensitivity knew no barriers of gender. Indeed he was fascinated, almost obsessed, by those infinitely variable masculine/feminine qualities which are to be found in both sexes. It is significant in this context that when he wrote his extraordinary eulogy of his bride-to-be in 1928 he remarked of her many qualities: '[. . .] a Nordic type of womanhood, half-boyish yet wholly womanly [. . .]. To meet her is to have all one's boyhood fairy-dreams & hero-dreams come true.'[7] In this instance, the juxtaposition of the feminine image of 'fairy-dreams' against the masculine one of 'hero-dreams' is very telling.

Similarly the emotional quality of his affection for his very closest friends knew no gender complications. In a letter to Herman Sandby in 1937 he makes the following comment concerning happiness:

> There are those that say that a man gets more perfect happiness with a man friend than with a woman sweetheart. George Moore says that there are few women a man would wish to meet in Paradise. I know nought of such sex differentiation. With me *it is the race*, not the sex, that matters [. . .]. If *the race* is right, & *the land* is right, I am in heaven.[8]

Grainger's letters are naturally the most revealing documents of his entire legacy and the cryptology he used (often wandering into Danish, Ancient Swedish, German, Icelandic, Norwegian, Maori and a bizarre language of his own devising amongst others) is difficult to decode. The affection he expressed for his close male friends in correspondence went far beyond the conventionally florid epistolary style of his day.

There were two further important elements in Grainger's sexual make-up, whose interconnectedness set them somewhat apart. Fortunately, perhaps, they were always to remain at the level of unrealized fantasy.

The idea of incest was obsessive with Grainger for most of his life — both before and after the death of his mother. He did not, however, harbour the desire to make this physical reality with his mother. Perhaps this may have been largely due to his knowledge of Rose's syphilitic condition, but certainly other indeterminable and unrecorded factors came into play. Rose retained her youthful looks for many years and she and Percy were often taken as being sister and brother or wife and husband. Whatever the physical attractions may have been between Rose and Percy they were certainly never given an explicitly incestuous outlet, but a mere glance at any one of many thousands of letters which they exchanged can leave no doubt as to the emotional qualities of the relationship. The contents of each and every letter are drowned in the most excruciating and mawkish sentimentality and if the reader were not aware of the fact that they were between mother and son, they could easily be mistaken for the most intimate of love letters — which, of course, in many cases they were. On this subject, perhaps it is sufficient to say that even in old age Grainger described the relationship as 'the only truly passionate love affair of my life'.[9]

Grainger's incestuous desires, however, became more conscious when he considered the possibilities of having children. He was in fact never to father any children, mainly for the reason that he simply did not want any. They would never have fitted into his scheme of life. But he was always obsessed with the idea, nonetheless, and on the few occasions on which he wrote about the possibility of having his own children it was always in connection with some form of deviant sexual relationship with them. A few years after leaving Frankfurt he wrote to a girlfriend:

> I wish to procreate independent children, if at all. [. . .] I long for no slave children of my own, thanks. [. . .] I propose this: Never to whip them till they are old enough to grasp the meanings of lots of things, then say to them: Look here! I want to ask a favor from you kids. I want to whip you, because it gives me extraordinary pleasure. I don't know why it does, but it does. It gladdens me more than eating even. I know it's rotten for you, but then: I am particularly kind to you kids. I've worked hard to make you free in life, so that your childhood not only may be jollier now than ordinary children's, but may last ever so long, if you're pure minded like I am, & don't grow worldly out of pure cussedness, or inherited 'throw-back'. I don't *deserve* any reward for all this, or for all the freedom I allow & encourage, for that is every grown up's duty to the young, but I say this to you: I'm kind & a good old thing, & polite & obliging. Now why not do me a great favor, as one equal to another, let me whip you; because, only, it gives me such unexplainable delight. Don't you think the children'd let me? I have hopes. Then encourage them to whip each other as a form of athletic fight. (They have a game like that in Japan, I've just lately read.) I believe one could easily get decent, plucky, blue-eyed children to do it [. . .]. You know that I long to flog children. It must be wonderful to hurt this soft unspoiled skin. [. . .] & when my girls begin to awaken sexually I would gradually like to have carnal knowledge with them. [. . .] I would love to explain things to them & open to their eyes in this area the whole way of the world without shame or shyness or cowardice. [. . .] Why should a man not be sensual with his own children? [. . .] All these mixed father — and lover — instincts I have had since I was 14/15. I have always dreamed about having children & whipping them, & to have a sensual life with my own daughters.[10]

As a complement to these desires, he always felt physically attracted to girls in their early and mid-teens. The mental effects of the reproductions of Rubens and Titian masterpieces and the copies of Greek statues which had adorned his Melbourne homes were augmented during his Frankfurt years by the many nude statues which were to be seen in museums and art galleries of that city. They set his mind and fantasy ablaze and their very inaccessibility increased his frustration. Writing of his own psychological development of this period Grainger remarked in retrospect:

So the body, the naked body as well as the clothed, became for me a vehicle of expression, a tally for life, a symbol of nature's world just as music, poetry & prose did. In art I saw the pure, the unspoilt, the natural, the unblemished exalted & deified, & in the talk of my parents & of art-loving friends I heard the artificial & the pretentious, such as artificial flowers, modern clothes, the use of scent, powder & rouge, derided & criticized. So as I grew up to be fourteen or sixteen or twenty years old I looked upon grown women with horror as being dirty with their beauty grease, foul in their powder & rouge, disgusting in their indolent grossness, repellent in their lovelessness and worldliness. Mid-teenaged girls were half-spoilt goods, but I looked upon girls of thirteen & twelve down to six & five as being the only representatives of womankind that answered the requirements of an art-wonted mind & eye. I was not anti-woman, I was only anti-filth, anti-decay. I was not pro-infantile, I was merely pro-pure, pro-clean, pro-fit, pro-natural, pro-sweet, pro-nice. I was not so lacking in manly feelings as to love the nasty for the nice, as to tolerate females looking & behaving as revoltingly as men.[11]

So with Grainger one of the pinnacles of his sex-fantasy was to unite the parental or filial with the lover's emotion. This he discussed with all his girlfriends and he wrote about it to a great extent in letters and in essays.

Despite his constant and firm rejection of the Christian view of life, he was consciously, consistently and wilfully self-critical. In letters he would often refer to himself as 'cowardly', 'sinful', 'weak', 'evil' or 'wretched'. In 1927 he wrote:

The outer shell of me (the part of me that faces the world) has learned to go thru the motions of acting the part of a grown man; I can earn money, I can build concert programs, I can force my concert-hearers ((audiences)), I can think out money matters, with a worldly eye & a seemingly grown-up, manlike air. But the core of me, my inner self, my senses have stayed like those of a child — a child that knows he is naughty & looks to be punished for it. I always feel 'the world' to be a cruel monster whose avenging ill-will I am just about to bitterly taste.[12]

And later he wrote:

I have dim twilight thoughts about God & justness [. . .] so when there are storms & lightning I feel afraid, feeling for the moment that God will wipe me out because I am evil. When a train goes fast I fear it will leave the rails because of me — to wipe me out wretchedly. I cringe & quail because of my awareness of my evils — the evil deeds I have done & the far more evil thoughts I feel within my bosom.[13]

The relationship between man, artist and art has always been and always will be one of the eternal incalculables that perplex the student of psychology, art and biography. Each inquiry discloses a vast quantity of infinitely variable factors. Whatever becomes manifest as a result of a study of Grainger's life is usually confirmed by his own admission at some point or other. It is difficult to believe that there have been many men possessed of such a profoundly self-analytical and self-critical intellect. In Grainger's case, it is easy to see that (in his eyes, at least) his sex urges were the very mainspring of his existence and of his art. Similarly it is evident that the relationship which existed between him and his mother was the motive force which sustained his every thought and deed.

Perhaps the most curious aspect of Grainger was the fact that despite the apparent inconsistencies of his thinking and the abnormalities of his psychological make-up, he was, nonetheless, a man of total integrity. It was his acute self-awareness both as a man and as an artist that made him so. He was aware that life, like art, does not consist solely of beauty, perfection, goodness, purity and truth but must also accommodate all the weakness and inadequacies inherent in humanity. Whatever his artistic or human aims may have been, he became overwhelmingly conscious at an early age that a denial or rejection of the darker forces which motivated him necessarily implied a negation of life itself. Grainger believed that he knew the nature of his innermost forces, though at times he seems to have lost sight of the totality at the expense of satisfying a minor obsession. He talked and wrote about the most intimate details of his life, thought and art to his mother and few close friends. A few years after the Frankfurt period he wrote a very self-revealing letter to a girlfriend who he felt did not understand him. It can be assumed that the views he expressed had largely been formed in his days in Germany:

I believe you think the sport-spirit, the war-relish, & all that is only surface deep with me, & that the real ME is human & meltable & capable of real sympathy. If you keep on thinking that (maybe you don't) you're only raising up a little disappointment for yourself one day. The shock to my vanity that that disappointment wld be doesn't worry me but the idea of yr ever being disappointed in anything does; & please don't let me be that thing. I am not a deep person. The only *real* thing to me is *love of pleasure*; it is very real, & almost deep. I am incapable of real sympathy, because real sympathy is 'with-suffering' & I am incapable of suffering. My life is one long war against disappointment. Therefore I am not really unkind. Pain, to myself or others, is a thing I instinctively fight tooth & nail; therefore I am a socialist, etc. But ask me to really *feel with* folk who suffer (the poor, or my dearest & nearest even) & I have to fail; I can join in all mirth with almost anyone, but I can sorry with none — not even myself; I've tried but I can't keep it up, my mind wanders. Also I am shallow in that I am a *luxurious beggar.* [. . .] All my pleasures (the sole genuine things in me) are luxurious ones. *War*; it destroys & wastes what has taken tons of toil to build up. *Sport*; the 'afterwork' spirit of man. The very scenery that stirs me & that I love is lifeless & unproductive (as far as any nature can so be), useless & unkind to man; — Australian deserts, S'African barren Veldt, Scotch dreary highlands, The Sea. Only the aftermath in the life struggle (the time for play, the lives that can be thrown away, the country that can be let go waste) delights me. None of the birthful, needed, earnest-rooted things (love, work, suffering, endurance) of life awake in me even a worth-listening-to echo [. . .] I can't be 'plain lovable human Percy', because I'm not at all *plain* & only a wee bit human; but as to lovable; you just pile on the love & I'll say 'Ta'. [. . .]

War & sport & wild country & race pride pick me up & carry me away & drunken me, & don't leave me half-filled & questioning & cold, & therefore I worship them & serve them & sing them & shall till I drop.

You must know that's a horrid lie, about the 'iron coat of armour'. You know *quite well* that I use no such feudal-like thing. I wear only pink & very thin skin in all my dealings with all folk; (& surely with *you*). No, 'the iron coat of armour' was not merited. Because I am by nature cold (tho' *keen*) you imagine I must be stifling God knows what feelings. I show all I feel *always*. I can't fake up ones, even to please friends.[14]

If but two factors are borne in mind this letter can begin to make sense and as a result many pieces of the jigsaw puzzle may start falling into their proper places. Firstly, it must be remembered that when Grainger talks about 'pleasure' he includes in that concept what other people might term pain, torment or agony. He was neither exclusively sadistic nor exclusively masochistic and these forces were operative on the emotional, spiritual and intellectual levels as well as on the physical — perhaps even more so. Life and art could only bear fruit as a direct result of strife and struggle. For Grainger this was a cardinal article of faith. And if life did not present him with adequate torment in the normal course of events, then he would invent it and bring it upon himself with a ferocity which at times was almost beyond belief.

Secondly, he believed that it was essential to separate the concept of love from that of lust and put them at either end of a 'sliding scale' of infinite variables. This was a lesson he was forced to learn as a result of his relationship with his mother. Each successive human relationship thereafter made him more fixed in his belief. It did not by any means provide him with the final solution where human relationships were concerned, but it certainly helped. On this subject he wrote:

> That's why I say I hate love, that love is the cruelest thing in human
> affairs. I like only those things that leave men & women perfectly free.
> The only kind of love I like is platonic love. But there was heaps of that
> between Mother & me. The reason why I say I worship lust but hate
> love is because lust, like platonic love, leaves people perfectly free.[15]

For a few years Grainger's awareness of his own sexual abnormalities
caused him considerable worry and it was not until 1900 when he visited
Amsterdam that he found a lasting peace of mind. Amsterdam was the
world's capital where pornography was concerned. Here could also be
obtained any number of books dealing with the psychology of sexual
abnormalities. The literary quality of these books varied (as it still does
today) from smutty sub-journalism to the serious scientific treatise.
Needless to say, when the eighteen-year-old Grainger arrived in
Holland's capital he had the literary feast of his life. But above all, the
newly found knowledge that his abnormalities had been shared by countless people throughout history brought solace and alleviation of his
growing feeling that he was the only person in creation ever cursed with
such obsessions. It gave him a special delight to read that so many great
artists, composers, writers and philosophers had had similar urges.

Grainger never embraced the Christian way of life, so he lived
unfettered by its moral dogma. The stigmas of guilt and shame had
little place in his life, though consideration for his mother and other
people sometimes involved repression or abstention despite his claims to
the contrary. Wildness, recklessness and unbridled savagery were the
keynotes of his existence, and from these stemmed all the tragedy, restlessness and torment of his life. In 1932 he wrote: 'It is no use living
merely not to die. One should live to really live.'[16] And in a letter to
Roger Quilter in 1930 he wrote: 'I live for my lusts & I don't care if they
kill me or others. Now (as when I was sixteen) I live only for fury &
wildness. I feel that a hot parched wind from the Australian desert has
entered into my soul & with a fury of heat I must go thru', burning
up myself & others. But what joy! That is how I live: following my lusts,
& composing now & then on the side [. . .] My life (if you count the
majority of its hours) is that of a slave, but no sadist can call life poor
or disappointing who can realize his cruellest, wildest dreams. When we
successfully follow & realize our lusts we are lords indeed. I would not
exchange with the angels.'[17]

In a letter to Cyril Scott in 1956, he wrote of the many obsessive fears
which he had faced all his life. He went on:

> As far as I am concerned I think it is true that my cowardice in so
> many directions is supported by knowing that almost all the stirs I am

moved by are considered evil by most people & that most people, if they knew my thoughts, habits & feelings would disgrace me & put me in prison if they could. It is not a matter of being weak & unable to 'resist temptation'. I am quite strong in being able to control myself in all sorts of ways & I do not do deeds that I disapprove of. But the fact is that I really worship evil & find everything else un-worth while. But it may (nay, must) be said that all my worship of cruelty cruises only around sex-instincts. Apart from sex I am not such a bad fellow. But as I am really not interested in anything else but sex it just boils down to this: that I hardly think of anything but sex & that all my sex thoughts are full of evil & cruelty. And one of the greatest & most continual worries is that I may die without the full evilness of my sex feelings being known to the world or recorded. If I knew of a country where I could publish an unabridged account of my sex-life & sex-feelings I would be a happy man indeed.[18]

Although Grainger often had a tendency to overstate his case, the fear of which he wrote was a stark and real one; and with that fear unassuaged he was to go to his grave.

# 5

## Grettir the Strong Flexes his Muscles

By his mid-teens the attitudes which Grainger was to hold for the rest of his life were all but crystallized. He still thought of himself as 'Grettir the Strong' and was by now developing an acute sense of discrimination between those elements in European culture which had Nordic or Anglo-Saxon roots and those which owed their existence to the cultures of Ancient Rome and Athens. The former he clung to, enshrined and worshipped; the latter he rejected out of hand. His life was to be ruled by Thor rather than Zeus or Jupiter. His concept of 'race' was as absolute as it was naïve. His belief that he was the product of a racially mixed marriage had already become something of a burdensome complex.

The Frankfurt years, however, brought about a strange twist in his ideas. He came to Frankfurt prepared to consider the Germans as the descendants of the Goths, but, as has already been pointed out, he was greatly disappointed. His initial disappointment soon turned to bitterness, hatred and finally fanaticism.

Grainger reacted sharply to the anti-British feelings which were prevalent in Germany at that time and which were whipped up to a frenzy just before and during the Boer War. Whilst he did not embrace the British cause during the Boer War and was horrified by the stories of British atrocities he was, nevertheless, made the object of much anti-British feeling by many of his German elders and fellow students. His case was an almost archetypal example of how a person can become a fanatic as a result of being the victim of fanatical ideas. He gradually assumed many of the characteristics of his self-appointed opponents; and, as fate often has it, fanatics of opposing camps frequently have more in common than they would care to own where the pure mechanics of thinking are concerned.

Every event that occurred, every person he encountered in life was looked upon from a racial point of view and was a confirmation and strengthening thereof. Just as a Marxist interprets history and decides to organize his life and relationships according to hypothetical forces which flow between and divide social classes, so did Grainger passionately think and feel in terms of races and racial types.

It is very probable that the Frankfurt years also saw the emergence of anti-Semitic feelings. As a child, Grainger had been forbidden by his mother to play with Jewish children after an incident when some Jewish boys had tormented him and demanded to know how much his mother had paid for a new pair of shoes of which he was very proud. In many German cities around that time Jewish communities still adhered to the isolationist way of life of previous centuries, and isolationism frequently leads to curiosity, mistrust and hatred. In those days, moreover, it was much less frowned upon to be anti-Semitic and in many circles it was almost the rule. In such surroundings Grainger's anti-Jewish feelings blossomed — feelings which did not, however, prevent him from cultivating Jewish friends in later years and expressing admiration for the work of such colleagues as Bloch, Gershwin and Rubin Goldmark.

Inconsistency of thought and utterance did not seem to bother Grainger. Of course, some of these difficulties are resolved if one is prepared to accept Graingeresque premises, but so often one is left with irreconcilable loose ends. These he simply accepted as such and regarded as all part of the natural hazards of life. In this fashion he could declare himself a socialist, pacifist and democrat in one breath and in the next could be found arguing on the side of racialism, violence and a kind of apartheid system which would have geographically separated Nordics, Jews, Latins, negroes and even homosexuals and heterosexuals. Shaw, Chamberlain, Whitman and Kipling can hardly be regarded as ideal bedfellows from either a literary or philosophical point of view, yet Grainger seems to have held each of these writers in equally high esteem.

By the end of the Frankfurt years he was already making conscious efforts to drop from his spoken and written English words which had been derived from Latin and Greek. This idea of 'purifying' the English language and turning the clocks back to pre-Battle-of-Hastings English found its culmination some years later in the evolution of what he proudly termed his 'Blue-eyed English'. He also devoted much effort and love to the compilation of a 'Blue-eyed' dictionary. This was a crank idea of almost fabulous proportions, but fascinating, nonetheless — as are many such ideas hatched in obsessive minds. It was a dream which he pursued with tireless scholarship and energy and in his last years when he looked back on the glorious monuments and shattered ruins of his life's course it was this that he numbered amongst the very few achievements for which he had a proud affection.

Perhaps the best assessment of the curious mechanics of Grainger's thinking and philosophizing is given by Storm Bull, a piano pupil and friend of Grainger's and a man of great human insight:

What seemed to be inconsistencies, I believe, were in large measure the difficulties of following his reasoning in so far as much of his logic was based on premises foreign to other people. I can remember tracing what I considered to be inconsistencies through the maze of reasoning and coming to conclusions that would permit me to accept the seeming inconsistencies as logical reasoning if certain Graingeresque premises could be accepted. [. . .] I can only say that even supposedly contrasting opinions given by Grainger take a considerable amount of rationalization to bring about a form of consistency. Whether an attempt to do so is justified I cannot say. [. . .] I see no great advantage in attempting to rationalize his inconsistencies by virtue of our logic. On the other hand, I think it is almost even less profitable to make a reader believe that Grainger was truly consistent. I believe that in large measure he was sincere in respect to being truthful. I also believe that in large measure these were not merely momentary reactions but were part of an over-all philosophy in trying to bring together irreconcilable opposites. After all, it takes a great deal of rationalization to defend the necessity for an Anglo-Saxon dictionary based on the opposition to Mediterranean language. On the other hand, it is relatively easy to defend an Anglo-Saxon dictionary on the basis of the need for such a dictionary. There is no question in my mind as to whether or not Grainger was entirely sensible; in my opinion, he was not; and I have no reason to believe that he thought I was sensible either.[1]

Burnett Cross, another close friend of Grainger's, has also written:

As to inconsistency, I found out that PG did not value it above other things. Mentally he did not believe in the adage 'look before you leap'. On the contrary, he thought it was important to make a mental leap on the basis of the information at hand and see where it landed you. If it landed you in an untenable spot, get out and try another leap in another direction. I think this willingness to stick one's neck out is far more valuable than the appearance of consistency. (But it was disconcerting in conversation with PG, when you weren't used to it.)[2]

In so many aspects of Grainger's personality the Peter Pan element is very evident and the problem of his philosophy is no exception. It is often the case that people in reaching maturity will moderate or modify the fervour of their youthful philosophies as a result of the tempering effects of years and the attendant experiences of life and humanity. Not so with Grainger. The flame of his views burned brighter as the years passed, so that what was a fire in his youth was a raging, uncontrollable self-immolation of super-Wagnerian dimensions in his last years.

To pile inconsistency upon inconsistency, it is essential to remember that Grainger's relationships with people he loved were mostly marked by a saintlike gentleness, sweetness and kindliness of nature. He seems to have spent his life helping countless lame dogs over stiles. He was generous beyond reason. In a strange sense, however, this fitted in very well with other aspects of his psychology, for he would be almost lavish (though discriminating) with his praise, affection and money, even though he knew he would be hurt by the fact that his generosity was so rarely reciprocated.

The literary influences were as powerful as ever during the Frankfurt years. The works of Otto Weininger[3] and Houston Stewart Chamberlain[4] were almost certainly encountered around this period and it is probable that he first read the works of Nietzsche whilst in Frankfurt. The first two writers were proto-Nazis of a particularly noxious variety, while almost the only versions of Nietzsche to be obtained in those days were the scandalously inexact editions by Nietzsche's sister. Many years later these editions of Nietzsche were credited with being amongst the philosophical and cultural antecedents of Hitler's brand of racial dogma. A more cruel injustice to a writer and philosopher of genius has perhaps never been perpetrated. There can be no doubt, however, that it was the works of Rudyard Kipling and Walt Whitman — encountered for the first time during these years — that were to have the most profound emotional and artistic influence on the young Grainger.


In his Melbourne years, Grainger had composed a few forgettable trifles bearing the heavy stamp of the earlier classical composers. He claimed, however, that at the age of eleven he had already thought out a polyphonic complexity which he called an 'Australian fugue'. Although this is indicative of an early leaning towards patriotism, it is greatly to be regretted that he seems to have bequeathed no exact details of what might have distinguished his 'Australian fugue' from a normal fugue. For a year or so after his arrival in Frankfurt he showed no signs of great originality in his compositional work; but during the years 1897 and 1898 there was a sudden and rather dramatic blossoming of original talent.

Grainger's musical antecedents are not easy to set forth. When Delius met him some years later in London, they were both startled by the harmonic and formal ideas they had in common. Their musical tastes were practically identical, they were both instinctive rather than traditional composers and both claimed that they had learned most from amateur rather than professional musicians. Yet before their meeting they had known nothing of each other's music and hardly anything of each other's existence. Neither Delius nor Grainger intentionally copied the styles of any other composers though as boys and young men they both had their musical idols. Undoubtedly Dr Russell provided Grainger with his first musical idol when he played works by Schumann so exquisitely. Bach, Handel and Grieg came next when Grainger studied under Louis Pabst; and the Frankfurt years brought into play the influences of Wagner, Brahms and Cyril Scott.

Whatever is Bachlike, Grieglike in me is mostly thickened by some sort
of Wagnerlike, or Brahmslike, or Schumann sauce & I put forward
that this never failing craving for what is rich & thick & he-high-
rangesome ((tenorlike in range)) in every timestretch of my toneart is
due to the childhood sway that Schumann [. . .] held over me by
means of Dr Russell's lovely & lovable playing at Killalah.[5]

It is significant to note that after this early flowering of music he did
not conceive, write or publish the first version of any original composition for solo piano with the exception of the *Jutish Medley*. His antipathy towards that instrument as a means of musical expression was
already showing its first signs. He wrote in 1938:

[. . .] and now, when my compositions are given in their original form,
I read some such press comments as the following: 'Mr Grainger (like
Scharwenka and Moszkowski) is a pianist who has the happy knack of
writing short piano pieces that please a certain type of amateur, and
whose pieces eventually appear in arrangements for all sorts of possible and impossible combinations.'[6]

He was always scrupulously careful to have printed below the title of
all his piano arrangements: 'Dished up for piano'. Yet despite this, the
sort of cruel misrepresentation typified in the foregoing quotation was
always cropping up and in later years he found this deeply hurtful.

The Frankfurt years, however, were decisive in Grainger's development as a composer. Many influences worked upon him to mould the
style of his creativity. He reacted sharply against the almost universally
held belief that whatever was good in Western European musical traditions was to be found in the current productions of German, Italian and
Austrian trained musicians. He also rejected the commonly held belief
which equated length with profundity, light-heartedness with a lack of
seriousness and musical insight with obscurity. In these cases, his association with Karl Klimsch initiated and strengthened his resolve to
produce works which for the most part were to display an astonishing
economy of notes and a transparency and pithiness of content which in
certain respects can be compared with the works of Anton Webern. In
Grainger's best works whatever 'point' there was to be made was made in
as concise a fashion as possible.

His personal experiences of the awesome power of the German tradition during this period were most important. He felt moved to reject
such tyrannical authority and from then on looked upon his artistic mission in life as that of a soldier to his calling. By the age of sixteen he had
committed himself to a battle against Western European traditions and
his compositions were to be his weapons. Although the literary and
musical influences which triggered off this change were strong and clear-

ly defined, it demanded above all a conscription of his inner artistic forces. He saw his role as that of a musical innovator rather than that of a person who perfected or distilled what had been bequeathed to him. He was an anarchist and revolutionary by nature rather than by training. It is for this reason that a quest for the purely musical antecedents of Grainger's music is more often than not doomed to be fruitless.

Perhaps because Percy had become so fluent in the German language and because he was accepted so wholeheartedly by many German families, Rose felt by 1897 that he was becoming too 'Germanized', and she wrote of this to her husband, who was now working in Perth. John, in turn, communicated this to a girl, Amy Black, with whom he had a very close relationship, saying: 'I am sending you a copy of Percy's last letter to me which I am sure you will enjoy. Rose says he gets more Germanized every day, so I shall have to touch him up a bit with "Rule Britannia" and "Hearts of Oak" etc. [. . .]'[7] He sent his son a patriotic book called *Deeds that won the Empire* and several Kipling books. The latter captivated Percy immediately and he soon started writing choral settings of Kipling's poems, especially those of the *Jungle Books*. Grainger wrote of these pieces:

> In these, above all 'The Beaches of Lukannon', I developed my mature harmonic style — that is to say, harmony in unresolved discords. To the best of my knowledge, such a procedure was unknown at that time & must be considered as an Australian contribution to musical progress. So through the books my father sent me in 1897, I became what I have remained ever since, a composer whose musical output is based on patriotism & racial consciousness.[8]

Grainger was to occupy himself with Kipling settings on and off for the rest of his life. He was constantly adding to and revising them, so that when eleven of them were published for the first time as a cycle, in 1947, they represented a whole life of compositional activity — very much in the way the *Songs of Travel* did for Vaughan Williams. When Grainger published a work of his in later years, he often added a long and informative programme note. The programme notes for these settings, however, which take just over nineteen minutes to perform, simply state: 'My KIPLING "JUNGLE BOOK" CYCLE, begun in 1898 and finished in 1947, was composed as a protest against civilization.' The quintessence of his harmonic and polyphonic ideas can be found within the pages of these works. Though they form a major contribution to twentieth-century choral music they are rarely if ever performed today.

The poetry of Walt Whitman had a very profound effect on the thought and art of many composers of this period. Delius, Holst, Vaughan Williams and even Hindemith were to come under the influence of the virile and sensuous lines of the American poet. In 1901 whilst still in Frankfurt Grainger began a composition which was not to be completed until 1915. This was to be one of his most remarkable works and bears the title *Marching Song of Democracy*. It is a strident and energetic work employing massive forces including organ, large percussion and wind sections and a mixed choir required to sing wordless 'nonsense' syllables: 'Ta - ra - di - ra - da - ra - rum - pum - pum - pam' and so on. Grainger wanted it to be a kind of modern and Australian version of the Gloria of a Mass and it carried the following dedication: 'For my darling mother, united with her in loving adoration of Walt Whitman'. Grainger's own programme notes, which are worth quoting at some length, clearly state his indebtedness to Whitman for its inspiration:

In 'A Backward Glance o'er Travel'd Roads' (Leaves of Grass) Walt Whitman wrote: 'The New World receives with joy the poems of the antique, with European feudalism's rich fund of epics, plays, ballads — [. . .] & though, if I were ask'd to name the most precious bequest to current American civilization from all the hitherto ages, I am not sure but I would name those old & less old songs ferried from east to west — some serious words & debits remain; some acrid considerations demand a hearing. Of the great poems receiv'd from abroad & from the ages, & today enveloping & penetrating America; is there one that is consistent with these United States, or essentially applicable to them as they are & are to be? Is there one whose underlying basis is not a denial & insult to democracy?'

When a boy of sixteen or seventeen I was greatly struck by the truth of this assertion, not merely as regards America & literature, but as applying no less to Australia & the other young Democracies, & to all the arts; & I felt a keen longing to play my part in the creation of music that should reflect the easy-going, happy-go-lucky, yet robust hopefulness & the undisciplined individualistic energy of the athletic out-of-door Anglo-Saxon newer nations.

When in Paris during the Exhibition of 1900 I happened unexpectedly upon the public statue of George Washington when strolling about the streets one day, & somehow or other this random occurrence galvanized in me a definite desire to typify the buoyant on-march of optimistic humanitarian democracy in a musical composition in which a forward-striding host of comradely affectionate athletic humanity might be heard 'chanting the great pride of man in himself', the underlying urges to be heroic but not martial, exultant but not provocative, passionate but not dramatic, energetic but not fierce, athletic but not competitive.[9]

It is possible that the sentiments and ideas which are to be found in the works of Kipling and Whitman (more especially the former) may ring rather hollow in our more cynical and positivist minds of today. Nevertheless, they had a profound influence on Grainger and thereafter became a major part of his credo, flag and armour. In his desire to be Whitmanesque in letter as well as spirit, it was his original plan to write his *Marching Song of Democracy* for voices and whistlers only (no instruments) and have it performed by a chorus of men, women and children singing and whistling to the rhythmic accompaniment of their tramping feet as they marched along in the open air.

Of the many startlingly fresh ideas to be found in the score of *Marching Song of Democracy*, it is important to note the irregularity of the rhythm. In the first eight bars (written whilst he was still a student in Frankfurt) there are seven time signature changes:

$$\frac{4}{4}, \frac{2}{4}, \frac{5}{4}, \frac{4}{4}, \frac{3}{4}, \frac{2}{4}, \frac{3}{4}, \frac{4}{4}.$$

This clearly indicates an early interest in complex and irregular rhythms which was to lead him towards the desire to dispense with regular metre and definable rhythm completely.

Grainger's settings of *Love Verses from 'The Song of Solomon'* also showed great rhythmic inventiveness and he said that his interest in irregular rhythms had had its origin in his listening to Roger Quilter reciting these Biblical passages as well as his experiences on the trains in southern France and Italy. From these roots he evolved what he termed 'Beatless Music'. His experiments with irregular rhythms were followed in 1904 by Cyril Scott's piano sonata. Scott achieved a considerable measure of success with this work, particularly on the continent of Europe, but Grainger's contention that Stravinsky and Schönberg were influenced in their turn by Scott's sonata is, to say the least, open to debate and certainly enquiry. Scott, however, gladly confessed his indebtedness to Grainger.

In later years Grainger persistently claimed priority in many of his musical innovations over practically all of the major composers of the twentieth century. There is every possibility that he was right, but to prove his claim a minutely detailed study of countless scores of many composers and periods would have to be made. Until such a quest is undertaken, Grainger's contentions will always remain within the realms of disputability. There can be no doubt, however, that most of the musical problems which he had resolved to his own satisfaction within a year or so either side of the turn of the century were similarly resolved by other composers and such resolutions have since become common currency in today's world of music.

Rhythmically, the most complex pieces that he was eventually to have published were the two *Hill-Songs* on which he commenced work in March 1901 in Frankfurt. They are both works of inspired genius and one day may take their rightful place amongst the finest works of their kind of the twentieth century. An example of the metrical complexity which proliferates in the *Hill-Songs* can be seen in a passage which was written just after he left Frankfurt in 1901. Within a space of forty-four bars there are forty-two time signature changes which run after this fashion:

$$\frac{5}{8}, \ 1\tfrac{1}{2}, \ 2\tfrac{1}{2}, \ \frac{3}{4}, \ \frac{4}{4}, \ \frac{2}{4}, \ 1\tfrac{1}{2}, \ \frac{5}{16}, \ \frac{3}{4}, \ \frac{5}{8}, \ 1\tfrac{1}{2}, \ 2\tfrac{1}{2}, \ \frac{7}{8}, \ \frac{5}{8}, \ \frac{4}{4}, \text{ and so on.}$$

By 1907, at a time when Stravinsky was working on his Symphony in E flat, Grainger had sketched a piece called *Sea Song* wherein rhythm had become almost indeterminable, not to say unperformable. The first thirteen bars—bearing, incidentally, the instruction 'Fast'—provide the following time signature changes:

$$\frac{1}{4}, \ \frac{7}{32}, \ \frac{3}{32}, \ \frac{5}{64}, \ \frac{5}{16}, \ \frac{3}{8}, \ \frac{7}{64}, \ \frac{3}{32}, \ \frac{5}{64}, \ \frac{9}{32}, \ \frac{3}{8}, \ \frac{7}{64}, \ \frac{5}{16}.$$

It was not only in rhythm, however, that the two *Hill-Songs* displayed innovation. In 1898 Grainger had been deeply impressed by the instrumental and vocal combinations he had heard in performances of Bach arias, Passions and Cantatas. The idea of small instrumental groupings wherein each soloistic voice could hold its own and at the same time blend with its neighbouring voices into a finely wrought polyphonic whole appealed to him greatly. Hereafter he frequently composed pieces which he called 'Large Room Music' (an Anglicized version of 'Large Chamber Music') and which demanded forces consisting of from about eight to twenty-five instruments or blends of single voices and 'Large Room Music' combinations. Such groupings are based on a completely different concept from that which underlies an ordinary small orchestra. It was in this form of instrumental grouping that he was to write many of his most effective pieces. For example, the *Hill-Song Number 1* requires twenty-one woodwind instruments and *Hill-Song Number 2* requires twenty-four wind instruments. Grainger was fond of pointing out that his 'Large Room Music' ideas were conceived and put into practice before the composition of such works as *On Wenlock Edge* by Vaughan Williams and *Pierrot Lunaire* by Schönberg.

During his trans-European tour with his mother in 1900, Grainger had heard some Italian double-reed instruments (at San Remo) and an Egyptian oboe (either at the Paris Exhibition or at Hampton Court) and the snarling nasal quality of these instruments had a great appeal for him. These experiences led to his free and extensive use of double-reed instruments (oboe, English horn, bassoon, contra-bassoon) in the scoring of the two *Hill-Songs* between 1901 and 1902 and the later re-scorings of 1921 and 1923.

Five other works for more or less conventional orchestral forces were also composed between the years 1899 and 1901. With subsequent minor revisions and additions made between the years 1942 and 1945 they were eventually published under the collective title of *Youthful Suite.* The suite contains the following items: *Northern March, Rustic Dance, Norse Dirge, Eastern Intermezzo* and *English Waltz.*

These pieces show a preoccupation with unusual harmonic organization—for example, there are extended passages of parallel triads (*Northern March*), a series of mediant progressions of parallel major triads over a pedal in *Eastern Intermezzo* and a fondness for closing on added sixth or secondary seventh chords. Curiously, Grainger considered himself a pioneer in the treatment of these chords as finals without apparently being aware of the work of Chopin, Liszt, Debussy and Mussorgsky, amongst others. In any event he used these chords with dogged persistence much in the way Delius was to several years later.

Apart from the purely academic interest of *Youthful Suite,* however, it is a most appealing work and it is strange that some of the constituent movements have not become favourites with the Promenade audiences. Any single piece of the suite's five movements or any combination thereof could easily be performed in concert, and the multi-metric high-kicking *English Waltz* makes a wonderful conclusion to this sadly neglected work.

Perhaps the most interesting overall point of style that made itself felt during this early maturity was a definite tendency to create music in forms where there was little, if any, repetition of thematic ideas. Instead, it is possible to see a continual flow of new thoughts, joined together only by likeness of mood or style. In other words, Grainger's music for the large part was linear or organic in concept as opposed to architectural. It is easy to understand why he and Delius understood each other so quickly and thoroughly when they met some years later and why they both despised the music of the Mozart/Haydn/Beethoven period so much. One of Grainger's early defined musical aims was to strive to make music a mirror of nature rather than a mirror of man's impressions of or feelings aroused by nature. A river-like flow and a gradual unfolding and transmutation of thematic material were to him far more 'nature-like' procedures than the idea of 'constructing' music in classically accepted forms.

Examples of this early innovation can certainly be seen in the two *Hill-Songs* and in a somewhat less inspired creation which he originally entitled 'A Lot of Rot for Cello and Piano'. The last piece was eventually reworked for a larger combination of instruments and entitled *Youthful Rapture.*

Grainger was still hearing in his mind what he called 'nature-echoing, gliding, scale-less and non-metrical sounds' which were suggested to him by the Australian experiences of waves lapping against the sides of the boats in the Albert Park lagoon and the lines of the hills in the deserts of South Australia. His Frankfurt experiments with Beatless Music were very much a part of the same process of drawing together various ideas and influences which were to lead to the first Free Music experiments of more than thirty-five years later. It is tempting to ponder what he might have made of these ideas if the history of science had miraculously slipped forward several decades or more and he had been given access to such wonderful inventions as multi-track tape recording and electronic synthesizers. As it was he remained fettered.

Grainger had some rather curious and highly characteristic comments to make concerning the general mood of his first compositions and his mother's reactions to them:

> I am glad to recall that when I first started to compose seriously in Frankfurt my mother thought much of my music sounded like hymn tunes. This is certainly true of early things like 'The Beaches of Lukannon', 'Tiger, Tiger', 'The Merchantmen' [. . .] I suppose most musicians turn to classical music as an antidote to the churchiness of their childhood, or of their parents or of their past. But I was not dragged to church against my will & did not associate hymn tunes or other churchy tunes with being bored. I heard the church music welling out of St Columb's Church, Glenferrie as we walked past & I found it bright & glorious. One thing I like about church music, it seems to include both men & women & does not typify drunken men, like many Opera Arias seem to do & does not suggest that mother's daughter has learned dancing as Mendelssohn's 'Spring Song', Elgar's elephantine suite dedicated to the Royal children, Tchaikovsky's 'Sugar Plum Fairy', Sibelius's 'Valse Triste' & even Grieg's 'Anitra's Dance' all seem to. One reason why things of mine like 'Molly' & 'Shepherd's Hey' are good is because there is so little gaiety & fun in them. Where other composers would have been jolly in setting such dance tunes I have been sad or furious. My dance settings are energetic rather than gay. They are more like Russian music than English music. They are sad like parts of Balakirev's 'Tamara' & fierce like the 'Trepak' in Tchaikovsky's 'Nutcracker'.[10]

Wherever Grainger's musical ideals took him, he never lost his affection for the works conceived during his youth. In 1936 he wrote: 'In these youthful musical thots of mine there are tucked away some flashes that are soul-revealing—occasional chords, melodic lines, phrases that are truly Nordic, truly British, truly new-world, truly Australian.'[11]

# 6

## 'The years before the war were *Hell*'

There were many forces drawing Grainger to England's capital. By the turn of the century most of the Frankfurt Gang had begun to drift back to England and Grainger realized that it was there that everything that interested him in the field of musical composition was about to blossom. He was anxious to be in the thick of it.

The opportunity of moving to London first presented itself in the late spring of 1901, when he received an invitation from the Australian soprano Lilian Devlin to play a few numbers at a concert she was to give at St James's Hall on Tuesday June 11 of that year. Grainger had known Miss Devlin in Melbourne and later in Frankfurt, where she had studied singing at the Hoch Conservatorium. Rose and Percy welcomed the invitation and in May left Germany to take rooms at 31 Gordon Place in Kensington. They hired a Bechstein piano and he began practising.

The concert took place in the afternoon and Miss Devlin had as assisting artists Innes Smith, Kennerly Rumford (who had recently married Clara Butt) and the distinguished Australian contralto Ada Crossley. This concert, which marked Grainger's first English appearance, was an unqualified success. The *British Australasian* remarked: 'In Liszt's "Rhapsody Hongroise" he displayed qualities of touch and tone that evoked quite a demonstration of applause.' The critic of the *Whitehall Review* wrote: 'the applause that greeted him at the close of his performance foretells that he will soon be a great favourite with all music-lovers.'

Ada Crossley was then at the height of her powers and fame, and this recital brought about an association with Grainger that was to last for a number of years. He had a genuine admiration for her musical talents, as did she for his. She soon became a frequent visitor to the Grainger home and a close friendship developed between the three. It was Ada Crossley who taught Grainger stage deportment, and doubtless she was helpful with social and professional contacts.

At the turn of the century England still had a very rigid class system. Cultured people were very largely drawn from the ranks of the aristocracy and landed gentry, and it was thus possible in those days to pack a London concert hall during the afternoon of a weekday—an unthinkable

idea today. London's 'high life' was marked by privilege and pretentiousness and it was necessary for a career-minded musician to work his way
up through the ranks of the nobility and ingratiate himself with such
people in order to be 'launched' on a successful career. Whatever artistic
talents were possessed by the musical aspirant, social graces counted
equally. Though some artists were able to escape this state of affairs,
Grainger was not, and regrettable though the situation seemed to him
and his mother they were forced to bury their antagonisms and comply
with the accepted methods of advancement.

It was not long, therefore, before Percy had become enmeshed in a
hectic round of at-homes, parties and *soirées musicales.* His charm, good
looks and pianistic talents acted like magnets in drawing round him an
almost hysterical gathering of society hostesses. Grainger often described
himself as a 'pukka' democratic Australian and the thought of being
taken up or 'lionized' by an aristocracy of any kind ran completely
against the grain with him.

Around this period he wrote to his mother, 'I have nought in common
with these ways of living, nor with the thought behind the ways. Give me
rather bugs in my bed, dirt in my dishes, soap on my spoons, life in my
limbs.'[1] In a letter to Eric Fenby in 1936 he remarked about Fenby's
newly published book, *Delius as I knew him:*

> There is one thing I cannot understand, if I may say so: why you
> describe the pre-war life as being sweeter, happier, more spiritually-
> solvent. The years before the war were *Hell,* in my finding—with
> infinitely more cruelty, sham & soullessness than our present age. In
> every present régime each government at least pretends to help the
> helpless. Before the war utter heartlessness seemed to me to prevail,
> & utterly drivelling & goalless attitudes were hand fed. [. . .] I don't
> think you would have liked the years before the war if you had been a
> grown man in them.[2]

Grainger's first engagement came about by accident—or so the society
journals of the day maintained. On the afternoon of July 3 1901 he and
his mother were invited to attend the first London recital of the Australian contralto Maggie Stirling, which was given in the beautiful home of
Lord and Lady Brassey at 24 Park Lane. Maggie Stirling, like Melba
and Crossley, had been a pupil of Mathilde Marchesi and it was probably
through Melba that Grainger and his mother had been invited. The
advertised accompanist for Maggie Stirling was unable to appear, so at
a minute's notice Grainger was called from the audience and asked to
deputize. Without any preparation, he played the accompaniments and
gave a fine rendering of Schumann's *Faschingsschwank aus Wien* as a
solo item. This recital marked the beginning of his career as a society
pianist—his greatest source of income during his years in London.

Percy Grainger's birthplace, New Street, North Brighton, Victoria. Percy with his nurse Annie

Percy aged three with his mother

John Grainger, Yates (an actor) and
Dr Henry Michael O'Hara

Collins Street, Melbourne, looking
east, with newly constructed cable
trams, *c*. 1890

Dr Robert Hamilton Russell

Percy Grainger aged about fourteen

Louis Pabst                    Adelaide Burkitt

James Kwast                    Ferruccio Busoni

Grainger's piano teachers

With Herman Sandby and Alfhild de Luce, the future Mrs Sandby, on tour in Denmark,
1905

With the Griegs and (*right*) Julius Röntgen, Troldhaugen, August 1907

Grainger with his leading folk-singers, Brigg Manor House, 1906: George Gouldthorpe,
Joseph Leaning (*standing*); Joseph Taylor, George Wray (*seated*)

'Here is a photo taken at a few minutes rest for tea last Sunday about 8 miles out from Sale.'—P.G., October 28, 1908

John Singer Sargent. Postcard sent to Percy Grainger and inscribed: 'This is the appearance I present when on the warpath'

Percy with his mother, summer 1917: Bandsman, 2nd Class, 15th Band, Coast Artillery Corps, Fort Hamilton, South Brooklyn

*Above* With the Danish folksong collector Evald Tang Kristensen, Vejle, 1922

*Right* With Delius, outside Domplatz 12, Frankfurt, April 1923

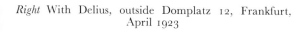

Melba's influence with England's aristocracy prevailed in his favour and it was not long before he was receiving more invitations than he could accept.

A few weeks prior to his first solo recital in London, he was invited by an eminent Australian artist living in London, Mortimer Menpes (a pupil of Whistler), to give a private recital at his studio. This took place during the first half of October 1901, and was well received by the gathering of celebrities who had come to hear him. The first public recital, however, took place at 3.00 p.m. on Tuesday October 29 in Steinway Hall, Lower Seymour Street.

Around this time, Rose and her son paid their first visit to Melba. The first words with which Melba greeted Rose were, 'Well, have you got rid of your funny old man yet?'[3] Grainger wrote to Melba asking her to come to his debut. She welcomed the invitation on the strict conditions that she was to be allowed to pay for her tickets and that the seats for her small party should be in the front row. Grainger, of course, was willing to comply with the great diva's wishes. Melba sent him a warm note of congratulation after the recital.

The critics of London's best newspapers were there and wrote enthusiastic accounts of his performance in the succeeding days. The critic of *The Times* wrote:

> Mr. Percy Grainger [. . .] has the gift of temperament, and no little individuality; he is evidently conscious of the importance of what he undertakes as the interpreter of the great masters' ideas, and in many passages of the group of pieces selected from Brahms's later works for piano solo, there was revealed rare intelligence and a good deal of artistic insight; [. . .] Grieg's 'Ballade' became quite interesting in his hands, and pieces by Scarlatti and Chopin were decidedly effective.

The *Morning Post* found his Bach playing 'excellent' and the *Illustrated Sporting and Dramatic News* thought it 'masterly'. Reservations, however, were expressed in some quarters as to the musical validity of his own transcription of Tchaikovsky's 'Flower Waltz' from *The Nutcracker*. The critic of the *Daily Telegraph* expressed the view that if Mr Grainger desired to be taken seriously, he would leave arrangements alone. Grainger did not leave arrangements alone and was to make many during the subsequent years. The Tchaikovsky arrangement was revised for publication in 1904 and its sales convinced him of the financial value of such publications. The piece was dedicated to the French piano virtuoso and composer Léon Delafosse. Delafosse popularized this transcription in France and in turn dedicated some of his Preludes to Grainger.

Grainger met Delafosse at the London home of Jacques-Émile Blanche. He had met Blanche during a weekend in France two years after his arrival in London and they had become firm friends. Blanche at that time was very firmly established as the doyen of the London society artists and was the first to produce a portrait in oils of Grainger. This was followed by one from the brush of Grainger's friend and fellow country-man Rupert Bunny.[4] Some years later, however, John Singer Sargent[5] produced a charcoal profile drawing which is perhaps the most remark-able portrait of Grainger and the one most often associated with him as a young man. The existence of an undated letter to Grainger from Augustus John indicates that a portrait of the Australian was planned by this British artist. No such portrait is known to exist and the plans were probably abandoned due to the outbreak of the Great War.

Jacques-Émile Blanche (like Sargent and Bunny) was a sensitive amateur musician, having been a pupil of Gounod, who would refer to him as his 'little Mozart'. Blanche was quick to see the significance of the music of Debussy, and by showing Grainger the score of Debussy's *Pelléas et Mélisande* at their first meeting in 1902 he opened up a new world for him. Grainger was intrigued by the harmonic innovation contained in this score, but felt that Debussy's experiments were not drastic enough. Despite his few reservations he immediately began to programme the solo piano music of Debussy and became the first pianist to give public performances of this music in England and later in Australasia, Scan-dinavia and South Africa. He also rendered a similar service for the piano music of Ravel, Scott, Albeniz and Granados.

In 1901 Grainger wrote to Herman Sandby in Denmark, suggesting that he should come to England where he felt sure he would establish his reputation as a cellist. Sandby was to cross the North Sea in 1902 and 1903 to engage in short tours of provincial cities with Grainger, and in England their joint efforts culminated in the receipt of a letter from the secretary of Queen Alexandra commanding them to play at Buckingham Palace. This was perhaps one of the greatest advances Grainger made in his early career as a society pianist. Royal patronage was the highest seal of approval, and thereafter Queen Alexandra often attended his public recitals and concerts in London. The two young musicians also played for Melba (a prospect Grainger always dreaded) at her London home at 30 Great Cumberland Place.

In his letter to Sandby of September 29, 1901 Grainger described the progress of some of his former Frankfurt colleagues and others he had recently met. He gave every indication of being intoxicated by the atmos-phere of creativity that pervaded London. Of Scott, he wrote:

He has certainly been influenced as regards form by my work, & himself asserts that his present period is entirely the outcome of the 'cello piece.[6] His last things are most original, chiefly of great un-broken flow. [. . .] He has written a piano sonata for me which I consider the only successful modern Klavier Sonata.

He also remarked that 'Hans Richter has really taken him [Scott] up and is performing "The Heroic Suite" in Manchester next month.' It was probably through Scott that a few years later he secured several important engagements with Richter and the Hallé Orchestra in Manchester.

Of Balfour Gardiner's latest efforts, Grainger wrote: 'Good ideas, but bad form, simply shitty. There is a nice warmth about his style, & he may improve in form, but I fear he has no formal conscience.' He was drastically to reform his ideas about Gardiner's music when he heard later works.

In this letter Grainger urged Sandby to persevere with his compositions despite his need to earn a living as a cellist, and in so doing he showed good insight into his own processes of composing:

I do not mean only compose, there are hundreds of other ways of developing composition-techniques besides actual writing, the chief thing is constant observation & thought for & on musical-creative matters; when you play music observe it always from the composer-standpoint, note modes of construction, develop *above all a sharp* criticism for 'musical ERFINDUNG': *inventiveness* is the seat of all musical strength, when you see forms & beauty in nature apply it in your mind to the forms & types in music, get to look on Poetry from the setter's stand-point, go for musicalness in Verse, & while reading, *always* take in the metre, rhythms & melodic lines contained therein, & when you *do* find poetry appealing to yr musical requisitions, *always* imagine it composed as you read it, continually think out *exactly* how it should be set, what type, what voices, what tempi, what *kind* of chordal type, what sort of melodic invention etc. etc. & when you feel fine emotions, or sweet noble impressions or think strong thoughts, *straight-away* translate them into yr musical language, at least in thought, think out *exactly* how a composition should be to express those lovely things in their fullness.

Thus you will slowly acquire a severe self-criticism, a quick absorption of the good in others & in nature, & when you ultimately proceed to actually compose, you will find you know what you want, can master yr form & expression, & are clearly conscious of what sort of stuff you need to create for a certain object. [. . .] The mistake is to compose not knowing what you want to make, to acquire the technique without feeling the necessity for it, & to get into mannerisms because you know not how to separate yr contrasting styles. If you think in this way you will find life full of the NEED of MUSICAL EXPRESSION, all emotions will require to become compositions. So it is with me. I have already *done* my thinking (the elementary part).[7]

The first engagement Grainger was able to secure as a soloist with an orchestra was on February 6 of the following year, 1902, when he was

asked to perform Tchaikovsky's First Piano Concerto with the Bath
Pump Room Orchestra under Max Heymann. The concert was preceded, on February 4, by a chamber music recital in which Grainger
and Heymann took part—the latter as a violinist.

Grainger journeyed to Bath alone and one of the most significant facts
about the engagement was that it marked the first time in his life when
he had been separated from his mother for more than a few days. He
enjoyed every moment of his trip to Bath; the concert was a great success
and whilst staying with the Heymanns he delighted in their conversation
and the long walks they often took together. He was to receive a cruel
and rude awakening, however, on his return to London, for when he told
his mother how much he had enjoyed his music-making and the company of the Heymanns she burst into an hysterical fit of anger. This form
of neurotic behaviour continued on and off for the rest of her life and
was repeated in a progressively more histrionic fashion whenever her son
enjoyed himself in her absence. When he returned from a recital tour of
Denmark with Herman Sandby a few years later—a tour which he had
thoroughly enjoyed—Rose's anger went unabated for several days. The
cause of these outbursts would seem puzzling had not Grainger himself
written extensively about his mother's attitude concerning them:

> Mother felt it was a disloyalty on my part to be so very happy the very
> first time I'd escaped from her apron strings. [. . .] On the other hand,
> she was never jealous of my happiness with such composer friends as
> Balfour Gardiner, Roger Quilter & Cyril Scott. What mother felt was
> disgust at my disloyalty, not merely my joy in being with other people
> than herself, but my joy in commonplace things & people. She had
> brought me up to enjoy superior things & people & here was I hilari-
> ously happy in getting close to common things & people. Hatred for
> disloyalty is not the same thing as jealousy. Alfhild [Alfhild de Luce—
> later to become Herman Sandby's wife] has written that Herman was
> hurt in his soul when he came to London to find that I had no manly
> freedom. What does a composer want with manly freedom? A
> composer needs protection so that he can forget outside things &
> concentrate on the much nicer things he has in his own mind.[8]

Except for the regular visitors such as Roger Quilter, who would take
tea with the Graingers each Thursday afternoon, and at the special
at-homes when all his friends were invited, it became increasingly
difficult for even his closest friends to gain access to Grainger during
these years. Cyril Scott has written that acquaintances who wished to see
him had to give advance notice and were invited to call, 'punctually,
please', at, say, 4.20 p.m. on a given day and not to stay after 4.40 p.m.
In subsequent years, Grainger began taking piano pupils (charging one
guinea an hour), and it has been recorded that if the pupil stayed one

minute over his or her allotted time Rose would enter the room and start
nervously pacing the floor.

'As this "How-do-you-do and Good-bye" arrangement, however,
savoured a little too much of a visit to the dentist,' wrote Cyril Scott in
*My Years of Indiscretion,* 'his friends decided frequently that they would
not come.'

Even in his Frankfurt days it is possible to detect that his closest friends
preferred to establish relationships which were 'at arm's length'. When
they understood his domestic situation, they soon realized that it was
Grainger's completely passive attitude towards his mother and her
domination and possessiveness of him that made him such an 'odd ball'.

The year 1902 also saw Grainger taking part in a series of provincial
concerts as a member of a touring party conscripted by the fifty-nine-
year-old Adelina Patti, then at the end of her career (she announced her
retirement in 1906). That such a young and little-known pianist as
Grainger should have been engaged is noteworthy and it is regrettable
that no evidence survives to indicate how in fact such a fortunate position
was secured. The concert party included the violinist Alice Liebman, the
tenor John Harrison and Charles Santley, the greatest English baritone
of his day.

A typical concert was given on October 6 in Birmingham Town Hall
when Grainger performed the Tausig arrangement of the Bach Toccata
and Fugue in D minor and Cyril Scott's *English Waltz.* For the former
Grainger received three recalls, and the latter had to be repeated. With
Alice Liebman he also performed the Allegro from the Sonata in C
minor by Grieg. His performances were welcomed throughout the
country and they certainly established his name in the provinces.

Grainger and Santley did not get along well when the latter declared
that he was indifferent to Kipling's poetical works and positively loathed
Walt Whitman. But Adelina Patti was greatly drawn to Grainger. She
would repeat to all who approached her that she felt as if she were his
mother, and in his presence (much to his embarrassment) she would
loudly declare to all around her 'I simply love that boy', and 'What a
glorious career you have before you', and so on.[9] Grainger wrote to his
mother of how Patti and he had often discussed Melba and how Patti
always spoke in glowing terms of the Australian singer. At the end of the
tour Patti presented him with an autographed photograph, inscribed:
'To Mr. Percy Grainger from Adelina Patti, Baroness Lederström —
1902'. On his return to London he was spared the kind of reaction that
he had had from Rose after the Bath concerts.

During these early years Grainger allowed himself little or no time for
recreation. He usually ran into town if he had a mission to perform or
if he was due to play at a recital. On these latter occasions he would slip
on a pair of running shorts and speed off with his evening dress rolled up
in a knapsack on his back. He always preferred to be in a state of nervous

and physical excitement before he played the piano. Running, in fact, was his main physical recreation and he soon became known as the 'Jogging Pianist'. He often undertook several circuits of the nearby Battersea Park, but because of his piano career his mother had forbidden him to play football — a sport which he had much enjoyed in Melbourne and Frankfurt.

Melba, of course, always sent complimentary tickets to Rose and her son whenever she appeared at Covent Garden and he was able to gain a fuller appreciation of her vocal talents during these years. In a radio interview which he made many years later he said:

> I think she had a very high standard of workmanship. She herself worked very hard at everything, knew all details and had mastered, I think, every technique of her art. I'm not particularly fond of opera singers as a rule, but I must say I've never heard anything to compare with the beauty of Melba's voice in any branch of singing. The top notes, of course, were very ringing and telling, as they are with a good many fine sopranos. But the curious thing with Melba was that her lower notes and her middle notes were equally telling. They had a quality all their own; and even when she was singing with a big orchestra, she was never wiped out. She had a tremendous carrying power and a tremendous beauty of tone and a very great refinement of workmanship in everything she did.[10]

In a more characteristic mood he wrote:

> Myself, I never liked Melba at all, I thought her rough & intender [. . .]. But I loved her voice as truly as I disliked her person. Her voice always made me mindsee Australia's landscapes, her voice having some kind of a peach-fur-like nap on it that made me think of the deep blue that forms on any Australian hill if seen a mile or more off.[11]

Occasionally he went to hear other pianists play. Around 1902 he heard the English-born violinist-turned-pianist Harold Bauer participate in a performance of the Piano Quintet in F minor by César Franck. At that recital he was won over to Franck and Bauer for life. He met and heard Bauer on many occasions in subsequent years and always regarded him as his model Schumann interpreter.

Whenever possible Rose and Percy would attend lectures given by George Bernard Shaw. They both liked his books and plays, and found a great appeal in his brand of socialism. Shaw unwittingly repaid their interest some years later when he chose *Mock Morris* and *Shepherd's Hey* as entr'acte music for the first London production of *Pygmalion* in 1914.

For lighter entertainment Grainger would take his mother to the music hall and later they would always make a point of seeing Harry Lauder when they had one of their rare free evenings. It was in the English music hall that jazz made its first European appearances. Of course, jazz in pre-First World War London had not reached the standards which it was to attain in the twenties and early thirties, but the influence of Afro-American rhythms was slowly beginning to filter across the Atlantic in the form of ragtime. One of his piano pupils from around this period recalls that Grainger used to improvise at the piano in a similar rhythmic style.

But it was not so much the rhythms that attracted Grainger to this new-fangled music as the delightfully curious instruments which were being used in the orchestra pit and sometimes on the stage of the music hall. In particular he was fascinated by 'tuneful percussion' instruments, which were then making their presence felt. During his London years he made an arrangement with Boosey and Hawkes whereby he would borrow from them a percussion instrument, master the necessary technique and return it in exchange for another novelty. Friends from this period have recorded that it was not an uncommon sight to see Grainger running home through the streets of Chelsea and Kensington laden with drums and xylophones. The experience he gained thereby was invaluable, for he was later to become a pioneer in the orchestral use of unusual percussion instruments.

On one occasion he was invited to play at a social gathering at a country mansion and was taken to see the wonderful collection of oriental instruments brought back by his host from overseas. Among the collection was a set of tuned gongs used in Balinese orchestras. He was fascinated by the sound they made and this experience reinforced his desire to incorporate 'tuneful percussion' instruments into his orchestrations.

It was also during this period that he met Donald Francis Tovey and heard him play some Bach keyboard music at a public recital. But though he admired his playing and his editions of Bach, Tovey's writings on musical matters, which appeared in later years, only elicited the most severe criticisms from Grainger. Tovey was a man of profound and extensive learning, but his enthusiasms and writings were nearly always restricted to the already accredited masters of music and he concerned himself little with contemporary musical developments. Later Grainger was to write: 'A man like Tovey who everlastingly rushes to the support of the victor is a musical abortionist.'[12]

In 1902, at a social gathering where he was invited to play, Percy met Mr H. Atterdale Grainger, the Agent General for South Australia in London. Atterdale Grainger insisted that Percy was a relative (in fact he was not) and decided to take him under his wing. He would take Percy to the Savage Club between 1902 and 1906, where he was frequently asked to play. Percy hated the Savage Club, Mr H. Atterdale

Grainger and being asked to play without preparation, so he would concoct fanciful excuses to avoid being taken there. It was at the Savage Club however that Percy had a profoundly stimulating musical experience: here he first heard the Mustel Reed Organ—a part for which he later incorporated in many of his compositions—when Mr Metzger, the London agent for the Mustel Organ, gave a demonstration around 1903 with a small group of wind and string instruments.

Grainger soon gained the friendship of many artists and actors. Roger Quilter introduced him to the young Ernest Thesiger, then an aspiring painter and later to become a stage and film actor—Grainger also remembered him as an exquisite embroiderer. They were to become very close friends.

Thesiger introduced Grainger to William Gair Rathbone—a banker and financier with refined cultural tastes. During the ensuing years Rathbone behaved like a father to Grainger, always inviting him to play at his musical gatherings in Cadogan Gardens. The relationship, however, did not rest on an employer-employee basis (as it did with most of the aristocrats for whom he played), for Rathbone was one of the most musically sensitive amateurs that he had ever met. It was Rathbone who continually drew the young Australian's attention to the latest music from Europe—France in particular. Rathbone also gave him his first Wagner scores at a time when out of diffidence and lack of funds he would not have dared to buy such luxuries. He also introduced him to the music of Gabriel Fauré and later enabled him to meet the Frenchman when he stayed with John Singer Sargent in London. To Rathbone Grainger dedicated *Handel in the Strand* and a 'Free Ramble' for solo piano on themes from a popular comic opera of the time called *In Dahomey* (subtitled 'Cakewalk Smasher'). In 1910 Rathbone gave him a letter and document box which had once been the property of Liszt. Grainger always kept the box standing on his piano in London and later in New York.

Thesiger also introduced Grainger to John Singer Sargent and it was largely through Sargent that he was able to earn his living as a society pianist. Of these two friends Grainger later wrote:

> It was Rathbone who continually engaged me as the solo performer at musical evenings at his house at which he did not torture me, as did many [. . .] by urging me to pianistic feats that I could not rise to. Rathbone & Sargent were my 'good angels' during these London years. I would be playing at some society 'At-Home' suffering sorely at my own pianistic inabilities & also horrified by, as I thought, the cruelty & inhumanity of the smart life around me. But when Sargent or Rathbone entered the room all changed for me. They were like shield bearers in my artistic life. I felt myself protected in their presence. It is significant that they both had American roots.[13]

Grainger frequently visited Sargent's studio in Tite Street and would sit entranced as the American painter played through the solo piano works of Albeniz and Granados. He often maintained that Sargent was the finest pianist he had ever heard where Spanish music was concerned. The painter leaned very much towards Latin culture and would have none of Grainger's worship of Nordic arts. Sargent continually complained that the whole of Norway smelt of fish.

By 1902 Grainger had befriended a lady who was to help him greatly with social introductions and who invariably employed him for her at-homes. The half-Irish, half-Polish Mrs Frank Lowrey was a tall and elegant lady in her forties and lived at that time in Cheyne Walk in a house once owned by Rossetti called 'Queen's House'. Vaughan Williams was to live in the same street at number 13, and probably met Percy through Mrs Lowrey. A great patron of the arts and particularly fond of helping young musicians, she held intimate musical evenings at her home and formed what she called 'The Queen's House Manuscript Music Society'. She made herself president of this society — understandably enough — and as vice-president she conscripted the services of her friend the Hon. Everard Feilding. Everard Feilding was the brother-in-law of the fine tenor Gervase Elwes, then relatively unknown.

When Grainger first met Mrs Lowrey she asked him to play the piano. He decided to deliver an impromptu piano transcription of *Love Verses from 'The Song of Solomon'*. This turned out to be a disastrous choice for as he played the last notes Mrs Lowrey fainted dead away, so overcome was she with the emotion of the piece. In later years Grainger recalled how silly he felt trying to revive her from what was probably more of a feint than a faint. The event set the tone for the whole relationship.

From that point Mrs Lowrey took him under her wing and saw to it that he met only the best people and heard only the best musicians. Mrs Lowrey was sometimes visited in Cheyne Walk by King Edward VII and though at this late stage it is impossible to determine the exact nature of these 'visits', the contact was useful to the extent that it enabled Mrs Lowrey to introduce Grainger to Queen Alexandra. Mrs Lowrey also took him to St James's Hall to hear Fritz Kreisler, whose playing she felt to be 'the coming thing'. Grainger, however, did not care for the violin in any case and took a very strong dislike to Kreisler's playing: 'I could hear nothing in his playing but out-of-tuneness & rasping bowing — a judgement I have never since gone back on. [. . .] I have always loathed the fiddle (a canary-like twitterer, not a man-high voice) & outsingledly all Jew-talk about fiddles worth gold-hoards (when I was sure that any one-pound-priced fiddle would sound just as well or better).'[14] The only aspect of Kreisler's performance that he liked was the way he came on stage holding his violin low down near his knees as if he was about to smash it.

On May 28, 1903 Mrs Lowrey organized a concert at her home in order to present the first performance of some of Grainger's choral works. Among the tenors on that occasion were Gervase Elwes and the composer, and the baritones and basses included Everard Feilding, Herman Sandby, Roger Quilter, Baron Clemens von Franckenstein (from Frankfurt days) and the Australian painter Rupert Bunny. Grainger often included parts for whistlers in his choruses and the whistlers on this occasion included Roger Quilter, Cyril Scott and Henslow Orchard. The works performed were three 'British Folk-Music Settings': *Irish Tune from County Derry, The Hunt is up* and *Ye Banks and Braes,* and two Kipling Settings: *The Running of Shindand* and *The Inuit.* Grainger also played the piano part in a performance of Cyril Scott's Sextet Op. 26.

This introduction to Gervase Elwes was useful for Grainger, for not only did the singer give the first performances of many of his works but his wife, Lady Winefride Cary-Elwes, was very interested in folk-music and played host to the Australian when he went folk-song collecting in Lincolnshire in subsequent years. On other occasions the baritone Harry Plunket Greene assisted at Queen's House concerts; he also gave some first performances of Grainger's songs. Ada Crossley, Ernest Thesiger and Frederic Austin often participated in these functions at Mrs Lowrey's house.

At another Queen's House concert, Balfour Gardiner took part in the singing of some of Grainger's part songs. Unfortunately, Gardiner was unable to keep to his allotted line of harmony and inadvertently followed the melody being sung by his neighbour. Eventually he discovered that the only way he could sing his part without being distracted was to put his hands firmly over his ears during the performance so as not to hear what was being sung by the others. The sight of Gardiner thus cut off from the world around him and Grainger thrashing about with clenched fists trying to obtain some form of order from the assembled choir must have been comical indeed.

There can be no doubt Mrs Lowrey helped Grainger considerably with social and professional introductions in his early London years. One night on returning home in a horse-drawn carriage after a concert, however, Mrs Lowrey let it be known that if he did not become her lover she would never help him again with his career. Mr Lowrey allowed his wife complete sexual freedom, and that night Grainger had his first sexual experience. Writing in an autobiographical essay, *Ere-I-Forget,* in 1945, Grainger reveals that it was not only his first sexual experience, but also his first orgasm, and throughout the act he felt as if he was going to die. Walking home in the early hours of the next morning, the only pleasing thought that could console him amid all the fears of a possible scandal was the knowledge that what he called his 'sexual equipment' did work after all and that his manliness had been proved. For Grainger, however, sex was to remain ancillary to flagellism, which was the true act of appreciation, joy and love. That his first orgasm took place at such an advanced age (twenty or twenty-one) can only confirm the suspicion that the cumulative effect of Rose's attitudes and actions (her fanatical possessiveness, her reluctance to touch him as a baby boy, her use of the whip) was one of emasculation. Perhaps Mrs Lowrey rendered a greater service to her protégé than was ever realized by anyone involved.

Mrs Lowrey would take him to an hotel in Maidenhead by the Thames, and sometimes she took him to Dieppe in France, where she rented a house. (It was here that he first met Jacques-Émile Blanche.) Rose, who was kept informed by her son of his every step, at first approved of the relationship for the sake of his artistic career, but soon registered her firm disapproval when she felt that Mrs Lowrey was taking unfair advantage of her obliging son. The relationship did not last much longer than two years and eventually it was brought to an abrupt halt by the ever-vigilant Rose. Towards the end of the relationship Mr Lowrey committed suicide when his financial interest in South African mining failed and, after this, his widow began to sink into ill health and social obscurity. A few years later she died of cancer.

Grainger had by now been away from Australia for eight years and he often felt a yearning for the wild countryside of his childhood. He longed to be in Melbourne once more to meet his old friends and experience anew the warm summer breezes as they blew in from the northern bush-lands heavily laden with the intoxicating scent of eucalyptus and wattle. It was therefore a joyful surprise for him to be invited by Ada Crossley to join her as a member of her concert party to tour Australia, New Zealand and South Africa during 1903 and 1904. The tour was to be organized by the Australian entrepreneur J. C. Williamson and Ada Crossley was to receive star billing throughout.

Before they departed, however, Percy became involved with Ferruccio Busoni, the German-Italian composer.

# 7

## The Twisted Genius and the Dinkum Aussie

Ferruccio Busoni was in his thirty-seventh year when he encountered Grainger. Italian born and German influenced, this charismatic figure was already being accorded respect and often awe in cultural centres as widely separated as Boston and Moscow. As a composer he has never been given the recognition that some have considered his due, but as a pianist it is generally regarded that he took his art to unprecedented heights. His career as a touring virtuoso had brought him to England in 1903. He wrote from London to his wife in Italy on February 24 of that year:

> [. . .] I am so looking forward to being in the South!! [. . .] I enjoy the thought of leaving an island which is an 'island' in every way. [. . .] I have made the acquaintance here of a young musician called Percy Grainger, an Australian. A charming fellow, highly gifted and a thinker. He became attached to me from the moment we met. He played me a very good Toccata by Debussy.

The meeting between Busoni and Grainger seems to have been contrived without the latter's knowledge by a friend of Mrs Lowrey, Mrs Matesdorf, with whom Busoni often stayed when giving concerts in London. Grainger was invited to meet Busoni at Mrs Matesdorf's house—a house known throughout London's musical circles as a rendezvous for visiting musical celebrities. It was not long before he was asked to give a display of his piano playing for Busoni—a request which Grainger always hated and which terrified him, especially in the presence of musical giants such as Busoni. Before this meeting, however, he had known nothing whatever about Busoni, so the only satisfactory escape the Australian could devise on the spur of the moment was to play a few pieces which he hoped the great pianist had not previously heard. He played his own harmonizations of two Scottish folk-songs[1] and *Irish Tune from County Derry*, which Busoni seemed very much taken by. His performance of the Debussy Toccata, however, completely captivated Busoni and thereafter they felt greatly drawn to one another.

Busoni was so impressed that he offered to teach Grainger free of charge if he went to Berlin. Grainger's concert engagements during the following months and the coming tour of Australasia precluded an extended period of study, but it was eventually agreed that he should journey to Berlin towards the end of June of that year.

He left his mother in London and arrived in Berlin about four days before the end of June. Here he stayed in a boarding house in the Lietzenburgenstrasse owned by Frau Kwast-Hiller, the ex-wife of James Kwast. His fondness for this woman typified his inconsistency for she was both German and Jewish. As a boy he had always sided with her in the frequent domestic squabbles with her husband and when poverty threatened her old age he made her a generous annuity which kept her in comfort for her remaining years.

Shortly after his arrival in Berlin, Grainger was surprised by the unannounced arrival of the ubiquitous Mrs Frank Lowrey. Initially she stayed in an hotel but was asked to leave by the manager, who objected to Percy's nocturnal visits and refused to be convinced by Mrs Lowrey's attempts to pass her young friend off as her nephew. At Grainger's suggestion she then moved to Frau Kwast-Hiller's boarding house, but not without some personal inconvenience to the landlady, who had been earnestly trying to interest the Australian in the physical attractions of her second daughter Evchen. The move thus fitted in well with Grainger's plans but thwarted Frau Kwast-Hiller's for Evchen and Percy, and when the possibility of earning some extra money from Mrs Lowrey's sojourn presented itself Frau Kwast-Hiller capitulated with a mixture of annoyance and admiration for Grainger's ploy.

The friendly relationship which had been established between Grainger and Busoni in London was not to last long in Berlin. Just as Grainger was a man essentially moved by primal urges and emotions, so was Busoni primarily a man of towering and sophisticated intellect. Busoni, moreover, was occasionally capable of dropping his mask of charm, sweetness and light to reveal a whole range of jealousies and antagonisms.

On his first visit to Busoni's house Grainger noticed how the Italian insisted on being regarded as undisputed master in all things and loved to surround himself with willing slaves. Whilst admitting that Busoni's motives might have been generous, he later remarked that the house was peopled with cripples and similar unfortunates — a strange assortment of 'The poor, & the maimed, & the halt, & the blind'.[2]

He was soon beckoned to the new concert grand piano and started by playing the Toccata of Debussy, but when he played next the *Irish Tune from County Derry* Busoni stopped him after only a few bars, saying 'Don't let us have anything sentimental. Play those dance tunes you played me in London.'

He then played the two Scottish folk-tunes, but was crestfallen when a girl said to Busoni after the performance, 'What a lovely tune! Is that because of the pianist or the piano?'

Busoni answered, 'It's my new piano, of course!'[3]

Busoni gave him Beethoven's 32 Variations in C minor to study, but the Australian seems to have had little intention of devoting his time to Beethoven or any other composer for that matter. It was about a week before Rose's birthday and he was by now in the habit of presenting her with a surprise collection of compositions for each birthday and at Christmas. For the next few days he occupied himself by putting the finishing touches to his setting of Kipling's verses *Mowgli's Song against People* — one of his finest choral works. He had wanted to have the setting ready for Rose's forty-second birthday on July 3, but he had been afraid to work extensively on the composition in London in case his mother overheard his work at the piano.

Grainger always insisted on designing the outer covers of his compositions himself and often went to great lengths to see that the lettering, lay-out and design were exactly to his liking. On this occasion he wanted the outer cover to be a certain shade of 'desert-brown', so he filled the bottom of the bath with a concoction of tea and coffee to his own formula and soaked the outer covers until they had taken on the desired hue.

In this fashion he devoted all his time to his Kipling setting whilst the Beethoven Variations lay unexamined on the piano. When he next went to see Busoni, the latter immediately detected that the Australian not only disliked the Beethoven work but had completely neglected it.

'Tell me, are you really working on these Variations?' asked Busoni, and Grainger admitted that he had not touched them because he had devoted all his time to the Kipling setting for his mother. 'When is your mother's birthday?' asked Busoni. He told him. 'Then come back to me on July 5,' said Busoni with no apparent trace of ill feeling.

Grainger then confessed that though he regarded the Beethoven piece as a work of genius, he disliked it all the same. 'Then what does interest you in the piano line?' asked Busoni.

'Your arrangements of Bach.'

Grainger took the Busoni arrangements of the four Chorale Preludes to the next lesson and Busoni was very pleased with his performance of them. 'Such pieces really suit you,' he said with obvious pleasure.[4] After this, Grainger and Busoni concentrated exclusively on the interpretation of Bach on the modern concert grand.

These were days well spent, for judging by Grainger's recorded legacy his interpretation of Bach was prodigious. And though he always claimed that it had been Pabst who had given him everything that was good in his Bach playing, there is also more than a little of the demonic power and logical clarity of Busoni's style. Busoni often gave demonstrations for Grainger of his skill with Bach's music and the Australian was dumbfounded by the pianistic genius that confronted him during these private auditions. He wrote:

[. . .] none of his pupils or other admirers could have admired Busoni as a pianist more than I did, for I admired him without reservations of any kind & revelled in everything he did pianistically. He was not a 'normal' player as Paderewski was & even de Pachmann was, unfolding the composer's music straightly and faithfully.[5] Busoni was a twisted genius making the music sound unlike itself, but grander than itself, more super-human. I cannot recall ever hearing or seeing Busoni play a wrong note. He did not seem to 'feel' his way about the keyboard by touching adjacent notes — as most of us do — he smacked the keys right in the middle.[6]

With the possible exception of Egon Petri, it is doubtful if any concert pianist ever gave more public performances of Bach-Busoni arrangements. Grainger continued to programme them long after they had been temporarily relegated to the realms of 'bad taste' by the dictates of fashion.

Grainger took him his first draft of *Hill-Song Number 1,* and Busoni expressed great admiration for it. But he particularly admired the Kipling Setting *The Merchantmen* for male voices, whistlers, strings, bassoons, four horns and contra-bassoon.

Grainger's attitude towards Busoni's compositions, on the other hand, was not in the least admiring, and it was perhaps this which proved to be the turning point in their relationship. He wrote:

As a composer he never interested me for one moment. I never heard a single musical phrase of his that had the least charm or pith of meaning. Perhaps he sensed my unfriendliness to his own compositions, & perhaps it was that that changed his initial kindliness towards me into scorn & hostility. On the whole Busoni was nice to me up to the end of the Berlin period. He gave me a lovely photo of himself & wrote on it, 'To my dear Percy Grainger (as dear as he surely will be great). Very affectionately Ferruccio Busoni'. He also gave me a full score of a choral setting by Liszt of one of the psalms. He worshipped Liszt.[7]

He found Busoni at his most tiresome when he took a few of his pupils out to a restaurant in the evenings. He liked to go to an Italian restaurant where an Italian tenor sang to his own guitar accompaniment.

[. . .] then Busoni would play very much the Italian as well as the great man, condescending to the folk level. I suppose it was only natural that Busoni, the Italian part of whose nature was still very well preserved, should want to relax in some Italianish way, but to my ears the singing & the common-place chords on the guitar were boring in the extreme.[8]

Robert Lewis Taylor in his book *The Running Pianist* described another incident which Grainger related to him concerning the disintegration of the relationship:

'It [the relationship with Busoni] was based on ridicule,' Grainger says [. . .] he was becoming increasingly eager to compose and correspondingly less interested in playing. This irritated Busoni who began calling in all his students when Grainger arrived for a lesson. 'We will now listen to Mr Percy Grainger, who does not like to practise, play some octave runs,' Busoni would announce, then nodding to Grainger, cry, 'So! Lay on!' 'My runs were, and still are, quite awful,' Grainger says. 'Busoni would laugh till the tears ran down his cheeks. I laughed too. We all enjoyed it thoroughly.' Grainger's ragged octaves were, however, often followed by an encore, very different in mood. 'Sometimes Percy would then play a slender little piece of Bach's or Mozart's' a musician who knew him in Germany said recently, 'playing it with that wonderful feeling that is certainly the essence of his genius, and Busoni's students would spontaneously burst into applause. They used to call Percy the Kreisler of the piano. It made Busoni furious. He was a terribly jealous man.'[9]

Whilst visiting the Busoni household, Percy developed a friendship with Busoni's wife Gerda, and he later wrote:

In Berlin, his Swedish-Finnish wife seemed to take a great fancy to me & her wide smiling face was like the sun shining & she certainly affected Busoni that way. When she was out of the house he would get sour & spiteful, but when the door opened & she appeared he rose with an exclamation of violent relief & greeted her with charming Italian manners [. . .] the presence of his wife transformed him utterly. She gave me my first J.P. Jacobsen books.[10]

It was also Gerda who presented him with a collection of her husband's Bach arrangements before his departure. Percy particularly welcomed the works of the Danish poet Jacobsen, for not only did they introduce him to a new field of literature which he was to relish greatly, but he was in the process of teaching himself Danish—the first of the Scandinavian languages he was to master. Until then the only Danish books he had studied were some H. C. Andersen volumes and a dictionary which Herman Sandby had given him.

Grainger also felt strongly attracted to Busoni's two sons Raffaello and Benvenuto. He remarked: 'When I saw them in Berlin, the two Busoni boys were as fair to see as children could be. Fine featured, bright eyed, soft limbed & no wonder with both parents so good looking.'[11]

Grainger and Busoni frequently discussed subjects other than music.

The Italian was very sarcastic about Grainger's interest in Danish and other such languages. 'What is all this interest in the art of small nations? Can't you find enough to interest you in the literature of great nations?' Busoni's question angered him intensely and he snapped back, 'No, I can't! The large nations all seem to me to be war-like minded, and I want to find out what are the influences that make some of the small nations happy in their peacefulness.'[12]

Grainger returned to London around July 23, and immediately began frantic preparations for his impending Australasian tour. He and Busoni were to meet on many occasions after the Berlin episode, but by then Busoni's attitude towards the Australian had distinctly soured. Often when Busoni was in London Grainger was away touring the provinces or abroad. Moreover, Busoni had been unable to find in him a willing slave or an adoring disciple — a state of affairs to which he had become accustomed in his other pupils. On one occasion Grainger went to congratulate Busoni in his dressing room packed with admirers after a London recital. Before he was allowed to speak, Busoni threw his arms up in mock surprise and exclaimed in a loud and biting voice, 'London's Society Pianist has deigned to pay us a visit!'[13]

Grainger remarked, however, that though Busoni was mostly teasing and scornful, he always expressed a great interest in his latest compositions and his criticisms were always thoughtful and generous. In 1907 they met and discussed the Australian's *Hill-Song Number 2*. Busoni played one part of the two-piano arrangement and later Grainger remarked that he read it from sight and that his reading of it was marvellous. After they had played it through, Busoni said in a rather sad and unwilling voice, 'That is a fine piece. I must admit it. That is a fine piece.' But Busoni criticized the way he had written the irregular rhythms by grouping them inside the bar. 'If you have irregular rhythms they should be presented to the eye as straightforwardly as possible,' said Busoni.[14]

The first time that Grainger became aware of Busoni's hostility towards him was in 1911 when he was booked to perform the Grieg piano concerto at the Zurich Town Hall under Volkmar Andreae (a composer as well as conductor). After the first rehearsal Grainger, who very much enjoyed the company of Andreae, invited him to lunch. He felt that Andreae had something on his mind and eventually, unburdening himself over coffee, Andreae said, 'May I ask you something very personal? What could Busoni have meant when he said, "You will make a laughing stock of yourself if you engage Grainger. He is nothing but a charlatan"? And certainly you are not a charlatan.'

Grainger replied, 'I suppose he meant just what he said.'[15]

Grainger's final assessment of the relationship was this:

In the eyes of a pianistic giant like Busoni I must have seemed no better than a charlatan—an ill-prepared man earning money under false pretences. But I would be equally justified in considering Busoni a charlatan as a composer. There was no need for hard feelings on Busoni's part towards me for our orbits never crossed each other. Each of us had what the other lacked. Busoni got brilliant results with next to no effort. I was slow & peg-away. Busoni impressed people immensely, but pleased few. I was able to please almost everybody including Busoni, but impressed nobody. Busoni was a big town artist, I a small town artist. My patience & humble stamina must have been just as annoying to Busoni as his flashy pretentiousness was to me.[16]

# 8

## Packed Houses and Zulu Warriors

The Ada Crossley touring party, consisting of Grainger, Jacques Jacobs (violin), W.A. Peterkin (bass-baritone) and Benno Scherek (accompanist doubling as tour manager), left England on the RMS *Omrah* of the Orient Pacific Line during the first week of August 1903. Grainger was able to practise his repertoire on the piano of the ship's lounge, and before they arrived in Adelaide on September 7 the entire party had given several concerts for the ship's passengers.

Wherever they went in Australia, New Zealand and South Africa they had an almost frenetic reception. Ada Crossley scored one of the greatest successes of her career and Grainger's triumph was no less enthusiastic. When in Adelaide Rose and her son stayed with their many relatives and in Melbourne they stayed with the O'Haras. In Adelaide, Percy spent a great deal of time with his Uncle Frank, whose mental development never went beyond that of a boy. They went on long walks together and Percy felt that in certain matters they had much in common. With the exception of Clara and Rose, most of the Aldridge family had little sympathy for Frank and would tease him until he could endure it no longer. After such tormenting Percy would usually find him in the bathroom or an outhouse gently sobbing. These were recollections of Percy's childhood and things did not change greatly on his return visits during adulthood. Percy liked Frank enormously and despite his uncle's retardation saw in him qualities he felt were recognizably those of the Aldridge clan. Frank kept scrap books and a simple diary and Percy regarded these as sacred documents in the Aldridge family history. He later inherited them and cherished them as if they were tablets of gold. In later years he settled on Frank and Clara sums of money large enough to free them from financial worry for the remainder of their lives.

Grainger also renewed his friendship with Robert Hamilton Russell, whose reputation in Australia as a surgeon was now secure. Rose for the most part did not travel with the Crossley party but stayed in Adelaide and Melbourne. The first leg of the Australian tour started with five concerts in the Sydney Town Hall. Five more concerts were given in Melbourne, followed by three in Adelaide and two in Brisbane. After each group of concerts in the state capitals the party proceeded to give performances in the far-flung country towns of the respective states.

The arrival of the Crossley party in Melbourne was greeted with the most extraordinary demonstrations of enthusiasm. It was, of course, Ada Crossley's show and her assisting artists hardly received a look-in. Apart from the few visits by royalty and Melba's tour in 1902, Melbourne had seen nothing to rival it. After the long journey from Sydney, during which the train was obliged to stop many times for the party to receive bouquets and the appropriate speeches from local dignitaries, the Sydney Express rolled into Spencer Street Station to be greeted by more than five thousand people. All the pomp and wild enthusiasm expected of such occasions were provided by Ada Crossley's fans as she stepped off the train on that warm October day. Union Jacks, potted plants, streamers, Reilly's Brass Band, the Lord Mayor and Lady Mayoress and a guard of honour formed by the Williamstown Boys' Brigade completed the magnificent scene and foot-police and mounted troopers were there to preserve order. As Ada Crossley walked down the platform the brass band struck up with *Home Sweet Home* followed by *See the Conquering Hero Comes*! At one moment it was thought that the crowd was getting out of hand and Ada Crossley was nearly pushed on to the railway tracks. As the reporter from the *Argus* wrote the following day: 'The police came forward, but even with the aid of Constable Holden, the strong man of Bourke-street west, they were powerless against the impenetrable wall of chiffon and lace.' On her arrival at the Menzies Hotel where another large crowd had gathered to greet her, Ada was overcome by the highly charged emotion of the day's events and in a very diva-like fashion finally surrendered to tears.

Five concerts were given in Melbourne and Ada Crossley gave the citizens a bonus by announcing that she would take part in a performance of *Elijah*. Each concert, of course, was sold out and the local music critics were lost for superlatives. Ada Crossley was in her home state (she was born near Tarraville, South Gippsland, in 1874) and Grainger was in his home town. They returned, they performed and they conquered.

Naturally, Grainger took with him to the Antipodes a bundle of musical manuscripts on which he was working at that time. He seized every opportunity to compose during the long train journeys and on the marathon walks he undertook. On his first visit to Brisbane in November, however, during a few days' break in concert-giving he was afforded the chance of relaxing and bathing in the warm blue waters off the Queensland coast.

In Queensland they went as far north as Townsville, several hundred miles into the Tropics. For most of the tour Ada Crossley and her party travelled by train, though Grainger would frequently set off in a singlet and a pair of running shorts immediately after a concert and walk to the next town, meeting the other members of the party the following morning or afternoon. Mostly he followed the roads, but sometimes when the railway tracks departed from the roadside he would prefer to take to the more remote bush country through which the train passed. He was glad of these diversions because walking on the rough, unmetalled roads which connected the main towns and cities of Australia wrought severe damage to his shoes and feet. In this way he developed an enviable first-hand knowledge of the native fauna and flora of Australia. He often chose to walk around towns rather than through them to escape the incredulous glances of the residents and, more importantly, the many dogs who seemed to take a fancy to his ankles. Grainger had been very fond of dogs, but the many unfortunate experiences he gained as a result of these long walks turned his affection for them into fear and loathing.

Certain parts of Queensland and the remoter regions of Eastern Victoria and Western Australia are even now inaccessible by train and the party was often forced to proceed by horse and cart, or, as in the case of several journeys in Gippsland, Eastern Victoria, by bullock dray. The story was frequently repeated for many years afterwards of the comical sight made by a rather disgruntled and bone-shaken Ada Crossley and party with all their baggage in the dray and the energetic pianist jogging along behind.

Rose joined her son for the trip to New Zealand, though again for the most part she travelled separately. It was in New Zealand that Grainger undertook most of his extraordinary jaunts. Once he walked from Oamaru to Timaru (fifty-six miles) between 2.00 p.m. and 6.00 a.m. the following morning, resting for only half an hour. On another occasion he walked from Masterton to Eketahuna (thirty-two miles) between 11.00 p.m. — directly after a concert — and 6.00 a.m. the next day without a moment's rest. In Eketahuna he put in about three hours' piano practice before boarding the train carrying the Crossley party bound for Palmerston North and an evening concert.

Grainger's physical stamina was astonishing and the fact that he enjoyed performing such feats well into his sixties was even more remarkable. On these trips he invariably carried his musical manuscripts and a plentiful supply of pens and pencils. He also included in his knapsack a lump of very hard cheese and some hardtack or stale bread. He always loved sour, stale and hard bread. Dangling from his belt would also be seen a canteen of water.

Whilst Grainger's boundless energy for work and walking was the source of much amazement among the rest of the party, he in turn was filled with admiration for the physical stamina of a different kind displayed by Jacques Jacobs. Jacobs was the violinist/leader/conductor of the orchestra in London's famous Trocadero restaurant and a great friend of Ada Crossley. The extra string that Jacobs had to his fiddle that drew so much admiration from Grainger was his success in seducing at least two or three different women each day throughout the tour.

He liked Jacobs in the early stages of the tour. They would play billiards at the hotels in which they stayed until five minutes before the concert was due to begin and at the last moment drop their cues, run to the concert hall, change and be ready for their opening duet. But Grainger grew tired of Jacobs's desire to upstage everyone — especially himself. Jacobs was taller and more bulky than he and fond of flexing his muscles, especially when ladies were present. Eventually they came to blows during a game of deck tennis on the return trip to England. Grainger, though not as strong, was more agile than Jacobs and suddenly found that he had thrown the violinist almost by accident. Whilst he had Jacobs's shoulders pinned to the deck, the Australian suddenly panicked for he felt that any revenge might be swift and brutal. At this point he let go. The unfortunate upshot of the fight was that whilst they were rolling around the deck one of the protagonists stepped on a mallet and it had flown up cutting the Captain's eyebrow so that the ship's doctor had to be called to stitch it up. By then Jacobs had aroused the animosity of many and Grainger was heartily congratulated by a host of people including the Captain.

The feeling of exhilaration and joy brought about by his New Zealand trip was somewhat marred when on the train to Rotorua Percy met, almost by accident, his father. He wrote to Roger Quilter of this meeting: 'My poor dear father is here on his way to hot baths. He's the totalest wreck I've ever seen. Had the narrowest shave. The cruellest overwork.'[1] Rose had previously written to her son when she was in Adelaide telling him that she had encountered her husband and warning Percy that he was about to leave Adelaide to receive treatment for syphilis in Rotorua. She instructed Percy not to touch or embrace his father as his hands and face were covered in an alarming and unpleasant rash. Nevertheless he was pleased to see John, who told Percy about his family history and much of his dubious past at that meeting. Percy's letter to Quilter about this meeting ended with an unusual, though characteristic statement: 'How I hope one day to earn such suffering as both my elders have gone thro!!'[2]

On their return to Australia, the Crossley party gave farewell concerts in the major cities of Queensland, New South Wales, Victoria and South Australia. These were perhaps the greatest successes of the tour and in Melbourne they broke all box-office records by drawing 20,000 people to the Exhibition Building on January 2, 1904. After the final concert in Adelaide, the touring party rested for one week. During this break Percy stayed with his Uncle Jim and slept for five days and five nights, only rising for meals. From Adelaide they sailed for Perth and Western Australia as it was to be another fourteen years before a rail link was forged across the seemingly endless Nullarbor Plain. The party visited major towns and settlements in this state including the twin goldfield towns of Kalgoorlie and Coolgardie.

Throughout the tour, Grainger had included Chopin's A flat

Polonaise Op. 53 in his repertoire and in the capital cities he had played it complete. In the small towns, however, he left out the rather wistful section which begins when the piece modulates to F minor. He did this partly to shorten the piece for the unspoiled ears of the smaller towns and partly because he found this section hard to remember when on the platform. But when he returned to Perth from the goldfields he heard that the pianist Mark Hambourg, who had just finished an Australian tour and was resting in Perth before his return to England, was to be present at the next Crossley concert in that city. Mark Hambourg was then enjoying the early successes of his career and was worshipped wherever he played. Grainger had met him in the 1890s when Hambourg had toured Australia as a child prodigy and had stayed with Robert Hamilton Russell in Melbourne. He had later studied briefly at the Hoch Conservatorium during Grainger's Frankfurt years. Grainger now debated with himself whether it would be wiser to let Hambourg hear him play the Polonaise with the cut or whether he should play the cut abominably. He decided to risk the latter. He claimed that it went horribly, though he was always absurdly over-critical of his own playing. Thereafter Jacques Jacobs referred to the cut as 'the bit you played to Mark Hambourg'.

With the Australasian part of their tour over, they boarded the SS *Wakool* and headed for the Indian Ocean and South Africa. When on ships Grainger usually kept fit by running round the promenade deck before breakfast and joining in the deck sports after that meal. On the voyage between Albany and Cape Town he exercised in this fashion and at other times continued with his studies of Danish, which he had taken up in earnest on the outward trip. He also spent much of his time at sea writing marathon letters to his friends in Europe. One he wrote in German to Karl Klimsch in Frankfurt ran to 129 pages. His letters around this time show the embryonic stages of the 'Blue-eyed English' which he was to evolve some years later. During these early years he referred to this strange form of his native tongue as 'no-outland-words-English', an Anglo-Saxonized distillation of English without words of foreign (Greek and Roman) extraction. In some ways it strangely resembled a literal translation of German into English without any attempt to use modern English idiom or to reorganize word order according to modern English usage.

He soon discovered that the deck sports and pre-breakfast running did not satisfy the desire for frenzied work which always descended on him in tropical seas. He persuaded the ship's captain, therefore, to permit him to shovel coal down in the boiler room. This he did — stripped naked — for an hour each day for several days until he developed whitlows on both hands — a very painful affliction of the fingernails. The ship's doctor ordered him to quit his coal heaving immediately, in case the complaint put his piano playing in jeopardy. Luckily the whitlows healed within the remaining ten days before the ship reached Cape Town.

Rose continued to Southampton since the party could not afford to keep her for the subsequent weeks in South Africa.

In South Africa Grainger continued his astonishing walking feats. Once he walked between Pietermaritzburg and Durban (about sixty-five miles) between midnight after a Friday evening concert and 6.00 p.m. just before the Saturday evening concert. On arrival at the hotel in Durban where he was expecting to stay, he discovered that the manager of the concert party had sent his luggage to another hotel. So he dashed off to the Durban Town Hall, where the evening concert was booked to take place. There he waited in his running shorts — startling early-comers to the box office — until the doors were opened and he was able to learn from the management where his belongings were to be found. Eventually he discovered the right hotel, changed into full evening dress and ran back to the Town Hall just in time for his entry.

Perhaps the most extraordinary South African incident resulted from an overnight jaunt, when he failed to arrive on the expected hour at a township where he was due to appear in the evening. Ada Crossley and the rest of the party walked to the edge of the township anxiously scanning the surrounding veldt with binoculars. Minutes passed and then quite unexpectedly a group of ferocious-looking Zulu warriors bounded over the horizon with Percy happily jogging along behind them. He wanted to invite his new friends to the concert, but had second thoughts when it was pointed out to him that such an action could have the entire party ignominiously drummed out of the country and possibly start another Boer War into the bargain.

In South Africa practically every major town and city was covered by the touring party and the critics were very enthusiastic about their performances. South Africa was at that time enjoying a wave of visiting celebrities, for within a matter of weeks of the Crossley tour the country was visited also by Madame Albani, Ben Davies and W. C. Fields — at that time a famous juggler.

The voyage home to Plymouth on the SS *Sophocles* was delayed considerably because the ship's keel and rudder had become fouled with weeds from the Brisbane river on its recent trip to Australia; this, coupled with the fact that the ship's engines were old and weak, meant that Grainger did not reach London until the beginning of May 1904. The concert party had given almost three hundred concerts in Australasia and South Africa and the reputations of Grainger and Ada Crossley had been reaffirmed and enhanced as a result. For Grainger the transition from child prodigy to mature artist was complete and he returned to England with renewed vigour.

# 9

## 'I am an Australian, not a Corsican!'

On his return to England Grainger once more took up his duties as a pianist to London's aristocracy. He had now come to accept his role with a detached and cynical tolerance.

The frantic address-changing which had marked his life in Melbourne and Frankfurt-am-Main continued relentlessly in London. Within four years of his arrival in London he and his mother had changed their home as many times. By 1905 they were living at 14 Upper Cheyne Row after having spent three short periods at Gordon Street, 26 Coulson Street and 63 Oakley Street. They had stayed in Cheyne Row for almost two years when they moved to 5 Harrington Road in 1907. On New Year's Day 1908 they moved once more; this time to rooms above a tobacconist's at 31a Kings Road. For the time being, at least, the years of restlessness were over in this respect and they remained at Kings Road until they left London in 1914. Throughout their London years they did not move out of the South Kensington and Chelsea area.

Cyril Scott vividly recalled seeing his Australian friend in the throes of several such moves. He remarked on Grainger's delight at watching a gang of perspiring men struggling with his grand piano on the staircase. The most noticeable effect that the sights and sounds of chaos had on him was to cause him to compose more than at any other time. He did not need peace and quiet for composition: working on trains he found almost ideal, and later, when radio came into being, he was frequently to do his best work with the radio turned up to full volume.

By the end of 1904 two famous conductors had begun to take an interest in Grainger and they were to help him become established as a concerto pianist over and above his reputation as a recitalist. Sir Charles Villiers Stanford first chose him as soloist at one of the Queen's Hall Sunday Concerts during the 1904/5 season, and Grainger became devoted to him. He arranged four of Stanford's *Irish Dances* and was the soloist chosen for one of the earliest performances of Stanford's *Variations on 'Down among the Dead Men'* for piano and orchestra.

A few years later Stanford asked him to go to America to perform at the Norfolk Music Festival. When he learned that he would be required to perform the *'Down among the Dead Men'* variations, however,

Grainger, who disliked the work, politely declined the offer.

Cyril Scott most likely introduced him to Hans Richter, the renowned Wagnerian conductor who was then attached to the Hallé Orchestra in Manchester. Richter had been very much taken by Scott and had given the first performance of his *Heroic Suite* in Manchester in 1902. The addressee of the following letter written by Richter on November 16, 1904 is unknown, but it is almost certain that it marked the beginning of his musical association with Grainger.

> I think you are mistaken if you presume I do not love pianists, just on the contrary: I love them, *if they play musical and follow respectfully the indications of the great masters* — but these pianists are in a great minority. After your letter of recommendation I must consider Mr Grainger as one of the rare species and noticed his address, 26 Colson Street, Sloane Square S.W. I shall come to London before Xmass and ask Mr Grainger to play for me. [. . .]

Richter heard Grainger and in the succeeding seasons he was often booked to play in Manchester under Richter's baton. He played the Schumann and Grieg concertos and the first two piano concertos of Tchaikovsky. In an undated letter to Herman Sandby around this period he wrote: 'Tonight I play here with Richter, & shall add a few words after it is over. [. . .] After concert — Had *huge* success. Old Richter shouting himself hoarse with bravos. Reengaged. Now my troubles are over.'

In 1905 he made his first extended concert tour of Denmark and it was during the summer and autumn of that year that he established one of the strangest relationships of his life, with Alfhild de Luce, who was later to become Herman Sandby's wife. She was a remarkable girl and already knew Percy from what Herman had told her some years before.

Alfhild had had a very solitary childhood. Her mother was a confirmed theosophist and spiritualist and had tended to look upon her youngest daughter Alfhild as a spirit and, though she was very proud of her child, never gave her the human warmth that she so desperately needed. She had no friends of her own age and her elder sisters were often away from home. As a result of her loneliness and her mother's theosophical and Swedenborgian ramblings she turned to art, music, literature and the Bible as the only anchors for her sanity. With the coming of Herman into her life she was spiritually reborn and they both fell deeply in love. Herman spoke to Alfhild of the 'Adonis from the Southern Hemisphere' and the 'Iceberg from Australia' in vivid terms. He also told her how Percy had sat in the audience at one of the student concerts at the Conservatorium when the teenaged Herman had played the Svendsen cello concerto. Grainger later wrote to Alfhild about this concert, recalling Herman's finely cut features, his mane of dark brown hair, his beautiful hands and in particular the soulfully melting tone he drew from his instrument: 'It cut right into me. It made me ill with envy.'[1] And again writing to Alfhild on November 11, 1905 Percy declared: 'Don't I just know his fire. I have sat eaten up by it time & again. There can be in his tone a quietly-ruthless slowly pushful & sending force that if I were a woman would lay me out wholly submissive, I wish I had the chance — I should be splendacious towards him of possibilities.'

When Herman returned to Denmark he worked hard at composing and began to give recitals in Denmark and Germany and joint recitals in England with Percy. In 1904 he spent his life savings on staging a joint concert in Copenhagen to introduce Grainger to Scandinavia. Herman immediately spoke to Grieg and Svendsen about the talents of his wonderful Australian friend.

Herman, however, had instinctively felt that it would be tempting Providence to have his sweetheart around whilst Percy was there. So before the Australian arrived in Copenhagen Alfhild was packed off to America, where she taught English to Scandinavian immigrants at a school in Brooklyn. Having saved as much money as she could she returned to Denmark in the spring of 1905.

Meanwhile Herman had made plans for a tour of provincial towns in Denmark for Percy and himself in 1905. The entrepreneur engaged to book the halls for the tour turned out to be slow and unhelpful, so Alfhild — by now Herman's fiancée — was conscripted to become the tour manager as well as Herman's accompanist. She was reluctant to do this at first for she was at that time enjoying a particularly creative period with her writing and painting, and disliked having the continuity of her work broken. But she was intrigued to discover more about Percy and was always prepared to desert her own work to help Herman.

When Percy came to Denmark Alfhild, who was then lodging with the Sandbys, moved out so that he could have her room. Percy proved to be a sensation with the entire family. A young man all the way from Australia who could converse in their native tongue and who knew Hans Christian Andersen to the extent of being able to recite long passages by heart was bound to succeed with them.

The trio was now complete and they would stay up late at night long after the elder Sandbys had gone to bed discussing art, philosophy and poetry. It was not long before Percy found himself greatly attracted to his best friend's fiancée and very late one night after the three had exhausted the topics of discussion Percy got up from his chair, went over to Alfhild, kissed her and paid her the highest compliment in his repertoire when he said, 'Really, Alfhild, mother must have looked something like you when she was young.'[2] Some years earlier when Herman had described Percy and his affection for him to Alfhild, she had become slightly jealous because of the terms in which he had described his Australian friend. Then Herman would comfort Alfhild by saying, 'You look a lot like Percy, dear

Alfhild. Your eyes are a different blue, your hair a different gold, but somehow [. . .] you are the Percy I love, in the shape of a woman.'[3]

The very nature of this *ménage à trois* was bizarre from the beginning and now with Herman deliberately casting himself in the shade in order to promote Percy's advancement, the stage was set for a tragi-comic episode such as could have taken place only with Percy involved. Alfhild, now living with a friend, would lie awake at nights and weep, not knowing why. And Percy would work himself up to a frenzy of passion on Alfhild's piano at the Sandby house. Herman, meanwhile, still kept himself in the background, seemingly unaware of the situation he had created. For Herman the kisses which Percy had bestowed upon Alfhild were as natural to him as an exclamation mark at the end of a stanza of poetry.

One day Percy and Alfhild visited Herman's brother in Regstrup and the Australian saw this as an opportunity to declare his feelings for her. In the presence of their host, Percy fell to his knees before her and tearfully said he loved her. Calmly she pointed out that Percy had his mother to care for him and even if she did grow to love him her loyalty to Herman was her first consideration. After this scene, their relationship entered a new phase — one of armed neutrality.[4]

Percy nevertheless persuaded Herman that Alfhild should go with them on the tour when Herman would have preferred his Australian friend as his accompanist. Percy wanted Alfhild's company and he wanted to set his seal of approval on his best friend's choice of a wife-to-be. He had previously been angered that Herman had chosen Alfhild without his consent.

The situation was only assuaged during the three-week tour which followed by Percy's and Alfhild's desire to talk at great length as their train crossed the vast heathlands of Jutland. Herman, who knew nothing of his friend's declaration of love to his fiancée, would calmly sit in a corner of the uncomfortable wooden box which passed as a railway carriage gently smiling as the other two debated philosophy, poetry and music. Percy would sometimes confide in Alfhild that Herman did not seem to resent his veiled advances.

Throughout the ensuing weeks the three lived on enthusiasm, fresh air and their youth. They discovered that their expenses were heavy, and despite full houses wherever they played the returns were slight. For much of their travels the food they consumed consisted largely of stale cheese sandwiches. Though Percy considered this a delicacy the frugality they felt forced to endure disturbed Alfhild to the extent of her once threatening to quit mid-tour if their expenditure on food was not increased. Her demands were met.

They would often travel by night with their heads cramped and jolted together on the third-class wooden bench of a railway carriage. A small crowd of people would gather at the stations to greet the party of musicians and Percy would astonish all by grabbing the heavy suitcases, jumping from the train before it had stopped and galloping off down the main street to the local hotel. The station porter with the light luggage, Alfhild with Percy's hat and Herman with his cello would follow on behind. On other occasions they would ride from town to town on the post-chaise. Then they would take long walks through the heather-carpeted fields of Jutland and sometimes row in the lakes till they feared they would have no strength in their arms for the evening concert.

As far as the music making was concerned, they ignored all criticism and played for the mere exhilaration of playing. Percy and Herman opened each concert with a movement from a sonata for cello and piano and the Australian would thump away quite unperturbed by the fact that he was supposed to be playing a duet. His sole concern was that the opening piece gave him the opportunity to loosen his fingers for the solo items that followed. Herman was fully aware of Percy's motives, but carried on comforted by the thought that he could shine when Alfhild accompanied him later on in the programme. Press criticism was generally excellent, though Percy could not understand why several country newspapers had suggested that he had dyed his hair a different colour for each concert. He was also amused by rumours that he and Herman were lovers.

There was one unpleasant incident during the tour. Percy frequently talked to Alfhild about his mother and once showed her a picture of them together. Alfhild made the drastic mistake of saying to Percy that his mother 'looked like a devil'. Percy immediately felt isolated and decided that just as he and his mother were one unit, so Alfhild and Herman were another. Those few words uttered by Alfhild cast the die for the future course of their relationship.

Grainger never forgot a remark against his mother and the new direction taken by his relationship with Alfhild underlined this fact. It brought out the very best and at the same time the very worst in both. Thereafter the friendship was conducted largely by post and the letters which were exchanged between them during the subsequent fifty years or so are most revealing and fascinating.

Percy was capable of writing the most venomous letters when the mood took him and as a consequence some of his friends were constantly apologetic or defensive when they wrote to him. Sometimes he would resurrect controversies which had originated as long as fifty years before. Sometimes he insisted that Alfhild should not write or try to contact him again even if it meant severing his relationship with his closest male friend Herman. But each time Alfhild's patience and tenacity won through. She would gently lecture him and sometimes bring down the wrath of her Christian piety on him. This, of course, infuriated Percy, who detested what he called 'Anglo-Saxon morality, goodygoodyness & cant — especially in women'. Once he wrote to Alfhild, who in a previous letter had lectured him about moderation in sex:

> I am very mild. I do not force my will on individuals or on the world. I
> am an Australian, not a Corsican! So I did not force my sex-will
> unduly upon you, did I? I let you see that I felt sexually towards you,
> but when you 'shooed me off' I did not get enraged at yr denial of me
> (as a Spaniard would have) but just made 'the best of it'.[5]

On another occasion when Alfhild had laced her letter with Biblical
and other religious quotations Percy replied:

> I was brought up in an atmosphere of artistic sophistication, in a
> mood of revolt against convention & morals. My grandmother was a
> blueeyed atheist & I was never taught enough religion to harm a cat.
> You can imagine my disgust when I hear from you, & lots of other
> women, maudlin conventional moralisings that my mother & grand-
> mother had turned their backs on *before I was born*.[6]

Alfhild also fancied herself as an amateur psychologist and often
attempted to analyse Percy according to Freudian methods. Percy reacted violently to such attempts and once wrote:

> I do not know what you mean by 'self' — I am not aware of containing
> any SELF. [. . .] I am sorry I cannot answer yr letter more intelligently,
> but I don't know what you are talking about, most of the time. You
> have a conventional moral training (acquired in U.S.A.) which my
> parents were careful to protect me against [. . .] you talk about
> 'glands' & 'instincts' anent sex. I am not aware I have a gland &
> certainly have never felt an *instinct* in connection with sex. [. . .] I am
> a complete enigma to myself, a riddle which I do not in the least wish
> to solve. My nature, my personality, does not interest me in the least. I
> only want to give a scientific *account* of myself, in music & in history.
> [. . .] I do not know what you mean by 'developing personality'. I was
> born of British stock. Isn't that enough? I know that all my feelings
> (even the hatred for my own race I sometimes feel) are British & that I
> will always know how to behave in the British way. I don't need the
> recognition of other people to give me confidence in this matter. In
> thinking of me, try to remember these things: I was born right — I
> don't have to 'develop'. I am happy thru & thru; Happy in my race,
> happy in my art. [. . .] I don't care a straw about god & eternity be-
> cause I am quite complete as I am. I don't have to behave morally — I
> am good. In other words, I am an Australian![7]

At the termination of the tour Percy mentioned to Herman that he
wanted to find a Scandinavian girl who resembled Alfhild. He was very

specific when he outlined that she had to be Scandinavian, artistic, musical and able to speak English. When he left for home he took with him a friend of Herman's, a beautiful young girl by the name of Karen Holten. She arrived in London wearing a blue velvet suit with a matching cape edged with fur. A tiny embroidered cap rested on her dark curly hair and sparkling blue eyes gazed from beneath her proud Nordic forehead. Rose liked her instantly. She stayed with the Graingers for a number of months studying piano with Percy. After a time Percy's romantic letters to Alfhild ceased. Percy's love for Karen lasted eight years but eventually she refused Percy as a lover and candidate for lifelong partnership because of the embarrassing scenes Rose frequently created during her jealous rages. When they parted, however, it was with a comradely resignation which enabled them to continue a lasting friendship.

At the close of the 1905 Danish tour Herman and Percy had provisionally set dates for a similar tour the following year, but various events caused Percy to withdraw. At the beginning of the tour he had persuaded Herman to come to live in London, but by the end of the tour he tried to persuade him differently, for he now felt that the presence of Alfhild would prove too much of a temptation for him. Percy also felt certain that a meeting between Alfhild and Rose would ultimately result in a clash of personalities. Herman, however, was determined at least to give London a try and Percy proceeded under protest to find separate accommodation for his friend and his fiancée.

When Alfhild first met Rose, she was stunned by the dogmatic terms of friendship which Rose immediately laid down. One day Rose visited her to check whether the accommodation which had been found for her was satisfactory. Her hopes of being able to visit Percy were soon dashed when Rose told her how busy he was and gave strict instructions that he was not to be contacted by letter, telephone or in person as every interruption of his work would be wasting his time. Alfhild was perplexed, but Herman was heartbroken when he received similar instructions. He was scarcely able to endure the loneliness and sadness he felt on realizing he could see his best friend only by Rose's leave. So Percy and Alfhild never met in these months' stay and Percy and Herman met only on one occasion. Even this single meeting became the cause of an almost total rupture in their friendship.

One of Grainger's most cherished aims, even at this early stage in his career, was eventually to earn enough money by his concert performances to be able to devote the rest of his life to composition. His piano playing was therefore a means to an end; as a result he had already come to hate and fear public performances. In fact, owing largely to self-determined circumstances, he was never able to free himself from what he called 'the rack of the concert platform'. Nevertheless he always aspired to this goal and many of his activities throughout his life were motivated by a desire for more money. It was this motive which contributed towards a temporary professional rupture with Herman.

Around this time Grainger had a chance encounter with a close friend of Pablo Casals and it was largely as a result of this that he finally decided to withdraw from the projected 1906 tour of Denmark with Herman. Casals's friend had told him that when the Catalan cellist had toured Europe alone the financial returns had been excellent, but when he had undertaken a joint tour with the pianist Harold Bauer the potential star attraction had been more than halved rather than doubled and their individual earning power had decreased accordingly. On July 22, 1906 Percy wrote to Herman informing him of his decision. Herman was deeply hurt and wrote accusing him of being a careerist and reminding him of the many kindnesses he had done for him whilst denying many opportunities to himself. Percy's reply was characteristic in its ruthlessness: 'I don't repay devotion enough to make it worth while [. . .]. Above all things, don't feel hard or bitter against me. Should you do so it would be wasted; as I would be wholly unable to return the feelings.'[8]

Herman and Percy did not part after this quarrel, however, and it was not long before they were corresponding again in their usual friendly terms. The suggestion of a joint tour was raised on various occasions thereafter, but it was not until many years later in America that they were to appear before the public again, this time as composer-performers.

# 10

## Unto Brigg Fair

It could never be said of Grainger that he engaged in any activity with the undeviating singlemindedness which characterizes the lives of so many other composers. He never found appealing the idea of specialization and took pride in being an 'all-round man' with several irons in the fire at any one time. This inability to undertake long bouts of concentrated work was perhaps a handicap that prevented him from scoring more unqualified artistic triumphs than he did. Nevertheless, the years between 1904 and 1910 saw his most intense compositional activity, his emergence (though not recognition) as the most important folk-song collector of his day and the beginning of his fame as an international concert pianist.

In 1905 Grainger was able to hear the first performance of one of his works when the Band of the Coldstream Guards rehearsed an arrangement of *The Lads of Wamphray* — a Scots Border Ballad by Sir Walter Scott which Grainger had originally set for men's chorus and orchestra. Hearing it for the first time enabled him to revise the score considerably. The following year he had the good fortune of being introduced by Balfour Gardiner to Fred Huish, who conducted the town band at Frome in Somerset. Grainger and Gardiner cycled around the local villages to rehearse the various sections of the band which were drawn from outlying district bands. It was here that the Australian first heard a saxophone and he loved the instrument from the moment he first heard it. On returning to the hotel that evening after the rehearsals he also first heard a nightingale. Gardiner was rapturous about this rare and wonderful sound, but his friend felt that it did not compare for sweetness with the Australian magpie.

The demand for Grainger's services at society at-homes was then at its peak and during these years he was appearing on the same programmes with such eminent artists as Hamilton Harty, Vladimir Rozing, Charles Santley, George Henschel, Maggie Teyte, Pablo Casals and even Harry Lauder. At one of these functions he met and thereafter befriended two young painters, Wilfred von Glehn and his wife Jane (on the outbreak of the Great War they changed their name to 'de Glehn'). They were both friends and admirers of Singer Sargent, who had introduced them to the Australian at one of his at-homes. The von Glehns in turn introduced Grainger to Lady Elcho, who was later to play host to him when he was collecting folk-songs in Gloucestershire and neighbouring counties. Lady Elcho was the wife of the Earl of Wemyss, and they had a fine town house at 62 Cadogan Square where they frequently entertained on a lavish scale aristocrats, statesmen, musicians, artists and actors.

Many of the society hostesses upon whose patronage Grainger depended were fearsome dragons who liked to position themselves at the centre of their small empires, from which point they would devour or, at best, collect people. Such women, whose intellectual gifts were often in inverse proportion to their social and cultural usefulness, thrived on scandal, gossip and petty intrigue. Lady Elcho, however, was in Grainger's view a cut above the average and he found that she 'measured up pretty well to the Australian standards of behaviour'.[1] Jane von Glehn often tried to persuade him to play at Lady Elcho's at-homes without pay, but Rose and her son did not see why he should. He regarded this side of his art as a business venture and refused to give impromptu recitals for people normally in the habit of paying for his services. Nevertheless Jane von Glehn was determined to engineer a situation where she felt he would be unable to refuse. To this end she once enlisted the talents of one of the guests, Mrs Patrick Campbell, to play her wiles on him. In the midst of a crowded room the great Shavian actress threw herself on her knees before him imploring him to play. Grainger, unable or unwilling to read any humour into the situation, continued to refuse and Mrs Patrick Campbell was forced to get up off her knees and make the best of an embarrassing predicament.

Meanwhile his public engagements were taking him throughout the British Isles and occasionally to Scandinavia. At a recital in London's Bechstein Hall on Wednesday November 15, 1905 he gave the first British performances of Debussy's *Pagodas*, Cyril Scott's *Lotus Land* and two of his own arrangements of the *Irish Dances* edited by Stanford. Later in the same year at the Assembly Rooms in Malvern he performed the Dvořák piano quintet with the Bohemian String Quartet, which included the violinist and composer Josef Suk, founder of the quartet and son-in-law of Dvořák. Still in the same year he began to make appearances at various Broadwood concerts throughout the country.

In 1906 he made a brief tour of some major cities with George Swinton and Gervase Elwes, and on March 13 of the following year he gave his first performance of the Schumann concerto at a Philharmonic Society Concert in the Queen's Hall. In January 1907 he was in London to hear an unforgettable performance of *Die Meistersinger* conducted by Arthur Nikisch. Shortly after this John Grainger turned up from Australia with an offer of divorce. Rose soon packed him off back to Perth.

In the autumn and following winter of 1907 Grainger made an extended tour of over eighty cities and towns in Great Britain and Northern Ireland as a member of another concert party organized by Ada Crossley. The party also included Evangeline Florence (soprano), John Harrison (tenor), Leon Sametini (violin) and S. Liddle as accompanist. The tour, though very exhausting, was but a prelude to yet another Australasian tour that took place during the following season with practically the same personnel. On the British tour Ada Crossley gave first performances of some of Grainger's recent arrangements of folk-songs. Shortly after this, Henry Wood began to include him as a soloist in the programmes of his famous Promenade Concerts at the Queen's Hall, and Dan Godfrey frequently invited the Australian to play concertos with his small but excellent orchestra at various south coast resorts.

Musical activities within Grainger's close circle of friends began on a very invigorating note, but seem to have deteriorated as the years passed. At their rooms in Gordon Street Rose and her son had organized musical gatherings once a fortnight to which they would invite Grainger's composer friends. They began quite simply as meetings where members of the assembled group were able to try out their latest part-songs and so gain compositional experience. The group included Cyril Scott, Roger Quilter, Balfour Gardiner, Herman Sandby (whenever in London), Frederic Austin, Everard Feilding, Alec Lane and Henslow Orchard. Norman O'Neill and Ralph Vaughan Williams also made rare appearances in these early years. The group seems to have been one of several ever-changing 'rock-pools' of musical talent that existed in Chelsea and South Kensington at that period.

As greater demands on Grainger's time as a concert pianist drew him more often from home, these gatherings became less frequent and eventually they were replaced by similar events at the London home of Lady Winefride Cary-Elwes in Hertford Street. Grainger was sometimes able to attend these but he was disappointed by the new character they had assumed. He later wrote: 'The meetings were called "Jambories" by Everard Feilding [. . .] and they had degenerated into play-sing-for-nothing tryouts for young and foreign musicians—that wretched entertainment so dear to the English where listeners who have paid nothing for the entertainment hear performances worth paying nothing to hear.'[2]

When Rose and her son moved into 31a Kings Road, however, the gatherings were resumed under Grainger's supervision. Whenever a concert engagement took him away from home it was Ralph Vaughan Williams who conducted Percy's works in his absence. The group took fresh impetus from other young composers such as the gentle and mild-mannered Gustav von Holst, the flamboyant Josef Holbrooke and the genial Arnold Bax. Before he had made his name as a composer and conductor Eugene Goossens was also a welcome guest in his capacity as a violinist.

Commentators have often described Grainger's London years as the sun at the centre of his life. To be sure, these years gave him the first taste of recognition as a composer — a recognition which he had deliberately delayed and the postponement of which he later regretted. His earning power as a pianist and the fame resulting from greater travelling increased manyfold and he was to have two partly satisfactory love affairs during this period. But he was still unhappy with life in many respects. Except for the artists and musicians he met, he constantly wanted to flee the 'high life' of London's aristocracy in which he had become entangled. Though at times he gave the impression of being enraptured by concert life, many factors contributed to a rapid disillusionment with his chosen career and instrument.

Grainger always feared that his memory would fail him in the middle of a concert and he often recalled the instance when at a south coast resort during a performance of the Schumann piano concerto he had vamped his way through the last movement. On another occasion in 1903 when he was practising on the pier at Bexhill-on-Sea for a recital due to include Cyril Scott's First Piano Sonata, his memory failed him again. He later wrote: 'As I sat and practised I could not remember the Sonata. As I heard the waves lapping under the pier and thought of my love for the sea and hatred of the concert platform and my love for my friend's composition and my unableness to play it, I felt such a strong urge to drown myself in the sea. Maybe the strongest suicidal urge I have ever felt.'[3] In later years he was often to remark that as he stood in the wings awaiting his entry he felt faced with the simple choice of shooting himself or quickly preparing a speech apologizing for the mess his audience was about to hear. His fear of audiences was almost pathological. At other times during a performance he would gently chuckle to himself, unable to understand how anyone could possibly take his piano playing seriously. It is true that he was never in the Busoni or Rachmaninov league where technical virtuosity was concerned, but his recorded legacy as a pianist testifies to the fact that his musicianship was one of the most individual of this century. The American critic, Harold C. Schonberg, has written:

> Grainger was [. . .] a whale of a pianist. [. . .] He had a free, easy swing at the piano, a superb tone, an effortless and completely natural technique. Naturally his playing had some romantic mannerisms, such as a tendency to ritard at phrase endings. But his recordings of Bach-Liszt (A minor and G minor organ fugues) are superbly clear and logically organized. His Liszt playing glittered; his Chopin and Schumann had strength, poetry and grace; and, of course, he was unapproachable in Grieg and in his own music. He was one of the keyboard originals — a pianist who forged his own style and expressed it with amazing skill, personality and vigor, a healthy, forthright musical mind whose interpretations never sounded forced and who brought a bracing, breezy and quite wonderful out-of-doors quality to

the continuity of piano playing.[4]

At times Grainger could turn out a massive tone, piling sonority upon sonority until the piano almost rattled—a talent he shared with Rachmaninov. A friend and host of Grainger, Poultney Bigelow, would often say to his other guests whenever the Australian was amongst them, 'We will now hear Percy Grainger tear the guts out of the grand piano!'

Grainger's strange and self-effacing modesty throughout his life as a concert pianist is puzzling. There can be no doubt that he genuinely disliked being lionized and that he had good grounds for lamenting the fact that his career as a concert pianist had overshadowed his talents as a composer. Perhaps the core of his discontent rested upon the fact that he had always wanted and intended his concert career to be a means to an end. The idea that 'next year' or 'in a few years' time' he would have earned enough money to devote the rest of his life to composing was always with him. But almost as soon as he had settled himself and his mother with little more than the necessities for the life of a travelling virtuoso he gave the rest of his earnings away.

Grainger could be curiously mean about matters concerning a shilling or two, but when he wanted to help a friend or relative or even someone he did not know but felt to be deserving he was lavish beyond reason. In this respect, no doubt, he had a good mentor in his friend Balfour Gardiner, whose generosity was legendary amongst those who knew him. But Gardiner was never so masochistically foolhardy. During the course of his life Grainger was to take on nine total dependants and about twenty partial dependants, and though he was aware of and sometimes regretted the misery this had caused him, he always proudly contended that he was motivated by what he called his 'racial duty' to relatives and friends.

The medical bills of both his parents were now considerable, but he was also handing out large sums of money to the Adelaide branch of the Aldridge family. When it became known that he was earning good money as a concert pianist a few of them even stopped working and decided to live off whatever he could send them. At first he would send them lump sums whenever he could afford it, but he later decided to put larger sums in trust so that they could live off the interest of the investments (with the provision that the invested capital should revert to himself on their demise). This proved to be unpopular with the Aldridges and on one of his subsequent visits to Adelaide they organized a deputation to try to persuade him to revert to the handout system. They did not win their case. In later years he would often send out cheques of $2,000 or more to a struggling and poverty-stricken composer whom he had possibly never met on the strength of a single letter explaining his plight.

But his antipathy towards his concert career did not rest solely on his fear of audiences or the difficult personal circumstances which he had brought upon himself. He came genuinely to dislike the piano both as a musical instrument and as a means of musical expression. Sometimes he described it as a nasty percussive instrument and at other times he would make statements such as 'I have always loathed the piano because I consider it an affront to destroy a melodiously conceived idea by trying to fit it into the limitations of two hands and a box full of hammers and strings.'[5] Listening to his records, however, it is almost impossible to guess that behind those remarkable sounds he could have nursed a deep-seated antipathy to the very idea of piano playing. One of his pupils, Storm Bull, has written: 'I do remember his frequently speaking of the instrument in that fashion, and it was only rarely that he gave indication of enjoyment in playing the instrument. Such enjoyment he had in the instrument was because of his essentially musical nature and the fact that it could from time to time, as far as he was concerned, be used for the purpose of communicating his musical thoughts.'[6]

Grainger was therefore torn more than ever between the creative and the re-creative arts. His mother's attitude only complicated matters. She behaved like a weather-vane. If he practised the piano too much she would ask him when he was going to compose again, and if he turned to composing she would say, 'Whatever will become of us if you neglect your piano practice?'[7] He was driven like a carthorse and the circumstances in which he had become enmeshed bore heavily on him.

Perhaps the only activity which brought any measure of true happiness and escape from his onerous public life was folk-song collecting. His most intense involvement with English folk-song collecting came between the years 1905 and 1909 — the halcyon days of what has since become known as the 'First English Folk-Song Revival'. During this period many young men who saw themselves as devotees of a dying art were scouring the English countryside for their material. Grainger's interest in this form of music, however, went back much further and the seeds may have been sown even in childhood. His encounter with Karl Klimsch and some of Grieg's settings of Norwegian folk-songs certainly stimulated this interest. In his Frankfurt years he had written some Kipling settings (for example *Dedication, A Northern Ballad, The First Chanty*) that clearly demonstrate a leaning towards the stark beauty and simplicity of the folk idiom. During his trip to Scotland in 1900 he had collected a handful of songs and arranged them for voice and piano before he returned to Germany, and when Roger Quilter gave him the two volumes of William Chappell's *Old English Popular Music* in June 1903 Grainger was already familiar with the famous Petrie and Child collections. Some credit must also go to Herman Sandby for opening his mind to the beauties of Danish folk culture. But it was not until he was introduced to that remarkable lady Lucy E. Broadwood in 1904 that he was fired with sufficient enthusiasm to do anything practical about the subject.

Lucy Broadwood's uncle, the Reverend John Broadwood, had published in 1843 his small collection of Sussex songs. The ripples created by the activities of this worthy cleric had moved others to perform similar tasks, not least his niece Lucy, who, with a small but significant body of 'field work' behind her, became editor of the *Journal of the Folk-Song Society* in 1904. The Folk-Song Society had been founded in 1898 by Lucy Broadwood, Frank Kidson, and Fuller Maitland amongst others, but had subsequently fallen dormant because of a lack of funds. Cecil Sharp was asked to join the committee in 1904 and he seems to have given fresh stimulus to the movement.

It is very probable that Grainger first met Lucy Broadwood at the London home of Gervase and Lady Winefride Cary-Elwes, who were particularly interested in the folk culture of North Lincolnshire. In March 1905 Grainger was invited to a lecture given by Lucy Broadwood for the Musical Association which she illustrated with some examples of her collecting and arranging. He later remarked that though her harmonizations were very simple they were very touching and he was sufficiently moved to approach her after the lecture to say that he wanted to do some collecting.

This was easily arranged, for Lady Winefride and her brother Everard Feilding had already organized musical festivals each spring for the previous six years at Brigg in North Lincolnshire, their country home. The organizing body was known as the committee of the North Lincolnshire Musical Competition Festival, and it was their job to lay down conditions of entry and judgement for each class of vocalist, instrumentalist, chorus and quartet. Grainger and Lucy Broadwood duly arrived a few days before the 1905 festival, which was held on April 10 and 11. At the instigation of Grainger and Everard Feilding the following event was included in the festival schedule:

> *Class XII.* Folk songs. Open to all. The prize in this class will be given to whoever can supply the best unpublished old Lincolnshire folk song or plough song. This song should be sung or whistled by the competitor, but marks will be allotted for the excellence rather of the song than of its actual performance. It is specially requested that the establishment of this class be brought to the notice of old people in the country who are most likely to remember this kind of song, and that they be urged to come in with the best old song they know.

1st Prize: 10/6          2nd Prize: 5/-          3rd Prize: 2/6

Frank Kidson from Leeds was the judge.

Four competitors entered and the event was won by Joseph Taylor, a seventy-two-year-old bailiff from Saxby-All-Saints, who produced a song called *Creeping Jane*. Grainger recalled that though Taylor's memory for words was not uncommonly good, he relied to a great degree on spectacular vocal effects. His singing was marked by sturdy rhythms, effortless high notes, complicated 'twiddles' and 'bleatings' and other rare devices of the folk-singer's art. The eighty-five-year-old and very deaf Mr W. Hilton of Keelby walked off with second prize for his rendering of *Come All You Merry Ploughboys* — although the *Lincolnshire Chronicle* incorrectly reported that it was *Early One Sweet May Morning*. As often with folk-singers, some items in their repertoire seemed to have an endless number of verses and Mr Hilton produced one such song during this event. When he had been on the platform for what seemed an interminable length of time efforts were made to stop him by the judge and other interested parties, but all was in vain. Eventually someone had to go on to the platform and roar into his ear that the judge had had enough and, somewhat puzzled, he was escorted down.

The third prize was collected by Dean Robinson of Scawby for *T'Owd Yowe wi' one Horn* (The Old Ewe with One Horn). The event also brought forth many other songs, eight of which were noted down by Grainger and Lucy Broadwood, Joseph Taylor's *Brigg Fair* being perhaps the most remarkable. Soon after his return to London Grainger began to make settings of what he felt were the most suitable items for chorus and voice and piano.

His first visit to Brigg seems to have been brief, but he was so moved by the whole experience that he decided he must give much more effort to collecting this material, which he realized now was on the very brink of extinction. The industrial revolution had dealt a blow to rural folk art, and the music hall and the gramophone were delivering the *coup de grâce*. He discovered that the younger generation no longer had to provide their own entertainment and showed scant interest in becoming legatees of the rich and varied art of their forebears. Lincolnshire had kept its folk culture in such a wonderful state of preservation because of its relative geographical isolation, being bounded by the River Humber in the north, the North Sea in the east, the River Trent in the west and the Wash and the River Welland in the south.

Back in London on April 13, Grainger wrote to Lady Winefride thanking her for the help and hospitality her family had offered at the Brigg Manor House and suggesting that the results of his collecting had proved so encouraging that he wanted to return in August of the same year to undertake a 'folk fishing cruise' on his 'byke' through that part of Lincolnshire. In the same letter he asked for the names and addresses of all the best singers in the area, and requested that someone note down all the words that had been sung at the festival.

Grainger returned to Brigg towards the end of August that year and stayed for about a week. Lady Winefride's two sons had been able to gather the names and addresses of many more singers and they accompanied him on most of his cycling trips around the countryside. He had a manner of approach which put the singers at their ease in his company and he was able to rescue a wonderful selection of songs. Sometimes he would calmly walk up to a man working in a field and ask him if he knew any songs. The farm-hand would then put down his implement and after a few minutes' thought would produce a song or two as he stood there out in the field. After a while Grainger developed a 'nose' for good singers and the best areas for collecting. On entering a village he would often be told that he would never find any songs there and by evening have collected sixty or seventy. On one occasion he visited one of his favourite singers, Mr Dean Robinson, to collect a particularly good variant of *Robin Hood Rescuing Three Squires.* Dean Robinson was so keen that the young collector should obtain the complete verses of the song that he wrote all the words on the wall and then ripped off nine feet of wallpaper and gave it to him. Grainger kept this souvenir until he died. He was always made very welcome whenever he visited Dean Robinson at Scawby, not the least reason being that the daughter of the household had taken a powerful fancy to the fine-featured young man. On another occasion he heard of an old lady who was supposed to have a large repertoire of fine and rare songs. When he approached her, however, nothing he did or said could persuade her to divulge one note of her treasure. Undaunted, he paid court to the old lady's beautiful granddaughter and persuaded her to smuggle him into the front room and hide him under the bed when the old lady was out. This part of the surreptitious operation completed, he waited under the bed with pencil and manuscript paper at the ready for the return of the old lady. The girl then asked her grandmother to sing her some songs and Grainger spent the remainder of the evening noting down the melodies she gladly sang.

He found some of his best singers in the Brigg workhouse and here he collected one of his most beautiful tunes called *Lisbon* from the singing of Mr Deane of Hibaldstow. Grainger's first attempt to collect it, however, was not very successful for when the old man had sung about a verse and a half he began to cry. Grainger did not persist because Mr Deane had not sung the song for many years and it worked him up to a state in which his weak heart might not be able to stand the strain. So for the time being he left the song rather badly collected.

Percy was as brimful of energy as ever and instead of walking down stairs he preferred to take a section in one giant leap. Once he lost his footing and fell, spraining his ankle in the process. This did not deter him in his collecting activities, for he organized several members of the Elwes household to round up a bevy of singers and had them arranged around his bed in a semicircle with each singer performing his songs in turn. These singers were justly proud and not a little jealous of their fine repertoires. On one occasion when he was collecting from his bed Grainger turned to one singer and asked him if he did not agree that the previous song rendered by his neighbour was very good. 'Ah, yes! It were very good. But he sang it wrong all the same,' replied the old man.[8]

Before his ankle had properly mended Grainger was obliged to return to London to prepare for the forthcoming tour of Denmark with Herman Sandby. Spurning Lady Winefride's offer of transport to the railway station, he bade farewell to the Elwes family and, jumping on his bicycle, pedalled off with one leg in the air. From Denmark he wrote to Lady Winefride: 'It is nice to be able to play to all these dear Danes the lovely tunes that your help allowed me to gather in & to think how few lands in Europe could boast such a crop. Good old supposed to be unmusical England. I write all this because I really think we really did a big thing by that week's work; more so than we realize, & I'm fearfully thankful to you for making it all possible (& so joyous).'[9]

The festival of the following year took place at Brigg Exchange Hall and the main concert on Monday May 7 employed the combined forces of several local choirs and the Brigg Brass Band. In the intervening period Grainger had worked hard at the preparation of choral and vocal arrangements of some of the songs he had collected the previous year. The soloists for this occasion included Miss Violet Londa, Harry Plunket Greene and Gervase Elwes. As a rule Percy did not like professional singers. It was his feeling that most often a singer who was skilful, technically brilliant and possessed a fine voice usually left him cold because of a lack of musicality, but on the other hand the truly musical singer was rarely in command of first-rate vocal equipment. He put Melba in the former category and Elwes and Plunket Greene in the latter. He was naturally fond of these two singers and warmed most especially to their art. Perhaps the fact that they included his works in their repertoires while Melba never once uttered a single note of his songs had more than a little to do with his likes and dislikes in this respect.

The 1906 Brigg Festival was one of Grainger's first engagements as a conductor and he led the soloists, choirs and band in first performances of his settings of *Marching Tune, Brigg Fair, Six Dukes went Afishin', The Gypsies' Wedding Day* and *I'm Seventeen Come Sunday*. In the programme notes were printed the names of the singers who had furnished him with the original material and when some of these arrangements were published later on a wider scale he made a special point of naming the origins of the melody and words at the head of the first page of music. His setting of *Brigg Fair* for tenor solo (Gervase Elwes) and chorus turned out to be the highlight of the evening's entertainment. It is one of the most haunting and supremely lovely folk-song settings ever written and he was happy to be able to give its first performance in the town whence it took its name. Shortly after the Brigg Festival he accompanied Gervase Elwes in a recital of his folk-song arrangements at London's Aeolian Hall. Many of the pieces had to be repeated and the newspaper critics were free with their praise.

For about ten days around the end of July and beginning of August of the same year he was again in North Lincolnshire. This time, however, he came armed with an Edison Bell cylinder phonograph and several boxes of brown wax cylinder blanks. He thus became the first folk-song collector in the British Isles to make live recordings of his singers. Madame Evgeniya Lineva, the Russian folklorist, was perhaps the first person ever to use the phonograph for field recordings, in 1897. This was closely followed in 1899 by Dr W. Fewkes's recordings of North American Indians; quite independently, recordings of native folk-music had been made in New Zealand and Tasmania before the turn of the century. It is possible, though not altogether certain, that Bartók may have started his sound recording activities after having read about Grainger's cylinder collecting. This system of collecting was almost ideal, but it proved to be a source of argument in subsequent years between Grainger, Cecil Sharp and other members of the folk-song 'establishment'. Not only did it throw into bold relief a sharp divergence of attitude to the basic folk-song material, but it threatened to expose the frequently hit-and-miss and sometimes dishonest techniques of other collectors. Grainger had little faith in the pencil-and-pad approximations of his contemporaries.

Now that he had his new recording machine Grainger found that he was able to collect a greater quantity of songs and also to play the cylinders back as many times as he wanted, which removed much of the guesswork when it came to the job of transcribing them. Sometimes he played them back at a greatly reduced speed in order to unravel the intricate problems of ornaments, slides, irregular rhythms and so on. He took with him a pitch pipe which was blown into the recording horn just after the cutting stylus had begun to make the groove and before the singer had launched upon his song in order to obtain the correct pitch on playback. He found that his singers quickly became used to the techniques of using the phonograph, and did not object when their heads were guided nearer to or further from the recording horn to avoid the dangers of 'blasting'. Although Joseph Taylor—his most seasoned recording artist—always gave of his unique and impeccable best, he said once, 'It's lahk singin' with a muzzle on.'[10]

Grainger, of course, made it one of his first tasks to return to the Brigg workhouse to record a complete version of *Lisbon* from Mr Deane, feeling that 'he might as well die singing it as die without singing it'. The old singer, however, was found in the hospital ward, with a huge gash in his head resulting from a fall: Grainger asked him if he would like to sing *Lisbon,* but the old man insisted that his head was too bad and he felt too weak to sing. 'All right, Mr Deane, you needn't sing yourself, but I would like you to hear some records made by other singers in these parts,' said Grainger. Before the first cylinder had played through, however, Mr Deane turned to the Australian and said, 'I'll sing for you, yoong mahn.' Grainger quickly set up the machine on his bed, exchanged the playback stylus for a recording stylus and the used cylinder for a blank and set the equipment going. Whilst the machine was still recording, Mr Deáne said into the horn at the end of the second verse, 'It's pleasin' muh.'[11] The old gentleman was not killed by his singing and Grainger's gamble paid the dividend of providing him with one of the loveliest and most precious melodies he had collected.

Despite the successes that his arrangements had had at the 1906 North Lincolnshire Festival, Grainger's main concern was that he should first publish his collection of material as it had originally been sung to him. In a letter to Cecil Sharp he wrote: 'Personally, I am very keen that the tunes I collect (barring now and then a choral setting or 2) should be publicly presented in as *merely scientific* a form as possible, for the time being. I don't wish to come forward as an arranger yet awhile, altho' in 15 to 20 years time I hope to myself publish a folkmusic book; settings etc.'[12]

Unfortunately Grainger's concert life and other activities kept him away from the task of transcribing the cylinders into manuscript form, and although he seems to have made a determined effort initially some thirty years were to pass before he had made further transcriptions of the collection. By the time he had come round to making copies of these manuscripts (less than half of the entire cylinder collection), either he or the world around him was lacking in sufficient interest to publish his treasure of folk-songs as a complete volume. Copies of the original incomplete manuscript collection, however, are to be found in hecto- graph form in several libraries in Britain and America but despite moves by various dedicated parties they still remain unpublished.

November 1907, April 1908 and July and August 1909 found Grainger in Gloucestershire on short visits to collect folk-songs. On each of these visits he stayed with Lady Elcho, whose husband owned a country home at Stanway in that county. A friend of Lady Elcho, Eliza Wedgwood (great granddaughter of Josiah, the Staffordshire pottery baron), who lived at Broadway a few miles away in the neighbouring county of Worcestershire, assisted him during these expeditions. His first visit conveniently followed a recital in Cheltenham Spa about twelve miles from Stanway. He had asked Eliza Wedgwood to round up a few folk- singers in advance since she had expressed the desire to become a col- lector. When he arrived with his phonograph to record the material, she had already noted the words of a selection of songs. His novel use of the phonograph elicited some delightful comments from the Gloucestershire singers. One old vocalist on hearing the playback of one of his songs said 'He's learnt that quicker nor I.' Another singer declared, 'It do follow up we wonderful.'[13]

Grainger had wanted to stay with Eliza Wedgwood at Broadway, where he expected to perform most of his work, but when he arrived he was taken to Lady Elcho's mansion. Lady Elcho was a friend of the cele- brated Mr H. G. Wells and his wife, who lived nearby. She was also the long-standing mistress of Arthur Balfour (Prime Minister between 1902 and 1904). Whenever Grainger was invited to stay at Lady Elcho's home these other distinguished guests also turned up and Percy, of course, was expected to perform on the piano like some dancing monkey. This he hated, but he was at least able to interest Wells and Balfour in his folk-song collecting activities. John Singer Sargent sometimes stayed at Lady Elcho's home and often watched Grainger and Eliza Wedgwood working. Sargent and Wells went with Percy to local workhouses to 'dredge' the inmates on several occasions. Wells was fascinated by Grainger's habit of jotting down the characteristic banter and mannerisms of his singers. 'You are trying to do a more difficult thing than record folk-song,' he said, 'you are trying to record life.'[14]

Arthur Balfour probably drove the group around in his new motor car, for Grainger once wrote to his mother from Stanway:

I've taken about 15 records so far. Quite good stuff most of it — though not outstanding. Got 'The Drummer Boy' from Mrs Hawker and a nice 'Green Bushes' variant. Got a very complete 'Lord Bateman', about 10 morris tunes. We've a big day before us today & Sargent is coming with us to the workhouse and is very keen and open to the poetry of it all. Mr & Mrs Wells were with me most yesterday. He tremendously moved by the sweet humanity of folksingers, and she is very charming, happy, kindly and observant. In all sorts of ways they are a very happy blue-eyed couple. Balfour's motor's a dream and he a dream beyond words.[15]

Grainger valued the help given to him by Eliza Wedgwood, though he was critical of the way she tried to combine her interest in folk-song with her passion for antique furniture. On their travels they often visited singers in their old country cottages and she would immediately scan the place for fine examples of old furniture. After one old lady had sung for them a version of *Polly Oliver*, Eliza Wedgwood said to her, 'Now, if you ever want to sell that chest of drawers over there, you just think of me.'

'Oh, no, Ma'am,' said the old lady, 'I never don't want to part with that. It was my mother's it was and I hope to keep it as long as I live.' Grainger later wrote: 'Why fussy and rather go-getting women like Eliza Wedgwood who used their fairly well-born-ness to further quite greedy and business-like aims are so admired and talked about I never will understand.'[16]

In a letter to his mother during one of his Gloucestershire visits he wrote:

Collected two phonograph records for the first time in my life of 'Bonny, Bonny Boy' from a Mrs Wixey at Buckland who was staying in Broadway, Worcestershire. Very, very peasanty, gloriously modal, so full of variety. She is a killingly funny old dear [. . .]. Mrs Wixy said 'It was really beautiful company, happy company, respectable company.' Yesterday evening we saw the school children do morris dances learned from Esperance Club teachers who owe all to Sharp. He has really done good work in this matter. I think the morris dances are charming. The two best, those two I sketched, [. . .] 'Shepherd's Hey' and 'Country Flowers' are just as jolly as Sharp's harmonic treatment of the tunes is revolting.[17]

As well as collecting in Lincolnshire, Gloucestershire and Worcester-shire, Grainger also noted down a few London street cries. Street vendors of milk, lavender, muffins and other such commodities were still a common sight in pre-First World War England and he preserved a few of these in manuscript form. Yet another kind of folk-music which interest-ed him was the sea shanty. He first obtained examples from a Mr Charles Rosher in 1906, but the best material came first hand from the singing of Mr John Perring of Dartmouth whom he discovered in Devon in 1908 when he was on a concert tour of that area. *Dollar and a 'alf a Day* and *Shallow Brown*—both brilliantly arranged by Grainger at a later date—were amongst the many splendid shanties he collected from John Perring. This 'deep-sea sailor', as he called him, could recall the days when it was not uncommon for ships' captains to vie with one another to secure the talents of the best available shantymen, whose sole job, it seems, was to lead the singing of the crew who joined in the choruses as they worked. Different songs accompanied different tasks on board ship; thus there were 'capstan shanties', 'windlass shanties', 'pumping shan-ties', 'hauling shanties' and so on.

Rose wrote to Roger Quilter in 1908 of the time her son had discovered John Perring: 'Last Saturday after Concert Perks found a Sea-Chanty Singer at Dartmouth & was so overjoyed that he sent me a telegram which arrived near midnight frightening our little household—it ran: "Found Genius Sea Chanty singing man—I in Seventh Heaven. Perks". He arrived here at $\frac{1}{4}$ to 5 (a.m.) and at once began singing me the songs [. . .]'.[18]

As far as Lincolnshire was concerned, however, 1908 was perhaps the last year in which Grainger was able to give any extended effort to collecting. He returned there for a few days towards the end of May and in Brigg was able to make a sizable body of cylinder recordings on May 25 and 26. Many of these were re-takes of previous cylinders and they in-volved nine singers, including four of his best—George Gouldthorpe, Joseph Taylor, George Wray and Joseph Leaning.

The previous year Grainger had had one of the most significant encounters of his life, his meeting with Frederick Delius, which probably took place at the London home of John Singer Sargent. At the time of the meeting Delius wrote to his wife:

I also met Percy Grainger, a most charming young man & more gifted than Scott & less affected. An Australian—you would like him immensely. We all met at his house on Thursday for music [. . .]. I have become acquainted with the musical critic of the Daily Telegraph—Robin Legge [. . .] I left him the score of Appalachia & he and Percy Grainger are quite enthusiastic about it. Enclosed a little note Grainger left at my house after he had run & played the score. He is impulsive & nice [. . .].[19]

The two took to each other immediately and their lives and thoughts were to become entwined at many points after this. They both had similar ideas concerning composition and harmony, as well as sharing a healthy disrespect for the music of Haydn, Mozart and Beethoven.

When they met, Grainger showed Delius a selection of his settings and compositions amongst which was his masterly setting of *Brigg Fair*. Delius took one look and said, 'But our harmonies are identical.'[20] He singled this item out for orchestral treatment and Grainger was delighted when Delius asked his permission to use the material. As well as reverting to Joseph Taylor's original tune, Delius took Grainger's harmonizations as used in his choral setting. It is perhaps to be regretted that, magnificent though Delius's orchestral rhapsody is, there can be no question that its fame has overshadowed Grainger's original setting. Delius made him the dedicatee of the English Rhapsody *Brigg Fair*.

On March 31, 1908 in a programme of Delius's music at the Queen's Hall Beecham conducted the New Symphony Orchestra in the first London performance of *Brigg Fair*. Grainger had Joseph Taylor come down to London for this performance and, together with Rose Grainger, Everard Feilding and Frederick Delius, they sat together in the hall. Legend has it that on hearing 'his' tune, Joseph Taylor immediately stood up and began to sing along with the orchestra. No attempt was made to stop him in his proud and touching flight of musical expression. It is alleged to have shocked a few of the arty stuffed-shirts present, but this was Joseph Taylor's day, a day when high art made a respectful and low bow to its humble folk origins.

It was also an important year for Joseph Taylor, for in 1908 he became the first folk-singer to have some of his songs recorded and issued commercially. Grainger had persuaded the Gramophone Company, for whom he had recently made some piano recordings, to engage Taylor to record some of his songs. Nine items were eventually issued that year on one 12″ and six 10″ records. Grainger had hoped that this would be the first of many sets, but it was not to be, perhaps due to small sales, for the Taylor recordings remain some of the most elusive collector's items and only two complete sets in their original form are known to exist today. They are priceless historical documents of a dead art. The recordings were accomplished at three sessions on June 20 and July 11 and 13 and the set was issued with an accompanying leaflet.

In May 1908 Grainger had published a selection of his folk-songs in the twelfth edition of the *Journal of the Folk-Song Society*.[21] It contained twenty-seven songs with their variants and texts, seventeen of which were from Lincolnshire. The collection was prefaced by a fascinating essay on the use of the phonograph as a folk-song collecting aid, which made some suggestions for its improvement. He looked forward to the day when an accurate and easily decipherable 'voice picture' could be made from the record. In this way he hoped that the most minute variation in rhythm or pitch could be translated into a visible form for analysis and study. He was aware that conventional music notation was inadequate when it came to the needs of the folk-song material he had collected, and made special reference in this essay to one of the songs, *Lord Melbourne*, a rhythmically erratic tune the conventional notation of which, in an attempt to be as accurate as possible, presented what he called a 'regrettably disturbing picture to the eye; whereas the impression of the actual performance is rhythmically smooth and flowing, though quaint and wayward'. Also in the preface to the songs were some charming word portraits of his singers. Grainger had the most profound love and respect for his singers and felt deeply moved by what were almost invariably their tragic circumstances. When in 1937 he came to write his masterpiece for wind band, *Lincolnshire Posy*, a work based on some of his Lincolnshire collection, his dedication read 'to the singers who sang so sweetly to me'. The preface to this work is written in a mood of rancour, 'at the memories of the cruel treatment meted out to folksingers as human beings (most of them died in poor-houses or in other downheartening surroundings) and at the thought of how their high gifts oftenest were allowed to perish unheard, unrecorded, and unhonoured'.[22]

In this touching dedication Grainger did not make public his feelings about the unjust treatment that the collectors themselves had meted out to their singers. Yet in his preface to the 1908 collection he touched upon some questions which caused considerable stirrings among the Folk-Song Society hierarchy and which eventually contributed towards his departure from their midst. In his efforts to go about his work in as scientific a way as possible he had come to a few inescapable conclusions which he felt obliged to present to his fellow collectors. They flew in the face of a host of fondly held beliefs and prejudices and he was regarded by many as a heretic when he challenged their dogmas. Even today his findings are far from being universally accepted, let alone understood. In brief his conclusions were as follows:

1.   That it was a heinous crime to collect a narrative folk-song consisting of several verses and then distil therefrom a 'normal' tune which was expected to hold good throughout the song. It was his experience

that a creative folk-singer would call upon an endless vocabulary of melodic, rhythmic and dynamic variations that would suit the emotional and, more importantly, the metrical demands of the words themselves within each verse. In other words, he believed that the collector should record the act of singing itself, not the impression of a song received by the collector.

2. That for most singers their songs were not spontaneous or haphazard improvisations that would change with their subsequent performances, but rather that their art was indeed somewhat formalized according to the traditions to which they had become the legatees. Even the most rhythmically irregular singer (here George Wray is singled out) would be surprisingly uniform in his use of rhythm, ornaments, dynamics and other devices in repeated performances of the same song.

3. That the performance of an entire narrative song consisting of several verses demonstrated a rhythmic continuity between verses and half-verses. This further suggested to Grainger that the singer viewed his song as a closely knit formal whole rather than a meaningless repetition of a single tune.

4. That folk-singers rarely used a scale of notes which fell easily within any of the accepted modes (Dorian, Phrygian, Lydian, Mixolydian, Aeolian, Ionian etc.); instead they tended to use a scale incorporating elements of them all, which Grainger referred to as a 'single loosely-knit modal folk-song scale'. It is clear that here he was suggesting that to assign a folk-song tune to a single mode was frequently inaccurate.

5. That a large vocabulary of ornaments was deliberately used by folk-singers and used in a bold and improvisatory fashion to lend emphasis to the words and melody, and that such ornamentation should be notated faithfully.

6. That except for shantymen (used to loud singing due to the habit of having to make themselves heard above the elements) all his singers made great use of a very wide range of accents and dynamics.

At some stage Grainger must have asked Cecil Sharp to send him any ideas and comments which had occurred to him as a result of his essay in the *Journal*, for on May 23, 1908 the latter penned a voluminous letter which, contrasted with the above findings, throws into bold relief the difference in their respective attitudes to the whole subject of folk-music. In his letter Sharp begins by warmly congratulating Grainger on his work and continues by stating his own reservations about the phonograph. Apparently he had attempted to use it the previous Christmas, but for a variety of reasons had abandoned its use. He believed that the machine was unreliable and that it made the singer nervous; his efforts had always ended in disaster. One wonders whether Sharp himself rather than the phonograph had made the singer nervous.

Then Sharp plunges right to the heart of their divergence of attitude: 'In transcribing a song, our aim should be to record its artistic effect, not necessarily the exact means by which that effect was produced [. . .] it is not an exact, scientifically accurate memorandum that is wanted, so much as a faithful artistic record of what is actually heard by the ordinary auditor [. . .]. No doubt it is much easier to note down the "great or slight rhythmical irregularities ever present in traditional solo-singing" from a phonograph than from a singer. The question is, is it worth doing at all?'

In his attitude to folk-song collecting Grainger was a solitary and courageous pioneer. Here indeed we have one of his most important contributions to the history of music. Not only are his feelings and ideas enshrined in what we know to have been his collecting activities, but they permeate every level of his art as a folk-song arranger. It is significant to note that from about 1909 he began to fade out of the folk-song collecting scene in England and sought ears more sympathetic to his radical ideas in Denmark and New Zealand. It is sad and curious that practically no recognition has been accorded Grainger's ideas until comparatively recent years. Benjamin Britten has stated that as far as the arrangement of folk-song is concerned he regards the Australian as his master in everything he does.[23] Patrick O'Shaughnessy and Bob Thomson, both ethnomusicologists of distinction and repute, were perhaps the first to point out the true greatness of Grainger's achievement in this field. A. L. Lloyd, the famous authority on folk culture, wrote in 1967: 'To vary the psychological climate he [the folk singer] would not as a rule put drama and pathos into his voice (though in fact the "showman" singer is not such a rarity in tradition as some make out); more likely he would convey the mood of the song by a small alteration of pace, a slight change of vocal timbre, an almost imperceptible pressing or lightening of rhythm, and by nuances of ornament that our folklorists, with the exception of Percy Grainger, have consistently neglected in their transcriptions; more's the pity.'[24]

Whilst Grainger was alive the world was silent about his innovations, and the stoniest of silences came from the English Folk-Song Society, its heirs and disciples. The Sharp dogma ruled over all.

# 11

## The Little Half-Viking

In a short essay written in 1938 Grainger described his knowledge of and feelings for Grieg's music before he met the composer:

> In my childhood in Melbourne I heard a great deal of Grieg played by my mother and our dear friend R. Hamilton Russell—the first exquisite pianist in my life. Indeed my mother played more Grieg than any other music in the years 1888-1895. But I did not think much of Grieg's music at that time, much as I would have liked to have admired it, for it would have suited me very well to see in Grieg's music the rebirth of the Old Norse Spirit I was worshipping then in the Icelandic Sagas. But I could not. I did not awaken to Grieg's greatness until I met Cyril Scott in Frankfurt-am-Main around 1897. He, chiding me for my then Handel-like style of composition, asked me if I didn't like modern music. 'What do you mean by modern music?' I asked him. And he played me Grieg's Ballade Op. 24 and Tchaikowsky's Theme and Variations for Piano. But the full range of Grieg's harmonic inventivity and the adorable wistfulness and tragicness of his nature were not revealed to me until Herman Sandby showed me Grieg's 'Norwegian Folksongs', Op. 66, around 1899. Then Grieg joined Bach, Brahms and Wagner in the firmament of my compositional stars. My Grieg worship deepened when William Gair Rathbone put Grieg's 'Norwegian Peasant Dances' Op. 72, into my hands around 1905.[1]

His first personal contact with Grieg was occasioned by a friendly act of Herman Sandby. Herman, a friend of Grieg, had met the ageing and infirm composer in Copenhagen in 1904 and shown him, unbeknown to Grainger, the Australian's first printed scores, which included his settings of *Irish Tune from County Derry* and *Two Welsh Fighting Songs*. Grieg was delighted with the younger man's work and sent him a signed photograph of himself inscribed 'To Percy Grainger with thanks for your splendid choruses'. Although Grainger was naturally thrilled by such a compliment, it would never have occurred to him to try to meet Grieg. He always preferred to worship his stars from afar.

In May 1906, however, Grieg came to London with his wife Nina to give two concerts of his music at the Queen's Hall. For the duration of his stay the sixty-three-year-old Norwegian and his wife were guests of Sir Edgar and Lady Speyer. Sir Edgar Speyer was an international banker and financier and was providing the sole monetary force which kept the Queen's Hall Orchestra afloat. Grainger had been pianist for many of their at-homes at 46 Grosvenor Street.

Grieg must have been somewhat difficult to entertain, for Lady Speyer remarked that for most of the daytime the curious little Norwegian gentleman would simply sit in the hall with his hat and coat on, rarely speaking with anyone. During one of their few conversations Grieg was asked if there was any musician in London he would like to meet. At first this question elicited the reply, 'No, thank you. I feel so weak and ill that I just want to get the concerts over with and go home.' On further reflection, however, he said, 'Yes, there is one person I should like to meet, this young Australian composer, Percy Grainger.'[2]

Grainger was duly asked to dinner in order that he might meet the 'Miniature Viking', as Stanford called him. The Australian was far from daunted by the prospect of meeting a man with whose music he had already discovered such a strong spiritual empathy. Of course, this affinity was strengthened by his ability to converse with Grieg in Norwegian, a language he had recently learned.

Grieg was surprised when Lady Speyer informed him that Grainger was a pianist as well as a composer, and he was even more thrilled to learn that the Australian included in his repertoire the *Norwegian Folk-Songs* Op. 66 and the *Peasant Dances* Op. 72. Grieg had given the première of the Op. 66 pieces two months earlier in Kristiania (Oslo); they had been given a poor reception and no other pianist in Scandinavia had attempted to play these modern and iconoclastic settings. Grainger immediately seated himself at the piano and began to play.

Grieg, who as a rule showed little mercy to executive musicians, was amazed at the stylish way in which Grainger played his latest compositions, and made the following entry in his diary for May 20:

For the moment, there is no Norwegian who can do the same thing. This is typical in more than one respect. It shows that we still don't have a Norwegian who has the understanding to take on such assignments, and if such an understanding is not present where it should be, in the country itself, then it exists outside, yes, indeed in Australia, where the wonderful Percy Grainger was born. All this talk of the necessity of being a Norwegian to understand Norwegian music, and in particular, to play it, is simply silly. Great music can transcend the purely national level whilst, nevertheless, retaining its nationalistic roots.

And in an interview with the Danish newspaper *Kjöbenhavn* on March 15, 1907 Grieg said: 'What is nationality? I have written Norwegian Peasant Dances that none of my countrymen can play and here comes this Australian who plays them as they ought to be played! He is a genius that we Scandinavians cannot do other than love.' It was this press statement perhaps more than any other which established Grainger's name as a pianist beyond the shores of Great Britain. Almost overnight he became an international pianist.

But Grieg was not entirely uncritical of Grainger's interpretation of his work. A year after their first meeting he was to say to the Australian, 'Mind you! You don't play the folksongs according to *my* intentions! But don't alter a thing. I love individuality.'[3]

An almost instant artistic and human rapport had been established. A spiritual kinship was felt by both parties. Grainger's superb piano playing—to Grieg 'like the sun breaking through the clouds'—its rhythmical clarity, robustness and tenderness, its broad tonal palette, its youthfulness, and his passion for folk-art, made him the personification of all Grieg's ideals and dreams. His feelings for the young Australian were such that on May 24 he was moved to write in his diary: 'I love [him] almost as if he were a young woman.'

Before he left London Grieg gave his new friend an autographed album of almost all his songs and similarly inscribed scores of the music that had been performed at the two Queen's Hall concerts. Despite his steadily worsening illness which was to strike its fatal blow the following year and his mood of sadness and embitterment resulting from the neglect of his finer works, Grieg was sufficiently stimulated by their meeting to invite Grainger to stay with him later on that year at his summer villa 'Troldhaugen' at Hop near Bergen. But it was not until the following year that the two musicians were able to meet again.

Grieg was so impressed with Grainger's playing at this first meeting, however, that he invited him to turn the pages for him at his 1906 London Chamber Music Concert. It is interesting to note Grainger's comments on Grieg's piano playing:

As a rule his tempi were faster than those heard in performances of Grieg's work by other artists; and invariably the enthralling wistfulness and poetic appeal of his renderings knew no trace of sentimentality or mawkishness. Strong and sudden accents of all kinds and vivid contrasts of light and shade were the outstanding features of his self-interpretations; while the note of passion that he sounded was of a restless and feverish rather than of a violent nature. Extreme delicacy and exquisiteness of detail were present in his piano playing; and although the frailty of his physique, in the latter years at least, withheld him from great displays of rugged force at the keyboard, yet, when the occasion required, he prized and demanded those resources in others.[4]

Following Grieg's return to Bergen they began to correspond and on June 30, 1906 the Norwegian wrote:

Let me say it at once: I like you. I like your fresh healthy outlook on Art, I like your unspoiled nature which not even 'High Life' has been able to corrupt, and then I like your deep feeling for folk-song and all the possibilities it carries within itself. Your conception of English folk-song is full of genius and contains the seed of a new English style in music. And then your taste for the Norwegian folk-songs and Scandinavian languages and literature proves that you are not wrapping yourself up in the cloak of onesidedness. On top of all that there is your magnificent piano playing and sympathy with the Slaatter. [. . .] It is your understanding of what I have wanted to do, even if I have not always been able to do it — it is that which makes me so happy.

Grieg usually signed his letters 'Your devoted friend' or 'Your old friend and admirer' when he wrote to Grainger. Soon the Norwegian was able to find a date in 1907 when the younger man could spend a few days at 'Troldhaugen'. He arranged for the Dutch composer Julius Röntgen to be there at the same time. Grieg also invited Herman Sandby to come for the same period, but by now the young Dane was recruit number 577 in the Danish army. The organizers of the 1907 Leeds Festival had invited Grieg to participate and he used this opportunity to suggest to them that he might conduct his piano concerto at the festival with Grainger at the piano. The authorities at Leeds needed no persuading.

Shortly before Grainger travelled to Norway, however, Grieg almost cancelled their meeting because in the hope of improving his health he had taken the Finsen Electric Light Bath treatment and instead his whole nervous system had suffered a drastic setback and he was troubled by asthma, sleeplessness and hallucinations. Returning to 'Troldhaugen', he slowly recovered thanks to the gentle solicitude of Nina Grieg.

At about 8.30 on the morning of July 25, 1907 Grainger arrived at Grieg's beautiful villa at Hop. The prospect of the Australian's pending visit had brought about a marked improvement in the older man's health, and though he was forced to delay his arrival for a few days the reunion proved to be every bit as rich and joyful as had been expected by both parties. The composer-conductor Julius Röntgen had arrived from his home in Amsterdam four days previously, and the meeting between Grainger and Röntgen prompted Grieg to make this entry in his diary on July 27: 'and so I had the joy of bringing these two wonderful men together who, I knew, would understand each other. Such vision as Julius has is a rare thing. What is important in Grainger's talent, in spite of his foreignness, was immediately perceived by Julius, who at once listened with eagerness to his music, his eminent piano playing, and his masterly and really original treatment of folk melodies.'

In a letter dated July 28 to Quilter, Grainger spoke enthusiastically of his impressions of Grieg, in language thick with early vintage Graingerisms.

> You dearest Rodg,
>
> Words can't describe the concentrated greatness and all-lovingness of the little great man. Out of the toughest Norwegianness, out of the most narrow localness, he spreads out a welcoming and greedy mind for all the world's wares. Such a fighter for freedom; so unauthoritative; so unfossilized in his lithesome yieldingness to the young and new [. . .].
>
> So sweetly and fatherly (and isn't he just my compositional forebear [. . .]) he enthuses at my things, 'Wamphray March' in partic. Here with dear Him and darling Her, I am with nought but what enfires, refreshes, stirs. I'm Englishing an old Norwegian folkballad for him. So often and often I'm thinking of how you'd be relishing the homely showings of the little half-Viking, and then again for his great-hearted largesse of sympathy and loving kindness towards your beloved and (you-)beloving Perks.
>
> Such things he says, and such flashing moments, situations blaze by with him. Weak, and threadbare now almost in his body, and nervously frail, his brain is yet whiplike and no health blemishes really break his gradually imposing patientness; nor his good-humouredness, which however (typically Norwegian, it seems) never reaches humorousness.
>
> All over this all-wooden house are books in every possible tongue. Such a wide sweep his inquisitiveness takes; all subjects; all standpoints. In himself I've no doubt he's got his narrowness; but by gum, his opinions! And they don't worry him, seemingly; and he's not for the turning on of force, or the driving home of authority . . .
>
> > Always lovingly,
> > yr. sometimes cold,
> > Perks.

Grainger would frequently plunge into the waters of the Nordasvannet lake below the house to rid himself temporarily of his eternally excessive energies—freezing cold as it may have been. He would also keep in physical trim by running each afternoon at 4 o'clock to Hop railway station and back to collect the post.

The two musicians also discussed the formation of a Norwegian Folk-Song Society. This was to be carried into effect during the following winter. Grieg was delighted and much impressed with the work done by the English Folk-Song Society and greatly admired many of the old melodies which Grainger had collected and preserved with the aid of a

phonograph. As the Australian sat playing selections from his Lincolnshire material on the Edison Bell cylinder phonograph he had brought
with him, Grieg was quickly convinced of the advantages of this new
scientific method of making 'field' recordings and lamented the fact that
no Norwegian had undertaken a similar project for Norway. Grieg,
conscious that his own health forbade his taking part in such work,
gladly hailed Grainger's offer to visit the remoter parts of Norway with a
phonograph in the summer of 1908, also promising to make arrangements of the best folk-songs and dedicate the collection to him, making
sure that Percy would be given the opportunity to première them.

Grainger also took with him to 'Troldhaugen' Delius's score of
*Appalachia*. Grieg buried himself in his friend's score with great satisfaction and was thrilled with the new work. It set him reminiscing about
the days when he and Delius had taken long walking tours in the
Norwegian mountains which they both loved so dearly.

During Grainger's stay Grieg suggested that together they should make
a grand concert tour of Europe the next year, the Australian playing the
piano in his concerto and he conducting. Grainger was profoundly
touched by this offer and willingly agreed. To this end — and with the
forthcoming Leeds Festival in mind — they worked long hours rehearsing
the piano concerto, which Grieg was rescoring to include a second pair
of horns. Grainger's studies with Grieg on this work were invaluable,
and some years later he brought out his own edition.

In the evenings a friend or two, occasionally Svendsen, would drop by
to take part in the discussions or listen to Grainger play; Nina Grieg
would often sing to the small circle. Grieg was ill during the whole of
Grainger's visit; a severe attack of pneumonia in his youth had left him
with the use of only one lung and asthma had complicated matters. In
the company of his infectiously ebullient friend, however, he seemed to
tap fresh reserves of strength, and as another relaxation from their joint
studies would row Grainger to the next tongue of land on the fjord where
his close friend Frants Beyer lived. Beyer was a well-known authority on
Norwegian folk culture and some years earlier had joined Grieg in his
folk-song hunts, the booty from which had been used by Grieg as the
basis for the Op. 66 and other folk-song arrangements. A further attraction of the Beyer household was the superb German concert grand piano
which he owned. Grainger often played on this glorious instrument and
on one occasion played one of the big Bach-Busoni organ transcriptions.
Grieg, who at one time or another must have heard most of the great
Romantic pianists — including Liszt, exclaimed, 'Now I realize that you
are a teetotaller! No alcohol drinker could ever keep up such a strain so
evenly, I am sure. It's colossal! Rubinstein was the nearest to it I have
heard, but he was much more haphazard and hadn't your reliability.'[5]

Grainger often discussed with Grieg matters relating to the Norwegian's compositional output. When asked which pieces of his he had the

greatest affection for Grieg replied unhesitatingly that he set greatest store by *Den Bergtekne* ('Taken by the Hills') for two horns, baritone solo and strings, the *Album for Male Voices* Op. 30, and the *Four Symphonic Dances*. They were never performed during the composer's lifetime and are rarely programmed even today. This made Grieg very bitter, but Grainger was wont to point out later that the Norwegian was very bitter about everything. 'I don't mean "bitter" in a bad sense, but he felt pained about everything. But that's the same with all Norwegian poetry, it's one long moan—the hero's moan, not a weakling's moan. The sadness of a hero.'[6] It was due to Grainger's efforts that some of these items were given their first American performances.

In later life Grainger was to remark of Grieg that he admired in particular his absolute insistence on a scrupulous attention to detail in his art and his constant striving for freedom and independence in all aspects of life. Persuaded by Grainger that many of the translations of his songs were very inferior and needed improving, Grieg would often spend an hour or two over the correct meaning of a single phrase.

Eventually the time came for Grainger to bid farewell to his beloved 'Half-Viking', and when, on the evening of August 4, 1907, Grieg accompanied him to the ferry in Bergen, no-one, except perhaps Grieg himself, had the slightest idea that this was to be the last time they were to see each other. The day after his departure, Grieg wrote in his diary:

What an artist, what a man! What a lofty idealist, what a child, and at the same time, what a broad and mature outlook he has on life. A future socialist of the purest water. Wagner's words: 'Aus Mitleid wissend, der reine Thor!' ['The pure fool, knowing through compassion'—*Parsifal*] fit him exactly. [. . .] As a pianist I don't know with whom amongst the greatest I shall compare him. But any comparison fails when the really great are considered. Grainger is himself. It is possible that I am partial to him, because he has actually realized my ideals in piano playing. If I had his technique, my conception of piano playing would be the same. Like a god he is exalted above all sufferings, all struggles. But one feels that they (the sufferings, struggles) have been experienced and conquered. It is a human being, a great soul, an aristocrat that is playing. May he prosper and succeed in life!

On August 11, 1907 Grieg wrote one of his last letters:

Dear Percy Grainger,

Thanks for your post-card! But above all, thanks for the days you gave us! I had so much wanted to get to know you more intimately, both as an artist and as a man, as I had the feeling that we would understand each other. And so it turned out. You have become a dear young friend to me, who has enriched the evening of my life. I have always found that they are mistaken who divide the artist from the man; on the contrary the two are indissolubly wedded to one another. In the man can be found the parallels of all the artist's traits. (Yes, even the most minute.) Even your subborn 'unnecessary' fifths (!) I could recognise again in my dear Percy Grainger! Not that I have the least doubt that they will sound well in your choral treatments.

I have again immersed myself in your folk-song settings and I see more and more how 'genial' they are. In them you have thrown a clear light upon how the English folk-song (to my mind so different from Scotch and Irish) is worthy of the privilege of being lifted up into the 'niveau' of Art; thereby to create an independent English Music. The folk-songs will doubtless be able to form the basis for a national style, as they have done in other lands, those of the greatest musical culture being no exceptions. [. . .]

Your devoted,
Edvard Grieg.

On August 16, Grieg wrote to Alexander Ilyich Siloti (cousin of Rachmaninov and pupil of Liszt) in St Petersburg: 'Recently I had a guest here, a young Australian. He is called Percy Grainger and lives in London. How he played! I have never heard such performances of Bach. And when he played my works, old Adam woke up and asked in astonishment, "So what I wrote is really that good?" And besides, he is a really important person. I beg you, remember his name. You will undoubtedly hear of him again. He is possessed, incidentally, by the same absurd idea as you are: he does not wish to be a pianist, but something different. In other words, "the grass on the other side of the fence is always greener".'

Grainger was the last guest at 'Troldhaugen'. Three weeks after his departure Grieg went to Bergen intending to take the ferry to England for the Leeds Festival. Though his luggage was already on board the ship, Grieg was too ill to follow. His attack was so severe that he could not be moved to his own home a few miles away. He died in the early hours of September 4. Later that day, Nina Grieg sent a telegram to Grainger containing the simple message: 'Burial Monday Greetings Thanks Nina Grieg—Bergen'.

Shortly after Grieg's funeral Grainger was back in Denmark, where he performed in a series of memorial concerts under the baton of Svendsen. At one concert fifteen members of Scandinavian and other royal families turned up to pay their final respects to Grieg. Whilst in Denmark he stayed with the Sandby family and when he returned to their home after the royal concert he ran around the sitting room shouting, crying and laughing, so overjoyed was he by the fact that Svendsen had embraced him at the end of the performance. He also played at the similar memorial concert in London and on the day of this performance he received Grieg's gold watch and chain from the composer's widow as a token of her late husband's love for him.

The programme notes for the Leeds Festival, which ran from October 9 to 12, 1907, proudly announced: 'The musical public will welcome the special visit of Dr. Edvard Grieg, the Norwegian Composer, who will conduct a first performance in this country of three scenes from his uncompleted Opera, 'Olav Trygvason'. He will also conduct his Pianoforte Concerto.' Sadly, the opera remained uncompleted and he was not to conduct. Sir Charles Villiers Stanford, the festival's principal conductor, stepped into Grieg's place for these two occasions.

The festival consisted of eight concerts, each being held at Leeds Town Hall. The cream of British singers had been invited to participate in this great North Country event which over the years had earned a reputation for excellent performances. The singers included Agnes Nicholls (later to become Lady Hamilton Harty), Mrs Henry J. Wood, Ada Crossley, Kirkby Lunn, Ben Davies, Spencer Thomas, Gervase Elwes, Plunket Greene and Ben Ffrangcon-Davies. For the choral works a choir of no less than four hundred voices had been assembled. And amongst the players of the 'Band' could be found A. E. Brain, Alfred Hobday and W. H. Squire, all three of whom were to make highly successful careers in later years.

Many British composers were there to conduct their own works, including Stanford, Boughton, Somervell, Vaughan Williams, Elgar, Bantock and Parry. The festival saw four first performances.

Grainger's performance, greeted with a boisterous manifestation of Yorkshire approval, came during the last concert of the festival, in which he accompanied Mrs Henry J. Wood in four songs by Grieg (*An das Vaterland, Warum schimmert dein Auge, Ich liebe Dich* and *Ein Traum,* plus one encore) before going on to play the Grieg piano concerto. The approval was not limited to Yorkshire, however, and the music critic of the *Birmingham Post,* Ernest Newman, was moved to write the following: 'Mr Percy Grainger accompanied the songs with exquisite taste, and afterwards gave the most brilliant and individual performance of the Grieg pianoforte concerto that I have ever heard. The fire and virility made one believe that Grieg was a bigger man than one had been accustomed to think him — though of course, the concerto is early Grieg, written before ill-health had made such a drain on his energy as it did later.' Indeed, every critic present was similarly ecstatic about his playing, which had proved a fitting tribute to Grieg's memory. Grainger was to remain a lifelong champion of the orchestral, vocal, choral and instrumental works of Grieg, including items of his in the programmes of his first London and New York solo recitals and his first and last Carnegie Hall concerts. He performed the piano concerto under Leopold Stokowski, Willem Mengelberg, Basil Cameron, Henry J. Wood, Sir Landon Ronald, Alexander Siloti, Ossip Gabrilowitsch, Hans Richter, Walter Damrosch, Alfred Herz and Josef Stransky among many others.

One of the most prominent characteristics of Grainger's life and thought was restlessness. It can be seen in his constant adoption of extremes, the almost unbelievable confluence of sheer genius and utter banality, and the labyrinthine tangle of what sometimes appear to be wildly inconsistent and illogical statements (albeit passionate and completely earnest for the most part). And when in 1938 he looked back and made a reassessment of the importance of his friendship with Grieg, he left a record from which we can obtain some idea of the extraordinary way his mind worked. Amidst the non sequiturs can be found a truth of considerable worth and perception. Many aspects of his personality and attitudes can be seen in this short extract; the utmost importance of the racial question, the spiritual masochism and finally the sense of defeat:

[. . .] Grieg's behaviour to me was flawlessly fatherly, tender and sweet from the first to the last. It just shows what close ties bind one Nordic composer to another, and it also shows the strange affinity that links Australia to Scandinavia. Their people like ours are a Colonial people. They are still colonizing their own great waste lands — in parts as sparsely populated as Australia — and the percentage of Scandinavians that colonize abroad, in the U.S.A. for instance, is a higher percentage of the home population than that ever sent out by Britain. It seems as if the Australian type in so far as it differs from its British forefathers is largely reverting to Scandinavianism. In Grieg's case there was the further fact that his Grandfather migrated to Norway from Scotland, the name was originally Greig, and that his music seems full of Scottish folkmusic inheritances.[7] It might seem that I should have been very happy at all that happened to me as a long result of these choruses of mine that Herman Sandby in his young artistic devotion to me showed to Grieg in 1904. Of course, I am very thankful for it all, but it brought me, like most happenings in my artistic life, mainly sorrow and disappointment. I had wanted to be Grieg's prophet, but instead he became my prophet. I had wanted critically and impersonally to proclaim the still-unsuspected, far-reaching importance of Grieg's compositional innovations, but instead became his protégé. And who believes in the impersonalness and criticalness of a protégé? So, in a sense, it would have been better if I had never met the Griegs, sweet and dear though they were to me.[8]

# 12

## 'Poor put-upon Percy'

For a short period in 1907 Grainger and his mother lived at 26 Coulson Street, in a quiet row of small Georgian houses running parallel to the Kings Road near Sloane Square. The following year he heard for the first time a chamber work of the French composer Gabriel Fauré and in March, when the Frenchman was staying in London, his host John Singer Sargent arranged a meeting with Grainger. Sargent had already shown some of the Australian's scores to Fauré, who had declared: *'Il a beaucoup de flamme* [. . .] *C'est une energie suprême'*.[1] A few days after he had met Fauré he wrote to Roger Quilter: 'You know I've always felt the English Dance as the whole land on the hop, the whole caboozle of football, factory furnaces, newspaper bicycling boys, fire engines; the general athletic pith of England whanging away. Of this Fauré knew nought, but his 1st words after my playing of it was "It's as if the total population was adancing". So he fished the true typical impression out of my rotten hammering out of it, somehow.'[2]

Earlier that year Grainger was invited to play at home for Sir Edgar and Lady Speyer, who with the help of Henry Wood had persuaded Debussy to come to England to conduct *'L'Après-midi d'un faune'* at Queen's Hall on February 1. The Speyers acted as hosts for Debussy. When Grainger had first performed his Toccata some years earlier in London it had been described by one critic as being like a day spent in the Battersea Dog's Home, but by this time public reaction was slowly coming around to accepting the new harmonies of Debussy and Grainger was glad to meet one of his musical heroes. He was disappointed, however, for he was amazed by the Frenchman's appalling manners and behaviour. Many years later Grainger said that on the occasion of their meeting he found him like 'a little spitting wild animal' and recalled that when he was asked to move with the others into another room for tea, he had replied, 'No I won't eat with anyone. Bring my tea in here so I can eat alone.'[3] Nevertheless this strange meeting did not prevent Grainger from continuing to include Debussy's piano music in his programmes, for he had by then earned something of a reputation for his interpretations of these works.

In January 1908 Rose Grainger received a visit from Mr Tait, the representative of J. C. Williamson who had organized the 1903/4 Australian tour for her son. His visit was to discuss the terms for a similar tour during the 1908/9 season. Percy made his terms clear. He wanted £40 a week and the condition written into the contract that a Steinway of his choice was to be transported wherever he went. His experiences of performing on antique and faulty instruments in the country towns of Australia during the previous tour had determined him to force the inclusion of this clause. Tait reluctantly agreed, but warned that as he had agreed to come that year in a supporting role to Ada Crossley, it would prevent his organization from taking him on a solo tour for the next two years. Rose was opposed to the idea of Percy's going, but eventually allowed him to accept. John Singer Sargent was one of several friends who threw a grand farewell party in his honour.

Before his departure for the second Australian tour, Grainger made his first entry into a recording studio. This took place on May 16, under the auspices of the Gramophone Company (later HMV). For his recording debut he chose an odd selection. A truncated version of Liszt's *Hungarian Rhapsody No. 12* occupied the single-sided 12″ record, and the two 10″ records consisted of his own arrangement of Stanford's *Irish March-Jig—Maguire's Kick* and the cadenza only from the first movement of Grieg's piano concerto. These earlier examples of Grainger's playing demonstrate clean fingerwork and ample fire and tenderness as and when required. They remain his rarest records.

Shortly before departing for Australia, he met the painter Charles Conder, who had lived in Melbourne between 1888 and 1890. He immediately felt the gentleness and charm which had had such a marked impression on Rose in Melbourne days. Conder was in an utterly crestfallen mood because the critics had torn his recent exhibition to shreds. 'But do you mean to tell me that a great and acclaimed genius like you still minds what a lot of ignorant swine like art critics write about your art?' asked Grainger. Condor began to weep. 'A little,' he said.[4] Within a few months the disillusioned and dispirited Conder was slain by the combined effects of syphilis and alcohol.

The meeting and the subsequent events had a profound effect on Grainger. His whole attitude towards newspaper critics jelled in a flash, and though he never stopped quoting their favourable opinions in his own publicity material, he ceased deliberately to court them thereafter. In private his opposition was, with rare exceptions, venomous, as evinced in the following example:

> Can nothing be done to hinder artmen from lending their ears to the braying of newspaper donkeys? Fancy that any real tone-birther ((composer)) should sink so low as to read the bilge written by such a nincompoop as Ernest Newman. I single out E.N. because I am not aware of his ever having written against me or my art. But I met him

around 1903-1905, in Manchester or Birmingham or somewhere, was told he was a rising light as a tone-art-judge ((music critic)), but could only see that he was a dull, clerk-typed man from whose mug nary a clever word about toneart could come forth. Much later on I read fulsome praise of Strauss by Newman [. . .] at a time just before the war when all the foolish world had made up its mind that Strauss was an all-right boy [. . .] I knew that he was a small flea that climbs on a big dog's back. But when, after the war, I saw that E. Newman was belittling Strauss *beyond* his earn-ment ((deserts)), just because it was fashionable to do so at that moment, then I knew for fair that E.N. was simply a bad worth-weigher ((critic)) who always shoots too far or too short of the mark, as well as being a bloody swine, a kicker-of-a-man-who-is-done, a weather-cock, a fair-weather-friend [. . .] it goes without saying that I have never seen a wordchain ((sentence)) written by E.N. that shows, or even hints, that Newman has any inner feeling for, or outer tonecraftsome knowledge of, tonecraft. Such a man is no better nor worse than a folk-mood-guesser, a backer of the winning horse at all costs.[5]

There were many times in Grainger's life when he nurtured the forlorn hope of forming a composers' guild whose members would agree to the printing on the first page of their works a list of the names of musicians who would be forbidden to perform their works and critics who would be forbidden to judge their music. He was never an élitist who felt that the creation, recreation and enjoyment of art should be restricted to those born with higher sensibilities and sensitivities, but he was always bitterly opposed to what he felt was unmusical professionalism and academic stuffiness and artiness. In fact he firmly believed that geniuses were not born but rather created by their environment — particularly the environment provided by their mothers during childhood.

With Rose in attendance Percy and the Ada Crossley touring party sailed from Southampton early in August 1908 on the RMS *Orontes*. As in the previous tour, they began with concerts in the capital cities of each state and then returned to offer their talents to the outlying towns and goldfield settlements. Grainger, of course, renewed his habit of walking from town to town during the tour of the outlying districts. His most publicized walk took place in south Victoria in the first week of November when, attired in belted shorts, double socks (well soaped) and boots, he covered the forty-six miles of unmetalled road between Yarram and Sale in eleven and a half hours.

In the last week of November, he received a blow when the tour's sponsor J. C. Williamson sent news to him that his services were no longer required. The letter of dismissal was sent to Adelaide, but he had left by then and was entertaining the goldminers and their ladies in Kalgoorlie, Western Australia. Williamson had found Grainger's fee too high and with the additional £60 weekly cost of transporting the Steinway from Sydney around the country towns he was not being adequately covered by box-office receipts. So, without even offering to renegotiate his contract, he simply sacked him. Grainger knew, however, that it would have been very bad publicity to leave in the middle of a tour without good reason and return to England earlier than expected without any European concert bookings. He therefore offered to reduce his fee to £30 a week and waive the piano clause. This satisfied Williamson and he was duly re-engaged.

In January of 1909 the troupe of artists sailed for New Zealand where they toured the main cities of both islands. Whenever he was able Grainger went to the Maoris to note down their music and in the North Island he secured the valuable services of Maggie and Pomeri, two famous Maori guides. It was in Otaki, however, that he unearthed his greatest treasure, as he explained in a letter to Roger Quilter:

I met a dear old man [. . .] born here, son of a settler, I should say, brought up in the country when Maoris swarmed & whites were scarce; ½ (at least) native in feeling, married to a Maori, very chummily pally with his handsome but erratic ½ breed sons, quite a card he is. Kind and easygoing to animals; they browse in his unkempt garden, doesn't kill flies if he can help it & takes phonograph records of every bit of native music he can. 2 years ago Raratongan natives were brought over to Christchurch (NZ) Exhibition. They sang gloriously. This old man phonographed them. Nobody else did seemingly. His name is Knocks [. . .] I came to hear his Maori records, but he made me hear the Raratongan records & I straightway noted them down in his cobwebby, dirty, manuscriptbelittled, brokenwindowed, queersmelling house from afternoon early to 5 the next morn. The old man stayed up to 2 o'clock with me, & he & ½ breeds & I had great fun manning the phonograph & chatting and getting on well together & feeding on tea & bread & butter. That old chap is a dear trustful tolerant (though a bit bitter against the whites) kindlisouled born artist nature; you don't find that sort in Australia.

These Raratongan things are the strongest impressions I've met since the Faerø dance tunes. These are dance music also. *But polyphonic.* They have *real harmony,* & of course tons of rhythmic delights. Sometimes their spirit is very sweet, rocking & kittenish, & at times fierce & rending like tiger claws, but always it is great larks [. . .]. Red flowers in shining blueblack hair, the easy graceful gait of Sea air bedewed coastdwellers, the bold free eyes of islanders, the dance instincts of folk shortly ago fighters & maneaters; there is lots of fun ahead. I am taking some phonograph records of Maori songs myself. *Not* sung in harmony ever as far as I can make out; but queer interesting intervals they use, & they sing & recite like heroes; such wantonness, laziness, energy, unselfbeknownst attack, & strong coaxing throbbing voices.[6]

When Grainger discovered the four and eight part polyphonic music of the South Sea Islands he was overwhelmed. He tried to get other people interested in the work of Knocks and to carry on with the work of phonographing the music that interested him so much. Many years later, when the New Zealand branches of the British record companies began to record the folk music of these parts, the folk culture had become diluted with European influences. The cylinders of Knocks and Grainger (now preserved in Melbourne) are among the few authentic recordings. But the polyphonic singing from Raratonga proved extremely difficult to transcribe and this work has yet to be completed.

Memory lapses afflict the finest solo instrumentalists at times, yet it is strange that Grainger had more lapses in the piano music of Schumann than in that of any other composer — for there can be no doubt that he loved and revered Schumann's keyboard writing. By April, Grainger and the touring party were back in Australia, where they performed their farewell concerts in the state capitals. In a performance at the Sydney Town Hall of Schumann's treacherous Toccata in C major Op. 7 he became completely lost and in a fury bashed his way to the end. For Grainger the ironic feature of the affair was that his performance was greeted with thunderous applause and the critics waxed long and poetic about his supreme command of the work. After this tour he never programmed the toccata again.

Shortly after his arrival in England on June 29, Grainger once more plunged into the tiring world of public recitals and concerts. That season he performed twice at Queen's Hall Promenade Concerts and in the autumn and winter embarked on extensive tours of Scandinavia, Holland and Germany.

His return to London after his Australian tour made him an even more eccentric-looking Chelsea figure than before. His encounter with the Maoris had given him the idea of getting his mother to make shirts and shorts out of brightly coloured towelling. He would often go running in these clothes and found them warm in winter and cool in summer. He also conducted his one-guinea-an-hour piano lessons in them.

After their meeting in April 1907 Delius was to exert a strong musical and personal influence in Grainger's life. Delius had immediately asked Grainger to go and stay with him at Grez in the spring of 1908, but the visit was not made until after the Great War. By 1908 Thomas Beecham had begun to programme Delius's works and whenever possible Grainger went to hear them. It is almost certain that Beecham's interest in Grainger's music came about largely through Delius's advocacy. The two composers often exchanged scores of new works. Whenever Delius was in

England he would visit the Graingers and he and Percy would talk endlessly of each other's artistic progress, and Delius even proposed a joint negro folk-song collection in America.

Delius later wrote to Ethel Smyth:

The Russians and French have tried to break away (from German classical traditions), and partly the Norwegians—Grieg. The English and Americans, however, go on stolidly creating dead works [. . .] and indeed the public is abruti to the degree that they will listen with respect and awe to any twaddle having Jesus or the Virgin Mary as a subject. And when it is more than usually dry and long they call it 'noble and severe'. Handel is the creator of this public and of the 'genre ennuyeux' which is still the bane of music in England, and every conductor in England flatters that public except Beecham. I believe there is lots of talent in England and that it will gradually become more daring and independent, but there is as yet very little to encourage it. I consider Percy Grainger the most gifted of the younger composers I have met, and he is again Australian. Have you met him?

This letter was written on March 15, 1909, and by then Delius was helping to set in motion a practical means of helping Grainger as well as many other young British composers. On March 23, 1908 a letter had appeared in *The Times* which was a call to arms for the cause of British music. It was signed by a body of notable musicians including Elgar, Delius, Mackenzie, Wood, Bantock, Pitt and O'Neill, and outlined the aims of and called for subscribers to a new musical society calling itself the Musical League. Its object was to hold annual festivals of new and unfamiliar compositions, and it was hoped that the first festival would be held in Manchester under the direction of Hans Richter. But the original plans were modified and the first festival took place in Liverpool (without the directorship of Hans Richter) in September 1909. Delius had accepted the position of vice-president of the organizing committee under the presidency of Elgar solely on the condition that some works of Grainger's were performed. Often enough Delius had said to him 'My lad, if you don't hear your things sung and played you will never know if you are scoring as you want to, or not.'[7]

The festival began with a chamber concert in the Yamen Rooms on the evening of Friday September 24. The following day in the afternoon an orchestral concert was held at the Philharmonic Hall, and in the evening the final event, a choral concert, took place at the same location. Vasco V. Akeroyd's Symphony Orchestra and the Welsh Choral Union were harnessed under the baton of Mr Harry Evans. Six works of young composers had their first performances at these remarkable concerts and Grainger took part in the first concert in the role of pianist. He had a marked success with renderings of the *Handelian Rhapsody* in D major by Cyril Scott and two of his four arrangements of Stanford's *Irish Dances*. His greatest success, however, came in the final concert when, sandwiched between works by Ethel Smyth and Havergal Brian, the tenor John Coates and the Welsh Choral Union under Harry Evans performed his settings of *Irish Tune from County Derry* and *Brigg Fair*. The performances were greeted with such a storm of applause that they had to be repeated. When the applause broke out again after the encores the audience began to call for the composer. He wrote many years later:

> [These] two little trifles were exquisitely sung and were (I think) the sensation of the festival. When I heard the outbreak of spontaneous applause I was furious—furious at the needless 10 years of compositional misgivings I had endured; misgivings fed by the mirth of most of my fellow-composers at what they considered the eccentricities of my composing methods, fed by the meanness of my rich friends—to none of whom it had occurred to 'stand' me a private rehearsal in which I might have put the effectiveness of my scoring to the acid test. And now (I said to myself) my eccentricities have been proved 'normal', my experimental methods sound. I ran into the top gallery and hid. The applause [. . .] must have lasted 4 or 5 minutes, and I was frightened as well as furious. But no one found me and I did not appear.[8]

When Grainger wrote this he had allowed to slip his memory the instance in 1907 when Balfour Gardiner had paid for the hire of Percy Hall in Tottenham Court Road and for the musicians needed to rehearse the *Hill-Song* material.

The Liverpool concerts of 1909 marked the starting point of Grainger's public life as a composer. His fame began to spread and Delius always spoke enthusiastically of him to his friends and professional acquaintances. Béla Bartók probably encountered the name of Grainger in connection with the Australian's pioneering work in folk-song and it is almost certain that Delius wrote to him shortly after the Liverpool festival mentioning Grainger's success. In an undated letter (probably written in August/September 1910) Bartók wrote to Delius:

> It is with great pleasure that I can tell you that your Brigg Fair is to be performed here [Budapest] in February—under a relatively quite good conductor (we have plenty of bad ones, and how bad). I should like to suggest some Grainger to this conductor for the following season—actually only because I should like to hear it myself. But I do not know how to come by a score etc., whether the composer will agree to a performance at all, what to choose.—Please advise me on this. And please mention me to Grainger when you have an opportunity; I

should like to write to him on the subject of folk-lore, and would not wish to do so as a complete stranger.[9]

Nothing has survived to confirm that anything came of this tenative approach of Bartók's; the two composers never met or corresponded, though their paths did cross many years later in the columns of an American music magazine.

Reynaldo Hahn turned up in London in November of 1909 and called on Grainger asking him to put him in touch with a selection of young London-based composers. Hahn was due to give a series of illustrated lectures in London and Paris on new music and wanted to build up a repertoire of songs, which he always sang accompanying himself at the piano. Grainger immediately contacted Cyril Scott, Balfour Gardiner and Roger Quilter suggesting that they send samples of their songs to Hahn. Percy thought him a great singer and, with a few reservations, a sympathetic composer.

In December of the same year, Nina Grieg came to London and stayed for two weeks with the Graingers in the Kings Road. The friendship with Nina Grieg was maintained until her death. The following year during his winter and spring tour of Scandinavia Grainger stayed with her at Bergen and after his recital on January 28 in Kristiania she introduced him to the King and Queen of Norway. He was asked a few days later to play at the Royal Palace. When he returned to Kristiania after a tour of the country districts the Queen was again in the royal box for a performance of the Grieg concerto. She asked him to sit with her after he played, and presented him with a handsome scarf pin. She wrote to Nina Grieg a few days later: 'We think he is as wonderful as an artist, as he is delightful and fascinating as a personality.'[10] This tour was a great success and he was re-engaged for a more extensive tour of Scandinavia, Holland and Germany during 1910/11. In that following season he worked for the first time under Willem Mengelberg — a mutually happy collaboration which was to continue for many years.

Grainger was back in London from his continental tours by April 1910 and on the eleventh of that month he was invited to the home of Sir Edgar Speyer, where Dr and Mrs Richard Strauss were staying. Strauss was in London for the first London performance of his opera *Elektra* under Beecham which had taken place on March 12. *Elektra* had scandalized London and it was the most talked-about musical event of the year. On the evening of April 11, an at-home was arranged, but this time Grainger was not one of the artists; he was merely a guest and enjoyed the opportunity of meeting Richard Strauss, whom he found charming and whose music he already knew and loved. It is possible that at this meeting Grainger showed Strauss some of his compositions; in any case, shortly after they next met in 1911 Strauss became the first German conductor to programme Percy's music in Germany.

The strange thing about Grainger's love affair with Karen Holten — taking place at this time — was that they rarely met more than once a year, conducting the relationship almost entirely by letter. It survived over eight years, however, despite the presence of Rose, whose meddlesome influence gradually discouraged Karen's visits to London and whose tantrums eventually killed Karen's love for Percy.

Grainger, of course, was never blind to the nature of his mother's affection for him and the poisonous effect it was bound to have on any love relationship he formed. He knew he could never leave her because of her possessiveness and her failing health and though she sometimes suggested to him that it would be a good idea to make a wife of Karen, Rose only spoke of such plans with a *ménage à trois* in mind — with her son's wife playing the least important role. Percy, of course, knew that no woman would accept such conditions. Occasionally Rose became quite insistent about Percy's need to get married, and the only way he could rid her of the idea was to catalogue his sexual deviations, laying strong emphasis on his lust for little girls. At this, Rose would temporarily shelve her plans for her son, but the tension for Percy was fearsome and unflagging. In the summer of 1909 Rose wrote to her son (at that time on tour) about her fears. The somewhat obscure reference to 'blue roses' is taken from a poem by Kipling which tells of a girl who taunts her suitor by rejecting his gifts of red and white roses and withholding her love until he can produce blue roses. For Percy and Rose 'blue roses' came to mean Percy's sexual deviations.

If only you didn't prefer blue roses, I should be happy — but ever since I knew that — I have never been really joyful — and when you are away, I fret very much about your strange fancies. When you are with me, and I see your sweet face, looking noble, and happy, I forget the wrong-coloured roses, and sometimes think it is all a horrible nightmare, and that I shall wake, and find reality again, as I used to know it. If you only had the power of loving me, as I do you, you could never indulge in your fancies, knowing that through them, all joy has left my life, and although I love you quite as much as I used, I am no longer proud of you, nor feel the same pleasure in mixing with my fellow creatures, as I feel so ashamed of having a child with such fancies as you have. If you were as I once thought you to be, you would be a grand man and outgrow them, remember one cannot stand still, and unless you overcome them, they will overcome you, as years go on, you will have stranger fancies, and God knows how you will end. I would sooner you were a dear, sweet, untalented person, with a love of right, than be gifted as you are, and be as you are. Strange when I wrote Kipling's little verse in the book I gave you, I little knew how near home the words were, and how often I would feel the bitterness of their truth. Don't think I am blind to all your splendid qualities, for I am not, and am ever grateful to you for being kind to me, and for having brought much, much joy to me in all the past years. I felt so confident that as you grew to manhood I should have every reason to be proud of you, and having only one child, took hourly care to watch over you, and tried to point out to you strange and weak qualities that showed up now and again — hoping that as your mind expanded, you yourself would hate what was ugly. I am so sad Darling about you, and would be a happy mother, if you could tell me that it was all a dream and passed. When you can tell me that, Darling — don't delay — will you my love? [11]

As late as December 31, 1940 Percy wrote his own commentary on this letter:

What troubled my mother was either my enjoyment of flagellation or my declaration that I, if I had any daughters, would probably establish a lustful relationship with them — either through flagellation or by incest with them. It is indeed true that I, seriously, felt the inclination to do this. But it is also true that I liked to exaggerate a little bit in this respect when talking to my mother. Like most adoring mothers she probably had two main demands — the first being to keep me all to herself (i.e. without my marrying, if possible without my falling in love seriously); the second, the yearning to see me 'happily married' with children of my own and all that. I for my part was convinced that my mother's entire happiness, her whole aim in life, would fade if I married. Therefore I allowed myself to frighten her a little (with a little exaggerated talk about flagellation and incest) when she advised me too strongly to marry. Not that there wasn't a good deal of truth in my exaggerations! With Karen I spoke a little differently — when marriage came up for discussion. To her I first and foremost mentioned my duty to my art as the reason why I refused to marry. I always understood quite clearly that my first duty in life was to keep away from marriage, as I was convinced that my mother's entire happiness in life was rooted in her possessing me tooth and nail, entirely to herself. It was rather difficult for me to refuse myself the pleasures of marriage, as I was rather in love with Karen and because at the time (as now and as always) only felt two needs — art and sex. It was particularly difficult when my mother pushed me too hard with advice about marriage. Therefore I had to cool her off a bit from time to time. And that it was all to no avail is equally obvious.[12]

Rose's lack of understanding of herself, her son and the relationship which existed between them was as tragic as it was huge. Percy's handling of the situation was often clumsy, but he felt that his technique of scaring his mother into dropping her frantic demands for his marriage was the

only manoeuvre left open to him. The thought uppermost in his mind
was that at no cost could he leave her. He often referred to himself as
'poor put-upon Percy'. This was a reference to the personal situation in
which he found himself as well as to the fact that his enslavement to the
concert platform took him away from composition and his loved ones.

At no time in his life after the age of about fifteen did Grainger abandon his sadistic and masochistic pleasure-seeking. Blood-letting was often
part of his activities and he nearly always laundered his own shirts because of the telltale bloodstains. With the possible exception of Mimi
Kwast, all his girlfriends were to be drawn into his particular form of
lovemaking and there is ample photographic evidence of this. Several
photographs exist which he took of himself after one of his frequent
bouts of auto-flagellation. An indication of his extraordinary mentality
can be detected from the fact that as he stood before the camera lens
with bleeding wounds he also held up a notice which gave details not only
of the exact time of day, location of session and number of lashes with
what kind of whip, but also the type of film used in the camera and the
exposure and aperture. Whenever he went on tour he took a selection of
several dozen whips with him.

One of Grainger's doctors has written:

Whip-lash marks were not infrequently evident at the time of his
examinations and treatments at the office. The explanations were
readily forthcoming and as the years went by I gradually learned his
own conception of himself. He would never ask me to try to cure him.
He did not consider it a disease. He considered it something that
might be deplored by some, yes, but it was also something to be enjoyed by him. He could not help it. To him it represented a biological
characteristic given to him to be exercised with no social infringements and with enormous personal joy. In addition he had the gift of
music; these two precious talents he felt should be exercised to the full-
est, and his was no split personality. [. . .] By accepting himself as he
was, biologically and sexually, he defused, so to say, a sizzling time
bomb within him which otherwise might have blown his personality to
bits. It might even be crucial for complete fulfilment of the love-action
that his love-partner had also met the 'approval' of his mother. He
knew well his love-action was never to be approved by his mother.
Neither her love nor her sorrows, however, could disengage Percy
from his compulsive sexual act. They thundered on [. . .] with a constant and searing feeling of guilt, not towards the characteristics of the
love-action, but towards the mother who felt so ashamed of the dark
side of her son. With these three people involved in a dark drama repeated again and again in different places at different times and with
a different female partner, it is not improbable that Percy would feel
relieved that his mother was aware, not to be able to prevent the act,

but willing to or insisting about participating by choosing the girl or
approving of her. Rose was thus personally involved — to Percy's great
relief. In such ambivalent situations arising from mother and son's
absolute dependence on each other, it might seem unbelievable that a
mother should be able to shoulder her mother responsibility, even to
the extent of advice regarding sex matters for the deviant offspring.
The letters indicate that she did. These are facts.[13]

Very few of his friends ever understood Grainger. This was perhaps because he was already becoming used to concealing his innermost feelings
from the world. He was skilful at sublimating his true emotions and
projecting them into his music, and conversational references to himself
were always heavily veiled. When he talked about Grieg's bitterness and
sadness he was also talking about his own — perhaps more so. Bitterness,
in fact, became the keynote of his feelings towards the world around
him. Introversion was his natural defence. In musical terms, his frustration and bitterness were expressed in a choral and orchestral setting of
Swinburne's Border Ballad *The Bride's Tragedy*. The story tells of a girl
who, about to be married to a man she loathes, is snatched from the
church door by her lover. They ride away, pursued by the bridegroom
and her family until they come to the banks of a swollen, angry river.
They dash in and try to cross but are drowned in the attempt. The first
half is full of speed and action, the second is a dirge for the lovers. Most
of the work for this fine example of Percy's original settings of poetry was
done in 1908 and 1909. In 1936, he wrote to Alfhild Sandby:

> I am particularly glad that you, Alfhild, like *The Bride's Tragedy*.
> That work was my personal protest against the sex-negation that our
> capitalistic world (assisted by mother, by you, & by numberless other
> well-wishers) offered to young talents like me. A man cannot be a full
> artist unless he is manly, & a man cannot be manly unless his sex-life is
> selfish, brutal, wilful, unbridled. But the main stream of thot in our
> age sets its face against such manliness as has always seemed right and
> proper to me. Well, there was no need to lose one's temper about it.
> But the situation called for a protest, I felt, & *The Bride's Tragedy*
> was my protest, & the angry chords on the brass (at the first singing of
> 'they lie drowned & dead') is my personal bitterness.[14]

In 1905, during his tour of Denmark with Herman and Alfhild,
Grainger had been introduced to Hjalmar Thuren, a masterly authority
on Danish folklore. This meeting opened up two fields of wonderment
for him. Firstly, Thuren himself had done extensive research in the area
of Faeroe Island folk-music, and Grainger was immediately taken by its
special qualities. Two undoubted masterpieces emerged from this field

of his studies: *Father and Daughter* and *Let's Dance Gay in Green Meadow*. The former is set for five men's solo voices, double mixed chorus, strings, brass and percussion plus a mandolin and guitar band. The guitar and mandolin band is very elastic in its constitution and is split into four sections each requiring the instruments to be tuned in four different ways. As many as sixty guitars and mandolins have been used for its performance, and, very characteristically, Grainger wrote on the score that the more instruments used the better it would sound but that the entire band could be left out at will. It was scored mainly between 1908 and 1909 and dedicated to his friend Singer Sargent. The tune is developed as a passacaglia and the work relies for its strength on progressive harmonic and contrapuntal exploration with each restatement of the tune. This technique was used in other works by Grainger, notably *Green Bushes* and *Scotch Strathspey and Reel*. Despite the spirited energy of *Father and Daughter* it is a grim tale of revenge telling of a man who kills his daughter's lover and is in turn killed by her. The tune is a narrative dance tune and is taken from a collection of Faeroe Island dance tunes which Hjalmar Thuren had made with a phonograph as early as 1901.[15] (It is almost certain that Grainger took his idea of folk-song collecting with a phonograph from the work of Thuren.)

*Let's Dance Gay in Green Meadow* is another Faeroe Island dance tune and was set by Grainger for four hands at one piano and in another form for band. Although the piece never saw public performance in any form during his lifetime, it is a masterpiece of stark, clashing harmonies and counterpoint. The ending is a stroke of genius: it simply leaves off at the end of a twelve-bar phrase, without any dynamic, rhythmic or temporal suggestion of a conclusion, thus giving the effect that the dance is something without end.

Grainger had wanted to find a printed source which would lead him to a fuller understanding of Danish folk-music and Thuren gave him the name of Evald Tang Kristensen. Tang Kristensen had been collecting since the 1860s and already had a body of published work behind him. Grainger devoured the Tang Kristensen collections and soon rated him the greatest genius known to him amongst folk-song collectors anywhere in the world—a view in which he never wavered.[16] What appealed so much to him was the way in which Tang Kristensen had noted down the tunes as they were really sung without watering them down to suit the rhythmic and modal preconceptions of the academic world. Tang Kristensen had been subjected to much stupid and uncalled-for vilification—being accused of incorrectly notating his folk-songs because of either faulty hearing or ignorance. When Grainger collected folk-songs in Jutland with him in 1922, 1925 and 1927, he discovered that the tunes were almost note for note the same as those collected by his Danish friend fifty years previously. For the time being, however, Grainger did not go out of his way to seek a personal introduction to Tang Kristensen. He felt that he needed to gain some experience from his own field-work before meeting his hero. Later, in 1914 and with a whole world of experience behind him, he ventured a meeting with the great man. They made plans for a joint collecting expedition and were at the stage of Grainger having shipped his phonograph and several crates of blank cylinders over to Denmark, when unfortunately a certain prince was assassinated at Sarajevo and the whole of Europe was plunged into a senseless waste of life and money. Grainger and Tang Kristensen had to postpone their collecting for eight years.

On Grainger's concert tour of 1910/11 he was greeted by sold-out halls and followed by laudatory reviews everywhere he went. He described the tour as 'painful but beriching'.[17] Rose was with him much of the time, and at Kristiania, where Grainger gave recitals in early October 1910, both Graingers and Nina Grieg were made guests of honour at a celebration given by a society for the preservation of the old Norse language. After toasts, speeches and presentations the hosting society gave a magnificent display of folk-songs and dances from Norway, Denmark and the Faeroe Islands. Nina Grieg then travelled with Grainger and his mother to Copenhagen where later that month he was introduced at the Danish Royal Court.

On October 28 Grainger's *Mock Morris* and *Molly on the Shore* were given their first public performances by a ladies' amateur orchestra in Copenhagen. (The string quartet version of *Molly on the Shore* had been performed in December 1909 before a small invited audience at the home of the von Glehns in Cheyne Walk.) Herman Sandby's brother Christian was the conductor, but he failed to please Nina Grieg, who was highly critical of the playing of the orchestra. At any rate works such as these were to become Grainger's bread-and-butter in future years. In his original arrangements they are tiny masterpieces of delicate scoring giving evidence of a spontaneous talent for counterpoint and variation, but like the later *Shepherd's Hey* and *Country Gardens* they were written with the idea of appealing to a wider, relatively unsophisticated audience, and contain few suggestions that the mind creating them was also wrestling with such problems as polytonality, complex rhythms, post-impressionist harmony and aleatory music. In later years, when bitterness mostly clouded his attitude towards life, Grainger looked back on the astonishing popularity of these small works with shame and remarked that they had been badly scored and ill-conceived. His attitude may be accounted for by the fact that the popular pieces had almost completely eclipsed the interest in works by which he set much greater store. As with Rachmaninov and *the* Prelude, works like *Mock Morris* very quickly became artistic liabilities.

During the summer of 1911 Grainger was approached by Balfour

Gardiner and asked if he would like to take part in a series of concerts the following year. He was overjoyed to have this chance and he set about choosing the works for inclusion. This series of concerts and a similar series which Balfour produced during 1913 were to shake the English musical establishment to its roots. Henry Wood, Dan Godfrey, Landon Ronald and Percy Pitt had been programming only a few items of British music, but even adding Beecham's championship of Delius to this, the total output of British music at concerts was pitifully small. The Anglo-Saxon habit of revering anything foreign and ignoring any home-grown talent was then at its height.

It was probably during the summer of 1911 that Grainger first met the sister of Dame Ethel Smyth, Mrs Charles Hunter. Charles Hunter owned coal mines and his great wealth enabled his wife to conduct a splendid social life at their seventeenth-century home Hill Hall in Epping Forest. It was John Singer Sargent who introduced him to Mrs Hunter and the Australian thus entered a new world of refined and aristocratic spirits. His job was to play the piano at her at-homes, where he was usually paid £25 for an evening's work, though they engendered in Grainger the usual feelings of extreme discomfort. The society hostess Mrs Hunter would often entertain Henry James and Grainger noticed how submissive he was towards her. Rodin was also a friend and frequent visitor to the Hunters' home and once made a fine bust of Mrs Hunter. At dinner Grainger was often seated next to Rodin, but this always bored the Australian for Rodin was then in his dotage. Mrs Hunter once paid Grainger £50 for an evening when she was entertaining Rodin, General French and the Duke and Duchess of Connaught.

Beecham was also a regular guest at Hill Hall, though he was thoroughly disliked by Charles Hunter, who referred to him as an 'insolent young pup'. George Moore, another visitor to Hill Hall, would run and hide or beg leave to go home if Beecham turned up. When Grainger met Beecham the talk would often turn to Delius. Once after they had been walking through the local forests and villages Beecham went to the piano at Hill Hall to illustrate some points from *Appalachia* which they had been discussing. Grainger was quite shocked when in his playing of the Delius extracts Beecham chose harmonies which, as the Australian himself said, were hardly worthy of Mendelssohn. It was Delius's harmonies that attracted him more than anything, and he was puzzled by Beecham's ignorance. Although he always maintained that Beecham conducted the works of Delius better than anyone, he never forgot the incident at Hill Hall. Grainger rarely expressed his dislike of anyone and Beecham continued to keep his company. Some time later, Beecham asked him if he would become his assistant conductor—a post which many young musicians would have eagerly accepted. But he turned it down, telling Beecham that his heart lay in composition rather than the performing arts and that piano playing was already more than he could cope with. Though hard to believe, the real reason for Grainger's turning down the offer — never confided to a soul, but it is to be found in some of his later writings — was: Beecham did not have blue eyes.

On July 9, 1911 Grainger was entertained at the country home of Edward Speyer (the cousin of Sir Edgar Speyer) in Shenley, Hertfordshire. This was probably the only occasion when he met Elgar for more than a brief moment, though nothing remains in either the Grainger or the Elgar legacies to inform us how they reacted to each other. Grainger certainly found Elgar's music extremely distasteful, with the exception of *Nimrod* from the *Enigma Variations*, which he arranged for piano solo in 1953.

In November he travelled to Holland to give his first Amsterdam concert with Mengelberg. By chance, on the train which took him to Amsterdam, Grainger met Georges Enesco, who was on his way to the same city to conduct his *Two Rumanian Rhapsodies* at the same concert. Although this was the only time they met, he liked Enesco greatly and also admired his work to the extent of utilizing some of Enesco's scoring techniques in his own compositions. From the *First Rhapsody* he took the idea of ornaments in parallel triads (used for example in *Colonial Song*), while the harmonic texture of the principal cadences in *Tribute to Foster* was inspired by the *Second Rhapsody*.

The most important event during his tour of Holland took place when he received a letter from his friend Roger Quilter, saying that he would like to use part of a legacy willed to him by his father Sir Cuthbert Quilter to help Percy publish some of his works. Rose Grainger and Delius had played their part in breaking down his resistance to the idea of publishing and this letter from his friend finally broke his resolve. In his absence Roger Quilter and Rose (who had returned to London earlier) had contacted Willy Strecker from the London branch of Schott and Company, who said he would be happy to add the Australian's name to their list of composers. When he was informed of this he was delighted, but pressed for a few conditions to be understood in all future agreements on publishing. After Quilter's original financial help, he wanted to pay half costs towards production. He also wanted to choose his own designs for covers and he wanted the freedom to use his own English expression marks. His works first appeared later that year in Great Britain and they included nine British folk-music settings, one Faeroe Islands dance folk-song setting, four Kipling Settings, one 'Room-music Tit-bit' and one setting of a poem by Swinburne. More works appeared during 1912 and soon his works were available both in America and Europe.

Despite Grainger's initial pleasure at the publication of his works, he retained a few doubts. The fact that, with rare exceptions, people refused to take him seriously and even fewer tried to understand his musical ideas made him increasingly guilt-ridden about various aspects of publication. Eventually he came to rue the day he had agreed to Willy Strecker's offer, particularly when he was persuaded to write piano arrangements of his works which, it was thought, would increase their popularity and sales. In 1945 he wrote:

[. . .] it is wrong for a tone-wright to put his puzzle-wifty ((complicated)) scores within the reach of know-nothing-y keyed-hammer-string ((piano)) players. In art, everything should be done to honour the clever, the hard-working, the learned types — those that learn to read scores. Nothing should be done for take-it-easy, know-nothing & care-less keyed-hammer-string-players ((pianists)). We tone-wrights should keep them out all we can, (be-shame them all we can). Allowing keyed-hammer-string dish-ups of my tone works (which, in their as-first-was ((original)) forms were always a-chance-for-all-y ((democratic)), & always group-minded) has wrecked my whole job-path ((career)) as a tone-wright [. . .] I should have gone on earning a half-good income as a half-good keyed-hammer-string player. I should have kept my pure tone-works out of the dirty keyed-hammer-string business altogether — as Wagner, R. Strauss, Hans Pfitzner & Arthur Fickenscher have done. So Roger, mother & Willy Strecker (for all their well-wishingness to me) did me an ill turn in planning the forth-printment of my tone-works. Yet as a greedy business man I real-see how much I owe to Roger everytime I see the big moneys roll in from Ascap, British Performing Rights Society, & from my forth-printers [. . .]. But when I was about 30 mother pleaded with me to have my works forth-sounded then & there. She said 'Your compositions are the only grandchildren I will ever have, it seems. I don't feel very well, & may not live to see you forty. I wouldn't like to go to my grave without having heard any of your compositions.' So I gave in [. . .]. It is the duty of an over-soul to shine like snow on a mountain-top, luring on beauty-loving men to strive-ment, struggle & keenness as it takes to climb to the heights. It is no use meeting lazy men half-way, bearing in one's hands titbits of beauty they have not worth-earned ((deserved)). Let them climb, or pine for nought.[18]

When Grainger's music was first published, his English expression markings became quite a talking point amongst other musicians. Rarely does he employ Italian terms and in these cases they are nearly always offered as alternatives. In fact the English expressions convey beautifully and precisely what he wanted and in many ways prove the so-called universal musical language of Italian to be woefully inadequate. Words and phrases of great originality crop up, such as 'louden lots', 'soften bit by bit', 'lower notes of woggle well to the fore', 'glassily', 'ripplingly', 'bumpingly', 'hammeringly', 'bundling', 'clatteringly', 'like a shriek', 'very rhythmic and jimp', 'rollickingly', 'hold till blown', 'jogtrottingly', 'easygoingly but very clingingly'. Some musicians were unable to take this seriously and have condescendingly spoken of 'golfing and culinary terms'. Some golf course! Some kitchen! It has been said that if any piece of music were to be opened at any page the only two musics which would be instantly recognizable are those of Percy Grainger and Max Reger. This is true, for with Grainger's music we are presented not only with the refreshingly different English expression markings but with balloons pinpointing one particular note within a chord needing special attention and other similar graphic directions. For intelligent economy in the use of staves his compressed orchestral scores are a wonder to behold.

The 1910/11 tour of the European continent terminated with a visit to Germany and performances in Cologne, Berlin, Dresden and Leipzig. Grainger was back in London by March and throughout the rest of 1911 gave only one performance in London, on May 29. He was present at the Queen's Hall on June 10 for the world première under Beecham of the complete *Mass of Life* by Delius, which epic work conquered him completely. At the end of the performance he went to see Beecham in his dressing room and gave him the score of his recently completed *English Dance*. On June 30 Beecham wrote saying that he liked the piece and that if he cared to have it done by him he would gladly give it at one of his concerts. Beecham also made some suggestions for amendments to the score, which Grainger gladly accepted. The first performance took place on Sunday afternoon February 18, 1912 with Beecham's own orchestra at the London Palladium. The previous Sunday Grainger had performed Franck's *Symphonic Variations* for piano and orchestra — his first appearance with Beecham.

Grainger's close friends in the days before his recognition by the general public as a composer had rather regarded his works as their private property. The admiration and understanding of his close friends were important to him and when after the *English Dance* première these were not sufficiently in evidence he felt that he was becoming alienated from them. His extended tours abroad took him away from Scott, Quilter and Gardiner much more than he would have wished. He loved these three deeply and greatly valued their artistic companionship. But in some senses he was not completely blameless. He had become a little suspicious of Scott and Vaughan Williams and for a time saw as little of them as possible. He felt they were taking his ideas and incorporating them in their own works without giving him credit. His friends, though never admitting it to him, were quite fearful of Rose and were saddened by the way she dominated her son. Gardiner would often appear from his country home, burst in on the Graingers delighted to see his friend and want to know what he had been composing lately. Rose would then politely interrupt and remind everyone that her son had to give the whole day to his piano pupils or practise for a forthcoming concert. For such reasons his friendships were deteriorating.

The winter season of 1911/12 saw Grainger back in Scandinavia and Germany. Again he performed to sold-out houses and before Scandinavian royalty, with whom he had become a favourite. His tour of Denmark was nevertheless an unhappy one for it was during this trip that he was finally turned down by Karen.

In February 1912 he returned to London for the two Beecham concerts and it was then that Beecham offered him the position as his assistant conductor. Beecham was obviously very much taken by the Australian's talents for he also asked him to write music for a performance by Diaghilev's Russian Ballet when they were next due in London. Beecham offered to provide the scenario, but Grainger became impatient and began to work on the composition in December 1913 after Beecham had delayed with his part of the bargain. As it turned out, Beecham never did provide the scenario and Grainger completed the music without it. It was not performed until some years later after he had left London. Eventually entitled *The Warriors—Music to an Imaginary Ballet*, this work, perhaps more than any other, has caused a deep division amongst the composer's admirers. Some regard it as a work of immense and prophetic genius whilst others cringe with embarrassment each time it is performed.

*The Warriors* employs vast forces including (if available and desired) an enormous section of tuned percussion instruments, three or more pianos and an off-stage brass choir. In a performance as Grainger originally intended it three conductors were required in order to control the various sections of the orchestra when they go their own ways in different keys and at different rhythms and tempi. In one performance, many years later in Chicago, thirty pianists playing nineteen pianos joined in the mêlée under the composer's direction. The work lasts eighteen minutes and though wrought in one movement is divided thematically and rhythmically into eight sections. Grainger's programme notes refer to 'an orgy of war-like dances, processions and merry-making, broken, or accompanied, by amorous interludes'.[19] It is dedicated 'in admiration and affection to Frederick Delius'. On the basis of this work, Grainger has been described sometimes as the Charles Ives of Australia. It is a wild and free work which occasionally wanders into cacophony and ends in an abrupt anticlimax. It has moments of splendour and tenderness and is an example of Grainger's organic 'continual flow' of thematic material. The difficulty that some people seem to have in appreciating and enjoying the work revolves around what might be described as its pointlessness, for it cannot be denied that it is easy to get the impression on a first hearing of a huge amount of human effort getting nowhere in particular. The score is replete with fascinating and bold experiments, but it is the kind of work which needs a great deal of sympathy for and understanding of Grainger's tonal and harmonic ideas to bring any measure of success to its performance. Perhaps it will remain the one big question mark amongst his works.

At this point it might be appropriate to remark that, in general, the variation principle underlies almost all of Grainger's best work. Several times he wrote in the form of a passacaglia (*Green Bushes, The Lost Lady Found, Let's Dance Gay, Father and Daughter*), while the strophic nature of many of the folk-songs which he set almost demands variation treatment, or a combination of variation and rondo principles. (See, for example, *Country Gardens, Shepherd's Hey, Molly on the Shore*, several movements of *Lincolnshire Posy, Bold William Taylor*.) Some of the wholly original works are written in a similar style (*Children's March, Mock Morris*) and only a handful of important works cannot easily be categorized in conventional terms.

Grainger was wont to describe certain of his works as 'Rambles'. Treating the term generically, we may include many of the 'problematical' works under this heading (*Pastorale, The Immovable Do, The Power of Rome and the Christian Heart, The Warriors, Marching Song of Democracy, To a Nordic Princess*). As Grainger tried to eschew 'classical' structures such as the sonata the onus was upon him to render his argument convincing by structures of his own devising. In shorter works his argument rarely fails, but in the longer ones he runs the risk of loquacity and there are times when the train of thought (or 'continual flow') in a work such as *The Warriors* seems to be confused because the haphazard structure will not support the dramatic content of the music. This, then, may account for the impression of glorious failure that *The Warriors* makes.


The Balfour Gardiner Choral and Orchestral Concerts of 1912 were an immense undertaking consisting of four concerts (March 13, March 27, April 17 and May 1) held at the Queen's Hall in London. Balfour Gardiner conducted most of the performances but Gustav Holst, Sir Edward Elgar, Arnold Bax, Arthur Fagge, Hamilton Harty, Charles Kennedy Scott and Norman O'Neill took charge of some works. The London Choral Society, the Oriana Madrigal Society and the New Symphony Orchestra provided the musical forces and Balfour Gardiner the entire financial support. The first concert, on March 13, was the most important for Grainger since five of his works were performed under his and Arthur Fagge's direction. They were *Irish Tune from County Derry, Father and Daughter* and three Kipling Settings. A band of thirty mandolin and guitar players was employed for *Father and Daughter* and the sight and sound created caused a sensation. The composer-conductor was recalled twelve times and the work had to be repeated twice.

The next morning Percy was surprised to receive a telephone call from his father, who had attended the concert. They met later on in the day and Percy found his father in poor health once more and on his way to

Harrogate to 'take the waters'. Percy tried to cheer him up by telling him of his latest successes, but John was merely scornful of his son's earning power. John told his son that he wanted to go to live in British Columbia. When Percy pointed out that his father knew no-one there John replied that that was precisely why he wanted to go.[20]

Between the first two concerts of the Balfour Gardiner series Grainger found time to fit in a round of orchestral concerts and solo recitals in Zürich, Basel, St Gallen, Heidelberg, Elberfeld and Amsterdam. The short tour brought him in touch with two fine conductors, Hermann Suter in Basel and Volkmar Andreae in Zürich. In Amsterdam he was the pianist in the first Dutch performance of his *Green Bushes* with the Concertgebouw Orchestra under Mengelberg. Back in London for the second Gardiner concert he played Tchaikovsky's First Piano Concerto. The third concert included a performance of *Mock Morris* and in the last of the series he conducted his *English Dance*.

Soon he was on the continent of Europe again, conducting a performance of *Green Bushes* and playing the Tchaikovsky concerto at Aix-la-Chapelle (Aachen) on May 10. This trip was very brief, however, for he needed as much time as possible to rehearse for the first all-Grainger concert in London, which took place at the Aeolian Hall on Thursday May 21 and for which he had conscripted a remarkable host of celebrity performers. The concert was to serve two purposes, first to give him a chance of trying out his compositions to hear if his ideas were sound and practical, and secondly to promote the sales of his new music which Schott had published earlier that year. The soprano Beryl Freeman sang two separate arrangements of *Died for Love*—an indication of how anxious Grainger was to experiment with different instrumental combinations for accompanying his vocal works. The Langley-Mukle String Quartet—with Eugene Goossens as its second violin—performed *Mock Morris* and *Molly on the Shore*. Gervase Elwes sang *Dedication* and one of Grainger's most beautiful arrangements, that of the old English song *Willow Willow*. George Baker, Frederic Austin and Hubert Eisdel performed in other settings. The concert ended with Balfour Gardiner conducting *Scotch Strathspey and Reel.* Roger Quilter and both Grainger and his mother played guitar in this work. It was around this time that the composer first started to use the name 'Percy Aldridge Grainger'.

The sea-shanty *What shall we do with a drunken sailor?* is the tune which knits *Scotch Strathspey and Reel* together, and underlying the main theme Grainger skilfully interweaves six Scottish and Irish folksongs. Although rather long the work maintains substantial interest by the brilliant contrapuntal interplay of the various themes. A key to Grainger's thoughts at the time of its composition can be found in his programme notes to the Aeolian Hall concert, where he asks the hearer to accept the suggestion that 'If a room-full of Scotch and Irish fiddlers and pipers and any nationality of chanty-singing deep-sea sailors could be spirited together and suddenly miraculously endowed with the gift for polyphonic harmonic free improvisation enjoyed for instance by South Sea Island Polynesians a rather merry friendly Babel of tune, harmony and rhythm would result.'

'Polyphonic harmonic free improvisation' is a noteworthy phrase, for it is this idea which links *Scotch Strathspey and Reel* to other works which Grainger was thinking about at that time. He was fond of incorporating passages where melodic lines or chordal sequences are sent off in different directions without apparent regard to each other. The resulting sounds often produce sudden discordant clashes which give the impression of having happened almost by accident—the more so when they occur in predominantly consonant stretches. Grainger himself wrote: 'My efforts, even in those young days, was to wrench the listener's heart with my chords. It is a subtle matter, & is not achieved by mere discordance [. . .]. Music is not made agonizing merely by sharp discords any more than literature is made agonizing by crude events [. . .]. It is the contrast between the sweet & the harsh [. . .] that is heart-rending. Perhaps these assaults upon the tenderness of men's hearts (as we find them in tragic poetry & music based on the same) will play their part in weaning men from massed murder of mankind in war, & massed murder of animals for food.'[21]

Perhaps the most important consequence of this theory was the idea of planned improvisation and indeterminacy and in 1912 Grainger began work on a piece called *Random Round*. Although one of his least known works, it certainly ranks amongst his more important.

*Random Round* is divided into several sections, each of which is begun when a Javanese gong is sounded. Within each section the thematic material is treated in ten to twenty variant forms and, to a harmonic ostinato strummed on a guitar, the vocalists and/or instrumentalists are at liberty to take any variant at any time, at any speed, and jump to another at will (but at the correct pitch). The variants are written so that some sort of harmonic whole might emerge from a performance. Throughout his life Grainger changed his ideas about instrumentation for this piece but the general idea remained the same. Although *Random Round* was almost totally neglected by the musical world, it is an important early instance of aleatory composition, planned in the same year in which John Cage was born and long before the advent of Berio and Stockhausen.

In September Grainger attended that memorable concert when Henry Wood conducted the English première of *Five Characteristic Pieces for Orchestra* Op. 16 by Arnold Schönberg. The performance was greeted with boos and hisses from the audience and the press hailed it as the advent of a musical Armageddon. Grainger, on the other hand, declared it a work of great beauty and genius—though he was never swung towards the German school of atonality he was always quick to jump to the defence of atonal experiments. Whenever Pierre Monteux was in town to conduct he would always book a seat, for he knew that the Frenchman would be bringing with him new works from Europe and especially those of Stravinsky, for which the Australian retained a lifelong love.

That year Grainger was due to give a series of recitals and concerts in Berlin and Hamburg. He arrived in Berlin with his mother on October 1 and they booked into an hotel. The following morning he began to walk to the hall where his first recital was to take place the next day. But he never arrived. His concern for physical beauty was so keen that the sight of what he felt were so many ugly faces in the hotel and in the streets made him turn around and head back to the hotel, where he telephoned his manager to complain of severe illness. His manager was left with the job of organizing the cancellation of the following day's recital and those due to be staged in Hamburg whilst Grainger hurriedly left town and returned to England. He never visited Berlin again.

Back in England he hid himself at the country home of a friend where he rested and took long walks in the sunshine and fresh air. He was fit enough by October 19 when he conducted a performance of *Green Bushes* at the Queen's Hall. At the end of this concert he was presented with a baton which had been owned by Joachim and used by Brahms and Wagner. During the last week of that month he travelled to Amsterdam and The Hague where he accompanied Ada Crossley in performances of his *Died for Love, Six Dukes went Afishin'* and *Willow Willow*. He also conducted *Molly on the Shore, My Robin is to the Greenwood Gone* and was at the piano again for *Handel in the Strand*.

After another brief rest he returned to Holland and Germany, where he gave recitals and concerts in Cologne, Koblenz, Frankfurt and 's-Gravenhage. Whilst in Holland he visited the Ethnographical Museum in Leyden. It was the first time he had seen in any great quantity the tuneful percussion instruments used in Indonesian orchestras. He was particularly interested in those instruments which encompassed the lower octaves, for he had long wanted to balance the high octaves of the glockenspiel and xylophone with warmer and more mellow tones of lower-voiced instruments. When he later included their European equivalents in his scores he became a pioneer in the orchestral use of tuneful percussion instruments.

At the end of 1912 Beecham took the orchestral score of *Mock Morris* to Berlin, thus introducing Grainger's music to Germany. The next year saw an explosion of performances of his works throughout Britain and on the continent of Europe. Balfour Gardiner held a further series of concerts at the Queen's Hall in February and March 1913; Grainger scored spectacular successes with *Colonial Song, Hill-Song Number 1, Sir Eglamore* and a new group of Kipling Settings. He was kept away from London by public engagements during two of these concerts and it was

Vaughan Williams who, in the composer's absence, conducted the choral works. (Balfour Gardiner was so nearly driven to distraction over the problems of staging these concerts that he threw up his hands and declared them to be the last he would organize.)

The year 1913 also saw the first performances of Grainger's works in New York, Minneapolis and Chicago. Frank Damrosch at the Institute of Musical Art was so interested in his works and reports of his piano playing that on July 10 he sent a cablegram to Percy asking if he would like to head the piano department of his establishment, working twenty hours weekly for thirty weeks between October 1913 and May of the following year. Although Percy was greatly tempted he turned down Damrosch's offer because of his heavy concert engagements for the winter and spring of 1913/14.

In September, October and November Percy took Rose with him for a tour of sixty concerts in Norway, Russia and Finland. Whilst Percy toured around the Norwegian country towns, Rose stayed in Kristiania, where she met Sibelius and attended his rehearsals with the National Theatre Orchestra. Percy never met him, for with the exception of the hymn tune from *Finlandia* he had disliked immensely all the Sibelius works he had heard. He liked Helsingfors, however, and was happy when he went to hear Georg Scheevoigt conduct Delius's *Life's Dance*. But he did not like Finland on the whole. He found it too German in temperament and culture.

In Russia on October 26 Percy played piano under Alexander Siloti at one of his famous St Petersburg concerts. Appearing on the same programme as Felia Litvinne (who sang Wagner's *Wesendonck Lieder*), he gave a performance of the Grieg concerto. Both Graingers had been in St Petersburg the previous week and on October 19 they had heard Siloti in the role of pianist. In a letter dated May 7, 1914 Grainger wrote to Siloti: 'I recall with great pleasure your remarkable performance of the Chaikovsky Concerto, which gave me such enjoyment [. . .]. I very much hope that I will have the opportunity some time of playing the Delius Concerto under your direction.'

In January 1914 his engagements took him to Saarbrücken, Pilsen and back to Holland. In Amsterdam Mengelberg conducted *Mock Morris* and the composer heard news that Schreker was about to perform *Father and Daughter* with the Vienna Philharmonic. Very soon Grainger's compositions and arrangments were included in the repertoires of such musicians as Eugen d'Albert, Ossip Gabrilowitsch, Rudolph Ganz, Mark Hambourg, Fritz Kreisler, the London String Quartet, Elena Gerhardt, Walter Damrosch, Josef Stransky, Frederick Stock, Nikolai Sokoloff and Alfred Herz. By 1914 his international reputation as a composer was secure.

Grainger's emotional life was still a source of endless complication and frustration. At the end of 1911 he had taken on as a pupil a girl named

Margot Harrison. A little over a year later, after his affair with Karen Holten had terminated, they were engaged. Margot was the charming and impulsive daughter of Peter Harrison, an art connoisseur, and close friend and patron of John Singer Sargent. Initially the engagement was welcomed by Rose, but her son was nagged continually by doubts. Rose's friendship with Margot's mother became unstable, especially when Mrs Harrison wandered around the Grainger home mentally appropriating items of furniture for the future home of Margot and Percy. Eventually Percy wrote a letter to Margot breaking off the engagement. Shortly afterwards, Mrs Harrison and Margot went to the Grainger home in Kings Road and Rose and Mrs Harrison tried to come to some arrangement about the relationship of their children. Rose had always felt the engagement to have been rushed, but she was happy when Percy and Margot decided to remain lovers. Rose—a believer in the then outrageous idea of 'free love'—motivated the curious plan whereby Margot would be required to live with the Graingers in Kings Road, and later that year (1913) travel with them on Percy's tour of Norway. The object seems to have been a trial marriage to enable Margot to get some idea of what life would be like as the wife of a travelling virtuoso. Margot was willing but when her father heard about it he immediately stepped in. Percy and Margot saw less of each other after this. Margot, furthermore, had become only too aware of Rose's influence over Percy and marriage was never discussed again.

On the whole, Grainger held out little hope for any of his piano pupils. He usually collected a handful of pupils on his trips to Scandinavia, and they would return to stay during the following summer at his home in Chelsea where he held lessons. In the summer of 1912, however, a tiny girl who had won a scholarship from the Melbourne Conservatorium turned up in London and Grainger immediately recognized and encouraged her talents. Her name was Katherine Parker and she came from Parknook in Tasmania. Through Grainger she met Hubert Eisdel, who was then at the height of his career and performing at many of Percy's concerts. Having married Hubert Eisdel shortly after this, she quickly gained fame as an accompanist and later wrote a collection of songs and solo piano compositions. Percy never lost touch with his beloved Kitty and eventually arranged one of her piano compositions for orchestra which he conducted at many of his concerts.

For relaxation Grainger still preferred the opera and music hall to all other entertainments. He began to hear the works of Puccini and, though it ran completely against the logic of his Nordic worship, the Italian composer had an enormous influence on his concept and handling of melody. The influence of Puccini's unashamedly full-blooded way of delivering a melodic punch-line is clearly seen in compositions such as *Colonial Song* and *To a Nordic Princess*. The operas of Richard Strauss also formed a large part of Percy's musical diet and he attended the

Beecham performances of *Salomé* and *Der Rosenkavalier,* as well as
*Elektra.* He once wrote an interesting little footnote which gives an insight into his feelings for the music of Strauss: 'It is my theory to like vulgarity—to think well of it, to champion it, to gird myself to always fight
on its side. It is my theory to think nothing can come to pass without a
pinch (or more than a pinch) of vulgarity. It would be quite in line with
the wonted path of my thought to make the point that Richard Strauss is
a greater, grander genius than Maurice Ravel because he (Strauss) has so
amply the vulgarity that Ravel lacks.'[22]

During April 1914 Grainger took part in a music festival at Torquay
organized by Basil Cameron, known then as Basil Hindenberg, and with
Cameron, Percy Pitt and Thomas Beecham as principal conductors.
*Colonial Song* and *Molly on the Shore* were conducted by the composer.
He had been practising the Delius piano concerto for about a year and
gave his first performance of the work at this festival. After the concert
Beecham, who had also conducted a performance of *Dance Rhapsody*,
wrote to Delius: 'Percy Grainger played your Piano Concerto and it went
fairly well in performance, and most successfully with the public. Percy
was good in the "forte" passages, but made far too much noise in the
quieter bits, rather to the poetic detriment of the work. The Dance
Rhapsody was also an immense favourite with the Public, who greeted
most of the novelties with the stoniest silence [. . .].'[23] Grainger obviously
had very definite ideas about the Delius concerto, for he loved it greatly
and performed it whenever he was given the chance.

Until the Great War Grainger never lost Beecham's friendship or his
championship of his music. In 1914 Beecham asked to see the score of
*Hill-Song Number 1* and immediately recognized its merit, liking it so
much that he decided to programme it at the Queen's Hall on December
7, 1914. Because of the outbreak of hostilities throughout Europe, however, this plan had to be cancelled. Grainger's heavy winter schedule in
Norway, Denmark, Finland, Russia and throughout Britain was also
cancelled. Delius continued to invite him to Grez but because of his
teaching and concert duties he was never able to take the rest. Nevertheless he continued to correspond with his friend, helping Delius to keep
in touch with musical events in Britain. For his part, Delius valued
Grainger's letters enormously. On April 29 he wrote:

What pleasure your letter gave me, dear friend! You are always the
one who sends me good news from England—I love your impulsive
letters—they are so entirely yourself & just like your music which you
know I love so much. I feel we have an enormous lot in common & that
you understand better than anyone what I am trying to do—I was so
happy to hear of your success in Torquay. Do you know that in Bradford they are giving a whole concert of my work. I proposed you
should play the Concerto—it is on November 27th & I do hope you are

not engaged [. . .]. Can't you come over here and pay me a visit with
your Mother. The spring has been simply divine — The garden is full of
Lilacs and Laburnums in full bloom — Try & come — I have 2 new
orchestra pieces — In June we come to London for a fortnight — you
must either come before or come back with me — you will love it
here — it is out of this world —

Ever so much love to you & your mother.

Your loving friend.

Frederick Delius.·

In mid-July Grainger was asked to play one of the pianos in a two-
piano four-handed recital of French music with the Princesse de
Polignac at her London home. Beecham attended and afterwards talked
with the Australian about the recent performance of *Colonial Song* at
the Torquay Festival. 'My dear Grainger,' he said, 'you have achieved the
almost impossible! You have written the worst piece of modern times.'[24]

That evening the Princesse told Grainger that all her army officer
friends in France had been mobilized. He did not believe that war would
follow. Events soon proved him wrong.

# 13

## 'Adieu Old World! I would hail a New World'

The Graingers' decision to leave London was made hastily. Only three weeks before they left, Grainger wrote to Delius saying that he had been chosen to play his friend's piano concerto on February 8, 1915 with the London Symphony Orchestra. The penultimate sentence in his letter was 'Here everything is normal, no signs of war.' The Great War was then six days old, and with matters quickly worsening, Rose became tormented with worry over her son's career prospects. Greatly concerned for his mother's health, Percy hurriedly decided on a trip to America; they joined the Cunard ship *Laconia* at Liverpool and reached Boston on September 8.

Grainger often explained his reason for leaving London. It was simple and logical. He wanted to emerge as Australia's first composer of worth and to have laid himself open to the possibility of being killed would have rendered his goal unattainable.

On arrival in New York they settled in the Hotel Calumet at 340 West 57th Street. One of Grainger's first tasks was to write to Hans Augustin, his European concert director, to cancel all his engagements for the forthcoming season. So that Augustin would not lose through his absence, he offered to pay the manager's commission from any booking for which a replacement could not be found. He also wrote many letters trying to contact Delius and eventually received news of his friend's safety, but was shocked to read that he had stayed at Grez until German guns had been within earshot.

The Schirmer music publishing house was the first contact he made in New York and with a letter of introduction from Willy Strecker in his hand Grainger soon found himself in the office of Rudolph Schirmer. The kindly music publisher took him under his wing and was soon on the telephone to his friend Antonia Sawyer who it was thought could well manage the Australian's performing career. The choice was a wise one, for she had once been an opera singer and had gained an enviable skill in picking her way through the tortuous world of concert management. Rudolph Schirmer soon took the Graingers to Mrs Sawyer's offices above the Aeolian Hall in West 43rd Street, and after Grainger had demonstrated his skills on an ancient upright piano a contract was drawn up and signed entrusting the management of his career to her. Concert halls in New York had been heavily booked for some time so it was not until the early part of 1915 that he was able to make his first public appearances. Rudolph Schirmer made considerable propaganda for his music and secured the rights to more than was hitherto available in America, while Antonia Sawyer, for her part, seems to have made it a condition that the vocalists in her care should perform at least one of Grainger's songs at their recitals.

In the meantime Percy attended a variety of interesting concerts. On the evening of November 7 he attended the first New York recital of the pianist Carl Friedberg, whom he had known in Frankfurt. Friedberg had been touring in England when war was declared and he was arrested and interned for a short period. With the help of influential friends he had obtained a release and immediately moved to America. From Friedberg and others Grainger began to hear stories of the excesses of patriotism to which the British had gone after the declaration of war. Willy Strecker at his own request had been imprisoned at Alexandra Palace in the company of two thousand waiters and hairdressers. He was to remain there for two years. Sir Edgar Speyer, who had poured £30,000 of his private fortune into the Queen's Hall Orchestra, had fallen victim to vicious attacks and eventually tendered his resignation as a Privy Counsellor. His resignation was initially refused by the King, but he soon left for America, where he added his voice to those opposed to the British cause. After the war his name was struck off the list of Privy Counsellors and his British naturalization was revoked. Grainger's friend Hans Richter returned his honorary doctorates of music to Oxford and Manchester Universities because of similar vilification.

Frederic Lamond was also in New York at that time, and Antonia Sawyer had secured the task of organizing his American tour. Lamond and Grainger met in her offices one morning and, surprised to see him, Lamond tearfully embraced the Australian as if he were a long lost son.

One evening Grainger was taken by Mrs Sawyer to Carnegie Hall to hear Fritz Kreisler. He recalled that it seemed that the entire German community of New York had turned out to hear their musical hero, who had been invalided out of the Austrian army. Kreisler came on to the stage limping, and Grainger found his playing as charmless and unmusical as he had in London. The only time that he fell completely under the spell of Kreisler's playing was about two years later when Kreisler played the viola to Zimbalist's violin in a performance of the Mozart *Sinfonia Concertante*.

It was not long before Antonia Sawyer also took Grainger to meet Busoni at his temporary New York apartment on Riverside Drive. He was later to write:

Then the war came & it was very hard on Busoni, for his sympathies were with Germany, yet he couldn't stay in Germany because his nationality was Italian. So he came to America & hated everything. He played the Liszt Concerto (which no one approached him in) with the New York Philharmonic Orchestra. He played a Chickering & it sounded simply stunning. But when I went round & told B. how marvellous the piano sounded he was furious. I'm not sure he didn't think I was making fun of him [. . .]. Busoni had surrounded himself with some half-talented composers & musicians as usual. I was asked there one evening & Busoni asked me to play, but I begged him to excuse me saying 'I have been busy composing for weeks & haven't played the piano at all & would hate to play badly to you who have been so kind to me.' He asked what I was composing & I told him 'Marching Song of Democracy'. 'Democracy' he repeated, aghast. I suppose democracy was the last thing he wanted to make the world safe for. 'When did you begin it?' Busoni asked. 'About 1900' I said. 'Is it a very long work?' 'No, it will play about 8 minutes, I expect.' Then Busoni dropped into a most sympathetic & earnest voice: 'Then I sincerely hope you finish it this summer.' I (like the idiot I am, never suspecting sarcasm) said 'Why?' 'Well, if you began it in 1900, & it's 1917 now,[1] & it plays 8 minutes, THEN I SINCERELY HOPE YOU FINISH THIS SUMMER.' By this time I was somewhat nettled, & said 'Fancy, it doesn't seem to me to matter in the very least when I began it, or how long it takes to finish it, as long as it is good when it's done.'[2]

Walter Damrosch and the Symphony Society of New York performed *Molly on the Shore, Irish Tune from County Derry* and *Shepherd's Hey* at one of their Saturday afternoon concerts on January 23, 1915, and the composer took the piano part in *Shepherd's Hey*. Although little personal publicity was made for this concert (Grainger being an integral part of the orchestra rather than a soloist), he was noticed and this appearance immediately brought him an enthusiastic following. By the time of his New York solo debut on February 11, a sold-out Aeolian Hall roared its approval of the newcomer. The music critics of all New York's newspapers were there, as was Enrico Caruso, who had asked for a box to be put at his disposal.

Grainger's programme consisted of the Bach-Busoni Organ Prelude and Fugue in D major, Brahms's *Handel Variations*, three pieces from Grieg's Opus 66 and 72, his own *Colonial Song* and *Mock Morris*, the *Opus Posthumous Study in A flat* by Chopin, Ravel's *Ondine*, and *Triana* by Albeniz. The critics were ecstatic—almost as much about Grainger's handsome looks as his playing. The following day James Huneker of the *World* described him as the 'Siegfried of the Piano' and Henry T. Finck of the *Evening Post* wrote: 'Hats Off! A genius! [. . .] in less than half an hour he had convinced his critical audience that he belongs in the same rank as Paderewski and Kreisler, sharing their artistic abilities, and yet as unique as they are — something new and sui generis. The audience was stunned, bewildered, delighted.'

The same programme was repeated at Boston's Jordan Hall on March 6, and the local press was similarly jubilant over his arrival in that city. Grainger had started his American career the hard way — at the top. He was delighted and amused by the fact that the best reviews of his New York début came from the *New Yorker Staatszeitung* and *Deutsches Journal*. He was shortly engaged to play the Grieg concerto with the New York Philharmonic Society under Josef Stransky and this performance confirmed his success. Offers began to flow into Mrs Sawyer's office for engagements for the following season. Sixteen concerts were booked for New York with the leading orchestras, as well as solo recitals, and more with the Philadelphia, Minneapolis, Boston and Chicago orchestras. It gave him a special pleasure when he secured an engagement with the New York Philharmonic to perform the Delius concerto on November 26, 1915.

In the first season Grainger's works received about a hundred performances, yet he was invited to conduct only once. Although the kind of success he was receiving as a pianist was unlike anything which Europe had brought him, he saw that such success was in danger of denying him any critical acclaim as a serious composer.

On May 13, 1915 Grainger and his mother moved to more comfortable accommodation at the Southern Hotel, 680 Madison Avenue. His main worry around this time was Rose's health. Her eyesight became worse and for a time it was thought she might go blind. Sleeplessness and headaches were also constant troubles. As the direct result of a conversation with a nature-cure specialist, she went on a diet consisting almost exclusively of green apples and nuts. Her headaches and sleeplessness left her and her eyesight improved.

Grainger always had mixed feelings about public concerts. He did not deny a sneaking sense of victory after a successful concert, but at the same time he disliked being lionized. In America his public acclaim was on a scale that he had never experienced before and it came with all the trappings that sickened him. The need to be polite to music critics whom he felt on the whole to be silly asses and the audience adulation were always repugnant to him. After the extraordinarily successful 1915/16 season he received more than two hundred invitations from the mothers of attractive and marriageable daughters to spend the summer months at their homes. He accepted none of them.

By May 1915 he was exclusively contracted to make piano rolls for the Duo-Art Company, whose artistic director W.C. Woods ensured that Grainger became one of their top artists. The Australian was unique in that he insisted on editing his own rolls, and although the reproducing piano was one of the most complicated pieces of pneumatic plumbing ever devised he grasped the mechanics of it in a remarkably brief space of

time. His musical output for the Duo-Art Company was largely duplicated by the records he was to begin to make for the Columbia record
label two years later. He cut six items from Grieg's Opus 66 as well as the
*Ballade in G minor* by the same composer. The solo part of Tchaikovsky's
First Piano Concerto was recorded so that a Duo-Art-equipped concert
grand piano could be coupled with a live orchestra, the solo entries of the
piano being triggered off by a button on the conductor's music stand.

Grainger soon persuaded Walter Damrosch and Leopold Stokowski to
perform some Delius pieces during the autumn and winter of 1915. The
performance of the Delius concerto with Josef Stransky was a tremendous
success and Grainger continued to make propaganda for his friend
wherever he went. He had ample opportunity to do this during the
1915/16 season for he was playing almost daily and his travels brought
him in touch with most of the important conductors of the period.

On January 17 and 20, 1916 in Boston and Pittsburgh he undertook
his only professional engagements with Nellie Melba. Their joint recitals
were in aid of field ambulances for the Allies. In March of the same year
in Chicago he gave the world première of John Alden Carpenter's
*Concertino for Piano and Orchestra* and a few days later he was commanded to perform before President Woodrow Wilson and his family at
the White House. In April he toured many cities with the Dutch soprano
Julia Culp. The two artists had met briefly in 1911 when Julia Culp had
been in London to participate in the first performance of Delius's *Songs
of Sunset* with Beecham.

When Grainger needed to travel he took the train. He loved railways,
for they gave him the space to spread his manuscripts out and compose.
After once being involved in a car crash, he avoided their use unless
absolutely necessary. He always travelled second class and rarely took a
sleeper, preferring to sleep sitting up. Sometimes he would leave the
train one station before his destination and give the difference in fare to
a local charity. His taste in hotels was similarly frugal and again he
would scrupulously calculate the difference between the tariffs of his own
hotel and those of the best hotel in town and gladly pay over the difference to a local children's home or negro charity. This spartan attitude towards life was reflected in his clothes. His underwear was bought at army
surplus stores, as were his boots and socks. Even in the most tempestuous
weather he would rarely wear an overcoat or hat. It was almost unthinkable in those days to go about without a hat and on several occasions he
was questioned (and twice arrested) by police officers who thought he
was a vagrant.

In June he was invited to take part in the Norfolk, Connecticut Festival
of Music. For his contribution he scored and put together an orchestral
suite which he entitled *In a Nutshell*. Some of the sketches for this piece
went back to 1905 and the suite was published eventually in four movements: *Arrival Platform Humlet*, *Gay but Wistful*, *Pastoral*, and *Gum-*

suckers March (originally entitled 'Cornstalks March'). Each movement makes use of the piano and a large section of tuned percussion, including four Deagan instruments (Steel Marimbaphone, Wooden Marimbaphone, Swiss Staff Bells and Nabimba). Despite the mood of jollity which colours the whole work it is serious in intent and contains some of Grainger's best and most characteristic scoring. The title *Arrival Platform Humlet* is explained as being 'The sort of thing one hums to oneself as an accompaniment to one's tramping feet as one happily, excitedly, paces up and down the arrival platform [. . .] of a belated train bringing one's sweetheart from foreign parts; great fun!'[3] *Pastoral* is one of the most successful works in which Grainger explores the harmonic possibilities of haphazardly crossing different thematic ideas in almost free rhythms. The beautiful main theme is drawn out in a trance-like, drifting manner and builds up to a powerful climax. *Gum-suckers March* is a huge romp of gaiety with some nostalgic backward glances to Australia when the theme from Grainger's own *Australian Up-Country Song* is quoted. The first performance was conducted by Dr Arthur Mees and Grainger was paid $500 for producing it.

At this festival he met the Alsacian composer Charles Martin Loeffler. In London John Singer Sargent and his friends had often spoken to him of Loeffler's talents, but Grainger had wondered whether Loeffler's music was really as good as they made out. When he came to America Sargent had given him a letter of introduction to Loeffler, so the Australian went to see him at his home in Medfield, Massachusetts. At that first meeting neither warmed greatly to the music of the other, but after the performance of the *In a Nutshell* Suite, Loeffler instantly recognized Grainger's talents and told him so. Grainger too heard and admired works by Loeffler in later years, particularly *Hymn to his Brother the Sun*. He was to meet Loeffler at the Norfolk Festival of the following year and again in 1922 at the Evanston Music Festival when they were both judges for a prize for composition. Grainger and Loeffler sat through a programme of Stravinsky's music and here the two composers did not agree about the value of one particular work they heard. Percy was thrilled by Stravinsky's genius, but Loeffler remarked, 'It's such awful old stuff to anyone brought up in Russia, as I was. There isn't a passage, an effect in the Firebird that he hasn't lifted bodily out of Borodin or Balakirev or some other source well known to musicians in Russia, but not always known to musicians outside of Russia.'[4]

It was at this festival that Grainger heard Kreisler and Zimbalist in the Mozart *Sinfonia Concertante*. Shortly after the concerts the music critic Richard Aldrich invited the Graingers to his home on the Hudson for a few days, and Percy was somewhat taken aback when he arrived to find that Fritz Kreisler had also been invited. Aldrich liked the *In a Nutshell* Suite, but found *Gum-suckers March* somewhat vulgar. Rose said, 'But there is always something vulgar about Percy. If it wasn't vulgar, it wouldn't be Percy.' Aldrich asked Kreisler what he thought about it and he answered, 'I think it is always a pity to be vulgar in art.'[5] Grainger's regard for Kreisler slipped even lower.

Around this time Kreisler asked Grainger if he would permit him to arrange *Irish Tune from County Derry* for violin. But Percy refused on the grounds that he didn't think his harmonies would suit the solo violin, and suggested instead that he did his own setting. This Kreisler did. Some years later, Kreisler asked him if he could make an arrangement of *Molly on the Shore,* and this time he agreed as long as he could retain his own violin and piano setting in print. Grainger once travelled from New York to Philadelphia specially to hear Kreisler play his own setting of *Molly on the Shore.* He wrote:

> [It] was a thousand times worse than I had fore-weened ((expected)), & I had not fore-weened anything good. Apart from its winsome folk-tunes, the charm of my setting lies in shifts from lively to wistful. In my fiddle dish-up the fiddle had its share of both moods. In Kreisler's dish-up the fiddle sawed away, fidgetingly, ALL the time, & never got its share of the wistful longer notes. These longer notes were all given to the piano, which's short-tone, sound-type could make nothing of them. I found in Kreisler what I have found in all 'foreign' (non-British, non-American, non-Scandinavian) tone-men who have messed around with my tonery (whether playing it like Stokowski, Stock or Gabrilowitsch, whether dishing it up, or re-scoring it, like Kreisler or Adolph Schmidt): an utter misunderstanding of the soul-stirs & craft skills in Blue-eyed tonery, a coarse fumbling of all its delicate points. They may be great boys—these foreigners—in some branches of tonery. But not in MY tonery, they're not.[6]

Towards the end of his heavy season of concerts and recitals in 1917, Grainger received news that his father had died on April 13. The last year of his life had seen John completely paralysed and for some time Percy had been providing his sole financial upkeep. Percy's father died leaving £267A and was buried unmourned in an unmarked grave in Box Hill cemetery outside Melbourne. The death certificate states that he died of chronic rheumatic arthritis—one of a handful of medical euphemisms commonly used in those days to cover the effects of tertiary syphilis.

On April 5, 1917 the United States joined the Allied cause when President Woodrow Wilson declared war on Germany. Grainger remained undecided on his course of action as a result of the new political situation. For a time he thought of returning to England or moving to Canada. He wrote to John Philip Sousa, who replied saying that he felt sure he could arrange a post for him in the Canadian army organizing military bands. On June 4 he wrote a letter to Delius which suggests that he was on the point of making a big change in his life:

> The thrills I have felt through your music, dear friend, have been the deepest & keenest feelings of my life [. . .]. Everything is uncertain now, & I don't know whether I shall have to go to Canada or England or where. Should anything happen to me, & you & I not meet again, know that I have loved you & yr art truly, have realized that you are one of the greatest musical geniuses of all time, & have responded to you passionately, both on artistic and personal lines.

On June 7 Grainger was at the Norfolk Festival of Music once more where he conducted the world première of his work *The Warriors*. The critics were at variance as to its worth and Grainger was less than jubilant. Frederick Stock had given a performance in February with his Chicago Symphony Orchestra of the *In a Nutshell* Suite and most of the newspaper critics had poured scorn on the work.

On the day of the first performance of *The Warriors* Grainger received a telegram from Melba in Australia asking him to set a patriotic Australian poem to music. He replied that he would be delighted. When a letter followed from Melba including the poem, entitled *The Flag*, Grainger shrank with embarrassment, for the work was appalling in content and cast. Melba had visions of some grand patriotic concert with herself singing and her compatriot conducting soloist, chorus and orchestra in a historic performance of *The Flag*. The subject was politely dropped.

Grainger often described himself as a conscientious objector; at other times as a coward. Wherever the truth lay, he knew that to return to England at that time was out of the question because of the public and private comments that had been made about his departure. Canada did not offer any more attractive prospects. He was not blind to the fact that as soon as war had been declared in America all pacifist organizations had been ruthlessly suppressed and to have remained a civilian would have been inviting severe criticism and a premature end to his career. More or less on the spur of the moment he bought a soprano saxophone on June 9 and walked to Fort Totten, where he enlisted as a bandsman. He was fitted out with a uniform and his hair was cut. The following day he was transferred to Fort Hamilton, South Brooklyn, to become a member of the 15th Band of the Coast Artillery Corps. The band leader was Rocco Resta, whom Grainger had known in civilian life, and the two became bosom friends. Unfortunately Percy was unable to play the saxophone, and in any case there were already adequate saxophone players in the band, so Resta gave him an oboe to practise. After he had gained a certain proficiency with the oboe he was promoted to 'Bandsman 2nd Class'.

When Grainger left London many of his acquaintances and friends had refused to reply to his letters because of what they felt to be his unpatriotic departure. His popularity fell in England, though Henry Wood included his works in his Promenade Concerts at the Queen's Hall throughout the war. After he had joined the United States Army, however, the friends who had neglected him began to write again as if the intervening period had never been. In many ways he felt that he had compromised his pacifist principles in joining the army, so he was grieved that these fine-weather friends had resumed their relationships only when he had proved his 'manliness' in what he felt was a degrading manner.

He often described the first few weeks of his army career as the happiest period of his life. On his pay of $36 a month he began to study all kinds of brass and reed instruments and when Rocco Resta was taken ill he was given the task of conducting the band on a few occasions. Rose was invited to live at Fort Hamilton with Resta and his wife and even played xylophone in some of the band concerts. She was to return to the Southern Hotel, however, early in 1918. For the moment, her son's greatest joy was that for the first time since his youth he had achieved relative anonymity and freedom from the concert platform. At 5 a.m. each day he would go to his mother's room where he would compose. Then after breakfast and morning parade he would practise his instruments. At the end of the morning there would be a band concert and in the afternoon he would usually continue with his practice or work on the band's vegetable plot. In the evening, after a second concert, he would return to his quarters and the company of other recruits. This was a particular joy, for when he talked with his fellow bandsmen he felt completely removed from the business-oriented world of professional musicians which he had disliked so much in civilian life. Throughout his entire army career the band never saw action, so Grainger's pacifist conscience was partly appeased.

It was not long, however, before a journalist spotted him at one of the evening concerts and soon it was revealed in the New York newspapers that the world-famous piano virtuoso was now a Bandsman 2nd Class in the 15th Band, Coast Artillery Corps. The spell of happiness was broken and soon he had to enlist the aid of the Fort Hamilton guards to prevent newspaper reporters from pestering him. Antonia Sawyer and Henry F. Davidson (President of the American Red Cross) had been summoned earlier that year to Washington to confer with members of the War Department where it was arranged for Grainger to undertake a certain number of concerts and recitals in aid of Red Cross funds. Eighty-five percent of the takings were to go directly to the Red Cross and the remainder kept for managerial expenses. He also gave other performances in Liberty Loan, War Bonds and Saving Stamp drives. In this capacity he undertook many concerts with such fine operatic stars as Claudia Muzio, Giovanni Martinelli and Margarete Matzenauer. He also gave several recitals with Margaret Woodrow Wilson, the daughter of the

President. On June 27 he took out first papers for American citizenship.

Grainger was given special dispensation to attend the première of his new work *Marching Song of Democracy,* which was given as part of the Worcester, Mass. Music Festival on October 1, under the baton of Arthur Mees. It was an immediate and emphatic success. The composer was called to the stage after the performance and amid tumultuous applause was made the recipient of a huge laurel wreath. Some newspaper reviews were characteristically idiotic: the *Christian Science Monitor* of Boston of October 6 went so far as to describe the work as 'a challenging reply to the insolence of the "Zarathustra" music of Strauss and the egoism of the "Siegfried" music of Wagner'.

Grainger's association with the Columbia Graphophone Company, which began on August 28, 1917, was to last fourteen years. The first items he recorded, his own arrangements of Stanford's *Irish Dance No. 1* and *Irish Tune from County Derry,* were never issued. The following day, however, he recorded the first part of Liszt's *Hungarian Rhapsody No. 2* which, when he had cut the second half, became his first record issued on this label. It is a straightforward, somewhat lumpy performance, but his later issues of works by Liszt display a sparkling technique despite the acoustic quality of the recordings. At his third recording session the entire 15th Band of the Coast Artillery Corps trooped into the Columbia studios for a recording of *Gum-suckers March.* Unfortunately this was never issued although initially it was marked 'O.K.'. At one time Thomas Alva Edison tried to lure Grainger over to his label, but by then he was already exclusively contracted to Columbia.

Cecil Sharp had been in America for some time and Grainger wrote to him in June 1918 about a new folk-song setting he had made. At the end of some of the Liberty Loan concerts he had improvised on one of Cecil Sharp's Morris Dance tunes called *Country Gardens* (a 'Handkerchief Dance'). The improvisation proved very popular and he wrote it down in time for it to be a birthday gift for his mother in 1918. Like all his folk-song settings it is 'lovingly and reverently dedicated to the memory of Edvard Grieg'. Grainger wanted Sharp to receive half the royalties as a token of his respect and gratitude for providing him with the tune and the encouragement he had given in the early days of his collecting activities. Sharp refused. Had he accepted, he would have probably become a rich man, for this setting was to break all records for sales in years to come for the Schirmer, Schott and affiliated publishing houses.

In later years when *Country Gardens* had achieved enormous popularity, Grainger tended to shy away from the acclaim it had brought him. Sometimes he would say that he had only written it to make money, and once he wrote: 'The typical English country garden is not often used to grow flowers in; it is more likely to be a vegetable plot. So you can think of turnips as I play it.'[7]

On June 3, 1918 Grainger became a full American citizen and in the same month he was transferred to the Bandmaster Students and US Army Music Training School on Governor's Island with the rank of Assistant Instructor. This transfer came just in time for Rose and her son because during the summer of 1918 there was talk of his band at Fort Hamilton being moved for duties in Europe. In such an eventuality Henry Junge of the House of Steinway had offered to organize a 'dummy position' for Rose at the Steinway offices in Paris. The principal at Governor's Island was Captain Arthur Clappé and Grainger's admiration for this man bordered on adulation. Captain Clappé was a Canadian who had studied music in the British Army at Kneller Hall. After a period of army service in Canada he had entered the Juilliard School of Music, leaving it to form the Army Music Training School on Governor's Island. Grainger recalled several times that Clappé was a Buddhist and man of gentle and saintly behaviour. When Percy was working at Governor's Island, Captain Clappé allowed him to live at home in the Southern Hotel with his mother. This meant that he was obliged to rise at 4.30 each morning and travel to his military duties. In September, Rose and her son left the Southern and took rooms at 309 West 92nd Street.

Perhaps the most important improvement which came with the move to Governor's Island was a greater opportunity to conduct and compose for the band. Those who worked under him in his capacity as a conductor remember Percy as a fine workman of the athletic variety. His own, perhaps tongue-in-cheek ideas on conducting were simple:

> The orchestra *plays the notes,* and all the conductor has to do is to listen to the orchestra, follow along with it and look inspired. (I can get up and conduct a piece of mine I haven't thought about for twenty years, without the least preparation. But I couldn't play the same piece on the piano, without preparation, to save my life.) That is why so many famous pianists have become conductors—to escape the endless misery and unreliability of keyboard memorizing into the comparative easiness and laziness of conductor-memorizing![8]

Although hostilities had ended by November 1918, Grainger was not immediately demobilized. Before he left the armed services he was offered the post of conductor of the St Louis Symphony Orchestra and the possibility of being appointed head of a projected school of music there. He declined on the grounds that he would be obliged to conduct so many items from the classical German, Austrian and Russian repertoires and he felt that no-one would want to listen to the kind of programmes he wished to present.

His compositional output from this period shows a sensitive ear for wind sonorities such as could have come only from a close association with these instruments. Both *Shepherd's Hey* and *Irish Tune from County Derry* emerged in arrangements for band and are models of wind writing. The exquisite harmonies of *Irish Tune from County Derry* are translated to suit the needs of the new combination of instruments with no loss of the original tonal balance, while the contrapuntal relief of *Shepherd's Hey* gains considerably from its new treatment. The *Children's March—Over the Hills and Far Away*—pure delight from beginning to end—is another product of this fruitful and happy period. Scored for wind, percussion and piano, it is perhaps the first composition ever written which incorporates the piano as an integral part of the band. The romping main theme is an original conception, though it has been suggested by some unkind folk that it is adapted from Smetana's *Vltava* or even based on a popular marching song of the eighteenth century — neither of these speculations is true. The work exploits in particular the sonorities of the lower brass and reeds and has a fascinating ending scored for tambourine, castanettes, snare drum and a bass string of the piano struck with a marimba mallet. The only mystery surrounding the work is the dedication, which honours 'my playmate beyond the hills'. Grainger left no clue as to the identity of the enviable dedicatee.

*The Power of Rome and the Christian Heart* was first sketched around this period and was directly inspired by the thought of young men being sent against their will to their deaths in the Great War. The title is, to say the least, unfortunate, for it does not illustrate well the ideas behind the work. Grainger was trying to put into musical terms the concept of the individual attempting to survive in an alien culture; the Nordic staving off the oppressive forces of Rome and Athens; the pacifist trying to hold on to his ideals during a period of war-mongering. It is difficult to reconcile these ideas with the obvious need he felt for the defeat of Germany in the war. The work itself is uneven, as are many of his original compositions, ranging in mood from the introspective to the histrionic. In later life he often mentioned that when he heard what he called the commonplace chords in this piece, he felt deeply ashamed and embarrassed. But there are many passages which, despite his own judgement, are astonishingly effective. Sections of agonizing discords contrast well with sweeter passages and the opening and closing passages played by the pipe organ are hauntingly sad.

Grainger's folk-song settings are easy to approach and many have acknowledged his supremacy in this field, but the original compositions have always been limited and divisive in their appeal. For the most part they stand up badly in the light of critical and academic analysis. As with Delius, it is of no importance whatsoever whether Grainger was able to write a proper fugue or cast his music in the sonata form or not; both these composers' music must either strike a sympathetic emotional chord or be left alone, and Grainger's style is particularly difficult to come to grips with if the emotional reaction is not felt. He must have been acutely aware of the misunderstanding and alienation his music sometimes caused, for he frequently went to great lengths to 'explain' it — a fatal mistake no doubt, because more often than not his explanations increased the puzzlement. Occasionally in his writings, however, he hits the nail squarely on the head. So few people were able to see the deeply tragic side of his life and work, and about this he once wrote:

> I think that young men in their teens respond (at least to the foreword of) my Conscientious-Objector piece 'The Power of Rome and the Christian Heart'. But on the whole I think the entire musical world is entirely oblivious of the whole world of bitterness, resentment, iconoclasm & denunciation that lies behind my music. If they were aware of it I am not sure it would make any difference [. . .]. I have always enjoyed composing, & always composed easily. No 'wretchedness' there. But the whole emotional stir behind all my music (except some 4-5 light, bright numbers, mostly folk-music) is so utterly the opposite of what the public wants (anywhere in the world) that a blast of fiery unwillingness meets every composition I put forward. [. . .] And the worth of my music will never be guessed, or its value to mankind felt, until the approach to my music is consciously undertaken as 'a pilgrimage to sorrows.'⁹

Grainger often remarked that in America neither he nor his music ever had a friend. It is true that the kind of friendship he knew in his youth with such young men as Quilter, Gardiner, Scott, Sandby and Thesiger was never to be recaptured, and the criticism his music received consisted mostly of journalistic inanities. There was one critic, however, who took the trouble to delve beneath the surface of Grainger's brilliance and popularity. Charles L. Buchanan, a freelance writer at one time attached to the magazine *Musical America,* wrote an article for the August 1917 issue of that publication entitled 'Analyzing the Greater Grainger' in which he demonstrated an uncommon degree of insight.

> There is no figure in contemporary music more picturesque and prolific, none so elusive, perplexing, inconsistent [. . .] Both works [*The Warriors* and *In a Nutshell*] are marked by an apparent dissipation of resource, a reckless dynamic exuberance, crudities of contrast and juxtaposition, errors in proportion and design. An undisciplined, unco-ordinated creature, Grainger's musical architecture often reveals a fundamental instability. (Witness the *Colonial Song* and the *Pastoral* from the *Nutshell* where an eloquent if somewhat premature climax is followed by a dawdling with evasive tonalities and modulatory obfuscations to the last degree inept and inconsequential.) On the other hand, *The Warriors* confirms our belief that certain valuable aspects of Grainger have been practically ignored by press and public. Grainger is the one considerable composer of contemporary symphonic music — the monstrous Richard Strauss alone except-

ed—who has not succumbed to the sterilizing obsession of mannerism. Whatever else his music may or may not be, one thing it indubitably is—alive with a restless assimilation of and experimenting with influences of a heterogeneous and conflicting character [. . .] Grainger is unquestionably one of the most expressive harmonists of his time, and the sound that he brings out of an orchestra is, for one pair of ears at least, the most beautiful sound that the contemporary orchestra can give us [. . .] By no means an obviously original harmonist like Debussy, for instance, Grainger blends, with an inspirational adroitness, existing material into an eloquent, often exquisite appeal [. . .] Grainger's predominant characteristic—and, it may well be, his invaluable service to our day and generation—is the relief he offers us from the perpetual and very premeditated thralldom of false intricacy and standardized formulas of expression. True, Grainger will have his fling with the best of them, and cacophony rules many a page of *The Warriors*. On the other hand, there are moments where a memorable outspokenness projects itself from this musical hodge-podge, a virility and directness of sound that we get from no other of today's composers [. . .] Grainger's contribution to the sheerly instrumental side of his art is obviously far and away the most important development in contemporary symphonic music. An inborn knack, a ceaseless practical intimacy with the orchestra and a utilization of a whole new army of percussive instruments [. . .] lend his orchestra an individual timbre of an exceeding richness of texture. Apparently a mere accumulation of the tendencies of the last score of years, *The Warriors* offers us at one and the same time an inconsequential debauch of a fertile but incoherent imagination and a wealth of tone color that appears to mark a new high record in the contemporary concert hall.

On February 6, 1919 Grainger was discharged from the US Army. No sooner had he hung up his khaki uniform, however, than he was caught up in an endless round of tours. In one sense he needed this, because when he left the army he was almost penniless. The earnings from the concert tours before the Great War had been spent on his own publicity and support for his ailing parents almost as soon as it came in. During his army days he had felt the urge to produce a series of concerts which would consist of 'Blue-eyed' music. His wish was that they would take the form of the Balfour Gardiner concerts from which he had benefited so much, with the difference that his own concerts would only contain the music he liked. To do this he needed money and he was resigned to the fact that such concerts would take some years of planning before they could be staged.

On June 6, he conducted the band of Edwin Franko Goldman in a performance of *Colonial Song* and *Children's March—Over the Hills and Far Away*. This event took place at Columbia University with Ralph

Leopold — a close friend from army days — at the piano. Though this was the first performance of the march with band, the composer had joined forces with Leopold for a two-piano/four-handed version at a Red Cross charity drive at the Aeolian Hall some months earlier. In July and August he was invited to conduct a five-week course in piano at the Chicago Musical College. It was the first of many summer music schools at which he was to teach and students fought keenly for places in his classes.

During the 1919 lectures in Chicago there was a deadly feud between the white and black workers in a meat packing factory brought about by the fatal stoning of a coloured man who was alleged to have broken a rule at one of the segregated bathing beaches. This affected the college students inasmuch as one of Grainger's students — a black girl — was frightened or forbidden to leave her home whilst feelings ran high. For the duration of the troubles Percy and Rose had baskets of provisions sent to the girl's home. The girl, in whose musical abilities he had great faith, was chosen to play the first movement of the Grieg concerto at the final Saturday morning concert of the course. He made sure that she was accompanied wherever she went until the time came for her to play. When her turn came she appeared in sheer black and the girl chosen to turn pages for her entered in a black skirt and white blouse. He himself then bounded on to the platform in white suit, shirt, tie and shoes. The contrast and implied protest were appreciated by all.

Grainger often gave his services free for concerts in aid of negro charities. On February 2, 1921 he wrote from Palm Beach in Florida to Roger Quilter: 'Your sweet little piece "Moonlight" was *loved everywhere* I played it, including a great Negro College where I played a free recital last Monday morning, they singing their own religious folksongs ("Spirituals") in return — the music and the surging sea of dark young faces (boys &.girls) one of the most deeply moving things I've ever been thru.'

Rose accompanied her son on his extensive tours of 1919/20 which took him to Oregon, British Columbia, New Mexico, California, Colorado and Ohio. After the final concerts in Los Angeles they escaped to Barstow, where they stayed for six days at the Casa Del Desierto Hotel. Even in old age Percy was to look back on these few days as one of the happiest times of his life. The surrounding countryside reminded him of the desert places of South Australia and he made some pastel and ink paintings of the area so that he could keep the wonderful colours with him after he left. He also worked on the military band score of *Molly on the Shore* for another Goldman Concert on the green at Columbia University on June 18, 1920.

In the autumn of 1920 he took part in a series of concerts staged by Carolyn Beebe with the New York Chamber Music Society, rescoring *Hill-Song Number 1* and *Green Bushes* for a chamber group. He wrote to Quilter, Gardiner and Sandby asking that they too should arrange some of their music for large chamber orchestra, but nothing came of this.

In October 1920 Grainger and his mother moved back to the Southern Hotel in Madison Avenue. Here they received a visit from Cyril Scott. On his arrival in America Scott had a bundle of letters of introduction, but when Grainger saw them he said, 'My dear man, letters of introduction are of no earthly good. I should burn the lot.'

'That's all very well,' answered Scott, 'but what will the people say who took the trouble to write them?'[10] During his stay in America Scott travelled to Philadelphia, where he played the solo part of his piano concerto with Stokowski conducting. He also made a unique piano roll in duet with Grainger of the latter's arrangement for four hands of Scott's *Symphonic Dance No. 1*. At about the same time Grainger wrote to Cecil Sharp asking if he could contribute part or all of the funds needed for the publication of folk-songs that Sharp had collected in the southern highlands of Scotland and the Appalachian mountains. Again Sharp turned down his offers.

Whilst they were living at the Southern the Graingers occupied rooms above those of the actor Lionel Barrymore. Eventually, out of consideration for his neighbours the pianist bought himself a dummy keyboard for practice. Grainger it seems created such noise with his new 'silent' keyboard, that Barrymore soon went to see the culprit to beg him to return to playing his piano.

In 1920 Grainger made plans with his agent in Amsterdam Hans Augustin to tour Holland, Sweden, Denmark and Norway in 1921. He also arranged with Evald Tang Kristensen to collect folk-songs in Jutland. Owing to the deterioration of Rose's health, however, these projects had to be deferred until the following year, and during the 1920/21 season Grainger went no further than Havana, where he performed four times during December 1920. Another plan of this period which was not realized was the idea of publishing a volume of arrangements for single voice and piano of English folk-song settings.

Between April 17 and 23, 1921 he became the first pianist of international fame to play at a moving picture theatre. This took place at the Capitol Theatre, which at that time was the largest cinema in the world, capable of seating almost five and a half thousand people. Grainger played to capacity audiences four times a day and the highlight of each performance was a rendering of the first movement of Tchaikovsky's First Piano Concerto which he played alternately with the Duo-Art piano roll being fed through the Steinway he was using. The Capitol Theatre Symphony Orchestra accompanied the pianist for these performances which were daily sandwiched between screenings of *Lyman Howe's Famous Ride on a Runaway Train* and the latest Mack Sennett comedy *Officer Cupid*. Many of Grainger's already popular favourites were played as encores alternately by the Duo-Art equipment and Percy himself. The concerts created a sensation and he was hailed as being instrumental in bringing a new phase of musical life to the country. Well over twenty thousand people each day participated in this exercise in bringing culture to the masses. Despite the vast audiences Grainger noted that those attending listened far more respectfully and quietly than those he had played to at Carnegie Hall, the Aeolian Hall and the Metropolitan Opera House.

In the winter of 1920/21 Mrs Sawyer organized a tour for Percy's friend the tenor Gervase Elwes. Rose staged several at-homes to introduce the singer to New York's musical personalities. After his successful New York recital in January 1921 Elwes was booked for an appearance in Toronto and, on the way to Canada, another concert in Boston. As he was leaving the train in Boston he accidentally picked up an overcoat which was not his own. Attempting to hand it back to the real owner on the train, which was just departing, he overbalanced and fell on to the track. His death was almost instantaneous. It was a heavy blow to Percy to lose his friend who had done so much for him.

On May 4, 1921 Percy and Rose bought a house in White Plains, which was then a township of considerable countrified charm about half an hour's train journey from New York City. The house at 7 Cromwell Place, a large gable-style wooden structure, was to remain Grainger's home for the rest of his life. Although there were times when he referred to the house as his prison, it was spacious and remarkably functional and very soon began to reflect his own personality. The grass around the house was cut once during his life and he refused to allow the house to be painted because he felt that the sight of natural wood was much to be preferred. The Graingers were at last able to ship over their London furniture which had been in storage since their departure from England at the outbreak of the war. In the summer months Rose and her son took their meals on the veranda and took great pleasure in feeding crumbs to the squirrels. Percy also found the veranda a congenial location for composing.

On December 22 a remarkable concert was staged at Carnegie Hall for the benefit of the poverty-stricken Moritz Moszkowski, who was very ill in Paris. The concert was arranged by the pianists Ernest Schelling, Harold Bauer and Ossip Gabrilowitsch, who on the night of the concert added their talents to those of Fanny Bloomfield-Zeisler, Ignaz Friedman, Rudolph Ganz, Leopold Godowsky, Percy Grainger, Ernest Hutcheson, Alexander Lambert, Josef Lhevinne, Yolanda Merö, Germain Schnitzer and Sigismond Stojowski. The mammoth piano circus was controlled by Walter Damrosch, who saw his job more as that of a traffic cop than conductor, and was such a success that it had to be repeated later in Philadelphia. Grainger's part in the concert was very small (*Over the Hills and Far Away* with his friend Ernest Hutcheson) but it gave him the idea of arranging works such as Bach fugues for many pianos and he was to organize many multi-piano concerts throughout his career. He found these concerts helped his students to trace the different voices in a complex fugue.

During his winter tours of 1921/22, Grainger became increasingly worried about his mother's health. She insisted on accompanying him on most of his tours, but for short trips of two or three days he invited Antonia Sawyer's niece Tonie and her husband Frederick Morse (who later built a house next door to the Graingers) to stay with her whilst he was away. Frederick Morse was a very able photographer and was responsible for most of the fine portraits of Grainger during his American years. Tonie Morse was to take over the organization of the Australian's concert life when Mrs Sawyer decided to wind up her operations in 1925.

# 14

## 'Your mad side has ruined us'

During the early part of 1922 there was a distinct deterioration in Rose's health. A two-month tour of the Pacific coast and Canada had been arranged by Antonia Sawyer. It was to begin early in March and promised to be the most lucrative of Grainger's career.

For more than a year Rose had complained to her son and her doctor of terrifying hallucinations and her sleep being continually broken by nightmares. Her day-to-day behaviour showed every sign that her mind was on the brink of collapse. Incapable of any extended period of concentration, she would become irritable and lose her temper at the slightest provocation. She was haunted by the fear that her future lay in the hands of doctors and nurses and that her sickness would be an intolerable burden to her son and his career. She was, however, determined to accompany him on his latest tour and it was only after a long and arduous debate with Percy, her doctor and Antonia Sawyer that she finally accepted the necessity of staying in White Plains, where a permanent nurse was installed during her son's absence.

On February 23 and 24 in Carnegie Hall he performed the Tchaikovsky B flat minor Piano Concerto under the baton of his friend Willem Mengelberg with the New York Philharmonic. No-one amongst the audience was aware of the turmoil in his mind. Often during concerto performances he would find it restful to work out and memorize railway timetables so that he could choose the best trains to take him from one concert engagement to another. Sometimes he could be seen taking out his diary and jotting down train times during an orchestral tutti, but he was never known to miss his piano entry.

During this period, Percy, who had always been particularly luckless with his love affairs, was going through the most difficult time of his life in this respect. There had always been a string of dizzy girls queuing for his affections and he usually managed to narrow them down to one or two specially favoured ones. Though radically different in most aspects of their personalities, they were all strong-willed, forceful and musical women. Most of them had been his piano pupils, and they were all to become disenchanted with Percy because of the immovable and overwhelming omnipresence of the third party—his mother. E—, for example, was an Englishwoman who had studied with him for a number of years in London and had recently been invited to stay with the Graingers at their White Plains house. This proved to be a fatal move because she had fallen in love with Percy at their first meeting and was now encountering the usual problems with Rose. Recently, however, there had been occasions when his mother had actively encouraged the idea of marriage. She had even offered to move out of their White Plains home and go to live in a New York apartment where Percy could visit her on his business trips and concert engagements. For Rose this was indeed a sacrifice. It would seem that in the later years of her life she was slowly becoming aware of the harmful effects her love had wrought on her son.

Nevertheless, if Percy needed a girlfriend or on the occasions when it was felt that he needed a sex-partner it was still mostly Rose who did the choosing. And just as capriciously she would terminate any relationship which she felt was in any way a threat to the love which existed between herself and her son. In one of the many remarkably frank letters which Grainger wrote to Alfhild Sandby is to be found a paragraph which sheds much light on his passive attitude towards his mother. Alfhild had recently sent him a play in first draft form which dealt with the conflicting loyalties a young man can experience when forced to choose between the attractions of his loved one and the iron will of his mother. (Alfhild almost certainly modelled the main character of the play on Percy, at least up to the point where the play's hero chooses to elope with his beloved.) Grainger was uncompromising in his criticism of the play and compared his own life and attitudes with those of the play's hero. He wrote:

> To me as an Australian (with possibly some influence early imbibed from Japanese and Chinese thought) it seems unbelievable that 2 young people should behave as your Leon and Varenka do: live for love (or passion) *in defiance of a mother's expressed wish.* That any young man or woman should be *disobedient to a parent* seems to me incredibly low. (When 'Mutiny on The Bounty' was shown in Japan they had to change the name to 'Heroes of The Pacific' & cut out all parts of the film showing actual mutiny. It is not *decent* for a Japanese to witness any form of mutiny, not even in a film.) I feel the same way. And I blush at the mere thought that two young people could dare to wish to *live together* against the will of a parent! I (in my life) have taken love action only when *advised to do so* by my Mother. Any other thought is sickeningly repugnant to me [. . .].[1]

His own involvement in the Mimi Kwast affair seems to have been forgotten for the moment.

Rose was completely ruthless in her demands for the most devoted filial affection and loyalty. Her bizarre and histrionic efforts to 'test' his love would take the most drastic forms. Often if he had been out of the house or the room, just before his return she would stretch herself out corpse-like on the floor shamming death. On discovering her in this state he would become tearful and panic-stricken and beg her to speak to him. The moment she was convinced she was not the object of indifference she would sit up and say, 'That's allright. I only wanted to see if you still loved me',[2] and go about her business as if nothing had happened. This 'test' she continued till around 1920, when Percy was nearly forty. Threats to make herself ill or commit suicide were frequent.

Rose was broken-hearted on her son's departure for his tour. She was cared for by the coloured house-boy they employed then, and E—helped the nurse in her duties. Antonia Sawyer called at Cromwell Place every evening on returning from her offices. Percy would write to her two or three times each day, and she would receive from him telegrams about the most trivial matters. He wanted to reassure her that she was uppermost in his mind. On April 2 he wrote to Alfhild Sandby: 'She is *a very little better* but still very ill & very weak & you can understand how miserable I am—a continent's width away [. . .].' Another letter which indicates her state of mind was pencilled by Rose to Roger Quilter some days later:

> I am still very ill, this nervous prostration is a terrible illness I only want to send you my fondest love—& to say that I am so glad that you and Percy are still so loving to one another. You will be glad to hear that he is a finer man now than ever he was, & would be fit to make a wife happy: having given up *all* those silly ideas & things he used to indulge in. In case I should not recover—I want you to know this dear friend—It was nice to see your portrait & I hope to see *you* again some day—but we never can tell, can we—I have been ill for over $2\frac{1}{2}$ months now. Dear Percy is in California—I had such a dear letter from him today.[3]

In the meantime, E—and one or two other women admirers of Percy, jealous of his love for his mother, had begun to spread rumours that the relationship was incestuous. E—'s jealousy had overwhelmed her by now, and though she knew her gossip was completely untrue she felt impelled to set in motion what proved to be a destructive chain of events. Amazingly, it had never occurred to either Percy or his mother that such an interpretation might be put on their intensely close relationship; but shortly after the rumours had begun circulating a friend tactlessly told the already unhinged Rose what was being said by the New York gossip-mongers.

Not knowing who had started or spread the rumour, she immediately sent imputative notes to several of her son's female friends. These pathetic and frenzied notes were mostly hurled back in her face, accompanied

by fervent denials and demands for apologies. One of the women immediately telegraphed Percy: 'The unmentionable has been laid at my
door.' Rose could not bring herself to an awareness of the fact that the
very person who had started the rumours was living under the same roof.

Frantic letters and pleas for help were pencilled on scraps of paper and
posted to her son. Towards the end of April her mind was beginning to
break under the strain of this torment. Percy did not help matters when
he sent letters and telegrams which would often end with phrases such as
'Longing to hold you in my arms once more' and similarly misconstru-
able sentiments. By now Rose was unable to organize her day-to-day
existence, and she telegraphed Percy begging him to stop sending her
passionate letters which she feared might be read by others. She also
asked him to destroy all her letters. Fuel was added to the fire when
E—stole one of Percy's letters which Rose had thoughtlessly left around
the house.

Antonia Sawyer was breakfasting on Sunday April 30 when Rose telephoned asking her how soon she could be taken for a ride into New York.
Rose said that she wanted to find a housekeeper for Percy's return and
needed to make the calls from Mrs Sawyer's offices. Aware that Rose was
behaving irrationally, Mrs Sawyer thought it best to humour her.

When they arrived at the Aeolian Building, they took the lift to the
offices on the eighteenth floor. In order to get to Mrs Sawyer's private
room they had to pass by a near life-sized portrait of Percy on the wall of
the outer office. Rose paused and stared. In the office she began to complain of severe pains and asked for medicine and a warm drink. Mrs
Sawyer left her lying on a couch and went down to a nearby drugstore.

Mrs Sawyer returned shortly after 11.00 a.m. but Rose was nowhere to
be seen. With the help of the liftman she feverishly searched the entire
floor of the building. Then the liftman noticed a high chair pushed up
against the window: he looked out and saw Rose Grainger lying on the
roof of the adjacent Central Building, fourteen storeys below.

When Dr Brodsky of the Flower Hospital arrived, he found Rose in a
concavity caused by her fall. She was still conscious, but, before he could
move her, she died from a fractured skull and multiple internal injuries.
At this time Grainger was playing before a full house in the Los Angeles
Philharmonic Auditorium. A telegram was handed to him when he
returned to his dressing room, applause still ringing in his ears. The
message stated simply that his mother had died, and requested that he
return to New York urgently.

It was only when Grainger was on the train that he read the details
of his mother's death. The *New York Times* quoted the official police
report's conclusion that Rose either jumped or fell. Although severely de-
pressed, he wrote a very long letter to Balfour Gardiner setting out every
detail of his financial and artistic estate and asking him to be his
executor should he die before reaching New York. Trying to sustain his

composure over the long journey, he wrote long letters mostly to his friends in Europe. He even sent a letter to Herman Sandby enclosing a cheque for $200 to help out with the publishing costs of some of the Dane's latest compositions.

On Friday May 5 Grainger arrived in Cleveland where he was met by Antonia Sawyer, Fred and Tonie Morse, who told him of the events leading up to his mother's death. Immediately on his arrival in New York he was taken to the funeral parlour where he asked Fred Morse to take several photographs of his mother in the casket.

Grainger at first wanted a private funeral, but he was eventually persuaded to invite Frederick Steinway and a few other well-known figures in the music world. The service was conducted by John Haynes Holmes, whom Rose had met some years previously. A few days later the body was cremated in accordance with her wishes imparted to her son some months prior to his leaving New York.

For several days afterwards the New York newspapers carried the most preposterous stories concerning Rose's death. Many reports stated that she had left $4 million in money and property in Australia to Percy; others declared that she had left a large sum to Cyril Scott. None of this was true (she had died leaving less than $3,000) and the whole affair greatly disturbed Grainger.

It was Fred and Tonie Morse, his Jewish neighbours, and Captain Clappé, his Buddhist friend and superior officer from army music school days, who brought most solace to Percy during this difficult period. In a letter to Roger Quilter three weeks after the event he wrote:

> She was a brave soldier always, fighting for 30 years a cruel disease (not of her Aldridge blood), & if, at the last, she felt her mind giving way, was she not a brave soldier to leap from the 18th floor? I say 'if', for nothing found so far shows any trace of intending such an act. Rather, all left behind shows plans for my homecoming & a clinging to life & a craving for health. I have searched relentlessly, with beating heart and dizzy head, for I want to be close to her in all things, to share whatever agonies she endured, to know all the horrors she knew, to probe all her thoughts, fears, reasons, motives. And in order to be able to do it all have done hard musical work, & taken long walks, eaten big meals & slept *all I could*, day and night — as an antidote.

Still later he wrote to Alfhild Sandby:

> I returned to New York, and heard the truth about E— from friends who told me that she had slandered me and my Mother in this disgusting way. Mother had been ill; her nerves were worn out; she hadn't long to live; the shock was too much for her; I firmly believe her mind gave way. She wanted peace; she took it.[. . .] I faced E— and told

her she was a despicable liar; I told her that I had never loved her and could never love her; and that I never again wanted to see her. What people believe I do not know; but in case I die before you, and you hear anyone accusing me and my Mother of having lived in incest, I want you to come forward & tell them what I tell you now. This is the sacred truth; & I want you to know it![4]

When Percy came to sort through her belongings, he found scores of draft letters, unfinished letters, letters completed but not posted and a drawer full of torn-up letters. When her son had pieced them together he perceived the entire sequence of events that had led to her death.

The relationship between Percy and his mother had been, in every sense of the word, unusual. The thousands of letters, notes and telegrams they exchanged present us with a fascinating, if frightening, picture which is almost impossible to grasp in its enormity and complexity. There is material enough here for a dozen dissertations on the psychological aspects of Mother Love. Before her death Rose was Percy's biggest single influence, and even after her death her memory served as the most sacred altar at which he worshipped. The umbilical cord was never completely severed.

One letter must be quoted in full. It was amongst the drawerful of torn-up material which Percy reassembled painstakingly after his return to White Plains. It was perhaps the last letter she wrote, scribbled in pencil, dated April 29 (the day before her death) but never sent.

My dear Son,

    I am out of my mind and cannot think properly. I asked L. over the phone whether you told her if I had any improper love for you? I did not want to say this, and knew it was untrue, but couldn't help saying it, and then next day told her I thought she had spread the rumour. I did not mean it, but couldn't help saying it. You must tell the truth, that in spite of everything I said—I have never for one moment loved you wrongly—or you me—not for one moment nor the thought of doing so. The whole thing has driven me insane—and I have accused myself of something I have never thought of. You and I never loved one another anything but purely and right. No one will believe me—but it is the real truth, as you know. It is quite unbelievable what I have said to L—, but I am insane—not on all points, but I cannot do anything any more—and only feel like lying in bed and thinking not sleeping—but just unable to do anything. I am insane. I am oh so sorry and want to do something to help you, but cannot. I doubt whether I will be able to dress myself in a day or so. Every day gets worse—I am an idiot, and no one seems to realize it. I am so sorry—I have loved you and so many others so dearly.

                Your poor insane mother.

P.S. You have tried so hard to be all that is noble—but your mad side has ruined us—dear God knows the truth—man will not believe the truth I am writing.

Percy carried copies of this and one other letter rolled up in a tiny container and hanging around his neck for many years afterwards, as if, like the Ancient Mariner, he needed his own albatross as a symbol of his judgement upon himself.

Percy Grainger was mad. And he was made mad by a mother who never allowed him to grow up. But great art is often the product of madness. His madness caused untold suffering for some and great happiness for others. Between these extremes, reactions from his fellow creatures varied from frustration, puzzlement, misunderstanding, ridicule and hero-worship to complete rejection. His basic humanity was little out of the ordinary. He had dreams, hopes and fears, but these are quite ordinary too. What made him stand alone was his obsessive determination to drag his fantasy into the world of reality. Yet mad though he may have been—and the present writer is aware of the disputable qualities of such an adjective—he was never certifiably or clinically so. He was a ruthlessly self-critical man and each mental and spiritual aberration seems to have been more than compensated by an intellectual and emotional strength.

The inconsistencies and contradictions of his endlessly complex personality were the results of an indiscriminate assimilation of all that flowed from the mother figure. When Rose died, Percy's inconsolable grief was due to her physical and spiritual absence. His ability to survive, however, was wholly bound up with the fact that, by then, Rose and he had become one spiritual unit—something which could not be changed merely by the cessation of the heartbeat of either one.

He was also a genius and he knew it. His mother had said so. His music was now inane, now inspired and sometimes both. His self-deprecatory attitude towards his piano playing, his inability to follow through his pioneering work on folk-song, his rejection of prestigious music posts and his obsessive fears all resulted from his sense of insecurity created by the emasculating effects of an overwhelming mother love. His dread of quitting a world which had forgotten or might forget him drove him to forge of himself the man of stature that he undoubtedly was. He lived in that strange realm where madness and genius merge imperceptibly.

# 15

## Beatless Music, Blue-Eyed English and a Nordic Princess

Grainger determined that the only way he could accommodate the grief of his mother's death would be by submerging himself in hard work, and he immediately set himself to planning his involvement with the Evanston Music Festival, five-week teaching session at the Chicago Musical College and his European tour. He slept and ate as much as he could and the few moments of rest he allowed himself were given over to reading the works of his friend Edgar Lee Masters. He recalled that he 'wept buckets' after reading Masters's *Children of the Market Place*.

Percy changed in many ways after Rose's death. He aged facially over a very short period. Although he remained remarkably handsome, the boyish looks which had stayed with him for the first forty years of his life gave way to more chiselled, manly features. He became less trustful of his fellows and rarely saw social acquaintances more than once a year. In England Cyril Scott was becoming recognized as an authority on nature curing, occultism and related paranormal subjects and about a year after Rose's death he wrote to Percy offering to act as intermediary with his mother on the spiritual plane. Scott claimed that he had established contact with her on many occasions. Percy declined the offer.

The works to be programmed at the Evanston Festival were *Green Bushes*, *English Dance* and *The Bride's Tragedy*. He attached most importance to the première of *The Bride's Tragedy*, not only because it was due to be performed exactly one month after Rose's death, but also because he regarded it as a requiem for her. He had forebodings about the difficulties of the passages which included irregular rhythms, and wrote to Roger Quilter on May 22: 'But I wonder whether it will not, perhaps, prove too tough a nut for Dean Lutkin & his forces.' At the concert itself Lutkin conducted all the quavers as crotchets and $\frac{2\frac{1}{2}}{4}$ came out as $\frac{3}{4}$, $\frac{3\frac{1}{2}}{4}$ as $\frac{4}{4}$ and so on. The applause, however, was overwhelming. The performance of *Green Bushes* was also successful: Grainger later wrote that for this he received the greatest ovation of his career in America — chiefly, he felt, out of sympathy for himself and as a tribute to his mother.

After teaching piano at the Chicago Musical College between June 27 and August 1 he returned to White Plains to prepare for his European trip. During this period at home Grainger made a dreadful mistake which he was to regret for the rest of his life. He made a bonfire consisting of several hundreds, perhaps thousands, of letters to and from his mother and himself. Both before and after this incident he collected all his letters with a passion that any magpie would have envied, yet, acting upon a caprice, he destroyed countless Grainger-Aldridge documents and with them much of the family history. It is one of the stranger ironies of Grainger's life that at about the same time as he destroyed these documents we first see the suggestion in letters to his friends that he wanted to create a Grainger Museum at White Plains.

Grainger left New York on August 10, 1922 on the *Oscar II* and as soon as he arrived in Denmark he travelled to Vejle, where he immediately began collecting folk-songs with Evald Tang Kristensen. Although some of the singers were persuaded to come to the Tang. Kristensen home for recording sessions, most of the material was gathered in the field as the two collectors travelled through Jutland. The Australian paid for the hire of a car and chauffeur and was amazed to see how well the eighty-year-old Tang Kristensen took to riding in the open-roofed vehicle even in the most inclement weather. For years Grainger had made a close study of the Jutland dialects and he was able to converse with the peasants in their own language; Tang Kristensen could note down the songs at lightning speed, and Grainger made cylinder recordings of half of the eighty songs they collected. In the evenings he returned to the Tang Kristensen home, where the day's activities were discussed. Tang Kristensen lived on a small pension and most of this went to the upkeep of a daughter who was confined to a mental hospital. The remainder of his yearly income, about 300 Kroner (in those days equal to £15), kept Tang Kristensen, his wife and son (born when Tang Kristensen was 65). Their lives were lived in the utmost frugality, but their house was a veritable museum providing Grainger with endless fascination, for Tang Kristensen had an enormous collection of pewter, china, broadsheets, old pictures and thousands of copies of his own folk-song books which he had been unable to sell.

Percy then moved to Norway and beginning with the first Kristiania recital on September 8 gave thirty-one performances in thirty-five days. Frederick and Jelka Delius were at his Kristiania recitals and his joy at meeting them after so many years' separation was only marred when Delius's rapidly crumbling health became apparent to him.

Grainger stayed at the Grand Hotel in Kristiania and there, quite by chance on September 12, he ran into Balfour Gardiner, who had been spending a few days with the Deliuses without realizing that Percy was still in Kristiania. He wrote of this meeting:

I had promised to go to the American consul's house that evening. I induced Balfour to go too, rather against his will. The consul's wife was a typical American, full of questions the answers to which meant nothing to her. I introduced Balfour as a composer & she asked him, 'What style of music do you write, Mr Gardiner?' Balfour squirmed for a moment, & answered 'Oh, the style of 1902, I suppose.' The consul's wife knew about 'Country Gardens' & asked me to play it, which I did. Balfour had not heard C.G. When I came to where the bass is fragmentary (because the left hand is looking after the tenor voice too) Balfour jumped up & said 'how awful', much to the embarrassment of the consul's wife, who had no conception, of course, of the outspokenness of composers to each other. Balfour explained that all such fragmentary, incomplete voices (the continuations of which are imagined but never heard) were the bane of piano music.[1]

Gardiner decided to join Grainger on part of his tour of Norway and was with him for ten days. On some occasions Gardiner travelled from town to town by horse and carriage with his friend trotting alongside.

Gardiner was a man of regular habits and could never take his evening meal before 8 o'clock, which was the time Grainger began each recital. The Englishman therefore made special arrangements to have his supper brought to him in his room, as the hotels and boarding houses served dinner at 6.30 sharp. This meant that he never arrived at the recitals until they were nearly over, though he always paid for a seat and apologized each time to Percy for turning up late.

Grainger wrote to Alfhild Sandby on October 4, 1925:

[. . .] in 1922 [Balfour Gardiner] said to me: 'You have grown too comfortable, too natural & too indifferent with your public. You must make sure they don't discover it. It might have disastrous results for you.' Of course, as we cross 40, & all see the futility of many of our hopes, & get tired of kicking out into empty space (of trying to light the fire in the public that will not burn for us) we get tired of driving ourselves and others.[. . .] In 1923 when I got back to U.S. after my year in Europe, I remembered B.G.'s warning and simply gave them hell that whole season, using all the fire and keenness I could muster.

At their leavetaking on the boat at Flekkefjord tears came to Balfour's eyes as he said farewell to his friend. Concluding his recollections of the Norway trip, Grainger later wrote: 'Balfour was a strangely queer mixture of not-to-be-expected-together things: heroic deedfulness, male harshness, womanly feelingfulness, fickleness, selfishness, endless benevolence, distressing self-criticism, unique politeness, secretiveness, downrightness, compassion, surging enthusiasm.'[2]

At the end of the tour of the Norwegian provinces he returned to

Bergen, where he stayed for a while with Nina Grieg.

After the war Nina Grieg had shocked her friends when she sold 'Troldhaugen' and most of its contents. Much of her late husband's music had been handled by a German publisher and wartime hostilities had cut off the royalties. When she died Grainger was to contribute substantially to the efforts made to return Grieg's ashes which Nina had had reburied in Bergen and to reopen the house as a museum with as many items of the original furniture as could be found.

Whilst in Bergen, Grainger encountered Ignaz Friedman and Joseph Szigeti, who were both giving concerts in Bergen at the same time. Before leaving Norway, he wrote to Roger Quilter: 'But my life is almost beyond me. My loneliness is overwhelming. Only lives such as mother & I [led], concentrating all on the closeness of love, could make possible such a torture.'[3]

He then travelled to Copenhagen, where he gave several concerts and met Karen Holten (now Mrs Kellerman). He refused to see Herman and Alfhild Sandby, however, because he remembered the remark Alfhild had made in 1904 about Rose's having 'looked like a devil'. He could not forget this, especially now when the slightest thing would send him into a mood of despair, and though he had misunderstood Alfhild he was to hold this remark against her for the rest of her life. After Copenhagen he moved to Amsterdam on October 20. Three performances of the Grieg concerto were given under Mengelberg in Amsterdam, The Hague and Haarlem. Then, after a solo recital in Zutphen, he ran away and hid in Dordrecht — a spot dear to him because previously he had spent several holidays there with his mother after gruelling European tours. In Dordrecht he began to clean-write the Jutish folk-songs he had collected with Tang Kristensen, but broke off this work for a short trip to London to hear Delius's *A Song of the High Hills* conducted by Albert Coates. The trip to London also afforded him the chance of briefly seeing Quilter and Scott.

Having returned to Holland he gave a few more concerts and recitals, then once more began his work on the Danish folk-songs. Before long he received a surprise visit from Ralph Vaughan Williams, who was in Holland at the time and, having heard of Grainger's loss, had sought him out and come to see him to render whatever comfort he could. A day or so later he received a telegram from Jelka Delius asking him to go to Frankfurt at once because the conductor who was due to rehearse the Rühlscher Gesangverein for a performance of some Delius works had refused to participate since he was not to conduct at the actual concert. Grainger left for Germany on January 8, 1923 — the same day that French troops reoccupied the Ruhr. In Frankfurt he found Delius living in the Domplatz opposite the cathedral and working on additions to the incidental music for Flecker's play *Hassan*. The noise from the cathedral organ constantly irritated Delius, but Grainger's visits provided a welcome distraction.

Grainger felt particularly uncomfortable rehearsing the chorus in *A Song of the High Hills* for Delius's sixtieth birthday concert, which was being financed by Heinrich Simon, owner of the *Frankfurter Zeitung*:

> The Rühlscher Gesangverein were as nasty to rehearse as a choral group could possibly be. They were poor readers, they talked all the time & I'm sure they hated the work [. . .]. Someone who was at one of my rehearsals with the Rühlscher said to me, 'You don't understand the Germans. If you bang on the lid of the piano a few times they would give you their attention.' I tried this in the next rehearsal & it had some effect. But one cannot act contrary to one's nature very long. There was one group of old ladies in the left back corner (second sopranos) that had a bit by themselves very soon after the chorus starts singing. I had more trouble with these old ladies than with anything else & when the Jewish-Danish conductor from Vienna had his first rehearsal with the choir & came to the spot where my old ladies became vocally exposed, he took one hate-filled look in their direction, made a big wiping-out-gesture & shouted 'Nicht mit-singen!' Neither the conductor, nor Delius, made any bones about letting me know that they thought the chorus thoroughly badly trained (by me), which of course they were.[4]

After the Delius birthday concert on January 29, in which Grainger played one piano of his two-piano arrangement of Delius's *Dance Rhapsody*, he settled down to what for him were more interesting tasks. During his stay in Frankfurt he lived with the daughter and son-in-law of Karl Klimsch in the Grünenbergsweg, but spent most of his time with Delius, showing him many of his latest scores. Delius liked them very much, but tackled the Australian on his use of the harmonium. 'If you go on using the harmonium in all your scores, they will all sound like that organ droning away over there. Your use of the harmonium suggests that you cannot accommodate your harmony voices in your orchestral texture.'[5] Grainger felt that the harmonium was essential in his scores and was hurt by Delius's suggestions. He defended the harmonium thus:

> If Wagner had 3 characteristic themes that had TO BE HEARD PROMINENTLY at one & the same time, it stands to reason that he had to have some non-prominently heard weaker-toned background instruments to play the harmonies for his 3 prominent themes. The 'modest' woodwind & horns sufficed in his case, because they were weaker than the trumpets, massed strings & massed basses that were forth-sounding his prominent themes. But in my large chamber music scores I often want my prominent voices to be played by *single* instruments, not massed instruments (because of the greater edginess of the

sound of single instruments). So I need a background instrument, to play the accompanying harmonies, that is weaker-toned than my prominent single instruments. In chamber music the harmonium seems to me perfect for this purpose, with orchestra the pipe or electric organ. Fancy that professional musicians have so deteriorated since Bach's time that they cannot hear that the harmonium, or reed organ, is the most essential of all chamber music instruments.[6]

The Deliuses were still hopeful of a cure for Frederick's syphilis at this time and Jelka was taking her husband from one highly respected doctor to another throughout Europe. Most of them turned out to be expensive quacks. Delius left Frankfurt towards the end of April for another course of treatment at a German spa town.

With inflation reaching phenomenal heights in Germany Grainger found it quite within his means to assemble and pay an orchestra to rehearse some of his works during April. The six rehearsals plus the occasional services of a conductor cost him £20. Alexander Lippay, the conductor (from the Frankfurt Opera House), at first refused to direct his *Hill-Song Number 1*, believing that no orchestra would be able to cope with the irregular rhythms. After the composer had demonstrated with the orchestra that such difficulties could be overcome, he conducted a variety of experiments with the piece by first giving the melody to the woodwind and the harmony to the strings and then changing the instrumentation around and so on. Similar experiments were made with *The Warriors* and *Marching Song of Democracy*. His habit, which he shared with Schumann and others, of cross-quoting thematic material is to be seen in both *Hill-Songs*. One of the most intriguing quotations used in these works is a thematic fragment from his Kipling Setting No. 1, *Dedication*. Kipling's poem is a fierce affirmation of filial affection and Grainger's accompaniment is stark and elemental. It is one of his most inspired compositions and was completed in two days in 1901. The words covered by the musical quotation are, prophetically, 'Mother o' mine!' To anyone familiar with Percy's works and life it becomes the most deeply moving section of the *Hill-Songs*.

In Frankfurt Grainger supervised the publication of a book entitled *Photos of Rose Grainger and of 3 short accounts of her life by herself, in her own hand-writing reproduced for her kin and friends by her adoring son Percy Grainger—also table of dates, & summary of her cultural tastes*. He had several thousand copies of this lavish production made and shipped to White Plains at a cost of £800. Copies of the book, which ended with photographs of his dead mother in the coffin, were sent to his friends. Even in those days when sentimentality was more commonly an element of human relationships, the receipt of this book caused no small amount of flesh to creep. It is at once touching and gruesome and perhaps tells us more about Percy than Rose.

Whilst in Frankfurt Grainger often visited his former teacher Karl Klimsch, who was then eighty-three. Although Klimsch had lost his entire fortune because of the devaluation of the German mark, he was in good health and spirits. The Australian's occasional gifts of a quarter of a pound of butter made the old man very happy, but not so happy as when his former pupil played his compositions over to him. He listened to *Colonial Song* with silent satisfaction and Grainger later remarked 'Perhaps he was the only friend my music satisfied.'[7] They were never to meet again.

In June Grainger returned to Dordrecht, then travelled on to Denmark to spend a few more days with Evald Tang Kristensen collecting, recording and transcribing Jutish songs. The period between July 21 and August 8 was spent in Norway with the Deliuses at their home in Lesjaskog. Delius was still working on the incidental music for *Hassan* and decided to ask his friend to write a dance movement for inclusion in the final work. On the basis of a tune given to him by Delius, he therefore sketched several pages for what was eventually included in the score as *Allgemeiner Tanz* ('General Dance'). Delius himself later filled out the instrumentation and completed the movement.

Delius at this time was almost blind, and his greatest wish was to see a mountain sunset before total blindness set in. On Saturday July 28 Grainger arranged for a chair to be slung between two poles and with the help of a strong Norwegian friend carried Delius to the top of the mountain Hovdalien at the back of his home. The party was joined by Jelka and they set out at 1.30, arriving at the summit at 6.20. Here the group was greatly disappointed because clouds were obscuring the sun, but they decided to sit around for a while and after about twenty minutes the skies cleared to reveal the most breathtaking sunset.

At times Grainger read to Delius or played the piano for him. Delius was very difficult to please and for no apparent reason would change his mind as to the selection he wanted played. However, he valued Percy's company so much that he begged the Australian to stay on with him. Delius was fearful of the day when his blindness and paralysis would lock up so much unwritten music inside his mind, and he wanted him to act as his amanuensis. But much as he loved Delius and his music, Grainger knew that to have stayed with him would have stifled his own creativity.

By mid-August he was back in White Plains, refreshed by having been in places and near to folk dear to his mother. His year in Europe had been a great musical experience. Apart from the experiments he had conducted with his own music in Frankfurt and the publication of his new works (*Hill-Song Number 1; One More Day, My John; Marching Song of Democracy*) he had taken a close look at new musical developments in Europe and had heard new works by Schönberg, Schreker (*Kammersymphonie*), Schelling, Hindemith, Pfitzner (*Palestrina*), Delius and Strauss (*Die Frau ohne Schatten*). Perhaps his greatest disappointment had been the unwillingness of all his English friends (except Balfour Gardiner) to visit him in Europe. Before he left Europe Hans Augustin had asked him to return in 1924, but Antonia Sawyer had by then filled his diary with American concert engagements and he had to refuse. He never returned to Europe as a major professional pianist or conductor.

Shortly after his return to White Plains he wrote a letter to Alfhild Sandby in which, at the same time as telling her that he never wanted to hear from her again, he said he was planning a series of concerts in which he wanted Herman to take part. Although he had not at that stage fixed the dates or the artists, he envisaged a series which would present not only his own works but those of Sandby, Delius, Gardiner, Scott and Quilter. He wrote to all these composers asking if they would be interested in turning up to perform in their own works and initially he received favourable replies. Delius was most enthusiastic and Grainger hoped that his presence, at least in the audience, would be the highlight of the series.

He gave only one New York recital during 1923 on December 5 at Carnegie Hall. As well as the works of Chopin, Schumann and Bach which usually appeared on his piano recital programmes, it contained one unusual item, Delius's *On Hearing the First Cuckoo in Spring*. The programme did not state whose arrangement was being used, but it was probably his own, though no manuscript has survived.

Among the audience at this recital was the young English composer Arthur Bliss, who was so thrilled by what he heard—especially the Bach playing—that he introduced himself to the pianist and congratulated him after the concert. Grainger was impressed with Bliss and they arranged to meet some days later at the home of a mutual friend. At this meeting he asked Bliss if he knew the Schubert piano duets. After the Englishman had replied that he did not, they spent the rest of the evening practising these pieces. For Bliss it was an unforgettable and enjoyable evening. Their acquaintance was not renewed until some years later when Bliss was in Paris with Constant Lambert for the first French performance of his ballet *Checkmate*. Lambert and Bliss were sitting at a pavement café sipping their coffee under the warm afternoon sun when Grainger chanced to walk past, having just returned from a visit to Delius in Grez.

A month or so later in 1924 when Grainger was touring Canada and the west coast of the United States, he included a piano version of his own *Colonial Song*. This piece is the first of a projected series of 'Sentimentals' which never seems to have got off the ground. He wanted to write a piece which typified Australian life as those of Stephen Foster had done for the American scene, and intended it to be suitable for what he felt were the relatively unsophisticated ears of Australian audiences. The great English contralto Dame Clara Butt in preparing for a tour of

Australia once asked Dame Nellie Melba for repertoire suggestions for her antipodean programmes. Although it was censored out of all but a handful of the first editions of Dame Clara's biography (the page was simply cut out), Melba's stentorian reply is alleged to have been 'Sing 'em muck!' Were *Colonial Song* not such a splendid work, one would suspect that a trace of Melba's attitude had crept into Grainger's mind during its composition. It contains a tune of which Puccini would have been proud and a climax which reminds one of Scriabin and doubtless owes more than a little in respect of melodic shape to those composers — men for whom Grainger had boundless admiration. It appears in various instrumentations and is perhaps most successful in the full orchestra version. *Colonial Song* provides another example of Grainger's practice of thematic cross-pollination, containing material in common with *Gum-suckers March, Australian Up-Country Song* and *Handel in the Strand.* It was perhaps the cavalier remark of Beecham which put an end to his continuation of the 'Sentimentals', though it is probable that an unpublished composition called *When the World Was Young* was due to be Sentimental Number Two. The scoring and instrumentation of *Colonial Song* serve the purposes of the melody very well indeed. The melody is beautifully nostalgic and sentimental and to criticize it for being so would be like criticizing Elgar's *Pomp and Circumstance* Marches for being pompous and circumstantial.

Mengelberg had begun his association with the New York Philharmonic Orchestra by 1924, and in the same season Grainger played the Grieg concerto with him. Percy often had the harshest things to say about professional conductors, but had nothing but glowing private and public praise for his Dutch friend. He was always happy to perform under Mengelberg, but refused to work under Toscanini, who eventually shared the conductorship of this magnificent orchestra. In time Mengelberg's American career was brought to an end by the neurotic tantrums of the Maestro. Mengelberg never returned to America after 1929 and Grainger never worked with the New York Philharmonic after that year. Toscanini was the victor and American audiences the losers.

Within a few weeks of performing the Grieg concerto with Mengelberg and the New York Philharmonic Orchestra, Grainger used the same orchestra in the most ambitious project of his career. The two concerts employed the 250 voices of the Bridgeport Oratorio Society and the ninety-four instrumentalists of the New York Philharmonic, first on April 28 in Bridgeport, Connecticut, and then two days later (the second anniversary of his mother's death) at Carnegie Hall in New York. The pre-concert publicity had stated that Delius would attend, but owing to ill-health he was ordered by his doctor to forgo the trans-Atlantic crossing. The programme was brilliantly planned and perfectly balanced, consisting of Grainger's *Marching Song of Democracy, Two North Country Sketches* and *A Song of the High Hills* by Delius, *Two Psalms*

Op. 74 by Grieg and two *Songs of the Church* (from the *Vespers*) Op. 37
by Rachmaninov. The Rachmaninov and the Grieg items were conducted by Frank Kasschau and Grainger conducted the rest. The Delius
works were being given their first American performances. The hire of
the chorus, orchestra and halls came mostly from Grainger's pocket and
cost almost $6,000. Large audiences attended and the critics on the
whole were generous with their praise, although Henry T. Finck of the
*New York Evening Post* was perhaps the only critic who made mention of
the Delius works; he especially liked *A Song of the High Hills*. About his
own *Marching Song of Democracy* Grainger wrote shortly after the concerts: 'I do not think that the audience cares much for this work, or that
other musicians prize it very highly — not even "Graingerites". But I like
it, & naturally care more for my own opinion than the whole world's.'[8]
Though unhappy to hear that after the concerts the Bridgeport Oratorio
Society had lost one-third of its membership, he was sufficiently encouraged to begin planning further concerts along the same lines.

In April 1924 he again urged Cecil Sharp to accept half the royalties
from *Country Gardens*, which was then selling at the rate of twenty-seven
thousand copies a year in the United States and Canada. Before Sharp
could be persuaded fully to accept, however, he was taken ill and died.
Sharp's colleague Dr Maud Karpeles eventually took up the offer and the
money Grainger gave was used partly to finance the publication of
Sharp's Appalachian collection and partly to subsidize a collecting trip to
Newfoundland. In a BBC broadcast the following year in memory of
Cecil Sharp Grainger's arrangement of *Shepherd's Hey* and a record of
Joseph Taylor singing *Bold William Taylor* were included.

On May 21 he sailed on the SS *Tahiti* for Australia. Tahiti was the first
port of call and Percy took the opportunity of climbing in his US Army
uniform the second highest volcanic peak on the island. He was entranced by the flowers and wild life, but found the slippery undergrowth
and the heat too much and was forced to abandon his climb about two
hundred feet from the top when leg cramps added to his difficulties. The
most exciting port of call, however, was Avarua — a luxuriant Raratongan island where, owing to the absence of a natural harbour, the ship lay
at anchor offshore and the passengers were collected in a fleet of native
boats towed by a tug. The volcanic island was administered by New
Zealand, but apart from officials no Europeans or Chinese were allowed
to settle there and consequently Avarua remained more unspoilt than
Tahiti. Grainger had hoped to hear some of the splendid singing to
which his New Zealand friend Knocks had introduced him by means of
the cylinders that had been made. He was, however, distressed to learn
that the native population of Avarua rarely sang their own songs when
ships stopped by, but merely sang and played along with the crews in
European-based material.

When the ship docked at Wellington he went to Palmerston North to visit a relative. On his return he decided to leave the train at Otaki because of a sentimental wish to see the house where Knocks had lived and where he had spent so many happy hours in 1909. In 1919 Grainger had written to Knocks, but, having received no reply, presumed him dead. His joy knew no bounds when he found a Walt Whitmanesque, bearded Knocks in excellent health and spirits. Knocks was one of Grainger's folk heroes. The old man was also a seer and, as had happened in 1909, he sat before Percy and told him many things about his life, mother, and future without hearing one word from the Australian.

The purpose of the trip was mainly to bury his mother's ashes and visit friends and relatives, though he did give a few lecture-recitals before specially invited audiences in Sydney, Melbourne and Adelaide with the aid of Duo-Art piano rolls. In Melbourne he stayed with Robert Hamilton Russell. During Grainger's days in Victoria Russell drove him to see a friend, J.W. Lindt, who lived on Black Spur in Healesville in the mountains to the north-east of Melbourne. Lindt had been a pioneer photographer in Australia and was one of the first men to take photographs of natives in New Guinea and the South Sea Islands. Percy was fascinated to see Lindt's remarkable collection.

The private recitals which Grainger gave at the Aeolian rooms in Adelaide, Melbourne and Sydney marked a new departure in his concert life. To begin with, they were the first lecture-recitals which he had given, and when talking about the piano reproducing machinery he mentioned the possibility of accurately cutting music which contained rhythms too difficult to be reproduced by a human performer. At this stage he termed the idea 'beatless music', and spoke of it as the music of the future. In his lectures he did not hesitate to sing the praises of American jazz — an easy short-cut in those days to becoming branded by academics as a musical buffoon or anarchist. His recitals included works played by himself and the Duo-Art equipment by Carpenter, Guion, Brockway, Dett, Sowerby, Dillon, Scott and Delius.

On a railway trip from Adelaide to Mount Gambier, Percy decided to walk part of the way. Garbed in what was partly his old army uniform, he covered the eighty-six miles between Tailem Bend and Keith carrying a 42 lb swag and sleeping mostly under the stars. Later he described the experience to Roger Quilter: 'The 2 nights, under the bright moon & stars, deeply frosty & the express trains roaring past nearby out of the utter silence — all unforgettable'.[9] One day, after a hard trudge through the South Australian desert, he tried to register at a bush hotel. The lady manager did not like the look of him, however, and was reluctant to allow him to have a room. After desperately trying to establish his good character, Percy said, 'I'll tell you who I am. I'm a musician and my name's Percy Grainger.'[10] The manageress seemed very pleased at this and remarked that she had heard he was a very good singer. When Percy explained that his line was piano playing, the good lady took him to the hotel piano and asked him to give her a tune. This convinced her that he was a man of some breeding, but Percy thought that she still cast him as a travelling piano-tuner.

In Adelaide Percy stayed with his Aunt Clara and Uncle Frank. Frank was bed-ridden and had spent most of the day crying when his nephew arrived, but Percy soon had him out of bed and in high spirits, taking him on long walks before he left. Percy bought them a phonograph with a small collection of records including Roger Quilter's *Children's Overture,* which they all liked greatly. In Adelaide Percy buried his mother's ashes in West Terrace Cemetery. A curious story surrounds the burial. There is no record in the cemetery books that Rose was ever buried there, and it is generally believed that Percy entered the place one night and buried her ashes with his own hands.

On his final return to Melbourne he signed a contract with the concert agents J. & N. Tait to undertake an extensive tour of Australia in 1926. Percy's trip in August and September from Sydney to San Francisco on the SS *Manganui* was brightened by the presence of Robert Hamilton Russell, who shared his cabin. Russell, who had pioneered a break-through in hernia operations was on his way to America to receive fellow-ships from the medical faculties of several universities in honour of his discovery. Percy and Russell spent most of the time talking about their sexual interests—flagellism and homosexuality respectively.

On his return to America in the autumn of 1924, Grainger imme-diately undertook another short concert tour beginning in Canada and moving on to the United States. In Detroit, where he played the Grieg piano concerto under Ossip Gabrilowitsch and later heard the orchestra play his *Colonial Song* and *Shepherd's Hey*, he once more encountered Russell. When he arrived in New York he was informed that he had earned the distinction of being the first non-Russian to have one of his works (*Country Gardens*) pirated by Muzgiz in Soviet Russia. Per-haps the most touching tribute he received that year, however, was a letter from Frederick Delius. For over two years Delius had been dictat-ing his letters to Jelka, but in a letter to Percy in May 1924 he had attempted his own signature in pencil. On October 20, however, Delius took great trouble to have sent to Percy what was almost certainly the last letter in his own handwriting to anyone. The letter is scrawled pain-stakingly in pencil and it is a deeply moving gesture which bears witness to Delius's love for Grainger:

Dearest friend
Just a few lines in my own hand to tell you I sent off to your address the full score of Eventyr, 3 preludes for piano & 2 Songs, words by Nietzsche—Many thanks for all the cuttings—We are again in Grez & longing for further news of the homeward voyage
With love from us both

Despite the fact that Delius's works were now being given more performances throughout Europe, the mood at Grez became more grim by 1925
owing to his continued deterioration in health. Jelka was beginning to
feel the burden of nursing a sick genius with so much music as yet
unborn. She urged Grainger to return as often as possible and to do what
he could to help her husband.

In 1924 Grainger became a vegetarian. Cyril Scott and Herman
Sandby, both vegetarians, had tried to convert him in his London days,
but his response had been to take great pleasure in eating huge slices of
roast beef swimming in rich red gravy whenever he was in their company.
It was perhaps Grainger's admiration of the writings of Bernard Shaw
that swung the pendulum the other way. During his autumn tour of 1924
he met a woman who turned the conversation to Shaw's ideas on vege-
tarianism, and from that time on he never knowingly consumed meat of
any kind. At times he had difficulties in reconciling his vegetarian and
pacifist ideas with his love of violence but this was explained (to his own
satisfaction) on October 13, 1946 in a letter to the editor of the *American
Vegetarian* which ended:

> But you may ask why I, who all my life have enjoyed warlike & violent-
> mooded literature, should be so much against war. One answer to that
> is that since war has ceased to be hand-to-hand fighting, its appeal to
> the savage side of our nature doesn't amount to much. It isn't sport-
> ing.
>      Yours, for meat-shun-ment & world-peace,
>                          Percy Grainger.

Percy's eating habits became fraught with difficulties because, though
he had become a vegetarian, he was not in fact particularly fond of vege-
tables. He did, however, eat large quantities of nuts, plain boiled rice,
wheatcakes, bread and jam, cream cakes, ice cream, oranges (which he
ate like apples, pith, pips, skin and all) and the occasional salad. He
usually jotted down in his diary the constituents of each meal as well as
the places where he ate. Percy's diaries afford an extraordinary insight
into the trivia of his everyday life. Though he rarely made notes of his
feelings or thoughts, his diaries contain the most minute details of such
things as his weight (an obsession), which items of clothing he had
washed and was wearing, whether and when he had shaved, train times,
taxi tips and his sex life. The details of his sex life are written in a curious
code. At the side of any one of many different symbols, each representing
a different sex act, he went to great lengths to explain the act. The explanation, however, was always in Danish with the letters of the key
words often slipped one place ahead or back in the alphabet. From the
late twenties and early thirties onwards, his diaries show that he had
become an ardent film-goer. His favourite film stars seem to have been

Marlene Dietrich, Ginger Rogers and Ingrid Bergman.

Stories about Percy's antics whilst on tour are legion. He would often arrive early for practice at the hall where he was due to play and when the time came for the concert, would be nowhere to be found. After frantic searches he would be found asleep either under or on top of the piano. In one mid-western town of America he was once found asleep on a rather commodious window ledge about twelve feet from the floor. Only when the first members of the audience were creeping in did he rise from his slumbers and disappear to the dressing room to prepare for the concert. Stories emanating from nearer his home in White Plains usually centre around what was thought to be his eccentric dress. The white duck trousers, the ex-army boots and the windswept uncovered hair were always a cause for comment. If he had a guest arriving by train he would turn up at the station with a garden wheelbarrow and place the guest's luggage in that contraption, running home with it along the centre of the road whilst his friend either jogged alongside or rode to the house in a taxi. For a number of years Percy used a remarkable item of clothing consisting of a jacket to which short lengths of string had been attached. From these he would suspend his manuscripts, pens, pencils and other personal belongings. (He did not like briefcases.) Unfortunately such charming but minor eccentricities were just the kind of nugget upon which journalists would eagerly seize and they helped to create a picture of woeful imbalance.

The year 1925 was marked by two further explosive letters from Percy to Alfhild, in one of which, dated December 1, he wrote:

[. . .] as a business woman, as a business help to Herman no terms are bad enough for what I think of you. You have not an ounce of business ability, & with your sharp tongue you do more harm in 5 minutes than you could right in 5 years even if you had business ability. [. . .] I don't like to hear you talk as if you knew what Herman's art lacks, that you tell him what to do, etc. I would not do so myself — yet artistic advice should only come from the EXPERT in that line.[. . .] You ought to be ashamed of yourself drinking coffee and smoking. Yourself a gifted woman & a fine woman as you are, and devoted to and married to a genius you should insist on realising health & your own talent above all things. Give up all great hopes, all dislikes, all impatience, walk 2 to 4 hours daily, never smoke, never drink tea, coffee or alcohol, always be in bed by 9.30 or 10 p.m. That is your duty (in my eyes) as a talent & as Herman's wife. Women are mad anyway and you are exceptionally mad. I do not say it is a bad thing, but you should not overdo it.[. . .] Don't talk to me about your bad heart & mention coffee in the same letter.[. . .] I shall not be writing, & I HOPE VERY MUCH you will not write to me either.[. . .] If you continue to write (except in an emergency) I shall have to go to the length [. . .] of sending them back to you unopened — a thing I have done before & a thing I shall not shrink from doing again.

And as he wrote these stinging letters to Alfhild he was also writing to Herman asking him again to come to New York to participate in a series of concerts he was organizing for the winter of 1925/6.

During the spring of 1925 Grainger staged two more remarkable concerts in the Little Theatre at 238 West 44th Street, New York City. The first, on April 26, was an all-Grainger affair with *English Dance, Hill-Song Number 1,* seven Kipling Settings, *My Robin is to the Greenwood Gone* and *Scotch Strathspey and Reel* being performed by soloists from the New York Philharmonic Orchestra, the Kasschau Solo Choir and pianists Ralph Leopold and Ernest Hutcheson. The second concert contained no works by Grainger, but the Canadian negro Nathaniel Dett conducted the Hampton Institute Choir in a performance of his own *Negro Folk-Song Derivatives* whilst the Australian conducted the orchestra in *Kammersymphonie* by Franz Schreker, *Memories of New Mexico* by Natalie Curtis, *Lost in the Hills* Op. 32 by Grieg and Hindemith's *Kammermusik No. 1* Op. 24, No. 1.

Grainger undertook his annual teaching session at the Summer Master School of the Chicago Musical College during June and July of that year. Each student paid $25 for a half-hour private lesson and scholarships were offered to the best pupils. Special emphasis was laid on the use of the middle (sustaining) pedal of the Steinway piano and 'fluttering' the damper pedal. His own special brand of humour was evinced once when he noticed his girl students having pedalling problems with their high-heeled shoes. He tried on the shoes of each of the female pupils until he found a pair that fitted and then proceeded to give a demonstration of difficult pedalling. At another session with a large class, the noise from a neighbouring studio where a pianist was practising *Country Gardens* at about quarter speed floated through the open window in the hot sultry Chicago air. The students soon began to laugh at the spectacle of Percy's apparent deafness to the neighbour's practising and when mirth overwhelmed the entire class he was forced to ask them what had caused it. He used this incident to demonstrate the need for powers of concentration on the work at hand. Indeed he sometimes asked two pupils to practise two completely different works side by side on two pianos. Whilst in Chicago at the Summer School he lived in his studio, sleeping and cat-napping on a mattress underneath (and sometimes on top of) his piano and taking his meals in the studio also. A keen rivalry and perhaps professional jealousy developed in later years when Rudolph Ganz joined the faculty. It was no secret that the two pianists did not like each other or their methods of teaching and it was partly because of this that Grainger eventually quit the Chicago teaching sessions.

In August 1925 he once more left for Europe, where he stayed for a few weeks with the Deliuses at Grez and Evald Tang Kristensen in Denmark. In Grez he was joined by Balfour Gardiner, who helped him entertain Delius with long hours of piano duet playing. On his return to America he undertook many concerts of his own and friend's works. These concerts covered the winter season of 1925/6, and Herman Sandby participated in many. At one of the most important of this series, in the Aeolian Hall on December 29, Grainger conducted whilst Sandby played the American première of Delius's cello concerto.

In 1925 the Columbia Graphophone Company issued its first complete instrumental sonata set of the electrical recording era. It was of Grainger playing the Chopin Sonata in B minor Op. 58. It is perhaps significant to note that on all but one of the sides of this six-sided set, Columbia and Grainger in their wisdom chose the first of the three takes recorded. The spontaneity was thus preserved. This performance has stood the test of time and is the recording to which connoisseurs always turn when Grainger's greatness as a pianist is being discussed. It is played with a ferocity and wild abandon that is at times frightening, and despite the judicious cuts, the few wrong notes and the characteristic doubled strike of the last chord (he did this in practically all his performances) it stands as one of the high points of recorded piano playing.

The February 1926 edition of the German language *Pult und Taktstock*, issued in Vienna by Universal Edition, carried an article by Grainger entitled '*Neue Schlaginstrumente*' ('New Percussion Instruments'). It gave rise to a considerable degree of interest amongst musicians and composers in Europe including Alban Berg, who said that he had long wanted to use a bass-xylophone and bass-glockenspiel in his works but had no idea that they really existed.[11] Later, when the 'elastic' score of *Spoon River* was published in 1929 it was prefaced by a truly prophetic article entitled 'To Conductors'. As well as dealing with tuneful percussion instruments the whole essay could be described as Grainger's credo where orchestration is concerned. Elastic scoring was an invention of his which revolved around the idea that many of his works could be performed by any number of instrumentalists from four to four hundred as long as the tonal balance of the work was preserved. The complete essay is reproduced in the appendix of this book.

The last orchestral concert given by Grainger during the 1925/26 season was the greatest success of the season. It fell on the fourth anniversary of his mother's death, April 30, and took place in Los Angeles. Under his direction the Los Angeles Oratorio Society with chosen instrumentalists and vocal soloists performed *A Song of the High Hills* by Delius, *Marching Song of Democracy* and, after thirteen years' absence from the repertoire, *Father and Daughter*. Performers, audience and critics were all sympathetic. The following morning he gave a free piano recital for Los Angeles schoolchildren.

Percy often quoted Cecil Rhodes, who believed that one should be able to afford one's ideals. He was now a rich man and at the peak of the previous season had earned $5,000 a week. In May he received another commission from the Evanston Festival, offering him $1,000 for a work. Adding such amounts to the royalties from his compositions, he felt able to undertake more concerts of his own works. He had now settled most of his needy relatives with annuities from invested capital sums and extended his generosity to Herman Sandby, on whom he settled $5,000. He even provided the upkeep of a former admirer of his mother's.

On May 5, he boarded the RMMS *Aorangi* and set sail for Sydney. On this tour he undertook lecture-recitals and concerts of 'Nordic' and 'Anglo-Saxon' music throughout the various states. He also made a few broadcasts. J. & N. Tait had arranged to have four specially built Steinways taken from city to city and the Melbourne piano was even shipped to Tasmania, where he gave a series of concerts and lectures in Hobart and Launceston. He was followed by newspaper reporters wherever he went and he delighted in throwing them paradoxes and characteristic Graingerisms on every subject known to him. It was on this Australian tour that he began to talk seriously and publicly about the superiority of fair-skinned and blue-eyed composers. In those days such opinions were treated neither very seriously nor with much suspicion.

In Perth he was invited to visit a religious community of Loreto to play for the nuns. The main purpose of the visit was to introduce him to the musical talents of a young girl of Tasmanian origin who was being cared for by the sisters. He was astonished by what he heard and immediately wrote to the most important newspapers in Australia about his 'discovery'. The girl's name was Eileen Joyce. A committee was set up under the chairmanship of no less a person than the State Premier to raise funds and decide the future of the prodigy. Grainger was summoned before the committee and earnestly requested that she should not be sent to Europe but instead that the essentially 'Australian' qualities in her playing should be developed either under the best Australian teachers at home or in America. He suggested that she should study with Ernest Hutcheson (who was then Dean of the Juilliard School of Music) and offered her a free scholarship for his own classes in Chicago. Not long after Grainger had departed from Perth, however, that city was visited by Wilhelm Backhaus, who suggested that she should receive a thorough German training. Backhaus's suggestions were followed and Grainger's ignored.

Whilst Percy was in Australia he gave a large quantity of money to old friends and relatives and made substantial financial donations to orchestras and choirs in Adelaide. Despite his generosity to relatives, one of his cousins in Adelaide had declined to walk with him in the street because of Percy's refusal to wear a hat.

In Hobart he had made a remarkable discovery; he had met one Robert Atkinson, whose ideas on language reform were practically identical to his own — hard though it may be to believe that there was actually more than one person trying to establish the use of 'Blue-eyed English'. So delighted was Grainger in meeting him that he eventually decided to pay him a small sum each time he received a letter from him in 'Blue-eyed English'.

It was not long before he had settled an annuity of £1,000A on Atkinson. The Tasmanian was encouraged by his benefactor to write a book on language reform and paid £20A each time he sent a chapter. Atkinson, however, did not complete the project and left instructions before he died that if the manuscript remained incomplete it was to be destroyed. His widow carried out these last wishes and Grainger was infuriated when he was informed, until he suddenly remembered that he had in his fireproof basement a carbon copy.

Having boarded the RMMS *Aorangi* in November to return to the American continent, he wrote to Roger Quilter: 'I am feeling very weary & down-hearted. My Australian tour was too wonderful, & after being on the high horse so long, treated like a real genius & all that, one must expect a mood-slump.'[12] To others he confided that his tour had been dire, that the Australian musicians had been next to impossible to rehearse and that his audiences and relatives had misunderstood his music and ideas. For most of the voyage he attended to letters, trotted around the promenade deck, slept during the day and read Houston Stewart Chamberlain at night. News had reached him that year of the deaths of Karl Klimsch and Mimi Kwast.

In Auckland as he stood in a queue to have his passport stamped, he heard the customs officer shout out 'Ström!' He turned around as the young lady behind him in the queue responded. It was for Percy a classic case of love at first sight. She was thirty-seven when they met, and radiantly beautiful, fair of skin and blue-eyed. A few days later in the Pacific Ocean as he was practising alone in the music room for a recital on December 3 in Honolulu, she entered and, thinking that he was the ship's band leader, asked him if he could show her some chords on her banjulele. Percy did not want to interrupt his practice, so they arranged to meet the following day, when Miss Ella Viola Ström, still ignorant of Percy's identity, was given a first-rate lesson. Some days later she learned who her teacher was and when she found him late one evening in the writing room she gingerly approached him to apologize. During this meeting they told each other a great deal about their lives and Percy was greatly struck by Ella's likeness to his mother.

> Every romantic thought of my life seemed to rise out of dim memories & rush towards her for fulfilment [. . .]. It may be she said to me 'Hello little boy' or some other playful greeting, her bright eyes sparkling. And how she left the thought with me that she sensed the boy in me — which is the only way I want to be thought of [. . .]. Likewise it was the

girl in her — the playmate, the sister, the skittish-one (not the woman) — that I loved and worshipped.[13]

Ella Viola Ström-Bandelius was born just outside Stockholm in 1889. After a period of education and employment in Stockholm she moved to London on a Bernard Shaw foreign student exchange scholarship to study at the Slade School of Art. During her London period she met and was influenced by Augustus John, who executed several sketches of her. Shorter periods of work in Berlin and Paris eventually led to some exhibitions of her paintings and ceramics, and her work with the Swedish diplomatic service brought her in touch with many different cultures and areas of the world. Able to do justice to a Martini with the best of them, Ella had circulated mostly amongst socialites, writers and artists. One of her most ardent suitors had been Prince Iyemasa Tokugawa of Japan.

Percy gave her two tickets for the Honolulu recital, but she came alone. He spotted her in the audience and recalled that her face had a 'pathetic, rapt' look about it. This, he felt, was because he was playing badly. Back on board they played deck-quoits, but he was disappointed because he could beat her so easily. He was disappointed also by her persistent request for him to play Chopin. During the sea voyage they only saw about four hours of each other, but Percy often spied on her from afar. Shortly before they arrived in Vancouver, he found her in the writing room with tear-stained eyes: she had just learned of the death of her lover in London. Percy did what he could to comfort her. Ella was on her way to London, so on arrival in Vancouver on December 9 he offered to guide her across the American continent by train. The trip, which took them through the Canadian Rocky Mountains and which for some time was held up due to snowdrifts, afforded them the chance to get to know each other.

Percy told Ella about his mother and showed her the letters which he carried around his neck. He read to her from *The Santa Fe Trail* by his friend Vachel Lindsay, and when Percy felt dispirited, Ella would get out her banjulele and serenade him with *I wanna be happy*.

Ella left the train at Albany and went on to stay with friends in Maldon-on-Hudson. Percy did not accept an invitation to visit her, but stayed in White Plains practising for his forthcoming tour. He did, however, turn up by surprise at the wharf on December 23, where her ship *Ascania* was waiting to take her to Southampton. He came bearing gifts of a $5,000 life settlement, books by Whitman, Masters, Lindsay, Isadora Duncan, the 'Rose Grainger Book' and *Keeping Fit* by Macfadden. Before the boat sailed Ella invited him to stay for a while during the summer of the following year at her house in Pevensey Bay. Although he wrote a letter originally turning down the invitation it was not sent and eventually he did stay with her for a while in England during the summer of 1927.

In March that year the hatless and scruffy Percy was arrested by a police officer at Grand Central Station in New York as he was carrying a heavy metal lamp to give as a present to Antonia Sawyer. After he had established his good character at the police station, he gave the officer a free ticket to a forthcoming New York recital. Still a little suspicious the policeman turned up and was amazed to see his former quarry march on to the stage in white tie and tails. Later the same month Percy played twice under Henri Verbrugghen and the Minneapolis Symphony Orchestra; amongst the cellists of that orchestra were friends of his from European days, Engelbert Röntgen and Carlo Fischer.

After strenuous tours and the usual teaching sessions at Chicago, Percy sailed for Europe on the *Leviathan*. Arriving in Southampton on August 7, he anxiously scanned the wharf for Ella, who was due to meet him. As he did so he was spotted by the American Ambassador to Turkey: 'I did not like anything to take me away from mindpointing ((concentrating)) upon Helen [Ella], yet I did not dare risk slighting a highstanding state-thane ((official)). (There one has my whole timid, shillyshallying life in a nutshell).'[14]

Together at Ella's seaside hideaway 'Lilla Vrån' at Pevensey Bay they spent two blissful months. In the autumn of 1927 they went to Grez to visit the Deliuses, and then Percy travelled alone to Scandinavia. In Denmark he undertook his last Jutland folk-song expedition with Evald Tang Kristensen. Whilst at sea returning to England on October 2, Percy wrote to Ella proposing marriage. She accepted.

On his return to America in November 1927, Percy began writing an autobiographical sketch which he called 'The Love-Life of Helen and Paris'. It was an account of his meeting with Ella and the subsequent events. The outstanding point about the essay, however, is that it is chronologically the first full-length document which he attempted to write in 'Blue-eyed' or 'Nordic' English. It begins:

> The English stretches of this story are written (as well as I can) in 'Nordic English'. I have always believed in the wish-for-ableness of building up a mainly Anglo-Saxon-Scandinavian kind of English in which all but the most un-do-withoutable of the French-begotten, Latin-begotten & Greek-begotten words should be side-stepped & in which the bulk of the put-together words should be wilfully & owned-up-to-ly hot-house-grown out of Nordic word-seeds [. . .]. Tho I have thot keenly about the matter of Nordic English for many years in a hap-hazard way & have sketched many Nordic forms & word-chains yet this is the first time I have stick-to-it-ively driven myself to overset my thot-plan into deeds.

# 16

## 'It's like kicking out into thin air'

Grainger's concert season of 1927/28 took some new musical directions, and the general picture of his concert-giving was slowly changing. He was now beginning to shun the generally accepted centres of culture and instead was striking out for the smaller cities. He was trying to drop the label of star piano virtuoso. He began to feel at home with music clubs, chamber groups, school choirs, college bands and country music festivals and often received more enthusiastic playing from such musicians than from professional organizations. Indeed he believed and preached the idea that mere technical skill and excellence were barriers to fine performances. He sought recognition as a composer of worth more than anything else and one of the practical means of doing this was to reduce his fees for playing a 'war-horse' concerto if the orchestra also played some of his own pieces in the same concert. Success, however, did not follow automatically, and he was to find that that which came his way was sporadic and often lukewarm. So anxious did he become in later years to taste the fruits of his compositional activities that he would frequently travel thousands of miles to play a concerto in order to get some of his choruses performed, doing so with only his second-class hotel and travel expenses paid.

He later expressed the belief that as a creative artist he had dried up by his twenty-fifth year and, similarly, that by the end of the 1920s he had 'shot his bolt' as a public performer (two highly contentious theories). With the concert-goers who flocked to witness virtuosos walking the tightrope he was to lose much irretrievable ground, yet there was a small but devoted core of music lovers in whose estimation his stature never diminished. Despite the light he kept burning, the conviction of his own genius, the bitterness deepened and he would exclaim, 'I run around like a headless chicken. It's like kicking out into thin air while the rest of the world is dying of "good taste".'[1] The concert halls of Vienna, London and New York were being filled weekly by super-pianists of the Hofmann, Rachmaninov and Horowitz ilk, yet Grainger was not interested. His solo appearances at Carnegie Hall ceased in 1931 and his association with the Columbia Graphophone Company ended in the same year. He firmly believed, incidentally, that it was due to his bad piano playing that that record company had gone bankrupt during the years of depression.

Although Grainger had already tried out some of the settings of the Danish folk-songs collected with Tang Kristensen, he began to programme them more frequently during the 1927/28 season. *The Power of Love* and *Lord Peter's Stable-Boy* met with great success. In the same season he included in his programmes a setting for solo piano called *Jutish Medley,* a collective arrangement consisting of five Danish folk-songs. This piano setting contains some of the most effective writing Grainger ever made for the instrument. At different moments, strong wrists, alert rhythmic precision, a singing tone and an ability to bring out inner melodies are needed. The songs were then set for 'elastic' scoring and eventually formed the last movement of the *Suite on Danish Folk-Songs.*

On May 14, 1928 the Plainfield Symphony Orchestra provided the forces for a work of a completely different character. At this concert Grainger conducted the first performance of a work he had provisionally entitled 'Bridal Song'. He had begun the composition as soon as Ella had left New York; eventually entitled *To a Nordic Princess,* it was written with his own wedding in mind and is a wayward, wistful ramble, delicately scored for massive forces with pipe organ 'at will'.

His teaching sessions at Chicago continued as usual during 1928. Students were arriving from abroad especially to work with him. Vera Bradford and Marshall Sumner from Australia and Storm Bull, a Norwegian American, obtained scholarships and greatly valued the tuition which enabled them to enjoy successful careers later on as teachers and public performers. Grainger's fees were now $250 an hour and in the Summer Master Classes only the violinist Leopold Auer charged more. Each season began with a concert in which at least one work of Grainger's was conducted by the composer. He usually chose a work which would enable as many of his students as possible to participate. Fifteen to twenty pianos and a vast collection of tuned percussion instruments were not an uncommon sound.

As a rule Grainger would not tamper with a student's technique if it was well developed, but he would seek to improve the students' awareness of certain technical problems (and their general musical knowledge) by prescribing a certain work which would highlight that special difficulty. Whilst he always paid great attention to pedalling, he also had interesting ideas about laying emphasis on one particular note which formed part of a melody yet was in danger of being lost within a chord. His method was to use rigid wrists and fingers with the finger playing the particular note held in a position slightly lower than the rest. This meant that that note would be struck a fraction of a second earlier than the others and at the same time absorb more of the impact, thus giving it prominence. (As teaching material he would generally employ Bach's *Well-Tempered Klavier* — like Beethoven and Liszt before him.)

Whenever he had a piano piece to play which involved a glissando, he carefully prepared his index and second fingers with domestic sticking plasters. At one concert he forgot to take this precaution and when the dreaded passage came upon him he whipped out a handkerchief from his top pocket to protect his finger. He found this such a good method that for a short period he attached his handkerchief by elastic to the inside of his top pocket in order to ensure a rapid return after it had served its purpose. This Chico-Marx-like effect never failed to amuse his students and audience.

At the end of the 1928 Summer School he prepared to rush off to Hollywood, where he was to be married. He rolled up his mattress and Storm Bull helped him carry his luggage down to the front of the Chicago Musical College Building. Here he hailed a taxi into which he placed his goods and ordered the vehicle on to the La Salle Street Station about a mile and a half away. Percy and Storm ran alongside the taxi and arrived at about the same time.

The Hollywood Bowl was the scene for Grainger's wedding. He was engaged to conduct and play there for the evenings of August 7, 9, 10 and 11 and amongst the unusual works he performed were the *Nordic Symphony* Op. 21 by Howard Hanson, Bach's *Brandenburg Concerto No. 3* (which the programme notes claimed was the first performance in Los Angeles preserving the tonal balance of the original score), *Suite: In a Mission Garden* Op. 52 by his friend and pupil Fannie Dillon, *Pavane* Op. 50 by Fauré, and *A Negro Rhapsody* by Rubin Goldmark. For the rest, the concerts were orgiastic riots of Nordicness. Ella, who had arrived from Australia a few days earlier, did not have the slightest idea what or where the Hollywood Bowl was when Percy suggested the place as a location for their wedding. She gladly agreed and fully expected a cameo wedding amongst a handful of friends.

The wedding itself took place on the stage of the Hollywood Bowl at the end of the concert of August 9. Percy conducted an orchestra of 126 musicians—the largest seen in the Bowl to that date. The last item on the programme was *To a Nordic Princess*. After the Swedish Lutheran pastor the Reverend J. Herman Olsson had performed the ceremony, the couple, paying guests and audience (variously estimated between 15,000 and 23,000) were entertained by an a cappella choir led by John Smallman. The American Stars and Stripes and the British Union Jack bracketed the stage. Ella wore a rose-pink tulle gown and sported three camellias in her hair. Fred and Tonie Morse acted as best man and matron of honour and the screen star Ramon Novarro, who had witnessed the ceremony, posed with the couple for photographers. Most of the assembled throng responded to the occasion in a light-hearted mood, yet some felt it was an unseemly, vulgar affair. A simple wedding supper followed at the Hollywood Plaza Hotel. A few days after the wedding the couple headed for Glacier National Park on a honeymoon of climbing and walking. They were accompanied by their friends the Morses and another couple called Greenwood.

At the time of their wedding Ella knew nothing of her husband's sexual interests, and when she discovered she was horrified. But she loved him nonetheless, finding it 'hell to be with him and hell to be without him'. There were even periods when, because of his demands, she left him for a short time. She discovered that her burden involved shouldering much more than Rose's mantle. Only she knew the full measure of his joys and frustrations, his saintliness and cruelty and his genius and aberrations. In the early 1930s he composed a letter which had instructions on the envelope that it was to be opened only in the event of his or Ella's or their both being found dead covered in whip-lashes. It explained that no blame should be placed on either since flagellation was for him the greatest pleasure and the highest expression of his love.

For the rest of the year Grainger undertook no public engagements. During December and January the newly wedded couple spent one month at a vegetarian sanatorium in Battle Creek, after which they left for Sweden to stay with Ella's relatives in Segeltorp. Using Sweden as a base Percy and Ella made tours of Iceland, Norway, Finland and Denmark. In Denmark they stayed with Herman and Alfhild Sandby. Grainger spent most of his time transcribing the cylinders of folk-songs which had been deposited with the Royal Copenhagen Library after Tang Kristensen's death. In Sweden he made the acquaintance of Hugo Alfvén and attended a concert devoted to his music. In Oslo he tried to meet the Norwegian composer Sparre Olsen, whose work *Six Old Rural Songs from Lom* he had purchased locally. The two composers were unable to meet, but Grainger wrote to Olsen for permission to make an English translation of one of the songs, *Mountain Norway,* because he wanted to perform it with choirs in America. The translation was made some years later and this was the beginning of Grainger's championship of Olsen's music.

Two months of the summer of 1929, however, were spent in England at Ella's home in Pevensey Bay. In June he went to London to hear Beecham with Beatrice and May Harrison rehearsing the Delius concerto for violin and cello. Shortly after this he took Ella to Grez, where they stayed for ten days with the Deliuses. Balfour Gardiner was also there. Eric Fenby had recently entered Delius's life and Grainger noticed that Delius's attitude to himself and Balfour Gardiner had changed. In a letter to Eric Fenby on December 6, 1936 about that first meeting, Grainger wrote:

It was the kinder of you to be kind to me in yr book because I behaved badly the summer you met me — partly because I was so anxious to rescore my Hill Song No. 2 & thus did not concentrate on D as I used to. But then, I saw there was no need to, since he had *you*. Before you came to Grez Fred always behaved nicely to me & Balfour. But with you there he behaved abominably. And I was *so delighted* to see it. It showed *how much he valued yr devotion & help*. His behaviour to B. & me clearly said: 'You boys could only give me 2 days or 10 days at a time. Now I have a young friend who gives me *all* his time. To Hell with you!' That *bragging* attitude showed me that he was still young & happy in his mind.

Grainger's biggest undertaking in England was to be present at a festival in Harrogate which he planned and organized with the help of Basil Cameron. The festival took place on July 24, 25 and 26 and the conductors were Roger Quilter, Frederic Austin, Cyril Scott, Norman O'Neill and Cameron. The four composers conducted their own music whilst Cameron took charge of other works. The works of Grainger conducted by Cameron were *Jutish Medley* (listed as 'Jutish Melody'), *Hill-Song Number 2, Spoon River* and the *Rhapsody for Cello and Chamber Orchestra: Youthful Rapture*. The soloist in *Youthful Rapture* was Beatrice Harrison, who a few months later recorded this strange, rambling little piece under Dr Malcolm Sargent. On the day of the performance of *Hill-Song Number 2* (July 25) Percy received an anonymous postcard addressed to 'Herr Percy Grainger' from someone whose patriotic fanaticism had not allowed him to forget the Australian's departure from England at the outbreak of the Great War. The writer referred to him as a 'white-livered pro-German' and suggested that he return to America at once.[2] Grainger was terrified and immediately went to Roger Quilter to ask him if he would sit next to him in his box that evening. But Percy's reluctance to tell him the reason puzzled Quilter and because of what he felt were obligations to friends he refused to comply with his request. Instead, Percy sat with Ella and the evening passed without incident.

By the autumn of 1929 Grainger had returned to America and once more plunged into a concert season which kept him fully occupied until June the following year when he began his annual teaching period in Chicago. During the 1929/30 season he participated in a concert with Beatrice Harrison and the Boston Chamber Orchestra at the Martin Beck Theatre in New York. Beatrice Harrison brought news that Balfour Gardiner had finally given up composing. The Englishman's grand piano had fallen through the floor of his music study into the room below and this had decided him to terminate his creative activities once and for all!

Ella was by now helping her husband at his concerts. As well as lending a hand in multi-piano performances, she taught herself to play various members of the tuneful percussion family so favoured by Percy in his compositions. She travelled with him on most of his tours and he found in her an ideal companion able to accommodate herself to most of his daily needs. She was with him in 1930 and 1931 when he visited Delius in France. Whilst at Grez in 1931 Grainger tried to get his friend's permission to set a selection of various Delius themes for violin and piano and at first Delius seemed agreeable to the idea. The following morning, however, he said, 'I have consistently kept myself aloof from the business side of music. I have never written to please the public. I have never done anything to make my music practical or to make it sell. And I think I had better stick to that policy to the end.'[3]

In November of 1931 Grainger received offers of senior teaching posts for the scholastic year 1932/3 at both Seattle and New York Universities. Eventually he accepted the offer from New York to be head of the Music Department there. (It was the music critic Richard Aldrich who was largely responsible for urging the authorities at New York University to make the offer in the first place.) He was glad of the position as it promised a stable income at a time when the concert situation was very uncertain owing to the Depression. On January 28, 1932 he wrote to Herman Sandby: 'Concert conditions here are quite mad, at present. People are panic-stricken & local managers do not keep to their contracts & think nothing of cancelling concerts at the last moment! [. . .] I have accepted the New York post (Sept 1932-June 1933) at $5000, to lecture on music & teach Advanced Composition 2 days a week.'

The year 1932 was an important one in Grainger's life in that it opened up to him a whole new world of music which was to become very significant in his compositional activities. The previous year he had visited the Haslemere Festival in England organized by the redoubtable Arnold Dolmetsch. Grainger already knew a considerable body of pre-Bach music and, at the other end of the spectrum, always kept abreast of new developments. He felt that 'progress' was an irrelevant concept where art was concerned. In a letter to the Reverend Frederick Hensley Belden about the composer Howard Hanson dated January 29 of that year, he wrote: 'I cannot see that period matters in art. Art is not a matter of "modern" or "old fashioned", it is a matter of expressing individual *feelings*. If we like those feelings, good. If not, it cannot be helped. I love some modern composers, dislike others. I consider Howard Hanson a very wonderful composer.'

In 1932 Dom Anselm Hughes, an English monk from the Anglican Benedictine community at Nashdom Abbey, Buckinghamshire, undertook a lecture tour of the United States and Canada. He was one of the world's leading authorities on English mediaeval music and was at that time secretary of the Plainsong & Mediaeval Music Society. His lectures and tours attracted great attention on the American continent. Professor Gustave Reese, the eminent American musicologist, who was then lecturer on mediaeval and renaissance music at the College of Fine Arts, New York University, showed Grainger some of the publications he had obtained from Dom Anselm Hughes. Grainger also heard some of the records made by the Nashdom monks, after which he immediately wrote to Hughes and became a life member of the society. He always visited Nashdom when he was in England, and when Hughes was in America on subsequent lecture tours he made a point of travelling to see Grainger in White Plains. The common interest of music enabled the wild Australian atheist and the urbane English Christian to establish a profound friend-ship. Grainger would sometimes give private piano recitals to the monks at Nashdom and on a subsequent trip to England in November 1936 addressed the general meeting of the Plainsong & Mediaeval Music Society at King's Weigh House Church on 'The old music from the stand-point of the modern composer'. The outcome of their friendship was a decision for Hughes to edit and Grainger to arrange a collection of six-teen items of early music, twelve of which were eventually published under the generic title of *English Gothic Music*. The idea was to make mediaeval music accessible to English and American choirs and chamber groups. Grainger worked slowly at the arrangements, conscious that an attempt to popularize a difficult music must not involve its cheapening, and the task occupied him on and off for the remainder of his life. It was his desire to rehearse each arrangement with as many different vocal and instrumental combinations as possible, and this doubtless slowed down his work considerably.

During a stay in Scandinavia in the summer of 1932 Percy and Ella hatched the idea of establishing a museum in Australia. His initial efforts in this direction took the form of writing to friends asking them if they would return any of his own or his mother's letters which they had kept. A few complied with his idea, some sent copies and others found the sug-gestion an outrage. Two copies of each document were made and de-posited in the twin fire-proof rooms he had constructed in the basement at White Plains. Manuscripts and odd musical instruments of all kinds were collected by Grainger with his museum in mind. Items which had no connection whatsoever with his own musical development were ear-marked for inclusion in this strange heterogeneous treasure house, and he bought up paintings by Rupert Bunny, Ernest Thesiger, Jacques-Émile Blanche, Jelka Delius and Tom Roberts as well as letters written before he was born by such men as Hans Christian Andersen and Tchai-kovsky; he also obtained a musical sketch by Liszt. The idea of a man creating a museum to himself during his own lifetime may seem odd and Grainger's has been described as a monument to his own vanity. Certain-ly Grainger was convinced of his own genius, but the purpose of the museum was never one of self-glorification. What he wanted to do was make available to those who were sufficiently interested as much docu-mentary, pictorial and other evidence as possible of the artistic and human influences of parents, relatives and friends which help to form any one creative human being. In his own case the Nordic and the maternal sways were strongly represented in his collection of artefacts.

Grainger returned to America at the end of the summer of 1932 and began work at New York University. He took his students through an extraordinarily wide range of new and ancient music and with the aid of recorded illustrations introduced them to a large body of the native musics of Africa, Asia and the South Sea Islands. In his lectures on composition he first put his own theories to the test. He began to talk about Free Music for the first time, gently hinting that his own pioneering experiments in irregular rhythms and complex harmony around the turn of the century had led, via Cyril Scott's piano sonata, to the creations of Schönberg, Hindemith and Stravinsky.

At one lecture Duke Ellington and his entire band were invited to illustrate some of Grainger's theories. It would seem that his lectures up to that point had not been especially well attended yet his lecture with Ellington was filled to overflow and extra-mural students were on the point of breaking down the doors to enter. To open the lecture Grainger jumped on to the stage and said, 'The three greatest composers who ever lived are Bach, Delius and Duke Ellington. Unfortunately Bach is dead, Delius is very ill but we are happy to have with us today The Duke.'

Grainger had expressed a great liking for the sophisticated jazz produced by such men as Paul Whiteman, Ben Pollack and Duke Ellington and this lecture enabled him to get to know one of the greatest jazzmen of all time. He once told Ellington that his jazz music bore striking harmonic resemblances to the music of Frederick Delius. This puzzled Ellington greatly because he had never heard Delius's name, let alone his music. Not being a man of narrow culture, the band leader bought all the available records of Delius and had many of the English Columbia records by Beecham imported. He listened to them all with intense interest. Although this made him a lifelong lover of the music of Delius, it did not convince him of any similarity such as Grainger had suggested.

In later years Grainger was to look back on his days at the university with a sense of disappointment. He felt out of place in the university atmosphere and detected that some of his students were at his lectures merely to keep up their attendance figures. There was, however, a small group of students who took him seriously and placed a high value on his advice and ideas. Two of this group, Bernard Herrmann and Morton Gould, attended his advanced composition and orchestration classes. They treated him more as a friend than as a representative of the stuffy academic establishment. Grainger did not place orchestration examples before them; instead he allowed them to choose their own pieces and gave them advice where and when needed. Herrmann, for instance, decided to orchestrate MacDowell's 'Celtic' Sonata and felt the need to employ the sonorities of a tenor tuba. The Australian knew little of this unusual piece of plumbing, so, together, they familiarized themselves with the instrument and found suitable moments to include it.

Grainger stayed on for the Summer Session of New York University's School of Education and on August 16, 1933 terminated his connection with that institution. He never returned to any academic establishment during the remainder of his life, though the offers continued to flow in. He also rejected the offers of honorary doctorates of music from a number of American universities. There can be little doubt that his experiences at New York University soured his feelings for academic institutions and it is easy to see why some of his students and fellow lecturers failed to take him seriously. His lectures (of which some notes still survive) and his published articles on musical history, theory and philosophy are based on a strange collection of premises and his arguments are sometimes developed with a tortuous logic understood only by himself. Few of his theories, moreover, departed very far from the implied or stated idea of the superiority of that music produced by blue-eyed, fair-haired composers. It was one of the great tragedies of his life — a tragedy caused solely by his mother — that though he was able to assimilate a profound knowledge of a truly phenomenal range of subjects, he was sometimes unable to organize or sift the constituents of this knowledge. His mind was teeming with ideas; many contained the germ of genius (see, for example, his essays on Elastic Scoring and Free Music), yet a few would be so crass and mulishly stupid as to make his friends and colleagues want to run and hide with embarrassment (for example, his article 'Melody versus Rhythm'). A few friends, such as Alfhild Sandby and Balfour Gardiner, took none of his nonsense and confronted him boldly whenever he expounded one of his more eccentric ideas. But the general reaction to Grainger's ideas was one that tended to reinforce his isolation. This tragedy is rooted in two closely connected origins; Grainger's uncritical and passive acceptance of his mother's views of life and his lack of any kind of formal education. Although he rarely diluted or changed his ideas, he sometimes harboured feelings of inferiority and insecurity about his own abnormal creativity, a fact which perhaps partly explains why he remained aloof from the mainstreams of so many of the fields he touched upon during his active career.

Around this period Grainger established distant links with Bartók. Grainger and Bartók had many things in common — both had a love and scientific reverence for folk-music, both were musical innovators and brilliant pianists. Each revered the music of Bach and delighted in writing complex, many-stranded textures as a result, and both composers' natural styles of melodic invention were strongly influenced by folk idioms. In September and October 1933, an American magazine called *Music News* published an article by Grainger entitled 'Melody versus Rhythm'. Beginning with one of those frustrating false alternatives he loved to toy with, he entertains and educates us by wandering through a

mass of inconsistencies, non sequiturs and Graingeresque logic to end in
a mire of barely digestible conclusions. Despite all this, however, one can
never deny the spectacularly broad sweep of highly individualistic intellect and knowledge upon which he drew for such articles. His main thesis
is that melody, which, in its purest form, attempts to follow the extended
utterances of human voice and thought, is that part of music which leads
us towards 'dreaminess, lovingness and compassionateness', whereas
rhythm is that aspect of music which enslaves us and appeals to the lower
aspects of our natures. He cites Arthur Fickenscher of the University of
Virginia, and his invention of a harmonium (the Polytone) capable of
five pitch divisions to the half-tone and quintet *From the 7th Realm* for
piano and strings which makes use of microtonality as pointers towards a
future of melody in music free of arbitrary scales and modes. Bartók was
shown this article by Storm Bull, one of Grainger's best pupils and now
with Bartók at the Liszt Academy in Budapest, and he was encouraged to
pen a reply. Published in the columns of the same magazine in January
1934, it was a short and simple refutation of Grainger's basic idea and
suggested that rhythm and melody never were nor ought to be in conflict
and that both had their parts to play in ancient, primitive and modern
music.

At the end of August 1933 Percy and Ella left America for a short stay
with Alfhild and Herman Sandby in Denmark. The holiday resulted,
however, in a quarrel which caused Herman and Alfhild to leave their
own home with Percy and Ella still there. Percy's feelings of democracy
had been offended, it seems, when Alfhild had suggested that she ought
to employ a home help whilst she had Ella and Percy as guests. Percy,
who at every stage in his life had needed a maid in his home for one
reason or another, had become enraged at Alfhild's suggestion. Alfhild,
not surprisingly, was unable to tolerate what she felt was hypocrisy, so
she left, taking her husband with her. But still Alfhild did not abandon
Percy completely. Doubtless she acknowledged that though a mixture of
extremes, he embodied many fine points alongside his strange shortcomings.

On September 23 Percy and Ella boarded the four-masted Aaland
brig *L'Avenir,* which took them on a 110-day trip between Copenhagen
and Perth in Western Australia. During the voyage on the 400-ton ship
Percy kept fit by involving himself in crew tasks and scrambling up and
down the rigging to the crow's nest. His literary recreation was the
composition of his second autobiographical essay, the 'Aldridge-
Grainger-Ström Saga'. He completed 130 pages of this article which
covered the period of his childhood in Melbourne. As with all his autobiographical sketches, it remained unfinished and is written in a fragmentary and haphazard fashion.

After the sea voyage, during which they had made only one port of call
at Tristan da Cunha, Grainger embarked on a memorable series of 56

concerts and recitals and 158 broadcast lecture-recitals in the main cities and towns of Australia and New Zealand. He stayed in Australasia for about two years with a short break during the winter of 1934/5 for a tour of the west coast of the United States and Canada. Most of his earnings were devoted to the building of the Grainger Museum in the grounds of Melbourne University. Whenever possible he would arrive at 6 a.m. to lend a hand with the bricklaying. During the early part of 1935 his building plans began to suffer from a lack of money which was not being made up by the income from his concerts. When he heard of this, Balfour Gardiner immediately placed £1,000 at Grainger's disposal in a London bank. Without this gift, he would not have been able to complete the building so soon.

Although an official opening ceremony took place in 1939, members of the general public were never admitted during his lifetime. The museum is often thought to have been Grainger's most spectacular mistake. While putting such a large and fascinating collection of documents and artefacts on display was without question a fine idea, the practical tasks of shipping the material to Australia and organizing the collection for display presented him at times with insurmountable obstacles. Although it would have been so much cheaper and less time-consuming to have erected his museum somewhere in America, it was his patriotism that forced his decision to build it in Melbourne. There is also much evidence to show that at times he planned to return to live in Australia towards the end of his life. This was prevented by increasing commitments in America and a fear that he would lose the royalties from American performances of his works were he not resident in that country. With the devaluation of money over the years the endowment he provided for the museum became insufficient to stave off increased costs of building maintenance, and silverfish, leaking roofs and official apathy began to gain the upper hand. As this book is being written a gigantic rescue operation is in progress to realize the enormous historical value of the collection.

The design of the building is odd, to say the least. In plan it looks like half a wheel with four spokes. The main source of light for the interior comes via glass blocks built into the masonry high up by the ceiling. This has doubtless contributed towards the oft-attached description of the architectural style as being 'London County Council 1930s lavatorial'. On more than one occasion people have arrived at the museum to find that some joker has daubed on the front of the building in white paint the words 'gentlemen' and 'ladies' with the appropriate arrows. A debt of gratitude is due to the graffiti-mongers of Melbourne that their good breeding and innate good taste have prevented them from writing merely 'men' and 'women'.

One of the main features of the museum was to be a display of first editions of his music. Eventually Grainger added a legend to this display — a lament for the fact that his best works had remained unplayed:

> I do not mind being 'found wanting', as long as I am 'weighed in the
> balance' first. But I (in common with most composers) do not like to
> be condemned unheard. And the non-performance of my serious
> compositions is the more insulting in view of the fact that several of
> my pieces are said to be 'known wherever music is made' [. . .]. This
> long display of the first editions of my published compositions may
> seem, to the thoughtless, a proof of my 'success' as a composer; in
> reality it marks the measure of my artistic defeat. The bulk of these
> works are not 'alive' — for music that is not heard is not alive, and the
> bulk of my music is never heard [. . .] where musical progress and
> compositional experiments are discussed my name is never mentioned.
> Can a more complete aesthetic failure be imagined? Not by me.

The broadcasts he gave and the articles he wrote sometimes raised a
fury of opposition. He dared to suggest that Mozart, Haydn and Beethoven were perhaps not such good composers after all, and he used his
fame to force his audiences to listen to a vast range of music from China
to Africa and from the thirteenth century to the contemporary music of
his friends. A synopsis of the lectures delivered over the air by the Australian Broadcasting Commission was published, entitled *Music—A
Commonsense View of all Types*. The breadth of his vision was remarkable; certainly Australia had never experienced anything like it, and perhaps no one in any country had delivered such a series of lecture-recitals
since the historic recitals of Anton Rubinstein in the 1860s and 70s.
The Australian lectures were largely based on those he had given at New
York University. Perhaps the most extraordinary piece of music he
demonstrated was a short sampling of his Free Music for four Theremins
or strings. The music was written on graph paper and in this instance was
performed by four strings under the direction of the violinist Percy Code.
For another broadcast he persuaded the ABC to squeeze twenty 'tuneful'
percussionists (including pianists) into its Sydney studio to demonstrate
some of the necessary musical examples.

At a morning rehearsal in Sydney Town Hall he gave a particularly
athletic performance of the Grieg concerto. During the orchestral tutti of
the first movement just before the cadenza he jumped down from the
platform, ran to the back of the hall, where he touched the rear door,
ran back again and in one bound was at the keyboard ready for the
cadenza. He did this probably to limber up or check the acoustics.
Whilst in Sydney he went to see the brilliant Australian artist Norman
Lindsay, whose fleshy, Bacchanalian paintings he had always admired.
The two men had much in common. Both were vigorously Australian
and opposed to the Australian brand of puritanism known as
'wowserism'. They were both passionate theorizers and philosophizers

and held a remarkable collection of racial ideas. But, unlike Grainger, Lindsay had arrived at his ideas largely as the result of a rejection of his mother's attitudes.

In Adelaide on July 23, 1934 Grainger organized a chamber music recital in memory of Frederick Delius, whose death thirteen days earlier had been a crushing blow to him. He performed the Delius Sonata for Cello and Piano with Harold Parsons (the director of the Elder Conservatorium) and the Sonata for Violin and Piano with Peter Bornstein. Other works included four songs by Grieg, the *Fantasy for Four Strings No. 4 in C minor* by Purcell, the *Fantasy for Five Strings No. 1 in D major* by John Jenkins, a Delius string quartet and Delius's *Dance Rhapsody* arranged for two pianos by Grainger. It was a touching last tribute to the man he had loved so much.

Despite the drain on his financial resources and the massive overwork to which he was subjecting himself, he was happy to be with his relatives and friends. He found he was still treated very much as the returning hero. The choirs and orchestras, which had been badly hit by decreased membership and finances because of the Depression, were only too happy to perform his works when he made a gift of the music to their libraries. At eight universities and colleges he established what he called 'Rose Grainger Libraries' in memory of his mother. This involved the donation of a large quantity of his own music and that of his friends.

His new works were well received wherever they were performed. A particular favourite with the Australian audiences was his *Tribute to Foster*, an adaptation of Stephen Foster's *Camptown Races* for chorus and orchestra in which use is made of men's voices behind the platform, musical glasses and a bowed metal marimba. As a child the melodies and words of Stephen Foster had made a deep impression on him, and it will be remembered that his mother had often sung him to sleep with *Camptown Races*. It then becomes understandable why the extended middle section of Grainger's setting is cast in the form of a lullaby in the minor key. The composer adds several verses of his own delightful words which end with: 'When I was a tot on me mammy's knee / She sung dat race track song to me, / Sung it to me sweet as a lullaby. / Hear dat song till de day I die!' The work fades into a diminuendo of side drum and 'Doo-dahs' and leaves a haunting memory.

By the end of 1935 Percy and Ella were back at White Plains and Percy immediately began preparing for a heavy concert season which was to last until April the following year. At this stage in his life his fees usually ran between $250 and $500 a concert and a broadcast concert would earn him as much as $1,000. His performing rights cheque for 1936 was $1,400 (rising to $8,000 in 1938) and *Country Gardens* continued to break sales records on both sides of the Atlantic. Ella constantly pressed him to quit the concert platform and he felt a deep urge to do so himself, but as always he spent his money very quickly—mostly on other people — and his slavery to the keyboard instrument he claimed to loathe so much was never to be broken completely. He continued to travel second class and sleep upright in day coaches.

Between May and December of 1936 Percy and Ella were in Europe and most of that time was spent at Pevensey Bay. For a short period they were hosts at 'Lilla Vrån' to Sparre Olsen and his wife. Olsen's recollections of that summer are touchingly recorded in a short memoir he wrote of Percy which was published in 1963. During that period in England, Percy attended many interesting concerts including the first performance at Covent Garden of Roger Quilter's light opera *Julia*, a suite for chamber orchestra by Herman Sandby at the old Grotrian Hall in London, Cyril Scott's *Ode to Great Men* and Delius's *A Mass of Life* at the Norwich Festival and a performance of his own *To a Nordic Princess* in Bournemouth. He also managed to fit in a trip to Sweden, Finland and France, a six-day walking tour of the Scottish Highlands and the complete Haslemere Festival organized by Carl Dolmetsch. A special event was his first BBC broadcast, when he shared the conducting of some of his works with Leslie Woodgate (Roger Quilter's former secretary). The works performed included *The Merry Wedding, Tribute to Foster, Love Verses from 'The Song of Solomon'* and *Marching Song of Democracy*.

The singer called upon to perform the solo part in *Love Verses from 'The Song of Solomon'* was drawn from the ranks of the BBC Chorus: the £6-a-week vocalist was the tenor Peter Pears. For his efforts Pears received an unsolicited autographed photograph from the Australian composer. Twenty-one years later Grainger was given a record of Peter Pears singing the Australian's arrangement of *Six Dukes went Afishin'*. He loved this record, playing it constantly; he wrote of Pears's singing: 'He has the sweetest voice which grows falsetto-ish as he rises into the higher notes, which is much more lovable than the Caruso method of forcing a mad-bull-type-of-tone into what Stokowski called "Purdah".'[4]

Grainger's heart was now firmly set on the fuller realization of his Free Music. In a letter to Everard Feilding around this time he wrote:

> In spite of a 1000 disappointments (& proofs of my own artistic feebleness) I still have a hardly sane belief in my own artistic greatness & a growing belief in the practicability & inevitableness of all the theories and plans I have ever held & I still believe that I shall bring my 'free music' (combining all the liberations effected harmonically by Schönberg, intervallically by Fickenscher & others and rhythmically by myself) to a triumphant end. I believe that free music will be more soulrevealing, more melodious, more truly tender & lovely than any music yet [. . .]. I am not very fond of my own music. It is seldom the kind of music I like. Most of it is only (like Mock Morris) a study in scoring, or some other technical preparation for the Free Music I've

been hearing in my head since a young boy & which only now I am technically equipped to embark upon [. . .]. My chief thought is always this! that the first 'free music' (towards which the whole path of all music always has been headed) shall be written by an Australian & the thought that Australian musical life can be freed from the absurdities, falsenesses, ignorance & good-for-nothingness that plagues European & American musical life.[5]

He was working towards what has been described by some as his only true claim to prophetic genius and by others as his ultimate folly. In following his dreams he would encounter many setbacks, as he foresaw in a letter of this period to Alfhild Sandby: 'You write of yr "long fight for recognition". There *is* no recognition for talent & genius. It is no good fighting for it, it will never come. Far better to turn round & *attack the world,* in bitterness, fury, & pride, as I hope to do.'[6]

During his periods of rest at Pevensey Bay he would receive visits from his old friends. Of a visit from Balfour Gardiner, he once wrote:

[. . .] when Balfour Gardiner and I sat in the bracken around Hurstmonceux castle (near Pevensey) & I told him of how my Free Tonery would (I hoped) tally the movements of clouds, water, trees, birds, fishes, & so on, he said: 'Yes. Keep to those clouds & trees & things. They will give you much less anguish than dealing with people'. And that takes my thoughts back to when Cyril Scott & I were staying with Balfour at Moody's Down, Barton Stacey (Hants?) around 1902 or 1903, when I was mulling over my first sketches for the Marching Song of Democracy. I asked Cyril and Balfour if they would climb a rise or knoll a few 100 feet away & sing in fifths the theme that starts at bar 105 of the finished work. They kindly did so & it sounded so wild, fresh & pure to hear the 'open-fifths' ringing out between the trees (somewhat magic-ed by the slight far-off-ness) [. . .]. That is what is so nice about young people; they are willing to do such things. Would they do it today? Maybe.[7]

Percy's indiscretions were monumental. On his return trip to New York during December 1936 he read Eric Fenby's *Delius as I knew him.* On December 6 he sent to Fenby what was mainly a charming and indeed touching letter about Delius and the book, yet in the middle of it he wrote:

Are you aware that Delius was one-fourth Jew? On the sailing boat on which we sailed to Australia (110 days) was (quite accidentally) a niece of Delius, a Miss Krönig—a straight-forward & utterly reliable middleaged woman from Manchester, & kinswoman on his Christian side. She said there was no doubt at all that D's mother was $\frac{1}{2}$-Jewish.

This (I think) explains his *hatred* of Christ [. . .] I think that also explains (in part) his dislike of markedly Christian composers such as Palestrina & Sibelius & Bach (at times, not always) & his *marked* liking for so many Jewish composers: Mendelssohn, Albeniz, Ravel, Bizet, etc. as yr book shows.

As early as 1924 he had suggested to Jelka that her husband was partly Jewish, but both she and Frederick utterly rejected the idea. He was so obsessed with this notion that he once tried to check Delius's ancestry for himself at Somerset House in London. His searches were fruitless.

On his return to White Plains in December 1936 he found a letter awaiting him from the American Band Masters' Association offering him a commission to write two pieces for band for their annual Grand Concert and Convention at Milwaukee in March 1937. He decided to make a new arrangement for band of *Lads of Wamphray* and compile a suite for band of five arrangements of Lincolnshire folk-songs which he entitled *Lincolnshire Posy*. The latter work is arguably his masterpiece and three of the movements were composed from scratch in the remarkably short time of four days. After frenzied work writing out all the band parts without a score (there was not time for both) he successfully rehearsed the entire work with the band of the Ernest Williams School of Music in Brooklyn and then raced off to Milwaukee. To his great disappointment, however, the entire concert was a fiasco. The bandsmen found the irregular and 'free' rhythms of two of the movements so difficult that these pieces had to be dropped from the final concert. Grainger remarked later that 'they were keener on their beer than on their music'.[8] Fortunately the work was performed three months later by the Goldman Band with complete success and this worthy bunch of musicians restored his faith in its practicality.

At times the bitterness so evident in Grainger's letters gave way to a mood of gentle nostalgia tinged with pessimism, especially when he was writing to his old Frankfurt friends. In a letter sent to Herman Sandby on December 9, 1937 he wrote:

The English have drawn together their empire thru hardness, greed, crime, & other sins. I rue such wickedness & would be glad to see our Empire (& all empires) fall apart & leave all races free and safe. Yet there is studiousness, gentleness, wit, spiritualness in the English that I love. They have some kinds of softness, yieldingness that belong to them alone — my old folk-singers, for instance, & the soft, free, gentle songs they sang. But the English are a mixed-blooded race, with different racial qualities inharmoniously crossed & at feud with each other. I could willingly see the English lose to the Scandinavians, or to any gentler race. But not to the swinish Germans. And my life was early dedicated to a war in music [. . .] though nobody noticed then, or today. For me the war (my war against Germany in music) began 14 years before 1914 [. . .] I had a hard time. And a still harder time when I lost my mother. I had done many hard things in the hopes *of not failing her.* Yet it seems I failed her so much that she had to leave this life [. . .]. But my duties (my war) still keep me in these hard lands, when (for me) life is but a nightmare, & no real life at all. There is so much that I admire in the English speaking life, but next to nothing *I enjoy.*

Grainger had hoped to travel to England in late September 1937, but he contracted pleurisy shortly before the date of departure and the entire trip was cancelled. He was always able to find activities to occupy his mind and instead of travelling he began to catalogue the material he wanted to send to the museum in Australia. During November he travelled to Seattle, where Basil Cameron had recently taken over the conductorship of the symphony orchestra. Cameron conducted a performance of Cyril Scott's *Festival Overture,* which the Australian immediately hailed as a work of genius.

In 1937 Grainger also began to work each summer at the National Music Camp at Interlochen, Michigan. Although he taught at Interlochen for eight consecutive summers, the relationship with that institution was not entirely a happy one. The response he obtained from the youngsters was far below average. He was unable to sway them from their deeply ingrained conventional musical attitudes. He eventually lost respect for the staff and patience with the students and quit after the summer of 1944.

The connection nevertheless had some use, for it enabled him to obtain a commission for Storm Bull to prepare two works for the camp of 1938. Storm had no previous experience of composing for symphonic band, so when it was decided that he would arrange a number of the Norwegian folk-tunes from Grieg's Op. 66, Grainger asked Glenn Cliff Bainum, the Director of Bands at Northwestern University, to have Bull's experiments tried out with his band. Bull took one of the Norwegian tunes, arranged it in about twenty different ways and had them all read through by the band. In addition to this, Grainger made many helpful suggestions concerning the orchestration of the Grieg pieces. When the works were performed the following year Bull stayed in the Graingers' chalet at Interlochen, later recalling that Percy drank large quantities of tomato and orange juice because he felt convinced (as he often did) that he was coming down with scurvy.

On January 6, 1938 Grainger was commanded to perform for the third time at the White House (the second occasion had been before President Calvin Coolidge). President and Mrs Roosevelt's invitation to dine before the recital was politely declined because he was unable to perform if he felt relaxed. (One practical method he employed to attain a state of physical excitement was to spend several minutes in a sitting position vigorously patting his knees with the flat of his hands.) The programme was shared with Elisabeth Schumann, who offered a selection of lieder by Mozart, Schubert, Langstroth and Richard Strauss. Grainger included David Guion's arrangement of the cowboy breakdown *Turkey in the Straw*, an eighteenth-century English hunting song called *The Hunter in His Career* arranged by himself, and the slow section ('Lullaby') from *Tribute to Foster*.

In 1938 Grainger's friend the composer Henry Cowell was sentenced to fifteen years' gaol on a morals charge. He responded quickly by writing to Cowell and visiting him in San Quentin as often as possible. Whilst Cowell engaged in the prison musical activities, Grainger and the band conductor Richard Franko Goldman sent him books and musical manuscripts and undertook to programme his music on a grand scale so that their imprisoned friend could benefit on his release from the accrued royalties. His release came sooner than anyone had initially expected, for as a direct result of Grainger's petitions to the legal authorities the American composer was paroled to him at White Plains in the spring of 1940. Grainger gave him a small salary and full board and one of Cowell's first tasks was to catalogue the English folk-song cylinders in preparation for their transfer to the Library of Congress.

Four months of 1938 were spent in Melbourne, where the building of his museum was completed. Grainger usually worked between 5 a.m. and beyond midnight of the following day. He needed little sleep and thrived on hard work. The museum was officially opened on December 10 by Professor W. A. Laver, who delivered an address to the assembled throng of dignitaries and friends. Amongst two hundred and fifty guests were Sir James Barrett, the Chancellor of Melbourne University and Miss Adelaide Burkitt, Grainger's old piano teacher. Grainger also made a speech in which he mentioned that it had been Ella's idea that he should build the museum in Melbourne; with this said he kissed Adelaide Burkitt and formally handed the building over to Melbourne University. After the ceremony the museum was promptly closed and Grainger returned to America.

In the winter of 1938/9 Percy stepped off a train in Wisconsin, where he was due to perform that evening. It was snowing hard and Percy wore his usual attire of white duck trousers, boots and a dark double-breasted jacket from which he had torn the lining. Of course he wore no hat or coat, but he made one concession to the inclement weather by unfurling a scruffy umbrella. A day or so earlier there had been a bank robbery in a neighbouring town and as a consequence of this Percy was picked up yet again by the police for questioning. When asked why he had taken so little protection against the weather, he replied indignantly, 'I do not eat meat, I do not smoke, and I do not drink, and therefore, I do not feel the cold.'[9] The police soon realized they had bitten off more than they could chew and he was released with all haste.

On another occasion during his tours of the 1938/9 season he performed with the South Bend Symphony Orchestra and their Australian-born conductor Edwyn Hames, and the consequences of this association were typical of what he was trying to do in his concert activities. His performance on April 28, 1939 of Tchaikovsky's First Piano Concerto was a considerable success and established for him an appreciative following in that city. On his return in January 1941 he used his localized popularity to negotiate a concert where he offered his services at a substantially reduced fee in return for programming music by English-speaking composers. The concert contained Cyril Scott's *Festival Overture*, Henry Cowell's *Ancient Desert Drone* and John Powell's *Natchez on the Hill*, as well as four of his own larger orchestral works. The local press were bitterly disappointed with the amount of modern music performed. This kind of reaction tended to amuse Grainger and when Edwyn Hames sent him some of the letters about the concert cut from local newspapers he replied by saying: 'When music can cause as much controversy as an athletic contest, music is in a pretty healthy state.'[10]

Early in 1939 he received a letter from Ella's niece, to whom the ownership of the Pevensey Bay cottage had been transferred some time earlier. She had received a letter from the British authorities asking what disposition they could make of the cottage in the event of war. Percy saw immediately that with preparations for war in hand he needed to collect all his belongings from England and bid farewell to his European friends. This mood directly prompted one of his most remarkable compositions, the *Duke of Marlborough* Fanfare. The stark beauty of the theme, initially stated on the horns, is gradually augmented with sharp harmonies and varied rhythmic treatments during its first and only restatement. This vivid and disturbing work carries the subtitle 'British War Mood Grows'.

In May Percy and Ella headed for Scandinavia, where they stayed with Ella's relatives in Sweden. In June they went to Bergen, where they collected Sparre Olsen and his wife for a walking trip to Aalvik, Roldal, Rauland and Heddal. Percy heard several Hardanger fiddlers and played the organs in some of the ancient churches they came across. After a return trip to Sweden and a further visit to Finland Percy and Ella returned to Oslo, where Percy began another walking trip taking the same route through the Norwegian countryside, this time with Balfour Gardiner. He felt that he could not possibly see anything more beautiful than Seljord and wanted to stay there always. After the second Norwegian trip he and Ella travelled to England to prepare the material which needed to be sent from Pevensey Bay to White Plains. He left Europe in August 1939 with a heavy heart, convinced that the whole of Europe was about to be engulfed in a destructive war and that he would never see his friends again.

# 17

## 'I shall go back to the joys of my teen-years'

The 1940s were for Grainger a decade through the first half of which he staggered and from the second half of which he began to emerge phoenix-like into a world more ready to accept his compositions. The war years put a temporary halt to many of his plans and he saw little financial return for the enormous amount of concert work he undertook. Performing royalties in Australia were largely turned over to his more needy relatives and English royalties were redirected to Cyril Scott, whose music had been suffering over the last decade from the adverse trends of fashion. During the war Grainger's concert duties included extensive performances for hospitals and members of the armed services. He once calculated that during his wartime tours he passed an average of four nights a month in a proper bed, the other nights being spent sleeping in railway station waiting rooms or second-class railway carriages. After his expenses had been paid, most of his earnings were donated to the Red Cross or other war charities. He even returned his piano to Steinway to help the war effort. His increased absence from home all but caused a complete breakdown in his marriage with Ella, but their friendship and need for each other survived greater difficulties before and after the war years.

In 1939 Dom Anselm Hughes embarked on his third tour of Canada and the United States. With the outbreak of war and the danger to Atlantic shipping he was left stranded in America. Grainger asked him to stay at White Plains for as long as he wished, and Hughes settled in at Cromwell Place for a few months. Eventually he received orders from his Abbot in England to remain in America for the duration of hostilities and soon he was put in charge of a small Episcopalian parish in Fredonia, N.Y. The convenience of geographical proximity enabled Grainger and Hughes to work with increased intensity on their *English Gothic Music*.

One morning in 1933 Grainger had sat down at his harmonium and discovered that the mechanics of the high C had broken and it was ciphering through whenever he played. Turning the fault to good use he decided to improvise around the note and very soon had created one of his most unusual and engaging compositions, which he eventually called

*The Immovable Do.* In the summer of 1939 he made an 'elastic' scoring version of the work and during the following season derived much enjoyment from trying it out with many different instrumental combinations at the rehearsals he conducted.

With war in Europe Grainger feared a possible invasion of the American continent, and when his tours took him to Springfield, Missouri in June 1940, he discovered and signed a six-month lease for rooms at the Wiltshire Apartments on South Jefferson Avenue. Before the move took place, however, he returned to White Plains and with the help of Fred Morse (who had largely taken over the duties of secretary) he began to make photocopies of the letters, documents and manuscripts in the fire-proof cellars of his home. In late September this work was temporarily interrupted when Henry Cowell announced that he had completed a catalogue of the folk-song cylinders. Grainger journeyed to Washington, where he worked with an engineer of the Library of Congress to transfer the entire collection to a record material more permanent than the brown wax of the cylinders. A system involving a photo-electric cell light beam was used for the transfers. The cylinders of Maori, Raratongan, English and Danish folk-songs with their disc transfers were later deposited by Grainger at various libraries throughout the world. Whilst in Washington he went to hear the Budapest String Quartet in an all-Beethoven programme. He sat with the generous patroness of the arts, Mrs Frederick Sprague Coolidge.

In November 1940 he engaged in a concert at Carnegie Hall given by the Australian soprano Marjorie Lawrence in aid of 'Bundles for Britain'. The last section of the programme was given over mostly to Grainger's own works and he played guitar and piano whilst Henry Cowell doubled on the same instruments. Willem Durieux played cello and conducted the Australian's setting of the English sea shanty *Shallow Brown*. In order to get permission to play the guitar, Grainger had been obliged to present himself with his instrument and give a short display before a board of the Musicians' Union. Although Marjorie Lawrence's mighty Wagnerian voice was hardly suited to the nimble requirements of Danish folk-song and she had shortcomings in the folk-song style, the audience nevertheless enjoyed the musical offerings, especially the encores of *The Old Woman at the Christening* and Grainger's arrangement of *Rule Britannia*.

Percy and Ella moved to Springfield late in November 1940. The new location had the extra convenience of being in a more central position for his tours, and it was to be their home for the next three years. The wisdom of his decision to move was confirmed for Grainger when America entered the war in December 1941. He was happy to be so far from the American coasts when the United States was faced with enemies on both (geographical) sides. In June 1942 Ella became an American citizen. For Grainger the most important event of that year was the performance in eight cities of his Kipling *Jungle Book* cycle with Adolph Nelson conducting the a cappella choir of the Gustavus Adolphus College from St Peter, Minnesota.

On April 20, 1943 Percy and Ella attended a meeting of the Musicological Society where Leopold Stokowski was the speaker and guest of honour. After the lecture Grainger met by accident the modern and experimental French-born composer Edgar Varèse. The Australian had tried on many occasions to establish contact with him, but Varèse had not answered his letters. Grainger wanted to talk over many ideas concerning his Free Music, but this brief meeting, about which no information has been handed down, was to be their only one. About three weeks later the Graingers were invited to dine with Beecham and Stravinsky in New York; Percy left a brief memoir of this meeting:

> The Stravinskys (he charmingly polite and nice-seeming) left first, whereupon Beecham felt called upon to say to his other guests: 'Stravinsky is a man who wrote a promising work — Oiseau de feu; a masterpiece — Petrouchka; an attempt at a super-masterpiece — Sacre du Printemps; and after that NOTHING!' I might say that the new version (Suite? for a string-&-wind-band) of 'Le Rossignol' I heard Goossens make a sound-disc of in Cincinnati, half a year ago, is a very pleasing form of nothingness. More mind-stirring was to hear that Stravinsky (tho born a Jew, as Beecham said) had become 'very devout' (Christ-believing).[1]

The wartime stringencies and especially a shortage of paper made Grainger's regular outlets less willing to accept his new works. It was not uncommon therefore to see him walking from New York publisher to publisher with a knapsack on his back filled with his latest scoring efforts. One morning he turned up at the offices of Eugene Weintraub of Leeds Music Corporation with a similar mission in mind. 'It's not very good,' said Grainger, innocent of Rule Number One of Salesmanship, as he began to spread a score all over the office floor. Weintraub was used to composers placing their works on his desk, but on this occasion no amount of suggesting, overt or surreptitious, could induce the Australian to follow the normal practice, and Weintraub's knees and back suffered greatly as a result of this interview.

As the musical discussion ended, they wandered over to the window and, gazing at the scurrying crowds beneath, they began to lament the sad state of affairs currently prevailing in the world. 'But there is hope,' said Grainger.

'Yes? What?' queried the publisher.

'Scotch Tape!' answered the Australian. The product had just come on to the market and he was intrigued by the possibility of correcting mistakes so easily. 'Just think what you can do with it. You can patch and patch and patch away,' he explained to the puzzled Weintraub.

Recalling Percy's departing gesture, Eugene Weintraub wrote:

> But what affected me most during this meeting was the last statement he made upon leaving my office. Knowing him to be perhaps the most gentle man alive I was flabbergasted and pained when he said, 'I am full of violence.' Remembering Thoreau's statement about 'quiet desperation' Percy's words should not have bowled me over so completely, but coming from him, I remember it to this day.[2]

About this time Grainger began to take a great interest in the music of Gershwin and towards the end of 1943 he was practising that composer's piano concerto, which he first performed publicly the following year. He also made several particularly fine piano settings of Gershwin's songs *Love Walked In* and *The Man I love*, which he was to use in years to come as encore pieces. Perhaps the most fruitful outcome of his interest in Gershwin's music came some years later when he prepared a Fantasy for two pianos on themes from *Porgy and Bess*. During his 1944 teaching session at Interlochen, he tried out a new setting he had made for tuneful percussion of Ravel's *La Vallée des Cloches*. (In 1928 he had arranged Debussy's *Pagodes* for a similar combination of instruments. The arrangement was designed deliberately to imitate the sounds of the Indonesian gamelan which had inspired Debussy in the first place at the Paris World Exhibition.) Although the effect was remarkably pleasing to the musicians who took part, Grainger took no steps to publish it.

He had the Gershwin transcriptions in mind when he began negotiations with Jack Kapp of Decca Records in October 1944 for a series of recordings. His return to the recording studios, however, was far from successful. He and the record company could not agree over many of the items recorded and which of them should be issued or rejected. The recording sessions were spread over a year and the resulting album did not sell at all well. The items by Cowell and his own Gershwin arrangements were never issued, and we can only lament what might have been. Instead the record company decided to issue a selection of the old potboilers. Grainger made several private approaches to the major record companies with the idea of preserving his interpretation of the Grieg concerto before his technique had deteriorated with the physical effects of age. No-one expressed an interest.

No music was too humble for Grainger to feel there was a case for its further investigation. In 1944 he became a member of the Society for the Preservation and Encouragement of Barber Shop Harmony. He always took great interest in such byways of musicianship. Yet at the same time the work of other pianists interested him very little. Apart from the few idols he had in his youth (D'Albert, Hutcheson, Harold Samuel, Lamond) he rarely went to hear other pianists play. An appearance by

Harold Bauer, Wanda Landowska, Ossip Gabrilowitsch or a few of his own pupils would sometimes induce him to a concert hall, but he avoided the rest like the plague. What he hated most, however, was the foreknowledge of the presence of another pianist in his audience. It made him feel quite wretched. But Harold Bauer always made a point of attending his concerts and going to see him after the event. Despite or perhaps because of Bauer's persistence they became good friends. On February 18, 1945 Grainger gave a solo piano recital in Miami and Bauer was in the audience. Of this event, Percy wrote:

> Ravel's 'Ondine' is honor-tokened ((dedicated)) to Harold Bauer. When I played it at a Piano Single-bout ((recital)) at the Blackstone Theatre in Chicago, in 1916 on my way to my first forth-see-ment ((appearance)) in California, H.B. was in the hearer-host ((audience)) making me wretched by his at-ness ((presence)). *Real* piano-players are egged-on to do their best when their fellow-craftsmen go to hear them, so we are told. But I (knowing myself to be a sham as a tone-show-player) always play my worst, if a piano player is in the hall. My heart sinks into my boots [. . .].[3]

The day after the Miami recital Bauer wrote to Grainger:

> Of course you know and you will never forget Delius' admiration for you. He revealed it to me one day in one of his characteristically explosive moments. We were talking about a number of contemporary composers whose work was then attracting considerable attention — 'What is lacking in every one of them,' burst out Fritz, 'is the one *indispensable* quality: originality. If you can't say of a musician, as the French do, that: *'il a une note a lui'* — he's no good! There are just a few who have this quality and one of them is Percy Grainger. I consider him a genius and one of the greatest composers.' [. . .] Frankly, I thought he was exaggerating, but later on I realized that he had said no more than the truth. Don't imagine, because all this went through my mind during your concert yesterday, that I was not listening — Everything you did was colored with that *'one indispensable quality'* and I enjoyed it all immensely. I never heard the Bach Toccata played so magnificently.

During these years Grainger received offers of honorary doctorates of music from the New York College of Music and McGill University in Montreal. He turned them both down and in his letter of April 24, 1945 to F. Cyril James of McGill University, he wrote:

> [. . .] it is with the deepest regret that I feel myself unable to accept a Doctor's degree, for two reasons. (1) The democratic Australian view-

point of my early years (for I have not lived there for over fifty years) makes me unable to accept any distinctions, and (2) the fact that I regard my Australian music as an activity hostile to education, and civilization leads me to regard myself as one to whom educational honours cannot apply. Also, as I have had only three months schooling in my life, I feel that my music must be regarded as the product of non-education. At the same time, I realize that there is always something inconsistent in any viewpoint such as the one put forth above; for although I have not been educated myself, I realize how much I owe to contact with beloved individuals who are highly educated. Nevertheless, the main facts and trends of my life as an Australian-born artist force me to take the stand I do.

Some years later he received an offer to appear in a film about his life and public career. Grainger feared that such a work would present him as a mere star pianist so he placed such awkward conditions on his appearing that the film company dropped the idea.

In the autumn of 1945 he wrote to Herman and Alfhild Sandby:

I have now been concertizing, more or less continuously, for about 53 years, and that ought to be enough. At the end of the season now just beginning I shall be 64, and I hope to end my main concertizing then. After that, I may play concerts for 3 months in the year; but not more, I hope [. . .]. But I have also come to despair of any response to our Nordic Music. Our people seem to me only stupid and I cannot see what there is to hope from them — artistically, racially, economically, emotionally.[4]

During the concert season of 1945/6 he included *Nola* by Felix Arndt and the *Warsaw Concerto* by Richard Addinsell in his repertoire and many of his admirers felt that in doing so he was deliberately pandering to 'middle brow' tastes. Yet Grainger liked the pieces and that was all that mattered. If he could play *Molly on the Shore* to the King of Norway and *Turkey in the Straw* for the President of the United States of America, then surely he could play *Nola* to the great American public. In July he worked with Stokowski at the Hollywood Bowl in performances of the Grieg concerto, the *In a Nutshell* Suite and the *Suite on Danish Folk-Songs*. The two men had not worked together for thirty years and the fruits of the present collaboration were preserved by a San Francisco radio station. The recordings show the pianist to have been in fine technical fettle with Stokowski giving very sympathetic support. Grainger loved working with Stokowski and was so happy on this occasion that he made no mention of the fact that Stokowski had failed to notice the glockenspiel player persistently coming in eight bars too soon in *Molly on the Shore* and that for the same piece the Hollywood Bowl librarian had given out the cello parts to the double basses.

During a visit to Chicago to conduct the Baylor University Symphonic Band in 1946 he accepted an invitation to visit Storm Bull (then holding a post on the music faculty of Baylor) and his wife at their new home. It was Storm's first house and being exceptionally proud of it he decided to paint the building in honour of Percy's visit. Across the road from the Bulls' home was a house which had remained vacant for many years and due to dilapidation had become something of an eyesore. When Percy arrived he took one look at the house opposite and said in all innocence, 'Isn't it surprising how people love to spoil wood through painting it. One loses all the charm of the grain.'[5] Storm always admired Percy's way of delivering an opinion with ruthless honesty and forthrightness and eventually came to agree with him on this issue. The only time Storm and Percy disagreed on a matter of importance was when the former announced his intention of marrying a girl with brown eyes and hair. Percy knew that the Bull family could trace their ancestry back through several hundred years of pure Norwegian blood and he felt that Storm was throwing away his Nordic heritage in marrying a 'Mediterranean type'. Storm, of course, ignored Percy's earnest pleas, but after many years when Percy had come to know and like Storm's wife he paid her one of the highest compliments in his armoury when he stared very firmly into her eyes and said, 'I don't think your eyes are brown at all, I really think they are quite green.'[6]

In August and September of 1946 Percy and Ella went to Europe for the first time since the war. Once again they stayed with Ella's relatives in Sweden. On his arrival in Gothenburg Percy was faced with the bewildering sight of a battery of newspaper reporters anxious to interview him. He was unable to fathom the reason for their presence as it had never happened to him before in Sweden. At that time Percy was not on good terms with Alfhild Sandby so he made no efforts to go to Denmark.

The next year saw a decided upturn in Grainger's fortunes as a composer. His wartime concert activities had brought him in touch with the United States Military Academy at West Point. Not only did he find it convenient to have a group of musicians so close at hand, but he also discovered that the standard of musicianship at the academy was as high as at any of the similar establishments he had worked with. The conductor and band were always happy to perform for Grainger, whom they began to look upon as their local celebrity. By 1946 he had attended unforgettable performances by the West Point Band of *Lincolnshire Posy* and *Hill-Song Number 2*, and in April 1947 the same band carried off a very successful performance of what is perhaps his most difficult work, *Hill-Song Number 1*. The conductor was Francis Resta—a former army colleague and younger brother of Rocco Resta who had been Grainger's band leader at Fort Hamilton during the Great War. By now Grainger had adopted the practice of short-cutting his correspondence work by sending photoduplicated 'round letters' to as many as twenty friends at a time. In a 'Blue-eyed English Round Letter to Kin and Friends' he wrote of this performance:

> The PG who writes to you today is a wholly other man than the one who wrote to you about tone-art matters some months ago — & for many years. For I have just passed a mile-stone in my tone-life [. . .]. Resta was not only able to carry his 24 single players (one player to each part) along at full speed (even in the hardest spots) but also to spell-bind them into playing with what seemed like utter freedom, singingfulness & rich feeling-show-th ((expressiveness)) [. . .]. It has left me with the feeling that I alone am right about everything & that it would be a waste of time (from now on) for me to doubt myself in any line any more. I feel that all the judgements that have been passed on me & my tone-works by tone-wrights such as Delius & Balfour Gardiner are wholly misleading [. . .]. But of course I care far more for the tone-thoughts themselves (in such a work) than for the tone-dress they clothe themselves in. My greatest joy lay in seeing how MOURNFUL the moods of the work are. It is shrouded in a large-size mournfulness — not mere wistfulness; it is sturdier than that. But never for a time-spot does the tonery seem to voice the mood 'God's in his heaven; all's right with the world'. Never (one feels) can the tone-wright be stopped in his wailing! [. . .] So the teachment of all these re-hearsals is the same: that the old stuff is all right & the older the better. So a great calm has come over me. I shall now give up testing things so carefully — I shall give up being a kind of tea-taster, or wine-taster, in tones. I shall go back to the joys of my teen-years, which was: trusting to my mind-picture-ment of tones, trusting to my 'inner ear' — the only thing in tone-life I really care about.[7]

In the same year — his sixty-fifth — his letters and diaries show the first indications of an overtaxed physical state: 'As for myself I feel dolefully out-of-sorts. I have pains in the nape of my neck, in the small of my back, in my guts, I feel giddy & unsteady on my feet all the time & have constant ringing in my ears. My mind fastens badly on to my jobs.'[8] Cyril Scott, who had now gained a considerable reputation in the field of 'nature curing', suggested he consume quantities of 'black strap' molasses. (Grainger would voice completely inconsistent attitudes about his own health. Sometimes he would say that he saw no special virtue in being healthy and at others that health was the most important thing anyone could possess.)

Grainger and Scott were again soon to meet, for Percy and Ella sailed for England on the *Queen Elizabeth* at the end of May 1947. Scotland never ceased to hold its fascination and he managed to spend a few days resting and walking in the more remote parts of that glorious country.

His brief stay in England enabled him to see all his old friends from Frankfurt days as well as Ralph Vaughan Williams, Dom Anselm Hughes, Dr Maud Karpeles, Arnold Bax, Frederic Austin and Ernest Thesiger. He also gave his first recital in England for thirty-three years, although it was a private one at a boys' school in Seaford, Sussex. On July 1, however, he appeared publicly at the Wigmore Hall in a programme of songs given by the Oriana Madrigal Society under the direction of his old friend Charles Kennedy Scott. He played the piano accompaniment to his own setting of *Shallow Brown*.

On August 23, a little over a month after his return to White Plains, he spent the day as guest of Harold Bauer in St James, Long Island. Much of the time was spent talking about Bach and his predecessors, but Grainger's diary entry for this day refers to two very unusual items of music: 'Talked with Bauer, balcony over sea. After lunch he showed me music. Delius MS of 1st Cello Sonata. Played me unknown last movement Schumann Sonata & his Bach Airs.' The 'unknown last movement' of the Schumann sonata was probably the 'Presto Passionato' in G minor which was the original last movement of the Sonata Op. 22 in the same key and rejected by Schumann at his wife Clara's suggestion. It was not completely unknown, however, because Horowitz had recorded it in London for HMV in November 1932 and sometimes included it in his programmes. But the Delius cello sonata is something of a mystery, because Grainger clearly states that he was shown the manuscript of the '1st Sonata', yet there is only one sonata known to have survived. Nevertheless, it is quite possible that Bauer did have a unique manuscript because not only was he a good friend of Delius in his Paris years, but he had made several concert tours with Pablo Casals and one could speculate that perhaps Delius had given the manuscript of an unknown early cello sonata to Bauer and Casals then had lost interest in the work. Alternatively it could have been an early version of the published cello sonata.

In November of that year Grainger received a letter from Bernard Heinze, then head of the Melbourne Conservatorium of Music, in which he informed him that the Elder Chair of Music at Adelaide University had fallen vacant and suggested that he apply for it. Percy sent a letter of rejection (December 3, 1947) which reads like a dirge cataloguing his troubles, problems and fears.

The year 1948 opened in what might have been thought of as splendid fashion. He had been commissioned by the New York League of Composers to prepare a work (*The Power of Rome and the Christian Heart*) for the Goldman Band concert in Carnegie Hall on January 3, to celebrate the seventieth birthday of Edwin Franko Goldman. The band played faultlessly, Grainger conducted well, the organizers had arranged it so that his work should be the central item of the evening, and the audience was warmly responsive. Ten days after the concert, he wrote in a round letter to his friends:

'Looking over the Karl der
Grosse Bridge towards
Sachsenhausen'; watercolour
by Grainger, Frankfurt, June
1896

With Karl Klimsch, Frankfurt,
1923

With folksong collector A. J. Knocks, Otaki, New Zealand, September 1924

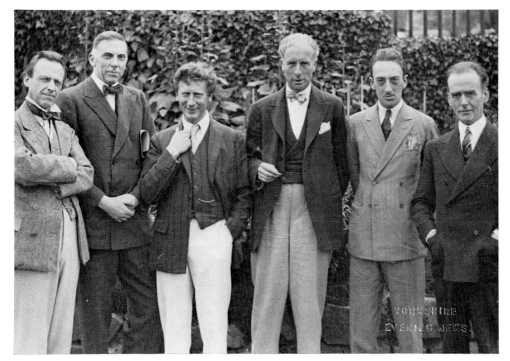

With Cyril Scott, Roger Quilter, Norman O'Neill, Edward Milner and Basil Cameron at the Harrogate Festival, 1929

Ramon Novarro congratulates Percy and his bride, the former Ella Viola Ström, on the day after their wedding at the Hollywood Bowl on August 9, 1928

With Duke Ellington, New York University, 1932

*Above left* Walking through the Ninety Mile Desert from Tailem Bend to Keith, South Australia, with a 42 lb swag, 1924

*Above right* Aloft on the Aaland brig *L'Avenir*, autumn 1933

*Right* On the Danish coast, August 1929

The earliest Free Music machine: three Melanettes coupled to a muted Pianola, 1948

With Ella at work on the Kangaroo-Pouch Free Music machine, 1952

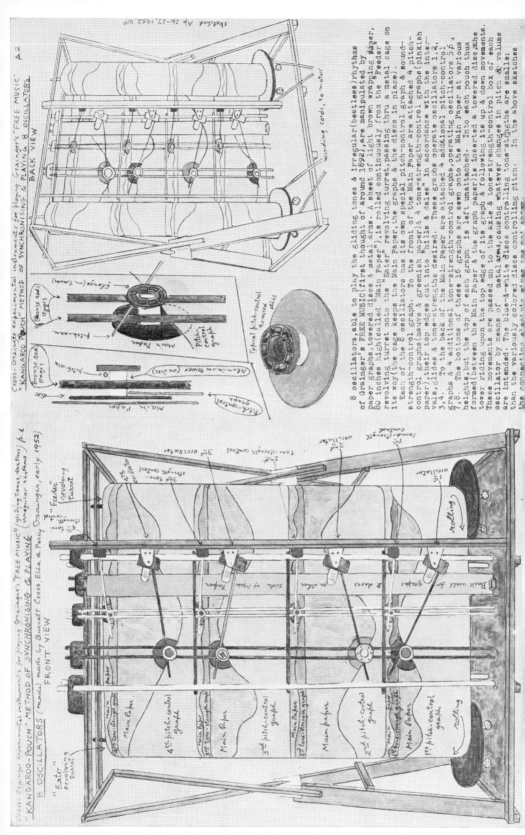

The Kangaroo-Pouch Free Music machine: Grainger's diagrams and explanation, April 1952

At the piano with the Blackwelder band, around 1955

With Douglas Kennedy of the Folk-Song Society and Ralph Vaughan Williams, Cecil Sharp House, May 1958

Conducting *Hill-Song Number 2* at Kneller Hall, Twickenham with the Band of the Royal Military School of Music, summer 1957

On what why-grounds ((reason)) I know not, but this Goldman tone-show had the power to make me more angry & adder-mooded than anything for a long long time. Of course, I loathe being hand-clapped & soft-soaped. I loathe big towns, be-famed tone-bodies like the Goldman Band (tho I must up-own that they were wholiy sweet to me), great halls like Carnegie, & above all I loathe the feeling that 'now everything must be done very well'. As for the piece itself, I loathed its every note. I hated its commonplace chords, its oily well-soundingness, its meaningless tone-lines. My tonery has been growing more & more commonplace ever since I was about 20 or 22 [. . .]. But one always gets something from all haps. What I got from the Goldman Band Tone-show was PURE JOY in hearing Milhaud's SUITE FRANCAISE, written straight for wind-band. What a bewitching work! What enthralling she-like little tunes darting about, what mastery of form & tone-color, what manly power in the use of 7-tone scales! [. . .] Sometimes I think Balfour was right, in making up his mind to turn his back on tone-art.

By now Grainger was earning practically nothing from his concert appearances. The system he had devised of offering his services as a pianist free in exchange for the performance or rehearsal of some of his works or those of his friends was operating at all but a few of his concerts. Hans Kindler and the National Symphony Orchestra in Washington, for example, performed (to great public acclaim) two items by Herman Sandby a few days after the Goldman concert. A few months earlier Grainger had enticed various Detroit musicians to perform works by himself, Cyril Scott and Balfour Gardiner. He also tried out in Detroit the band version of *Marching Song of Democracy* and found the work completely satisfying: 'The piece sounds more tone-clash-ful on the band than it does on the voices, wind-&-string-band orchestra & organ for which it as-first-was written.'[9]

On July 3, 1948 Percy and Ella boarded what he called the 'burst-gas-gin-ship' (motor ship) SS *Stockholm* and headed for Gothenburg. After about three weeks in Sweden with Ella's relatives they travelled to England, where they stayed for four months. In London Grainger's music received considerable exposure when he participated in a series of BBC broadcast concerts, again sharing the conducting duties with Leslie Woodgate. On August 10 he played the piano part in a performance of his *Suite on Danish Folk-Songs* under Basil Cameron with the London Symphony Orchestra at a Henry Wood Promenade Concert in the Albert Hall. In a letter to Herman Sandby six days before the concert he wrote:

I feel awfully disgruntled over this pending performance in London of my Danish Folkmusic Suite. If there is anything I hate it is listening to my own silly music and having to sit there like a fool while I see how much others also dislike it. And if it were not due to the fear of being poverty stricken I would never again have anything to do with any performance of any piece of mine. I would listen to a rehearsal now and then but always disappear before the performance. But I don't dare risk it yet. I feel that our financial future hangs on so slender a thread that I feel duty bound to back up Cameron or anyone else who takes upon himself the burden of producing music that pleases as little as mine does [. . .]. Lack of money is the only impression I carry of life on this Globe.

Grainger played exceptionally well and the work was thunderously applauded by the London 'Promenaders'. Perhaps the only real joy he received from this concert was the knowledge that amongst the Albert Hall audience was Johannes Tang Kristensen — son of Evald. He had personally seen to it that the Dane attended the European première of a work which owed so much to his father's efforts.

Whilst in England Grainger went to see Vaughan Williams and took colour photographs of his eyes. This was the first of a set of photographs he had taken over the next two years of the eyes of William Walton, Josef Holbrooke, Arthur Bliss, John Ireland, Cyril Scott, Ernest 'Jack' Moeran, Roger Quilter, Frederic Austin and Balfour Gardiner. These pictures were destined for display in his museum to demonstrate that really worthwhile composers had blue eyes. In September he was with the Central Band of the RAF during a broadcast performance of *Marching Song of Democracy*. On September 18 he attended the last night of the Henry Wood Promenade Concerts standing in the 'bull-ring' promenade section. The work he went to hear was Delius's *Summer Night on the River*. A few days later he was with Eric Fenby, who handed over to him a number of Delius manuscripts for the Melbourne museum. They included the 'Florida' Suite, *On hearing the First Cuckoo in Spring, Songs of Farewell, Avant que tu ne t'en ailles, Air and Dance, A Song of the High Hills,* a sketch from a string quartet, Delius's exam books from Leipzig and a number of photocopied manuscripts.

In November he returned to Sweden. The following month brought him the keenest pleasure when he attended a complete performance of Wagner's *Ring* in Stockholm. Although he was spiritually uplifted by this musical feast, he was still feeling physically unwell. In London he had experienced acute bladder pains, and on December 14 he went to a noted surgeon in Stockholm for a thorough medical check-up. (As he sat in the waiting room he read poetry by Schiller.) The surgeon's verdict was that though there was a tiny heart irregularity, he was physically fit and that there was no symptom which should cause alarm. He warned him, however, not to haul any heavy luggage — advice which, of course, Percy ignored.

Before leaving Gothenburg for New York, Percy and Ella finished clean-writing the score and orchestral parts for his *Youthful Suite* in preparation for photocopying for the publishers, a task which had taken them well over eighteen months. On his return to White Plains Grainger found waiting for him a letter from Stokowski, who was anxious to make a record of some of his works but had been distressed to note that most of the orchestral works on sale at Schirmers in New York had been those re-orchestrated by other people:

> Would you be willing to orchestrate them *yourself* and make an entirely new version of them through an orchestration that has your great skill in orchestrating? My thought was that each time a theme is repeated, *fresh* instruments would play. Also, I thought that such instruments as Vibraharps, Marimbaphones, Saxophones, Celestes — and in fact all the colourful instruments of the modern orchestra could be employed.[10]

It is hard to determine exactly how Grainger felt about this suggestion and even more difficult to know how he felt about the finished product, because sometimes he went into raptures over the record and at other times expressed utter shame for his involvement and anger that Stokowski had not thought his original orchestrations fit to record. Whatever the truth may have been, he set to work immediately, producing fascinating versions of six of his most popular pieces. During the preparation work for the recordings, which were eventually made in 1950, he often visited Stokowski at his home in Gracie Square, New York, while the Maestro made frequent appearances at Cromwell Place. A young physics teacher, Burnett Cross, was present on one occasion when Stokowski visited White Plains, and of this memorable occasion he wrote:

> Stokowski and Percy were working at the dining room table, going over a score. I was sitting on the floor beside the phonograph turntable (a table model that we usually kept on the floor), and playing whatever bits of Percy's pieces that they wanted to hear: for instance, Percy's arrangement of 'Early One Morning' for three solovoxes. Every so often Percy would dash into the music room about 30 feet away to knock out something on the piano, bringing out a line on the recording, or something of that sort. Instead of simply saying to me, 'The phonograph's too loud', or something of that sort, to adjust the balance between my phonograph and Percy's piano, Stokowski gave me my cues by conducting me — at the phonograph — with his well-known hands. I enjoyed every moment of it.[11]

Although Grainger was the pianist in *Handel in the Strand, Country Gardens* and *Shepherd's Hey*, because of some regulations of the Musicians' Union he only received the fee of a rank-and-file member of the

orchestra. He tried to interest Stokowski in some of his more difficult
works, but because of the conductor's heavy international commitments
nothing came of their discussions. Nevertheless, whatever Grainger may
have said or thought about the record itself, the orchestrations are quite
the best he ever did of these pieces for large orchestra, and Stokowski's
sympathetic conducting contributes no small part to the project's success.
The arrangement of *Early One Morning,* the only work which was built
up completely from scratch especially for the recording, is a beautifully
conceived exercise in sliding chromaticism between consonance and
dissonance. Sadly, it is unpublished.

In May 1952 after the Stokowski RCA record had been issued Columbia Records approached Grainger asking him if he would conduct for a
longplaying record of his own compositions. Somewhat overwhelmed by
this sudden windfall he immediately agreed and began making fresh
arrangements of some of his more 'saleable' works. The Columbia plan,
however, was nipped in the bud, for when RCA Victor heard of the possible new record he was asked to sign a contract which precluded him
from taking part in any other recording session of the works on the
Stokowski record. As far as recordings of Grainger's works are concerned, complete justice was not done until the late 1950s, when Mercury
Records engaged Frederick Fennell and his Eastman Rochester musicians
to make an all-Grainger record. The same musicians also recorded
*Lincolnshire Posy* and *Hill-Song Number 2* for issue with works by other
composers on two other records. These Fennell records will always stand
as definitive accounts of his music.

Grainger's work in the concert field by the end of the 1940s was almost
wholly concerned with performances of his own compositions and to this
end he continued playing for a reduced fee or nothing at all. The days
had long passed when publishers would keep a piece of music in print
simply because it had musical value. If a work did not sell well, then it
would be allowed to go out of print as soon as it was out of stock.
Grainger was terrified that this fate might befall his best compositions, so
his concert work during the last years of his life was part of a constant
struggle with his publishers to prove to them that his works were being
performed. At times his efforts in his composition tours would bear fruit
and he would bask in uncommon moods of joyfulness:

> I want my dear friends to know that I am U T T E R L Y  H A P P Y in my
> now-time-y life [. . .]. I like to be kow-towed to, & I like all the treat-
> ments that come to one with old age [. . .] I must say: now that time-
> beaters & other tone-show planners know that I set store only by my
> tone-works & not by my piano playing (even if I still play a concerto
> for them — as a 'sop' to their listen-hosts & to weigh up against the un-
> pleasing task of having to play my tone works) they try to be awfully
> nice to me about it — they really DO try to please me & give me hope-

fulfilment [. . .]. I shall be glad when the last rehearsal, the last tone-show, is over & when tone-writing for me again means nothing but the shaping of tone-thoughts & the writing down of them.[12]

In 1949 Burnett Cross contributed towards another source of joy. The Australian had always felt in his mind that his setting of *Bold William Taylor* was a model for the setting of narrative folk-ballads, yet the practical results had always been disheartening whenever he had tried it out. Cross expressed a great interest in English folk-music and Grainger had often planned to set up a 'Percy Grainger Prize' for the most authentic-sounding and stylistically accurate singer of folk-songs. Together they worked on a plan to produce a satisfactory performance of the elusive *Bold William Taylor*. The setting of the song was too high for Cross's voice and since it could not be transposed because of the tonal qualities of some of the instruments in the arrangement, they made a home recording of the work one whole tone lower and at a slightly slower pace than the original, with a skeletal accompaniment on the harmonium provided by the composer. Cross's singing was remarkably good and his grasp of the Lincolnshire dialect pleased Grainger enormously. The Australian then took this record on his tours and rehearsed various orchestras by having them accompany the record with the speed of the playback increased so as to bring it up to the correct pitch. Grainger was wholly satisfied with these experiments and they restored his confidence in the work.

On Tuesday, December 6, 1949 the English conductor Richard Austin and the Philharmonia Orchestra gave the first European performance of *Hill-Song Number 1* at the Royal Albert Hall in London. The event passed almost unnoticed in London's musical circles but Grainger in his state of battle-scarred isolation earmarked it as a red letter day when one of his more unruly children had finally come home to roost. A few months earlier he had visited a doctor in White Plains about his abdominal pains. The doctor found several small growths which he suggested should be removed in a series of monthly operations. Percy ignored the doctor's advice and wrote instead to Cyril Scott, who replied with the address of a lady in New York City who could administer 'bloodless surgery'. Because of his love and loyalty to Scott, he spent many dollars on and a great deal of time with this lady when a few operations at this stage, as the doctor had suggested, might well have extended his life by many years.

# 18

## 'Your loving but defeated, Percy'

The last years of Grainger's life were in many ways the most interesting because they were the first which brought him any measure of fulfilment and happiness. This was due mainly to his work on the Free Music machines, and despite many frustrations caused by ill health there were even rare moments when his continued concert life gave him simple pleasures:

> And Oh! The joys of old age! Being able to work with my funny machines and doing other things one likes even if others do not think them worth while. And when I take part in a concert the concert-givers are only glad that one doesn't have a stroke on the stage and they don't expect one to play all the right notes any more. All this is very soul-satisfying![1]

The Goldman Band and many other symphonic wind bands were now programming his works of their own volition and the composer was sometimes invited to these as the honoured guest. Once he turned up at a Goldman Band concert not knowing what the programme was, and was surprised to see that Richard Franko Goldman was due to open the second half with his *The Lads of Wamphray*. Grainger could not face the idea of hearing what he had come to regard as an annoying piece so he left during the interval.

The joy he derived from working on his Free Music machines was made possible by the technical help of Burnett Cross and the patience of Ella in allowing her home to be turned into a huge do-it-yourself sonics laboratory. Ella was only too delighted to see her husband away from the concert hall and working at home on his inventions. His absence on long gruelling tours (most of which Ella felt were unnecessary) had more than once brought her to the point of leaving her husband. On February 9, 1950 she wrote to Dom Anselm Hughes about this problem:

> Yes, I have often wondered how ever I could help Percy to take things a little easier, to spare himself. But I have absolutely no influence over him, he does everything according to his own opinion, and, as I always

think him quite clever in everything he does, I let him decide what he wishes to do. Except that in many cases it is a heartbreak for me to see him overdoing his strength. In fact, for the last five years it has always been a constant trouble to me to see Percy still 'in harness'. I always say to him to give up trying so hard for business, but he has so many schemes, for the good of music mostly, so I cannot really insist that he should remain inactive when he is so full of good intentions! And I am not a very forceful character.

As a youth, Burnett Cross had heard Grainger give a solo piano recital at the White Plains High School while he was a student there. A little later, when Cross was a timpanist in the Columbia University Symphonic Band and an undergraduate at Columbia College, his band was billed to play *Lincolnshire Posy*. The conductor knew that he lived in White Plains so he was asked to stop by at Cromwell Place to collect some band parts for the work. Apart from the Graingers' being very charming and cordial, he had no other vivid memory of that meeting. But towards the end of the Second World War Cross met Grainger on the platform of White Plains station while waiting for the train to Grand Central, and they sat together and talked mainly about folk-song during the train journey into Manhattan. That was in June 1945; their friendship and co-operation lasted and deepened until Grainger's death.

The first job Cross was enlisted to perform was the repair of Grainger's photocopying machine, which was kept in the cellar at Cromwell Place. Cross was astonished to see this black monster of great proportions and antiquity brooding in the depths of Number Seven. He was also highly amused to see that Grainger's method of timing a certain part of the copying process was to sing a specific number of bars from Wagner's overture to *Die Meistersinger,* at the end of which the process would be complete. Cross was quick to see, however, that behind the public image of an eccentric piano virtuoso was a man of immensely broad intellect and curiosity—a mind which had developed unfettered by formal education. He was often present when distinguished visitors and friends arrived at Cromwell Place and in his memory no subject was ever discussed (except highly technical sciences) which found Grainger out of his depth. Nothing was said which the Australian could not either cap or capsize.

Grainger had a natural talent for making technical drawings and the surviving reproductions of his machines are minor works of art. He was most anxious that his mechanical creations should be appealing and interesting to the eye, and constantly strove to make what he called 'pretty machines'. These machines were remarkable devices and would have made Heath Robinson and Roland Emmett envious. Ella, Burnett and Percy vied with one another in suggesting improvements and solving problems and the three made a happy working trio. Grainger was a very resourceful man and this was reflected in the ideas and materials used in constructing the machines. All kinds of junk were utilized as well as the more common items which were bought at local hobby and hardware stores. At times Ella and Percy would don their finest clothes to avoid police suspicion and spend part of an evening rummaging amongst the piles of rubbish by the back doors of department and furniture stores. Eventually the machines employed such improbable articles as pencil sharpeners, milk bottles, bamboo, roller-skate wheels, the bowels of a harmonium, linoleum, ping-pong balls, children's toy records, egg whisks, cotton reels, bits of sewing machines, carpet rolls, a vacuum cleaner, a hair dryer and, of course, miles of strong brown paper and string. It took Grainger, the devoted amateur, to teach Cross, the scientist and academic, that lashing two or three pieces of wood together with rope produced a stronger joint than did nuts and bolts. Grainger, naturally, was well to the fore in devising colourful names for his creations, and his diaries were filled with such titles as 'The Inflated Frog Blower', 'The Crumb-catcher and Drain Protector Disc' and 'The Cross-Grainger Double-decker Kangaroo-pouch Flying Disc Paper Graph Model for Synchronizing and Playing 8 Oscillators'.

Each improvement was noted down in his diary and a great improvement meant the declaration of a 'Red Letter Day' or even an 'Ultra Red Letter Day'. Work never stood still, Grainger was rarely satisfied and new ideas were constantly being put to the test. Many visitors to Cromwell Place were shown the latest model and he was always happy to demonstrate. Cross feels that few if any of those who saw the Free Music machines went away with the slightest idea of what Grainger was aiming for. Some went away convinced that madness and senility had finally overtaken the poor man, but Grainger did not give a damn for those who did not understand him. He was happy in the thought that he was finally working on the most urgent and important task of his life. One day it may become generally recognized as such, but for the moment, and except by a few imaginative people, his experiments in Free Music are usually dismissed as the eccentricities of an old man.

Cross gradually became a member of the Grainger household and eventually he would spend three or four days each week there, being paid a small retainer fee. He himself admits that it was some time before even he realized what Grainger was aiming for, yet once the ideas jelled in his mind the two men worked in perfect harmony with the talents of the one complementing those of the other. For much of the time that Cross worked with Grainger he was also earning a living as an educational consultant and writer of scientific textbooks.

The roots of Grainger's Free Music, as has already been mentioned, went back to his childhood, the rolling hills of South Australia which he saw from the train that took him from Melbourne to Adelaide, the water which lapped at the sides of the rowing boat in Albert Park lake, and above all the sounds of the wind as it howled through the telegraph wires on the Australian country roads. Often he thought to himself that just as the sounds and shapes of nature knew no arbitrary scales or metres so there should be no reason why in its search for full emotional expressiveness music should not enjoy a similar freedom. Just as a painter could move from one colour to another by either a gradual blending of tints or an abrupt transition, so should a composer be able to move from one note to any other by a gliding tone as well as by a leap if he so wished. Grainger wanted the means at his disposal to reproduce any note or group of notes within the physical limits of the given apparatus and proceed to the next by whatever kind of jump or glide took the composer's fancy. The glides he had in mind, however, were not haphazard, and he wanted to be able to specify very exactly the duration and slope. Just as he wanted to be able to reproduce any pitch within a certain range without the confines of scale or mode, so did he want also to be able to space notes in time without the limitations of regular metre. The same freedom would also apply to the question of dynamics. Such music obviously could not be reproduced by conventional instruments and in his own words he wanted to 'free music from the tyranny of the performer'. Conventional music notation also became redundant, for he wanted to translate his musical ideas directly into sounds. In other words, he wanted a composer's machine, not a performer's machine.

The question is often asked why Grainger and Cross remained aloof from the developments in electronic music which were being made in America and elsewhere at that time. The question is rather inapposite because whilst Grainger constantly remained aloof, he never fell behind in his knowledge of such developments. He and Cross often travelled far to meet this professor or that who had devised some kind of synthesizer or similar piece of equipment. Grainger also read extensively about new music and frequently attended lectures given by the darlings of the avant-garde. On November 3, 1958, for example, he sat in rapt attention amongst the audience at the McMillan Theatre, Columbia University whilst Stockhausen delivered a paper on 'New Instruments and Electronic Music'. Grainger's comment entered in his diary for that day was simply 'good'. And in his pursuit of new electronic instruments he even went to (and greatly enjoyed) the latest rock and roll films. At one time the two experimenters toyed with the idea of using film sound-track to reproduce Free Music. Whilst this means was never pursued in earnest, some of the ideas obtained from their study of the technique were exploited — particularly in their final instrument. The sound effects used in the Disney film score of *Forbidden Planet* interested Grainger so much that he went to see the film several times in 1956. Yet despite all this he and his collaborator struggled on alone.

The reason was twofold. Firstly, all the synthesizers and machines he saw were endlessly complicated and cost many thousands of dollars to build. Grainger wanted a practical machine which would fit into his music study, which did not cost much to build and which did not need an army of super-electricians and engineers to rush to its aid if anything needed adjusting or repairing. And secondly, but much more importantly, he felt that these elaborate machines had been invented prior to any consideration of musical needs. The inventor produced his scientific creation, then looked around for a composer or performer to extract some kind of noise from it. Grainger tackled his problem from the other end. He had already composed his music; now all he needed was a machine which would realize the musical thoughts which he had carried in his mind for more than fifty years.

Grainger and Cross became pioneers in electronic music almost incidentally. Had Grainger been able to obtain his music from a team of Egyptian singing cats he would probably have been quite happy. Electronic machinery in itself did not particularly interest him, it just so happened that ultimately this was the only means he could find to play his music. At first he was not even particularly interested in the timbre of the notes produced (though Cross certainly was). This was a consideration which was to come later.

The first experiments began gropingly around 1946 and by the end of Grainger's life he and Cross had achieved by their own criteria a large measure of success. The machines they created fall roughly into four main types. The first two types are, in essence, children of the Duo-Art player-piano system and reflect Grainger's thorough understanding of this mechanism. First he tuned three Melanettes (later to be substituted by Solovoxes) one-third of a half-tone apart and placed them pyramid-fashion on top of a muted pianola. The keys of the pianola were connected by cotton thread to the keys of the electronic instruments above. When the piano roll (specially cut by Grainger) was fed through the pianola the movement of the lower keys would in turn activate those of the electronic instruments. This contraption, of course, could only simulate a glide, but it was an important first step and was in working order by 1948.

Over the next five years Grainger and Cross worked on two machines, the first of which was again based on the piano roll system but utilized pneumatics instead of electronics to produce the sounds. Grainger called it the 'Estey reed tone tool'. This machine involved four large rolls of brown paper being fed over boxes of harmonium reeds tuned one-eighth of a tone apart. The thirty-six-inch-wide paper rolls had been prepared with holes punched again by Grainger and were passed over the reed boxes at a constant speed. The machine could operate with up to four reed boxes all blown by a vacuum cleaner (which he called a 'dust-suck-gin') thus enabling the inventors to obtain multiple voices and glides working contrapuntally. These simulated glides and jumps were very effective, but dynamics always proved difficult with this machine. With too much air pressure it was easy to tear the paper roll. It was, however, on this machine that they first reproduced a fragment of Grainger's Free Music in 1951 and, as Cross said, it was no longer a mechanical contraption but a definite musical instrument.

Grainger believed that this was a moment of considerable historical import and there is no reason to think him wrong. The glide was a phenomenon foreign to the traditions of Western European music. Portamento as used in performance with stringed instruments is on the whole a device of purely momentary worth and its use is dictated often more by fashion than by the composer's wishes. Bartók is an exception. Apart from the trombone it is scarcely encountered in wind music. Glissandos written for keyboard instruments or the harp are generally ornaments. Curiously, the only form of music which consciously made use of gliding tones to any extent was negro jazz, and in this field Duke Ellington was the leading exponent. His recorded versions of *Soliloquy* (recorded April 30, 1927) and *Black and Tan Fantasy* (recorded February 9, 1932) are fine examples of how gliding tones may be incorporated into the musical structure of a piece without being merely incidental to it. Grainger, who was always a great admirer of Ellington, must have been aware of the work done by this great tunesmith. Of course gliding tones may be found in some non-Western music — particularly vocal music.

The next machine to roll off the stocks was Grainger's most elaborate device in its purely mechanical aspects and at the same time a pure delight to the eye, a definite embodiment of his idea of 'pretty machines'. This was the previously mentioned 'Cross-Grainger Kangaroo-pouch' system. In essence it consisted of two huge vertically mounted carpet rolls around which had been wound two strips of strong coloured paper whose specially cut 'hill-and-dale' upper contours corresponded to the pitch and dynamic needs of the music. The two carpet rolls, graphically termed by the inventors the 'Feeder' and 'Eater' revolving turrets, took the rolls of 'hill-and-dale' paper through two metal cages wherein mechanical means were provided to track the undulations and activate the pitch and volume of eight oscillators. This machine was operative by the early months of 1952, yet, splendid though it was, it did not answer all Grainger's requirements for his music. Whilst within its pitch and dynamic range the instrument could produce beautiful gliding tones with multiple voices set at any interval, it could not produce instantaneous leaps in pitch.

The 'Kangaroo-pouch' machine was so called because the two rolls of paper carrying the 'hill-and-dale' information were sewn at various heights on either side of a master roll. Into each pouch formed by the stitching was placed a disc 'rider' which followed the undulations of the outer 'message' rolls. Upward slopes as steep as forty-five degrees could be accommodated and downward slides were as quick as the 'rider' could drop. Gradients steeper than this tended to buckle or tear the paper roll and it was this limitation that led the two experimenters to move on to another machine. The development of two machines sometimes ran concurrently and Grainger often turned back to the Solovox machine because the tone it produced was sweeter. Children who passed along Cromwell Place to and from school soon began to notice the strange sounds coming from the Grainger home. He was delighted when he heard them singing and whistling glides in imitation of his invention.

The final machine was the most sophisticated and worked almost entirely from electronic sources, though it incorporated the Duo-Art idea of a roll being fed over a device which translated messages (in this instance purely graphic) into sound. During the 1950s Cross began to catch up on transistor technology and with this latest machine took over almost completely from Grainger the question of design. The new instrument consisted of sealed-beam spotlights playing their light through tuning sticks and a roll of clear plastic on to which Grainger had 'painted' his music in water-soluble black plastic ink (the pitch and dynamics 'messages' being on separate levels). The amount of light which then filtered through as the plastic roll travelled through the machine was picked up and translated into sound by photo-electric cells and amplifiers. Grainger's death ultimately prevented this instrument from being fully developed into the seven-voiced machine that was originally hoped for.

There were, of course, many stages in between these machines and the full story of the experiments has yet to be told. Many visitors who saw the machines during Grainger's lifetime were tempted to dismiss his work simply because they had come expecting a science-fiction-type laboratory of glass, flashing lights and puzzling dials. When they saw his crude (but eminently practical and workable) instruments they tended to lose interest. Grainger filled his letters during the last ten years of his life with diagrams and explanations of his latest developments, but the seeds of his proud and enthusiastic inventiveness fell on stony ground. Some of his English friends, Vaughan Williams included, thought he was working himself into an irredeemable artistic quagmire. The loss was theirs, not Grainger's, for by this stage in his life he had come to an awareness of the worthlessness of recognition by the musical establishments. In his youth perhaps he would have been discouraged by the scorn of his friends and teachers, but now, despite the bitterness and despite the pall of increasing deafness and ill health, he had achieved a kind of inner peace which enabled him to sail on according to his own ideals and aims.

Burnett Cross was also anxious to help Grainger in a variety of other projects. One of his ambitions had long been to find a way of making a minutely accurate analysis of the pitch and metre of his folk-singers' cylinders. Cross possessed some home recording equipment and with this they were able to make 'sound-on-sound' recordings of a greatly slowed down re-recording of the folk-song added to which were metre counts made in Grainger's voice and with the sound of Ella striking carefully calculated notes on a marimba. These experiments were not entirely successful and were abandoned after a time. A much more successful project, however, was the construction of a remarkably simple device to aid Grainger's failing memory. He saw no reason why he should not be able to have the printed music before him at concerts and recitals but was worried about the dangers inherent in page-turning: accidentally turning over two pages at once and leaves of music falling over the keyboard are nightmares not unknown to performing artists. So he set about the construction of a desk roller in which all the pages of music were glued end to end and continually advanced as the music progressed by the activation of a foot roller connected to the music stand by a speedometer cable. This piece of equipment, of course, created great interest and amusement wherever he used it. It was once demonstrated in his only TV broadcast from the BBC television studios in Birmingham during an interview with Sidney Harrison.

The concert life which Grainger continued to undertake during the 1950s wrought severe damage to his health, but there were times when he took great delight in being a catalyst to the careers of younger talented artists. One such occasion was when he was called at short notice to give a recital in place of an orchestral concert due to be conducted by a young Italian prodigy. Grainger was asked if he would mind sharing the spotlight with two twelve-year-old twin brother duo-pianists. He gladly consented. Arriving in Auburn at 6.00 a.m. on the cold morning of March 18, 1950, he made his way to the home of the duo-pianists, Richard and John Contiguglia. With snowdrifts all around he walked into the house without snowboots or overcoat and sat down to a hearty vegetarian breakfast. Following a period of practice, he talked with the boys and treated them with an adult seriousness and respect that amazed and delighted them. When they remarked on the paucity of printed music available for two pianos/four hands, Grainger wrote out a list of music with its publishers for the future benefit of the young aspirants.

The rehearsal during the afternoon in the Emerson Hall had the boys watching in wonderment, not only at his remarkable playing but also at the way in which the sixty-seven-year-old pianist would leap from the five-foot platform and march out of the hall in the most matter-of-fact manner. When the twins went to collect him before the concert they took with them a copy of Country Gardens for him to autograph. They found him lying supine on his dressing room table, but he refused to autograph the music, saying that he wanted to hear them perform first. After the first half of the concert, which was taken up by Grainger's solo recital, he stood in the wings listening intently to every note played by the boys. When the concert was over he not only signed their copy of Country Gardens but saw to it that they were sent a large body of his own multi-piano music. It came with such personal inscriptions as 'To John and

Richard Contiguglia from their admiring colleague, Percy Grainger'.
Before he left Auburn he gave an interview to newspaper 'reporters. The
following day these journals made considerable play from such quotations as: 'All great music is painful', 'Happy music is inferior music',
'Pain and death are common and dominant in our life today'.

A little over three months later his friend Balfour Gardiner was dead,
and when Grainger visited Europe for three months later that year he
journeyed to Fontmell Hill at the request of Gardiner's nephew to sort
through the Englishman's literary and musical legacy. The days he spent
there helped rescue several unpublished scores which were performed
later at a London memorial concert with the Philharmonia Orchestra
under the baton of Richard Austin, son of Frederic. The trip to Sweden
and England afforded him a blessed rest after the three-month American
concert tour he had felt necessary to undertake simply to persuade his
publishers that he was still alive. During the three months of touring he
spent eighty nights sleeping in trains, buses and railway stations. His sole
income was a fifteen per cent royalty on the music sold. He felt trapped.
To add to his misery he was pulled into an out-of-court settlement which
involved his paying several thousand pounds to an Englishman who had
persuaded his lawyer to bring a 'prima facie' case of 'inciting to disaffec-
tion' involving his wife.

In the spring of 1951 Grainger toured the eastern seaboard of America
and in March appeared in the Spring Music Festival of the University of
Miami. He assumed, as was his habit in those days, the triple role of
pianist, composer and conductor. The reviews in the local press following the concert were harsh and almost give the impression that the
critics wanted to drum him ignominiously out of town. The *Miami
Herald* of March 20, for example, commented:

> The overpowering flood of sound and fury that we had anticipated did
> not materialize [. . .]. This may have been due to the state of tentative
> awe with which many of the young musicians approached the strange,
> disruptive, oddly expressive and often nebulous Grainger music with
> which they were dealing [. . .]. 'The Merry Wedding' which utilized
> two conductors [. . .] emerged as a totally unsynchronized work, which
> was quite to be expected under the conductorial circumstances [. . .].
> Mr. Grainger played the first movement of Tchaikovsky's B flat minor
> Concerto with extreme matter-of-factness, a galloping rhythm, and no
> bother at all about emotional content, and the orchestra [. . .] sawed
> through it with small grasp of its content and obviously insufficient
> preparation.

Grainger, of course, was not touched by such remarks — in fact he was
quite pleased that at last the critics were telling what he felt was after all
nothing more nor less than the truth. Still, no record can be found of his

ever having returned to Miami, and it is a sad fact that despite his herculean efforts the last ten years of his life brought him some decidedly unkind reviews.

The day following the Miami concert he arrived at 5.00 a.m. in a small seaside settlement he greatly loved called, oddly enough, Melbourne. He walked around the town until dawn, then took a swim. When he returned to White Plains he felt so run down with work and saw ahead of him so many projects to keep him at home that he decided to cancel a trip to Australia that he had planned for himself and Ella that year. They had booked to sail on the *Aorangi* on which they had met twenty-five years earlier. Above all he wanted to work on the Free Music machines and perform further work on the English Gothic Music which he had neglected for so long. In a letter to Dom Anselm Hughes that year he wrote:

> Think of all the lovely melodies you & I have set circulating in the world—things that enrich the national wealth & bring even money to all sorts of people. Yet people will pay untold sums to universities & colleges & famous teachers to learn mere platitudes & non-facts while, with apprenticeships to such as you & me, they could learn, for nothing, the nature of the melody, the true history of music & the mastery of fields of art from which they could later reap a rich harvest—if that's what they want. But no, people are always suspicious of genius & put their trust only in mediocrity.[2]

During the autumn of 1951 Grainger embarked on a singularly bizarre project when he ordered the construction of life-sized wood and papier-mâché dummies of himself, Ella, Cyril Scott, Balfour Gardiner and Roger Quilter. Clothing his English friends in suits which he had begged from them in real life, he chose to adorn the dummies he had made of himself and Ella in the towelling suits which they used when relaxing around the house. The task of shipping these grisly objects to Australia— for it was for display in his museum that they were intended—was fraught with complications, not the least being the twitching curtains of neighbours and the incredulous glances of passersby as the quasi-corpses were loaded on to a pantechnicon.

The following year showed further signs of failing health. On July 4 he noted in his diary: 'Don't feel very well these days, feel listless & only want to eat & sleep.' On the previous day he noted: 'Beloved mother would have been 91 today.' During that year he developed a fear of burglars as a result of hearing noises during the night. To cope with this he installed a mattress under his grand piano which was draped with Free Music bits and pieces. (One of his upright pianos had been used contemptuously as a dirty linen basket for a number of years). Thus concealed he slept in peace.

The view we have of Grainger in old age can be interpreted as one of the fallen mighty. A man who was once a star artist for Columbia Records was now bequeathing his last musical testaments on a slightly out-of-tune upright piano with the aid of a home recording machine. A man who could once dazzle capacity audiences at New York's Carnegie Hall and London's Royal Albert Hall was now staggering amidst infirmities of the body from one Women's Afternoon Club to another. The American high school gymnasium had taken the place of the European royal courts. Grainger's Australian chauvinism and Nordic bigotry grew narrower and more pathetic with advancing years and it is remarkable that he retained as many friends as he did. His constant complaint that neither he nor his music had made any friends since his arrival in America must be taken with a large pinch of salt. The issue of both the Stokowski and Fennell records gave him immense pride and pleasure in his old age and these two musicians were undisputed friends of his music. His letter-writing increased with advancing years and he conducted most of his social life through the medium of voluminous and rambling round letters. These monstrous epistles were often full of venomous railings against a world which he felt had refused to understand his muse or accept him as an artistic leader and pioneer. The more he thrashed about, the more he alienated his potential friends and admirers.

In adulthood Grainger was never a poor man. He was to die leaving almost $50,000 — a fact which gives the lie to his persistent complaints about being near to poverty. He earned huge sums and spent on a generous and grand scale. It is true that some of his music was being allowed to go out of print before his eyes, but publishers, after all, must consider the profitability of a work as well as its artistic merit. It was his fear of poverty perhaps more than anything which drove him to the limits of his physical stamina during the last fifteen years of his life to keep his name before the public eye. All his life, Grainger had a talent for making pig-headed decisions and a positive genius for hitching his waggons to the wrong stars. But with a mother like Rose it cannot be said that he had had a good start. It is difficult to name anyone in the twentieth century who made such a splendid mess of a career which had such portentous beginnings. It is surprising that he was able to salvage so much.

For a number of years Bernard Heinze, who was then director of music for the Australian Broadcasting Commission as well as Ormond Professor of Music at Melbourne University, had tried to persuade Grainger to undertake a concert tour of Australia. He had on many occasions rejected the plan and at other times agreed and later cancelled. The explanations he offered to Bernard Heinze were usually to do with illness or increased commitments in America. The real reasons were more centred around the fact that had the ABC had their way it would have involved him in endless repetitions of 'war-horse' piano concertos for a miserable fee; he would have been so much happier had he been asked to conduct works of his own or those of his friends. In January 1953 Heinze even travelled to White Plains to attempt a personal approach in organizing an Australian tour. The trip was not entirely fruitless, for he got Grainger to translate Mahler's German markings in a symphony he was due to conduct on his return to Australia.

In the late spring of 1953 Percy's White Plains doctor Kaare Nygaard advised a prostate operation. A bed was booked in the famous Mayo Clinic, a surgeon organized, and a date arranged for the operation towards the end of July. All was set for a course of treatment when Percy suddenly reversed all his decisions and wrote instead to Dr Kai Holten (Karen's brother) who was then medical supervisor of the Aarhus Kommunhospital in Denmark. Percy wanted to have the operation performed in Denmark and be under the care of his former sweetheart's brother. He was utterly terrified at the thought that he might wake up in the Mayo Clinic after the operation to find a Jewish doctor standing over him. Dr Holten agreed and Percy and Ella sailed for Scandinavia on July 29. Two days before his operation on August 20, he gave a private recital for the doctors and nurses of the Kommunhospital.

The operation was not a great success and Percy did not respond well to the treatment. Dr Holten wrote to Dr Nygaard that after investigations and further consultations with an eminent surgeon, Professor Aalkjer, his findings were that an extensive cancer had established itself in the prostate gland. The letter confirmed Dr Nygaard's suspicions, but Percy was not informed at this stage. He was in constant pain for about a month after the operation and Ella tried to take his mind off things by reading poetry to him. By the end of September he was recovering and fit enough to be writing characteristically strong and forthright letters to his friends, including some rather unkind remarks reserved for, of all people, Herman Sandby. (One is instantly reminded of Percy's letter to Eric Fenby when he explained that he was entirely pleased when Delius behaved badly to him at Grez, for it indicated to him that Delius was therefore well and happy inside.) Grainger wrote:

Another matter: Debussy, Ravel, Balfour Gardiner, Gabriel Fauré, Respighi, & myself divorced ourselves from the filthy Sonata-Symphony form. Why did you, Cyril, John Alden Carpenter *join* Sibelius, Carl Nielsen, Sir Hubert Parry, César Franck in *crawling on yr knees* once more to the Germans, *accepting a German form* once more, after geniuses like Grieg, Debussy etc had repudiated? What magic is it that these Germans have that all people want to crawl on their knees before them — them, the murderers of our young men, not once, *but repeatedly*, 1860, 1870, 1914, 1938? I shall never understand it. You gave me *so much more* than I was able to give you! You gave me Denmark (1904), Sweden (1904), large chamber music (1901), Grieg Op. 66 (1901), personal friendship with Grieg (1905). You gave me the materials of leadership, but you would not accept my British-Nordic, anti-German leadership. So all my compositional life I have been that miserable thing: a leader without followers! One might be tempted to say: These Nordics are too free to follow a leader. But not when it is a matter of following Germans! Then you are all born thralls [. . .]. The English were wrong in the Boer war & lost much of their empire as a result. The Germans have murdered our peoples & broken the link of German unity by *deeming themselves our superiors.* As long as the Germans refuse to acknowledge their *lack of superiority* over us other Germanics, so long should we refuse to use their artforms & creep on our musical bellies before them [. . .]. I shall never understand why you do it. Your loving but defeated, Percy.[3]

Two days after Grainger had written this letter Roger Quilter died, and, after he had seen her once, Karen Holten died two weeks later. Shortly he boarded a ship to take him to New York. For the last three days of the voyage he was gripped with chronic abdominal cramps which pained him as nothing had done before. Within an hour of the ship's docking at New York he was rushed by ambulance to White Plains hospital, where he was operated on once more. This was the first of a long series of operations at both White Plains hospital under Dr Nygaard and in the Mayo Clinic under Dr Cook. Against the strict orders of Dr Nygaard, however, he performed the Grieg piano concerto with the Dutchess County Philharmonic Orchestra under Ole Windingstad in a concert of Norwegian music on October 31 at the Carnegie Hall. At the end of the concert the Norwegian Ambassador to the United States delivered a message of greeting from King Haakon. It was Grainger's last performance at Carnegie Hall. The following year King Haakon awarded the Australian the St Olav medal for his services to Norwegian music. Grainger never again went against the advice of Dr Nygaard: he ended a letter to Herman Sandby dated December 30, 1953 with the sentence: 'Darling Herman, I have always been a stupid unlucky man, & it will not be otherwise with my illness.'

During his stay in the Mayo Clinic in 1954 Grainger occupied his time in writing the last pages of yet another rambling (but fascinating) series of autobiographical essays which eventually fell under the generic title 'Grainger's Anecdotes' (a work to which the present writer freely acknowledges his indebtedness). The last three essays, entitled 'The Things I Dislike', 'What is behind my music' and 'Why "My wretched Tone-life"', contain the quintessence of his artistic and philosophical genius and madness cemented by his unique form of venom. At one point he writes:

As I review my life as a whole (humanly & artistically) it seems nothing but tragedy, futility, heart-break—due to my wickedness, pig-headedness, cowardice, clumsiness, lack of skill. But I am (& always have been) kept going by my interests. Tho my conscience tells me I should kill myself, there is always some pending rehearsal, or something that anchors me to life. These days, of course, it is my Free Music gins. They, like my marriage, 'entirely satisfy' (as Kipling makes his Indian Hillman say of the 1st German War). Ella & I are bound for the Mayo Clinic (Rochester, Minn) & the operation I expect to have done there, is one many have died from. Yet I am less afraid of this operation than I am of playing before an audience. So this bears out what I have always thought: that I am more afraid of playing in public than of anything in the world.

In 'The Things I Dislike' he ends:

In other words, religion is the ruination of life. All our dark & needless belief in sin stems from religion, while our disastrous ambitions stem from the fighting spirit of the Old Testament. The world of modern doctoring, modern machines, modern art, modern amorality would be just paradise if we could only shed the blight of religion. As long as men are religious, moral, ambitious, meat-eating & warlike I shall regard every moment spent with them as a shameful waste of time. And I shall welcome every calamity, defeat & loss-of-face that may befall them.

In November that year while recovering from his operation he received a visit from Vaughan Williams. It is curious that on the two occasions when Grainger was under the greatest physical and spiritual stress, this gentle English composer, who was not, after all, a very close friend or a great admirer of his music, should have appeared to render solace. Before he left, Grainger arranged for Burnett Cross to take another close-up photograph of Vaughan Williams's eyes.

For relaxation, Percy never abandoned his great passion for the films. In June 1955, he went to see a film of Verdi's *Aïda* — an event which occasioned him to write in his diary: 'Rotten, dull show, filthy music, loathsome singing'. In old age, however, his love of Rachmaninov's music grew to a point where it ranked in his esteem almost with that of Delius.

In September of the same year he and Ella left for Australia. Although they stayed for nine months it was one of the most disheartening periods of his life. What he had always liked so much about Australia was its British qualities. What he now found was a country aping the worst aspects of American culture and flooded with the kind of European immigrants he disliked most. On one occasion an Italian tram conductor in Melbourne threw a tantrum with Grainger because he had handed the wrong money for his fare. Percy had recently been overtaken by slight deafness, and he now found this condition a great blessing for the first time. Australia's unique architecture had been savagely defiled since the pre-war period. Many of the charming artisans' cottages had been torn down to make way for characterless boxes and much of the delicate cast-iron lacework which adorned the house terraces had been requisitioned during the war to make armaments. He lamented this deeply. Many of his relatives and friends had died or were crippled. For the first time he felt a stranger in the country of his birth.

Percy and Ella devoted most of their time to organizing the exhibits at the museum. He bought his usual workman's early morning pass for the trams and arrived for work at about 6.00 a.m. and stayed there with Ella for between twelve and fourteen hours each day. When they arrived in Melbourne they had done so without informing any relatives and booked into a small hotel near the Albert Park Lake. When his relatives eventually discovered their presence in town, they were asked to stay alternately with his cousins Gordon and Norman. Percy and Ella were so absorbed in their museum work that almost certainly they would have foregone a midday meal had not Gordon and his solicitous wife Evie taken them biscuits and a flask of hot soup each day. Percy went to Adelaide on two occasions mainly to sort out the legacy of his late Aunt Clara.

Although Grainger still gave much love and care to his museum, there were times when even he regretted his pre-war decision to have it built in Melbourne. The Australian Customs and Excise Department sometimes halted material sent from White Plains and his pleas once went as high as the Prime Minister's Office in order that some material should be released. His return to a museum with leaking roofs and silverfish beginning to devour his precious documents hurt him terribly. His continued requests to his friends to return early letters were often refused outright. The enormously valuable letters to Herman and Alfhild Sandby were stubbornly withheld by the owners. He pleaded with his friends to write their letters and music on transparent paper to make the job of photocopying easier. He even went to the trouble at one stage of including a sheet of transparent paper with each letter he sent, but most continued to reply on normal paper.

Grainger often got into the most appalling mess with his original musical manuscripts. There were times, for example, when one section of a two-piano/four-handed work would be sent to Melbourne whilst the other remained in White Plains, and sometimes different versions of the same work would be similarly split up. The problem was made even worse after his death when many of the remaining original manuscripts at White Plains were scattered throughout various libraries in America, Europe, South Africa and Australia. After the Grainger Museum was built there was never a single location where every manuscript could be referred to, even in photocopy form. In the last years of his life Grainger would sometimes forget where he had sent or taken an orchestral score, and he began to lose valuable documents in this way.

Before Grainger left Australia Bernard Heinze again approached him about the possibility of a 'Grainger Festival' sponsored by the Australian Broadcasting Commission, which again would have involved featuring him as solo pianist rather than as a composer. He was offered £75A for a concerto and £50A for a solo recital. In a letter to Cyril Scott he wrote: 'The Australians must be aware that I have behaved badly thru life. But they would prefer to brag about me than to censure me. At least, that's what I think. So I am thankful that I am too old & too tired to be tempted to embark on the Grainger Festival — thus avoiding, I hope a colossal repudiation of myself & my music.'[4]

The Olympic Games were being held in Melbourne in 1956 whilst he was still working in his museum. The organizers of the games and most of the Australian newspapers were desperately searching for an Australian composer to write a suitable piece for the opening ceremonies. The young Australian composer Keith Humble put forward the name of Percy Grainger. The suggestion was received as a joke. Humble reflects today: 'I regret that I didn't have the knowledge or the force of character to insist on it, as Grainger is the beginning of Australian music.'[5]

Grainger's last job before he left Australia was to deposit a small parcel with a Melbourne bank. Instructions were left that it was to be opened ten years after his death. It contained an essay and a large collection of photographs giving full details of his sex life. His single hope had been that after ten years had elapsed the world would be sufficiently broadminded to accept such things without guilt or shame and that a rational enquiry could be made into all aspects of deviant sexual behaviour. He requested that the material be handed to an institute of psychology where a proper study could be made. In the same year that the parcel was eventually opened with all due ceremony at the Grainger Museum, a bookshop owner in Sydney was arrested by the New South Wales police for displaying a poster of Michelangelo's *David* in his window.

In June 1956 Percy and Ella returned to America via Suva, Honolulu, Vancouver and San Francisco. He had left Australia vowing never to return. The remainder of the year was spent mostly on the Free Music experiments. At various stages in the development of the instruments Burnett Cross made recordings on his home recording equipment. The music they made is quite unlike anything produced by other instruments either before or since. The music to which it can be most closely compared is what has become known in the pop world of the 1970s as 'progressive' music, where an attempt is made, often by electronic means, to fuse the best elements of classical music, jazz and popular music. Had Grainger lived longer and been able to continue his experiments with more sophisticated equipment he would not be very far removed today from some of the electronic extravaganzas of such groups as

Pink Floyd.

Towards the end of 1956 (his seventy-fifth year) when Grainger was continuing his formidable touring duties by train and bus, an event took place which scared him considerably. Asleep on a Greyhound bus one night he was being tormented by some frightful nightmare and in the throes of this experience he began to belabour the lady sitting next to him with many and hefty blows. On being woken he was puzzled but soon very apologetic when he realized what had taken place. Apparently he had dreamed that he was conducting a bad performance of *Hill-Song Number 1*.

On January 5, 1957 Percy and Ella sailed on the *Queen Mary* for Southampton, but by early February he felt so ill that he moved to Denmark. In Aarhus he was given radium injections and later, in Stockholm, X-ray treatment. During his stay on the continent of Europe he travelled to Frankfurt and Mainz to see old friends from his youthful days. The changes that had taken place in Germany were a shock to him almost as devastating as that upon his return to Australia two years earlier. But Grainger, too, had changed. In the pre-war days he had been able to amuse his friends' children by performing cartwheel after cartwheel; now they were faced with a slightly deaf, poor-sighted and occasionally lame man. Yet he was always moved to maintain contact with young people and his powerfully chiselled yet sympathetic features held a great attraction for those who could still detect the boy behind the mask. While in Frankfurt Ella and Percy travelled to Hochstadt, about fifteen kilometres away. It was a nostalgic trip for Percy because Hochstadt was the little walled mediaeval village which he and Rose had once come upon by surprise when cycling through the apple orchards of the surrounding countryside. It had survived the war.

Before leaving Denmark he performed the Grieg concerto and the *Suite on Danish Folk-Songs* with the Aarhus Symphony Orchestra under Per Drier. The entire concert was recorded. Some years after his death the tape was made available to the Vanguard Recording Society and immediately created controversy within the Vanguard offices. Whilst it demonstrated the unique and spectacular pianistic qualities of which Grainger was capable, it was a performance which, owing to the pianist's age, was not as technically accomplished as it might have been in his prime. Many performing artists (such as Melba, Butt, Patti, Cortot, McCormack, Moiseiwitsch) have been tempted to enter (or be wheeled into) the recording studios when long past their technical best. Yet it is just these precious records that are most sought after and cherished by the connoisseur and collector. When they no longer have the physical equipment to dazzle their listeners, the artists are forced to draw on the deeper musical qualities of the work and of their own art to lend conviction to their performances. Many, including Benjamin Britten and the present author, regard the Aarhus performance of the Grieg concerto as the noblest ever committed to record. Yet a generation of pianistic typists have attuned the ears of most critics and audiences to expect faultless performances these days, and Grainger's performance of the Grieg concerto (which, let it be admitted, is liberally sprinkled with lapses and avalanches of wrong notes) would doubtless be treated with scorn and derision were it made generally available. Thus the staff of Vanguard were split into two different camps. Whilst they all recognized its great musical and historical values, some felt that it would have rendered a disservice to the memory of the pianist had it been issued. Their view prevailed, but only just in time, for several hundred copies of the record had already been pressed.

In May Percy and Ella went to England, where, apart from his TV appearance in the BBC's Birmingham studios (performing *Handel in the Strand* and Grieg's *To the Spring*), he was given the chance of rehearsing two British Army bands in works of his own. Lieutenant Colonel McBain invited him to conduct the band of the Royal Military School of Music at Kneller Hall, Twickenham and Captain C.H. Jaegar asked him to conduct the band of the Irish Guards. It was becoming widely known that Grainger made almost yearly trips to Europe and it was seen that such opportunities should not be missed. That year he also received an invitation to play with the Oslo Philharmonic Orchestra in a concert to mark the fiftieth anniversary of Grieg's death, yet he had to turn it down because of ill health. Later in the year when his health improved, he mentioned to an English acquaintance that he would be happy to record anything from his repertoire free of charge. Unfortunately neither the money nor adequate recording facilities were available, so the opportunity was missed. He was most anxious to record some of the more obscure solo piano works of Grieg, for performances of which the Norwegian composer had praised him many years earlier. Eventually Burnett Cross recorded some of these (with Grainger introducing each one), and despite the home recording quality and the upright piano they are perhaps the most beautiful records he made.

At the end of May, Percy and Ella returned to New York, again on the *Queen Mary*. A few days after his arrival in White Plains he suffered several new kinds of terror. One night he woke up to find himself sitting on his bedside reaching for a painful spot on the side of his head. He touched instead an open wound covered in blood. He had either fallen out of bed or fallen as a result of sleepwalking. He never knew exactly what happened, but two nights later, on June 17, he entered in his diary: 'Going to bed, started to read, couldn't control my speech, talked nonsense, (very frightening).' On July 3, he wrote 'Beloved mother would have been 95 today. I have felt the tragic influence of her death more in this year 1957 than in any other year.'

In October, he was once more on the operating table for a bilateral orchiectomy (castration), but made speedy enough recovery to undertake

twelve concerts throughout the winter season in Michigan, North Carolina, Texas, Cincinnati, Wisconsin and California. Before his operation
he was informed that he had cancer. Grainger's first reaction to Dr
Nygaard on being told this was, 'You can do anything to me you feel will
have to be done — but remember, you mustn't change my music.' Some
time after the operation Nygaard felt obliged to ask if anything had
changed. Grainger replied, 'As to the music, absolutely no. As to my well
being, greatly improved.'[6]

In January 1958 he made one of his infrequent trips into New York
City to hear Leonard Bernstein conduct the New York Philharmonic
Orchestra in a performance of Webern's *Six Orchestral Pieces* and
Stravinsky's *Rite of Spring*. It was the first time he had heard either work
(he claimed!) and he enjoyed them both immensely. In February he
played the solo part in the Delius piano concerto in an otherwise all-
Grainger concert at the Baylor University School of Music. In the first
half of the concert he was one of the three pianists in a performance of
*The Warriors* and in the second half, after the Delius work, he heard the
orchestra and band perform three movements from *Lincolnshire Posy*
and *Marching Song of Democracy*. It was just the kind of concert he enjoyed most and he regarded the whole evening as a great success.

In April Percy and Ella returned to London for a stay of two months.
Except for one formal function at Cecil Sharp House (headquarters of
the English Folk-Song and Dance Society) where he met Vaughan
Williams, all his engagements were informal social meetings. As well as
seeing his old friends he made a new one when he met Benjamin Britten
for the first time on May 20. On the morning of the day he took the train
from Waterloo Station to collect the liner SS *Maasdam* from Southampton, he felt the urge to pay a final visit to the Victoria and Albert
Museum. He went with one object in mind; to spend a few moments
gazing at what he sometimes described as 'the best painting in the world'.
It was *The Mill* by Burne-Jones. He felt a close affinity with this school of
painting and often described himself as a pre-Raphaelite composer. It
was a painting he had been to see many times when living in London and
one from which he drew much solace and spiritual strength.

In 1959 he had intended visiting Sweden and the Aldeburgh Festival in
England, but his leg and back became painful in late May and he took
the earliest ship back to New York, after a stay of only six weeks. In
White Plains he was given X-ray treatment and in September he decided
to draw up his Last Will and Testament. It was one of the most extraordinary documents he had written and contained the following declaration: 'I direct that my flesh be removed from my bones and the flesh
destroyed. I give and bequeath my skeleton to the University of Melbourne, Carlton N.3., Victoria, Australia, for preservation and possible
display in the Grainger Museum.' This request was ultimately denied
him.

Grainger continued to make long journeys (many of them alone) during the 1959/60 season in order to give concerts wherever he knew his own music would be programmed. He continued to avoid air travel and preferred trains and buses. He once refused outright to see a close relative if she travelled to see him by aircraft. He disliked the fact that aircraft were unable to go backwards, sideways, or directly up or down. He felt this was a serious limitation. One night during that season when he had stretched himself out to sleep along three seats in a train compartment he fell off his resting place and cut his head.

On Friday April 29, 1960 Grainger gave his last public performance at the Dartmouth College in Hanover, New Hampshire as part of the Third Annual Festival of Music. In the morning he gave a talk entitled 'The Influence of Folk-song on Art Music' and illustrated it with two-piano versions of *Let's Dance Gay in Green Meadow*, *Spoon River*, *The Lonely Desert Man*, *La Cucuracha* and *English Waltz*. In the afternoon he conducted a performance of *The Power of Rome and the Christian Heart*. His appearances passed almost without a whisper.

In May he wrote to Stokowski asking if he could help him find a lost copy of the score and parts of his *In a Nutshell* Suite which he felt he might have left at the Hollywood Bowl when the Maestro had presented it fourteen years earlier. He ended the letter by saying that Schirmers had allowed it to go out of print and were not likely to reprint it. He was very low on copies.

Percy's health deteriorated rapidly towards Christmas 1960 and he was eventually admitted to White Plains Hospital.

Dr Nygaard has written of him during his last months:

> [. . .] there seemed to be an increasing weakness physically as well as mentally. His usually clearcut statements related to all topics and not only to music would at times seem to start a bit of wandering. Wrong words might slip in. Associations would appear unexpectedly and uncoordinatedly. It was soon clear that Percy was slowly developing metastases of the brain also. It seemed that the iron curtain had started to descend very slowly upon this brilliant mind although to one who did not know him intimately he might only have appeared as a frail gentleman, pale and weakened and tired out.[. . .] Of course he was a genius — whatever that actually means. Among many other things he also impressed me as being almost a human Saint.[. . .] When it came to thinking, Percy was able to refer to that inner light which shone with a clarity dimmed only by the last year of his suffering. And even then he was a Saint.[7]

As Ella sat patiently by his bedside, Percy turned to her and said, 'You're the only one I like.'[8] These were his last words. On the morning of February 20 he finally submitted to the greater strength of abdominal cancer. His body was flown to Sydney in a hermetically sealed crate and then taken by train to Adelaide. At the Christian burial service conducted in the Anglican St Matthew's Church, Kensington Road, Marryatville, on March 2, the chief mourners were Ella and Burnett Cross. The undertaker then walked ahead of the hearse to Adelaide's West Terrace Cemetery, where Percy was laid to rest in the Aldridge family vault.

Thus Percy, a lifelong atheist, had had his other last wish refused him: 'I request that there be no public or religious funeral, funeral service or ceremony of any kind or nature.' Even beyond the grave, it seems, he still feared public performances more than anything else.

# Notes

### 1. 'Bubbles'

1  I am deeply indebted to Michael Cannon, upon whose excellent book *The Land Boomers* (Melbourne University Press, Melbourne, 1966) I have drawn for much background material in this section.

2  Grainger, 'Aldridge-Grainger-Ström Saga', located Library of Congress, dated 1934.

3  Grainger, *Photos of Rose Grainger and of 3 short accounts of her life by herself, in her own hand-writing* (Frankfurt am-Main, published privately 1923).

4  Grainger, 'Grainger's Anecdotes', being a handwritten collection of autobiographical jottings variously dated between 1949 and 1954, located Grainger Archives, White Plains.

5  'Aldridge-Grainger-Ström Saga'.

6  Grainger, undated, untitled notes located Grainger Archives, White Plains.

7  'Aldridge-Grainger-Ström Saga'.

8  Ibid.

9  Letter from Grainger to Alfhild Sandby, March 30, 1940.

10  Legend to 'Percy Aldridge Grainger's published Compositions, 1st editions' being Desk One in Grainger Museum (University of Melbourne), November 2, 1938.

11  'Grainger's Anecdotes'.

### 2. Doctors and Dustbin Lids

1  Grainger, notes on A.E. Aldis, located Grainger Archives, White Plains, dated December 3, 1936.

2  From a recording of a lecture entitled 'Personality in Art' given by Grainger possibly c. 1943, located Grainger Archives, White Plains.

3  Grainger, notes on Thomas Sisley, located Grainger Archives, White Plains, dated December 15, 1936.

4  Grainger, 'Sketch for Article: English Pianism and Harold Bauer', February 19, 1945, Jacksonville, Florida, located Grainger Archives, White Plains.

5  Grainger, notes on John H. Grainger, located Grainger Archives, White Plains, dated November 8, 1936.

6  'English Pianism and Harold Bauer'.

7  Ibid.

8  Grainger, notes on Louis Pabst, located Grainger Archives, White Plains, dated November 23, 1936.

9  'Legend to 1st editions'.

10  Ibid.

11  Ibid.

12  Notes on Louis Pabst.

13  Frederic Lamond: b. Glasgow, January 28, 1868; d. Stirling, February 21, 1948. One of Liszt's last pupils and generally considered to have been one of the finest

Beethoven pianists of his generation.

14   Letter from Mrs N.A. Hill to author, February 15, 1970.


### 3. 'Perks' joins the Frankfurt Gang

1   Letter from John Grainger to Percy Grainger, October 4, 1895.

2   Mainly remembered as the teacher of such fine cellists as Beatrice Harrison, Boris Hambourg (brother of Mark), Maurice Eisenberg and Carlo Fischer. Also toured with Ellenor Gerhard, Artur Schnabel and Ferruccio Busoni.

3   Heermann numbered amongst his pupils Bronislav Huberman.

4   Louis Brassin, who is solely remembered today for his literal but effective transcription of *Magic Fire Music* from *Die Walküre*, had been a pupil of Moscheles, who had taught Felix Mendelssohn.

5   Hoddap later became a pupil of Busoni. Also toured with Jan Kubelik and recorded for Polydor under the name Frieda Kwast-Hoddap.

6   'English Pianism and Harold Bauer'.

7   Ibid.

8   More commonly written *Leschetitsky,* Theodor (b. Lancut, Poland, June 22, 1830; d. Dresden, November 14, 1915). Like Liszt, had been a pupil of Czerny, who in turn had been a pupil of Beethoven. Became one of the most famous piano teachers of all time and included amongst his pupils: Paderewski, Friedman, Brailowsky, Gabrilowitsch, Hambourg, Horszowski, Leginska (née Liggins), Moiseiwitsch, Ney, Schelling, Schnabel, Wittgenstein.

9   Melba's assertion that 'Georgie' (George—her first son, born October 16, 1883) was twelve years old and her guess that Percy was 'about 14' indicate that the letter was probably written during the summer of 1896. Percy, however, added the following note to the letter many years later: 'Nellie Melba to Rose Grainger (1897?)'.

10  Cyril Scott: *The Philosophy of Modernism* (Kegan Paul, Trench, Trubner, London, 1917)

11  Grainger notes on Karl Klimsch, located Grainger Archives, White Plains, dated August 19, 1936.

12  Ibid.

13  Ibid.

14  Letter from Grainger to Cyril Scott, March 23, 1955.

15  'Grainger's Anecdotes'.

16  Cyril Scott: *My Years of Indiscretion* (Mills & Boon, London, 1924).

17  Scott had given Grainger a copy of *Leaves of Grass* as a birthday present in 1897.

18  Cyril Scott: *My Years of Indiscretion.*

19  Franckenstein's brother Sir George Franckenstein later became Austrian Minister in London before the Nazi annexation.

20  Hans Pfitzner (b. Moscow 1869; d. Salzburg 1949): composer and conductor of great distinction in Germany, perhaps best known for his opera *Palestrina*.

21  'Grainger's Anecdotes'.

22  Ibid.

23  Letter from Grainger to J.H. Petersen, February 19, 1932.

24  Letter from Grainger to Alfhild Sandby, December 26, 1936.

25  Grainger, 'Ere-I-Forget—Jottingsdown (for use in the "Aldridge-Grainger-Brandelius Saga") of small closeups ((details)) that otherwise might [go] un-writ-hoarded ((unrecorded))'. Located Grainger Archives, White Plains, variously dated 1944/5.

26  'Legend to 1st editions'.


### 4. Saint and Sinner

1   Grainger, 'Birds-Eye View of the Together Life of Rose Grainger and Percy Grainger'. Located Grainger Archives, White Plains, dated variously during 1947.

2   'Grainger's Anecdotes'.
3   Ibid.
4   Ibid.
5   During the Great War, Grainger started work on a piece later entitled *The Power of Rome and the Christian Heart*. He often described this as the first specifically conscientious objector music ever written.
6   Newspaper cutting in possession of the author, the date and name of which, however, have been cut off.
7   Program-Note to *To a Nordic Princess*, Coatsville, Pa., USA, January 16, 1928 (G. Schirmer Inc., New York).
8   Letter from Grainger to Herman Sandby, December 9, 1937.
9   Letter from Grainger to Alfhild Sandby, November 26, 1929.
10  Letter from Grainger to Karen Holten, November 6, 1908. (translated in part from the original Danish text by Dr Paul Ries, Faculty of Modern and Medieval Languages, University of Cambridge).
11  'Bird's-Eye View'.
12  Grainger, 'The Love-Life of Helen and Paris'. Written variously during 1927/8, located Grainger Archives, White Plains.
13  'Aldridge-Grainger-Ström Saga'.
14  Letter from Grainger to Alfhild Sandby, November 1905.
15  'Bird's-Eye View'.
16  Letter written by Grainger on August 21, 1932 to be opened in the event of his being found dead.
17  Letter from Grainger to Roger Quilter, July 20, 1930
18  Letter from Grainger to Cyril Scott, July 23, 1956.

### 5. Grettir the Strong Flexes his Muscles
1   Letter from Storm Bull to author, November 26, 1969.
2   Letter from Burnett Cross to author, November 9, 1975.
3   Self-styled philosopher and founder of cult of 'charactology' or 'racial typology' based on a neurotic and almost hysterical opposition to women and Jews.
4   English-born son-in-law of Richard Wagner. Alleged philosopher whose writings concerned history, music and fanatical anti-Semitism. During the Great War, Chamberlain remained in Germany and became a political pamphleteer for the German cause. Greatly admired by Adolph Hitler.
5   'Aldridge-Grainger-Ström Saga'.
6   Letter from Grainger to Alfhild Sandby, March 30, 1940.
7   Letter from John Grainger to Amy Black, April 22, 1897.
8   Notes on John H. Grainger.
9   Program-Note to *Marching Song of Democracy*, Universal Edition, 1923.
10  'Grainger's Anecdotes'.
11  Letter from Grainger to Alfhild Sandby, November 13, 1936.

### 6. 'The years before the war were Hell'
1   Letter from Grainger to Rose Grainger, July 7, 1906.
2   Letter from Grainger to Eric Fenby, December 6, 1936.
3   'Aldridge-Grainger-Ström Saga'.
4   Rupert Charles Wolsten Bunny (1864-1947), b. & d. Melbourne. Studied in Australia and later in Paris under Jean Paul Laurens. Lived most of his life abroad, but returned to Australia in 1933. Also composed music.
5   John Singer Sargent, b. Florence, 1856; d. London, 1925.
6   Almost certainly 'A Lot of Rot for cello and piano' (unpublished), later reworked, retitled and published as *Youthful Rapture*.
7   Letter from Grainger to Herman Sandby, September 29, 1901.

8   'Bird's-Eye View'.
9   'Grainger's Anecdotes'.
10  Grainger radio interview in author's collection. Date and source unknown.
11  'Aldridge-Grainger-Ström Saga'.
12  'Ere-I-Forget'.
13  Grainger, notes on Sargent and Rathbone. Located Grainger Archives, White Plains, dated November 22, 1936.
14  'Ere-I-Forget'.


*7.  The Twisted Genius and the Dinkum Aussie*
1   Later used in *Scotch Strathspey and Reel.*
2   St Luke (14:21).
3   'Grainger's Anecdotes'.
4   Ibid.
5   When one listens to Paderewski's or de Pachmann's records today, Grainger's use of the word 'normal' to describe their playing may need a little explanation. Not only was their more sentimental style of playing considered normal around the turn of the century, but Grainger almost certainly would have heard de Pachmann and Paderewski in their prime when they were both considered the greatest miniaturists of their day (and before they made the records by which they are best remembered).
6   'Grainger's Anecdotes'.
7   Ibid.
8   Ibid.
9   Robert Lewis Taylor: *The Running Pianist* (Doubleday & Co. Inc., New York, 1950).
10  'Grainger's Anecdotes'.
11  Ibid.
12  Ibid.
13  Ibid.
14  Ibid.
15  Ibid.
16  Ibid.


*8.  Packed Houses and Zulu Warriors*
1   Letter from Grainger to Roger Quilter, December 7, 1903.
2   Ibid.


*9.  'I am an Australian, not a Corsican!'*
1   Letter from Grainger to Alfhild Sandby, May 15, 1947.
2   Letter from Alfhild Sandby to Grainger, December 6, 1936.
3   Ibid.
4   Ibid.
5   Letter from Grainger to Alfhild Sandby, December 26, 1936.
6   Ibid.
7   Letter from Grainger to Alfhild Sandby, March 30, 1940.
8   Letter from Grainger to Herman Sandby, undated but probably July/August 1906.

*10.  Unto Brigg Fair*
1   'Grainger's Anecdotes'.
2   Ibid.
3   Grainger, undated, untitled notes located Grainger Museum, University of Melbourne.
4   Harold C. Schonberg: *The Great Pianists* (Victor Gollancz, London, 1964).
5   Letter from Grainger to Robert Langham, October 23, 1927.

6   Letter from Storm Bull to author, November 26, 1969.
7   'Grainger's Anecdotes'.
8   Letter from Percy Grainger to Rose Grainger, April 26, 1905.
9   Letter from Grainger to Lady Winefride Elwes, September 17, 1905.
10  Grainger: quoted from his article in *Journal of the Folk-Song Society*, III/12 (May 1908).
11  Program-Note to *Lincolnshire Posy*, Schott/Schirmer, August 1939.
12  Letter from Grainger to Cecil Sharp, November 2, 1906.
13  Article in *Journal of the Folk-Song Society*.
14  Grainger: 'The Impress of Personality in Unwritten Music', *Musical Quarterly*, (July 1915).
15  Letter from Percy Grainger to Rose Grainger, April 4, 1908.
16  'Grainger's Anecdotes'.
17  Letter from Percy Grainger to Rose Grainger, August 1, 1909.
18  Letter from Rose Grainger to Roger Quilter, January 22, 1908.
19  Letter from Frederick Delius to Jelka Delius, April 21, 1907.
20  Grainger, interview with John Amis, BBC, June 14, 1959.
21  Article in *Journal of the Folk-Song Society*.
22  Program-Note to *Lincolnshire Posy*.
23  Benjamin Britten, BBC broadcast (in conversation with Peter Pears, Ella Grainger and John Morris at the Red House, Aldeburgh-on-Sea, Suffolk), June 15, 1966.
24  A. L. Lloyd: *Folk Song in England* (Lawrence and Wishart, London, 1967).

### 11.   *The Little Half-Viking*

1   Grainger, tablet of notes on Grieg, located Grainger Museum, Melbourne, dated December 8, 1938.
2   BBC Amis interview.
3   'Grainger's Anecdotes'.
4   Grainger: 'Glimpses of Genius', *Etude*, XXXIX/10 (October 1921).
5   Grainger's diary, August 2, 1907.
6   BBC Amis interview.
7   Grainger often investigated the racial aspects of the musical antecedents and influences of other composers. He made this idea known to Grieg, but the Norwegian gently but firmly refuted it.
8   Notes on Grieg.

### 12.   *'Poor put-upon Percy'*

1   Letter from Grainger to Roger Quilter, March 25, 1908.
2   Ibid.
3   BBC Amis interview.
4   'Aldridge-Grainger-Ström Saga'.
5   Ibid.
6   Letter from Grainger to Roger Quilter, January 31, 1909.
7   'Legend to 1st editions'.
8   Ibid.
9   Translated from the original German by Lionel Carley.
10  Letter from Rose Grainger to Roger Quilter, February 19, 1910.
11  Letter from Rose Grainger to Percy Grainger, August 30, 1909.
12  Translated from the original Danish by Dr Paul Ries.
13  Letter from Dr K. K. Nygaard to author, December 2, 1975.
14  Letter from Grainger to Alfhild Sandby, November 13, 1936.
15  Hjalmar Thuren: *Folkesangen paa Faeroërne* (Andr. Fred. Host and Sons, Copenhagen, 1908).
16  Program-Note to *Lord Peter's Stable Boy*, G. Schirmer Inc., 1928.

17  Letter from Grainger to Roger Quilter, January 19, 1911.
18  'Ere-I-Forget'.
19  Program-Note to *The Warriors,* Schott & Co., 1923.
20  Notes on John H. Grainger.
21  'Grainger's Anecdotes'.
22  'Helen and Paris'.
23  Letter from Thomas Beecham to Frederick Delius, April 20, 1914.
24  'Grainger's Anecdotes'.

### 13. *'Adieu old World! I would hail a New World'*

1  Grainger is clearly wrong here in his recollection of dates. This meeting almost certainly took place at the end of June or beginning of July 1915, after Busoni had decided to return to Europe.
2  'Grainger's Anecdotes'.
3  Program-Note to *Arrival Platform Humlet,* G. Schirmer Inc., 1916.
4  'Ere-I-Forget'.
5  Ibid.
6  Ibid.
7  Letter from Grainger to Michael Harrington, November 20, 1937.
8  Letter from Grainger to Michael Harrington, February 6, 1941.
9  'Grainger's Anecdotes'.
10  Cyril Scott: *My Years of Indiscretion.*

### 14. *'Your mad side has ruined us'*

1  Letter from Grainger to Alfhild Sandby, March 30, 1940.
2  'Grainger's Anecdotes'.
3  Letter from Rose Grainger to Roger Quilter, April 11, 1922.
4  Letter from Grainger to Alfhild Sandby of unknown date, and quoted in a typescript entitled 'Percy Grainger, Romantic Friendships' by Alfhild Sandby.

### 15. *Beatless Music, Blue-Eyed English and a Nordic Princess*

1  'Grainger's Anecdotes'.
2  Ibid.
3  Letter from Grainger to Roger Quilter, October 2, 1922.
4  'Grainger's Anecdotes'.
5  Ibid.
6  Ibid.
7  Notes on Karl Klimsch.
8  Round letter from Grainger 'to my fellow-composers', May 25, 1925.
9  Letter from Grainger to Roger Quilter, September 30, 1924.
10  *Adelaide Advertiser,* July 24, 1924.
11  Letter from *Pult und Taktstock* to Grainger, March 8, 1926.
12  Letter from Grainger to Roger Quilter, December 5, 1926.
13  'Helen and Paris'.
14  Ibid.

### 16. *'It's like kicking out into thin air'*

1  Letter from Grainger to Michael Harrington, April 26, 1928.
2  'Ere-I-Forget'.
3  Ibid.
4  Letter from Grainger to Michael Harrington, June 20, 1957.
5  Letter from Grainger to Everard Feilding, February 7, 1936.
6  Letter from Grainger to Alfhild Sandby, December 26, 1936.
7  Round letter from Grainger 'to Kith and Friends', July 27, 1948.

8  Edna Horton: 'Rare Music of Early Age Restored', from *Musical Courier,* October 1, 1939.
9  Letter from Storm Bull to author, November 26, 1969.
10  Letter from Edwyn H. Hames to author, May 5, 1969.


*17. 'I shall go back to the joys of my teen-years'*
1  'Ere-I-Forget'.
2  Letter from Eugene Weintraub to author, February 3, 1970.
3  'Ere-I-Forget'.
4  Letter from Grainger to Herman and Alfhild Sandby, September 14, 1945.
5  Letter from Storm Bull to author, July 21, 1969.
6  Ibid.
7  Round letter from Grainger, May 21, 1947.
8  Round letter from Grainger, August 16, 1947.
9  Round letter from Grainger, July 27, 1948.
10  Letter from Stokowski to Grainger, January 17, 1949.
11  Letter from Burnett Cross to author, February 15, 1970.
12  Round letter from Grainger, June 7, 1949.


*18. 'Your loving but defeated, Percy'*
1  Letter from Grainger to H.L. Cavendish, May 12, 1951.
2  Letter from Grainger to Dom Anselm Hughes, September 6, 1951.
3  Letter from Grainger to Herman Sandby, September 19, 1953.
4  Letter from Grainger to Cyril Scott, August 10, 1956.
5  James Murdoch: *Australia's Contemporary Composers* (Macmillan Company of Australia, Melbourne, 1972).
6  Letter from Dr K.K. Nygaard to author, September 9, 1975.
7  Ibid.
8  Letter from Stewart Manville to author, November 9, 1975.

# Select Source List
(Published works only. See Notes for unpublished sources.)

Aldrich, Richard: *Concert Life in New York 1902-1923*, Putman's Sons, New York, 1941.

Aldrich, Richard: *Musical Discourses from the New York Times*, Humphrey Milford, Boston, 1928.

Bauer, Harold: *Harold Bauer, His Book*, W. W. Norton & Co., New York, 1948.

Bax, Arnold: *Farewell, My Youth*, Longmans Green & Co., London; Greenwood Press, Westport, 1943.

Beecham, Sir Thomas: *A Mingled Chime*, Putnam's Sons, New York, 1943; Hutchinson & Co., London, 1944.

Beecham, Sir Thomas: *Frederick Delius*, Hutchinson & Co., 1959; Vienna House, New York, 1973.

Buchanan, C. L.: 'Analyzing the Greater Grainger', *Musical America* (August 25, 1917), p. 6.

Buchanan, C. L.: 'Play Boy Grows Up', *Independent* (July 28, 1917), p. 132.

Busoni: *Letters to his Wife*, trans. Rosamund Leg, Edward Arnold & Co., London, 1938.

Clemens, Clara: *My Husband Gabrilowitsch*, Harper & Bros., New York, 1938.

Covell, Roger: *Australia's Music*, Sun Books, Melbourne, 1967.

Cross, Burnett: 'Grainger's Free Music Machine', *Recorded Sound* (BIRS), Vols. 45/6 (January, April, 1972), pp. 17-20.

Damrosch, Walter: *My Musical Life*, Scribner's Sons, New York, 1926,

Delius, Clair: *Frederick Delius*, Ivor Nicholson & Watson, London, 1935.

Dent, Edward J.: *Ferruccio Busoni*, Oxford University Press, London, 1933.

Dorum, Ivar: 'Grainger's Free Music', *Studies in Music*, University of Western Australia Press, No. 2 (1969), pp. 86-97.

Elwes, Lady Winefride and Richard: *Gervase Elwes*, Grayson & Grayson, London, 1935.

Fenby, Eric: *Delius as I knew him*, Icon Books, London; Vienna House, New York, 1966.

Finck, Henry T.: *Grieg and his Music*, John Lane, London, 1909; Blom, Benjamin, New York, 1910.

Finck, Henry T.: *My Adventures in the Golden Age of Music*, Funk and Wagnall, New York, 1926.

Finck, Henry T.: *Richard Strauss, The Man and His Works, with an Appreciation by Percy Grainger*, Little, Brown & Co., Boston, 1917.

Forsyth, Cecil: *Orchestration*, Macmillan & Co. and Stainer & Bell, London, 1914; Macmillan Pub. Co., New York, 1936.

Gibson, Frank: *Charles Conder—His Life and Works*, Bodley Head, London, 1914.

Goldman, Richard Franko: *The Band's Music*, Pitman Publishing Corp., New York, 1938.

Goldman, Richard Franko: 'Percy Grainger's "Free Music" ', *Juilliard Review*, II (Fall, 1955), pp. 37-47.

Goossens, Eugene: *Overture and Beginners,* Methuen & Co., London; Greenwood Press, Westport, 1951.

Grainger, Percy A.: 'Arnold Dolmetsch: Musical Confucius', *Musical Quarterly,* XIX (April 1933), pp. 187-98.

Grainger, Percy A.: 'Collecting with the Phonograph', *Journal of the Folk-Song Society,* III/12 (1908/09), pp. 147-242.

Grainger, Percy A.: 'Culturizing Possibilities of the Instrumentally Supplemented A Capella Choir', *Musical Quarterly,* XXVII (1942), pp. 160-4.

Grainger, Percy A.: 'Foreword', *Concerto for Piano, Opus 16,* by Edvard Grieg, G. Schirmer, New York, 1920.

Grainger, Percy A.: 'Foreword', *Five Part Fantasy No. 1,* by John Jenkins, G. Schirmer, New York, 1944.

Grainger, Percy A.: 'Foreword', *Psalms, Opus 74,* by Edvard Grieg, C. F. Peters, London, 1949.

Grainger, Percy A.: 'Foreword', *Six-Part Fantasy and Air, No. 1,* by William Lawes, G. Schirmer, New York, 1944.

Grainger, Percy A.: 'Glimpses of Genius', *Etude,* XXXIX/10 (October 1921), pp. 631-2.

Grainger, Percy A.: 'Grieg — Nationalist and Cosmopolitan', *Etude,* LXI/6 (June 1943), pp. 386, 416-18.

Grainger, Percy A.: *Guide to Virtuosity,* G. Schirmer, New York, 1923.

Grainger, Percy A.: 'The Impress of Personality in Unwritten Music', *Musical Quarterly,* I (July 1915), pp. 416-35.

Grainger, Percy A.: 'Impressions of Art in Europe — Article 1 — Finland', *Musical Courier,* XCVIII/22 (June 1, 1929), p. 8.

Grainger, Percy A.: 'Impressions of Art in Europe — Article 2 — Sweden and Norway', *Musical Courier,* (July 6, 1929), p. 8.

Grainger, Percy A.: 'Impressions of Art in Europe — Article 3 — Delius Reaps His Harvest', *Musical Courier,* XCIX/13 (September 28, 1929), pp. 8, 31.

Grainger, Percy A.: 'Impressions of Art in Europe — Article 4 — Music in England', *Musical Courier,* XCIX/17 (October 26, 1929), pp. 10, 12.

Grainger, Percy A.: *Music: A Commonsense View of All Types,* ABC, Melbourne, 1934.

Grainger, Percy A.: 'Never Has Popular Music Been as Classical as Jazz', *Metronome,* XLII/13 (July 1, 1926), p. 10.

Grainger, Percy A.: 'Percy Grainger: On Music Heard in England', *Australian Musical News,* (June 1949), pp. 32-4.

Grainger, Percy A.: 'The Personality of Frederick Delius', *Australian Musical News,* XXIV/12 (July 1, 1934), pp. 10-15.

Grainger, Percy A.: 'The Grainger Tracts', 6 vols and 1 folio. British Museum, Cup 21 c 3.

Grainger, Percy A.: *Photos of Rose Grainger and of 3 short accounts of her life by herself, in her own hand-writing reproduced for her kin and friends by her adoring son Percy Grainger,* private publication, Frankfurt-am-Main, 1923.

Grainger, Percy A.: 'The Specialist and the All-Round Man', *A Birthday Offering to Carl Engel,* ed. by Gustave Reese, G. Schirmer, New York, 1943.

Grainger, Percy A.: 'What Effect is Jazz Likely to Have Upon the Music of the Future?', *Etude,* XLII/9 (September 1924), pp. 593-4.

Guerrini: *Busoni,* Florence, 1944.

Hee-Leng Tan, Margaret: 'The Free Music of Percy Grainger', *Recorded Sound* (BIRS), vols 45-6 (January, April, 1972), pp. 21-38.

Holst, Imogen: *Gustav Holst,* Oxford University Press, London, 1938; Vienna House, New York, 1976.

Howes, Frank: 'Percy Grainger', *Recorded Sound,* 1/3 (Summer 1961), pp. 96-8.

Howes, Frank: *The English Musical Renaissance,* Secker & Warburg, London; Stein & Day, New York, 1966.

Hudson, Derek: *Norman O'Neill. A Life of Music*, Quality Press, London, 1945.

Hughes, Dom Amselm: *Septuagesima*, Faith Press, London, 1959.

Hull, A. Engelfield: *Cyril Scott*. Kegan Paul, Trench, Trubner & Co., London, 1918.

Hutchings, A.: *Delius*, Macmillan & Co., London, 1948; Greenwood Press, Westport, 1949.

Jahoda, Gloria: *The Road to Samarkand*, Charles Scribner's Sons, New York, 1969.

Karpeles, Dr Maud: *Cecil Sharp*, Routledge & Kegan Paul, London; University of Chicago Press, 1967.

Klein, H.: *The Reign of Patti*, Century Co., New York, 1920.

Lee, Ernest Markham: *Grieg*, G. Bell & Sons, London, 1908.

Leonard, Neil: *Jazz and the White Americans*, University of Chicago Press, Chicago and London, 1962.

Lloyd, A. L.: *Folk Song in England*, Lawrence and Wishart, London, 1967; Beekman Pubs., New York, 1975.

Monrad-Johansen, David: *Edvard Grieg*, translated by Madge Robertson, Tudor Publishing Co., New York, 1938.

*More Folk-Songs from Lincolnshire*, edited by Patrick O'Shaughnessy, Oxford University Press in conjunction with the Lincolnshire Association, London 1971.

Olsen, Sparre: *Percy Grainger*, translated by Bent Vanberg, Norske Samlaget, Oslo, 1963.

Parker, D. C.: 'The Art of Percy Grainger', *Monthly Musical Record*, XLV/537 (1915), pp. 152-3.

Pound, Reginald: *Sir Henry Wood*, Cassell, London, 1969.

Reid, Charles: *Thomas Beecham: An Independent Biography*, Victor Gollancz Ltd, London, 1961.

Sawyer, Antonia: *Songs at Twilight*, Devin-Adair Co., New York, 1939.

Schonberg, Harold C.: *The Great Pianists*, Victor Gollancz Ltd, London, 1964; Simon & Schuster, New York; 1966.

Scott, Cyril: *Bone of Contention—the autobiography of Cyril Scott*, Aquarian Press, London; Arc Books, New York; 1969.

Scott, Cyril: *My Years of Indiscretion*, Mills & Boon, London, 1924.

Scott, Cyril: *The Philosophy of Modernism*, Kegan Paul, Trench, Trubner & Co., London, 1917; Richard West, Philadelphia, 1973.

*Seven Lincolnshire Folk Songs*, collected by Percy Grainger, edited by Patrick O'Shaughnessy, arranged by Phyllis Tate, Oxford University Press, London, 1966.

Slattery, Thomas C.: 'The Wind Music of Percy A. Grainger', Ph.D. dissertation, University of Iowa, Iowa City, Iowa, 1967.

Slattery, Thomas C.: *Percy Grainger—The Inveterate Innovator*, The Instrumentalist Co., Evanston, 1974.

Smyth, Ethel: *Beecham and Pharaoh*, Chapman & Hall, London, 1935.

Sorabji, Kaikhosru Shapurji: *Around Music*, Unicorn Press, Greensboro, 1932.

Taylor, Robert Lewis: *The Running Pianist*, Doubleday, New York, 1950.

Thesiger, Ernest: *Practically True*, Heinemann, 1927.

*Twenty-One Lincolnshire Folk-Songs*, collected by Percy Grainger, edited by Patrick O'Shaughnessy, Oxford University Press, in conjunction with the Lincolnshire Association, London, 1968.

Warlock, Peter (Philip Heseltine): *Delius*, Bodley Head, London, 1952.

Willetts, Pamela J.: 'The Percy Grainger Collection', Reprint from *British Museum Quarterly*, XXVII/3-4 (Winter 1963-4), pp. 65-73.

Young, Percy: *Elgar, O. M.*, Collins, London, 1955.

# Appendices

APPENDIX A

# Grainger's Published Compositions

That which follows does not pretend to be a complete catalogue of Grainger's compositions. His original compositions are still scattered to the four corners of the earth in museums, libraries and private collections. This is the first problem and one which no compiler of a Grainger catalogue has yet overcome with complete success. To attempt an 'armchair' catalogue moreover would be impossible at this stage because not all of the custodians of the individual holdings have published satisfactory inventories of their collections. Next is the question of size. Grainger's creative output was such that the inclusion of a comprehensive list would have constituted almost one third of this book. Thomas Slattery in his book *Percy Grainger—The Inveterate Innovator* included what purported to have been a complete catalogue of Grainger's compositions, but it contained errors and omissions. Without doubt the most valuable leap forward in Grainger scholarship so far has been Teresa Balough's *Complete Catalogue of the Works of Percy Grainger* which is published by and available from the Music Department of the University of Western Australia. It is hoped that a future publication from this establishment will list any necessary adjustments to cover the few shortcomings of this excellent first edition. The largest and most important holding of original Grainger manuscripts rests with the Grainger Museum in Melbourne and the archivist there has begun the enormous undertaking of rationalization and cataloguing. The published results of these efforts are eagerly awaited. In order to avoid copying previous lists or pre-empting the work being undertaken in Melbourne, it was thought best to include in this book a selected list of published compositions only.

The list that follows is arranged alphabetically and divided into (a) original compositions and folk-song arrangements, and (b) arrangements by Grainger of compositions by other composers. This list does not contain arrangements by other composers of Grainger's works. Grainger often worked on many compositions at once, returning to any one of them a number of times over a period of many years. For the purposes of this list, only the first and final dates are included. In the instances where a composition was published a number of times, only the earliest known date is listed except when a revised edition was issued for a subsequent publication. I wish to thank David Stanhope, Leslie Howard, Stewart Manville and Kay Dreyfus for their help and advice in preparing this list.

J.B.

## LIST OF ABBREVIATIONS

| | |
|---|---|
| AFMS | American Folk-Music Settings |
| BFMS | British Folk-Music Settings |
| DC | Dolmetsch Collection of English Consorts |
| DFMS | Danish Folk-Music Settings |
| EGM | English Gothic Music |
| FI | Faeroe Island Dance Folk-Song Settings |
| FS | Free Settings of Favourite Melodies |
| GV | Guide to Virtuosity |
| KJBC | Kipling's *Jungle Book* Cycle |
| KS | Kipling Settings |
| OEPM | Settings of Songs and Tunes from William Chappell's *Old English Popular Music* |
| RMTB | Room-music Tit-bits |
| S | Sentimentals |
| SCS | Sea Chanty Settings |

(a) Original compositions and folk-song arrangements

| Title | Instrumentation | Date of composition | Publication |
|---|---|---|---|
| Anchor Song (KS 7) | Male chorus or 4 single voices, solo baritone & piano or orchestra | 1905-21 | Schott (1922) |
| Arrival Platform Humlet | (i) Piano solo | 1908-12 | Schirmer (1916) |
| Arrival Platform Humlet | (ii) Orchestra, piano & tuneful percussion | 1908-12 | Schirmer (1916) |
| Arrival Platform Humlet | (iii) Two pianos (4 hands) | 1908-12 | Schirmer (1916) |
| Arrival Platform Humlet (RMTB 7) | (iv) Viola solo or massed violas | 1908-12 | Schott (1916) |
| (N.B. Versions (i), (ii) & (iii) incorporated as 1st movement in the 3 versions of 'In a Nutshell' Suite) | | | |
| At Twilight (P. Grainger) | Unaccompanied mixed chorus with tenor solo | 1900-9 | Schott/Schirmer (1913) |
| Australian Up-Country Song | Unaccompanied mixed chorus | 1905-28 | Schott (1930) |
| The Beaches of Lukannon (KS 20 & KJBC 5) | Mixed chorus with 9 or more strings, harmonium at will | 1898-1941 | Schott (1958) |
| The Bride's Tragedy (A. C. Swinburne) | Double or single chorus & orchestra (or piano) | 1908-13 | Schott (1914) |
| Brigg Fair (BFMS 7 — Schott edition only) | Tenor solo with mixed chorus | 1906 | Forsyth Bros (1906)/ Schott (1911) |
| British Waterside (The Jolly Sailor) (BFMS 26) | (i) High voice & piano | 1920 | Schott/Schirmer (1921) |
| British Waterside (The Jolly Sailor) (BFMS 26) | (ii) Low voice & piano | 1920 | Schott/Schirmer (1921) |
| Children's March—Over the Hills and Far Away (RMTB 4) | (i) Piano or massed pianos & military band | 1916-18 | Schirmer (1919) |

| Title | Version | Date | Publisher |
|---|---|---|---|
| *Children's March—Over the Hills and Far Away* (RMTB 4) | (ii) Two pianos (4 hands) | 1916-18 | Schirmer (1920) |
| *Children's March—Over the Hills and Far Away* | (iii) Piano solo (short version) | 1916-18 | Schirmer (1918) |
| *Colonial Song* (S 1) | (i) 2 voices at will, harp, band | 1905-13 | Schott (1913) |
| *Colonial Song* (S 1) | (ii) 2 voices at will, violin, cello & piano | 1905-13 | Schott (1913) |
| *Colonial Song* (S 1) | (iii) 2 voices at will, harp, 3 strings & orchestra | 1905-13 | Schott (1918)/Galaxy (1928) |
| *Colonial Song* (S 1) | (iv) Piano solo | 1905-13 | Schott (1913)/Schirmer (1925)/Allan (?) |
| *Colonial Song* (S 1) | (v) Military band | 1905-13 | Carl Fischer (1921) |
| *Country Gardens* (BFMS 22) | (i) Piano solo | 1908-18 | Schott/Schirmer/Allan/Hansen (1919) |
| *Country Gardens* (BFMS 22) | (ii) Piano solo (easy version) | 1908-30 | Schirmer (1943) |
| *Country Gardens* (BFMS 22) | (iii) Piano solo (especially easy version) | 1908-32 | Schott (1967)/Schirmer (1943) |
| *Country Gardens* (BFMS 22) | (iv) Two pianos (4 hands) | 1908-32 | Schott/Schirmer (1932) |
| *Country Gardens* (BFMS 22) | (v) One piano (4 hands) | 1908-36 | Schott/Schirmer (1938) |
| *Country Gardens* (BFMS 22) | (vi) Two pianos (8 hands) | 1908-36 | Schott/Schirmer (1938) |
| *Danny Deever* (KS 12) | Men's double chorus or baritone solo & men's single chorus, orchestra or piano | 1903-22 | Schott (1924) |
| *David of the White Rock (Traditional Welsh Song)* | Voice & piano | 1954 | Schott (1963) |

| | | | |
|---|---|---|---|
| *Dedication* (KS 1) | High baritone or tenor & piano | 1901 | Schott (1912) |
| *Died for Love* (BFMS 10) | Woman's voice, piano or various instrumental trios | 1906-7 | Schott (1912) |
| *Dollar and a Half a Day* (SGS 2) | Unaccompanied male chorus | 1908-9 | Schott (1923)/Schirmer (1922) |
| *The Duke of Marlborough (British War Mood Grows)* (BFMS 36) | Brass band or brass choir of military band 1939 or symphony orchestra & suspended cymbal | | Schott (1949) |
| *Eastern Intermezzo* | (i) Piano solo | 1899-1922 | Schott/Schirmer (1922) |
| *Eastern Intermezzo* (RMTB 5) | (ii) Two pianos (4 hands) | 1899-1922 | Schott/Schirmer (1922) |
| *Eastern Intermezzo* | (iii) Orchestra with piano | 1899-1945 | Schott (1950) |
| *English Dance* | (i) Orchestra with organ | 1899-21 | Schirmer (1929) |
| *English Dance* | (ii) Two pianos (6 hands) | 1899-1921 | Schott/Schirmer (1924) |
| *English Dance* | (iii) Room-music 9-some | 1899-1909 | Schirmer (1924) |
| (N.B. any parts of (i) may be combined with (ii)) | | rev. 1924-5 | Schirmer (1929) |
| *English Waltz* | (i) Two pianos (4 hands) | 1899-1947 | Schott/Schirmer (1947) |
| *English Waltz* | (ii) Orchestra with piano | 1899-1943 | Schott (1945) |
| *The Fall of the Stone* (KS 16 & KJBC 1) | Mixed chorus, 2 violas, 3 cellos (or 2 alto saxophones), 2 bassoons (or 2 baritone saxophones) (English horn, euphonium, harmonium, piano at will) | 1901-23 | Schott (1924) |
| *Father and Daughter* (FI 1) | Five men's single voices, double mixed chorus, strings, brass & percussion (mandolin & guitar band at will) | 1908-9 | Schott (1913) |

| Title | Version | Date | Publisher |
|---|---|---|---|
| *Gay but Wistful* | (i) Piano solo | 1912-16 | Schirmer (1916) |
| *Gay but Wistful* | (ii) Orchestra & piano | 1912-16 | Schirmer (1916) |
| *Gay but Wistful* | (iii) Two pianos (4 hands) | 1912-16 | Schirmer (1916) |
| (N.B. Above 3 versions incorporated as 2nd movement in the 3 versions of '*In a Nutshell*' Suite) | | | |
| *Green Bushes* (BFMS 12) | (i) Room-music: 22 solo instruments/ orchestra | 1905-21 | Schott/Schirmer (1931) |
| *Green Bushes* (BFMS 25) | (ii) Two pianos (6 hands) | 1919 | Schirmer (1921) / Schott (1923) |
| (N.B. any parts of (i) may be combined with (ii)) | | | |
| *Gum-suckers March* (Originally 'Cornstalks March') | (i) Piano solo | 1905-14 | Schirmer (1916) |
| *Gum-suckers March* | (ii) Orchestra & piano | 1905-14 | Schirmer (1916) |
| *Gum-suckers March* | (iii) Two pianos (4 hands) | 1905-14 | Schirmer (1916) |
| (N.B. Above 3 versions incorporated as 4th movement in the 3 versions of '*In a Nutshell*' Suite) | | | |
| *Handel in the Strand* (*Clog Dance*) (RMTB 2) | (i) Piano, violin, cello, (viola at will) or two pianos & massed strings | 1911-12 | Schott (1912) |
| *Handel in the Strand* (*Clog Dance*) (RMTB 2) | (ii) Piano solo | 1930 | Schott/Schirmer (1930) |
| *Handel in the Strand* (*Clog Dance*) (RMTB 2) | (iii) Two pianos (4 hands) | 1947 | Schott/Schirmer (1947) |
| *Harvest Hymn* | (i) Chamber, full or massed orchestra, voices at will | 1905-32 | Schirmer (1940) |
| *Harvest Hymn* | (ii) String quartet or string orchestra, & piano, or harmonium or organ | 1905-32 | Schirmer (?) |
| *Harvest Hymn* | (iii) Violin & piano | 1905-32 | Allan (1940) |

| Title | Arrangement | Dates | Publisher |
|---|---|---|---|
| *Harvest Hymn* | (iv) Violin, cello & organ or harmonium or piano | 1905-32 | Schirmer (?) |
| *Harvest Hymn* | (v) Chorus | 1905-32 | Schirmer (1940) |
| *Harvest Hymn* | (vi) Piano solo | 1905-36 | Schirmer (1940) |
| *Harvest Hymn* | (vii) One piano (4 hands) with solo voice(s), or unison chorus at will | 1905-38 | Schirmer (1940) |
| *Hassan: General Dance* | Orchestra | 1923 | MS sketches British Museum folio 50879 |
| *Hill-Song Number 1* | (i) Room-music 22-some | 1901-21 rev. 1923 | Universal Edition (1922) Universal Edition (1924) |
| *Hill-Song Number 1* | (ii) Two pianos (4 hands) | 1901-21 | Schirmer (1922) |
| *Hill-Song Number 2* (based on material from *Hill-Song Number 1*) | (i) a) Solo wind ensemble, 23 or 24 wind instruments & cymbals    or b) Band    or c) Symphony orchestra omitting trombones, tuba & violins | 1907-46 | Leeds Music (1950) |
| *Hill-Song Number 2* | (ii) Two pianos (4 hands) | 1907-22 | Schirmer (1922) |
| *The Hunter in His Career* | (i) Double men's chorus & orchestra | 1904 | Vincent (1904) |
| *The Hunter in His Career* (OEPM 3) | (ii) Double men's chorus, 2 pianos (orchestra at will) | 1904-29 | Schott/Schirmer (1930) |
| *The Hunter in His Career* (OEPM 4) | (iii) Piano solo | 1904-29 | Schott/Schirmer (1930) |

(N.B. Contributed number to the revised version of the incidental music by Delius. Full score in hire library of Boosey & Hawkes, London. Piano vocal score published by Universal (No. 4, *General Dance*, pp. 27-33 inc.))

| Title | Scoring | | |
|---|---|---|---|
| *The Hunting Song of the Seeonee Park* (KS 8 & KJBC 8) | Four-part male chorus (optional wind parts added 1941 & optional plucked strings added 1956 for publication of KJBC) | 1899-1922 | Schott (1922 & 1958) |
| *The Immovable Do (or The Ciphering C)* | (i) Band or mixed chorus with or without organ, or full orchestra or string orchestra or wind choir | 1933-40 | Schirmer (1941) |
| *The Immovable Do (or The Ciphering C)* | (ii) Piano solo | 1933-40 | Schirmer (1941) |
| *The Immovable Do (or The Ciphering C)* | (iii) Pipe, electronic or reed organ | 1933-9 | Schirmer (1941) |
| *The Immovable Do (or The Ciphering C)* | (iv) Small or full orchestra | 1933-42 | Schirmer (1942) |
| *The Immovable Do (or The Ciphering C)* | (v) Clarinet choir (saxophones at will) or woodwind choir | 1933-9 | Schirmer (1941) |
| *I'm Seventeen Come Sunday* (BFMS 8) | Mixed chorus with brass band or concert brass (also piano version of brass accompaniment) | 1905-12 | Schott/Schirmer (1913) |
| *'In a Nutshell' Suite* (See *Arrival Platform Humlet, Gay But Wistful, Pastoral & Gum-suckers March*) | | | |
| *The Inuit* (KS 5 & KJBC 4) | Unaccompanied mixed chorus | 1902 | Schott (1912) |
| *Irish Tune from County Derry* (BFMS 5) | (i) Unaccompanied 6-part wordless chorus | 1902-11 | Schott (1912)/Schirmer (1927)/Allan (?) |
| *Irish Tune from County Derry* (BFMS 6) | (ii) Piano solo | 1902-11 | Schott (1911), Allan/Schirmer (1939) |
| *Irish Tune from County Derry* (BFMS 15) | (iii) Room-music (10 strings & 2 horns at will) | 1902-11 | Schott (1913) |

| Title | Scoring | Date | Publisher |
|---|---|---|---|
| *Irish Tune from County Derry* (BFMS 20) | (iv) Military band, pipe organ with women's chorus & men's unison chorus at will | 1902-11 | Carl Fischer (1918) Schott/Schirmer (1937) |
| *Irish Tune from County Derry* (BFMS 29) | (v) Elastic scoring (3 instruments to full orchestra); optional wordless chorus | 1920 | Schott/Schirmer (1930) |
| *Jutish Medley* (DFMS 8) (N.B. Including *Choosing the Bride, The Dragoon's Farewell, Husband and Wife (A Quarelling Duet), The Shoemaker from Jerusalem & Lord Peter's Stable-Boy*) | Piano solo | 1927 | Schott/Schirmer (1928) |
| *Jutish Medley* (DFMS 9) (N.B. See *Suite on Danish Folk-Songs*) | Elastic scoring, including material for 2 pianos (6 hands) | 1923-9 | Schott/Schirmer (1920) |
| *Knight and Shepherd's Daughter* (BFMS 18) | Piano solo | 1918 | Schott/Schirmer (1918) |
| *The Lads of Wamphray* (Sir Walter Scott) | (i) Men's chorus with small orchestra or 2 or massed pianos | 1904-7 | Schirmer (1925) |
| *The Lads of Wamphray* | (ii) Wind band | 1904-38 | Carl Fischer (1941) |
| *Let's Dance Gay in Green Meadow* (Unnumbered FI) | (i) Piano (4 hands) | 1905-43 | Faber Music (1967) |
| *Let's Dance Gay in Green Meadow* (Unnumbered FI) (Publisher's name 'Faeroe Island Dance') | (ii) Band | 1905-54 | Schirmer (1969) |
| *Lincolnshire Posy* (BFMS 34) | (i) Wind band | 1905-37 | Schott/Schirmer (1940) |
| *Lincolnshire Posy* (BFMS 35) (N.B. Including *Lisbon* (mistitled in some editions as *Dublin Bay*) (Sailor's Song), *Horkstow Grange* (mistitled in some editions as *Harkstow Grange*) (narrating local history), *Rufford Park Poachers* (Poaching Song), *The Brisk Young Sailor* (returned to wed his True Love), *Lord Melbourne* (War Song), *The Lost Lady Found* (Dance Song)) | (ii) Two pianos (4 hands) | 1905-37 | Schott/Schirmer (1940) |

| Title | Description | Date | Publisher |
|---|---|---|---|
| *Lisbon* ('Dublin Bay') (BFMS 40) | Wind fivesome | 1931 | Schott (1972) |
| *Lord Peter's Stable-Boy* (DFMS 1) | (i) Elastic scoring (from 3 instruments to full orchestra) | 1922-7 | Schirmer (1930) |
| *Lord Peter's Stable-Boy* (DFMS 1) | (ii) Band (by virtue of conductor's synoptic score) | 1922-7 | Schirmer (1930) |
| *Lord Peter's Stable-Boy* (DFMS 7) (N.B. See *Suite on Danish Folk-Songs & Jutish Medley* (DFMS 8)) | (iii) Voices & room-music | 1922-7 | Schirmer (1930) |
| *The Lost Lady Found* (BFMS 33) | Mixed chorus or single voice(s) with a variety of accompaniments | 1910-38 | Schott (1949) |
| *Love Song of Har Dyal* (KS 11) | Woman's high voice & piano | 1901 | Schott (1923) |
| *Love Verses from 'The Song of Solomon'* | 4 soloists, chorus, room-music or piano duet | 1899-1931 | Schott/Schirmer (1931) |
| *Lullaby* from *Tribute to Foster* | Piano solo | 1915 | Schott/Schirmer (1917) |
| *Marching Song of Democracy* | (i) Organ, orchestra with mixed chorus | 1901-7 | Universal Edition (1924)/ Schirmer (1917) The Boston Music Co. (1917) |
| *Marching Song of Democracy* | (ii) Band with or without mixed chorus | 1901-48 | Schirmer (?) |
| *Marching Tune* (BFMS 9 – Schott edition only) | Mixed chorus with brass choir (3 cornets, 4 horns, tuba) or piano or brass band | 1905 | Forsyth Bros (?)/ Schott (1911) |
| *The Men of the Sea* (KS 10) | Low or medium voice & piano | 1899 | Schott (1923) |
| *The Merry King* (BFMS 38) | (i) Piano solo | 1905-39 | Schirmer (1939) |
| *The Merry King* (BFMS 39) | (ii) 10 or more strings or wind or both, with piano (organ at will) | 1905-39 | Schirmer (1939) |

| Work | Instrumentation | Date | Publisher |
|---|---|---|---|
| *The Merry Wedding (Bridal Dance)* | 9 solo voices, mixed chorus & orchestra (organ at will) or piano | 1912-15 | Oliver Ditson (1916) |
| *Mock Morris* (RMTB 1) | (i)  6 or 7 strings | begun 1910 | Schott (1911)/Schirmer (1914) |
| *Mock Morris* (RMTB 1) | (ii)  Piano solo, concert version | begun 1910 | Schott (1912) |
| *Mock Morris* (RMTB 1) | (iii)  Piano solo, popular version | begun 1910 | Schott (1912) |
| *Mock Morris* (RMTB 1) | (iv)  Violin & piano | begun 1910 | Schott/Schirmer (1914) |
| *Molly on the Shore* (BFMS 1) | (i)  String 4-some or string orchestra | begun 1907 | Schott (1911) |
| *Molly on the Shore* (BFMS 1) | (ii)  Full orchestra or theatre orchestra | 1907-14 | Schott/Schirmer/Allan (1914) |
| *Molly on the Shore* (BFMS 1) | (iii)  Voice, strings & guitar | begun 1907 | Schott (?) |
| *Molly on the Shore* (BFMS 19) | (iv)  Two pianos (4 hands) | 1907-47 | Schott/Schirmer (1948) |
| *Molly on the Shore* (BFMS 19) | (v)  Piano solo | 1907-18 | Schott/Schirmer/Allan (1918) |
| *Molly on the Shore* (BFMS 23) | (vi)  Military band | 1907-20 | Carl Fischer (1921) |
| *Morning Song in the Jungle* (KS 3 & KJBC 2) | Unaccompanied mixed chorus | 1905 | Schott (1912) |
| *Mowgli's Song Against People* (KS 15 & KJBC 11) | Mixed chorus & 10 or more instruments (revision of instrumental parts in 1941 & 1956) | 1903-23 1903-56 | Schott (1924) Schott (1958) |
| *My Robin is to the Greenwood Gone* (OEPM 2) | (i)  6 strings, flute, English horn | 1912 | Schott (1912) |
| *My Robin is to the Greenwood Gone* (OEPM 2) | (ii)  Piano solo | 1912 | Schott (1912) |

| Title | Scoring | Date | Publisher |
|---|---|---|---|
| *My Robin is to the Greenwood Gone* (OEPM 2) | (iii) Violin, cello & piano | 1912 | Schott (1912) |
| *The Nightingale and the Two Sisters* (DFMS 10) | (i) Elastic scoring | 1923-30 | Schirmer (1931) |
| *Night-Song in the Jungle* (KS 17 & KJBC 3) | Unaccompanied men's foursome or 4-part chorus | 1898-24 | Schott (1925) |
| *Old Irish Tune* (N.B. Early title for *Irish Tune from County Derry*) | Single mixed chorus, unaccompanied | c. 1904 | Vincent Music (1904) |
| *One More Day, My John* (SCS 1) | Piano solo | 1915 | Schott/Schirmer/ Universal Edition (1916) |
| *The Only Son* (KS 21 & KJBC 10) | Soprano, tenor & large room-music (mixed chorus at will) | 1945-7 | Schott (1958) |
| *Pastoral* | (i) Piano solo | 1907-16 | Schirmer (1916) |
| *Pastoral* | (ii) Orchestra with piano | 1907-16 | Schirmer (1916) |
| *Pastoral* | (iii) Two pianos (4 hands) | 1907-16 | Schirmer (1916) |
| (N.B. Above 3 versions incorporated as 3rd movement in 3 versions of '*In a Nutshell' Suite*) | | | |
| *The Peora Hunt* (KS 14 & KJBC 7) | Mixed chorus & optional accompaniment of a) harmonium & piano b) 2 bassoons (or 2 cellos) (1st bassoon — baritone saxophone) & piano or harmonium c) 1 or 2 bassoons (1st bassoon — baritone saxophone) strings & piano or harmonium d) Strings & piano or harmonium | 1906 | Schott (1924) |

| Title | Scoring | Date | Publisher |
|---|---|---|---|
| *The Power of Love* (DFMS 2) | Elastic scoring | 1922-41 | Schirmer (1950) |
| *The Power of Rome and the Christian Heart* | Band, organ & optional strings | 1918-43 | Mills Music (1953) |
| *The Pretty Maid Milkin' Her Cow* (BFMS 27) | (i)  Voice & piano (high (original) key) | 1920 | Schott/Schirmer (1921) |
| *The Pretty Maid Milkin' Her Cow* (BFMS 27) | (ii)  Voice & piano (low key) | 1920 | Schott/Schirmer (1921) |
| *Recessional* (KS 18) | Mixed chorus, optional keyboard accompaniment | 1905-29 | Schott/Schirmer (1930) |
| *Red Dog* (KS 19 & KJBC 6) | Unaccompanied 4-part men's chorus | 1941 | Schott (1958) |
| *A Reiver's Neck-Verse* (A. C. Swinburne) | Male voice & piano | 1908 | Schott (1911) |
| *The Running of Shindand* (KS 9) | Unaccompanied male chorus | c. 1902-3 | Schott (1922) |
| *La Scandinavie (Scandinavian Suite)* (Including: *Swedish Air and Dance*, *A Song of Vermeland* (Swedish), *Norwegian Polka*, *Danish Melody*, *Air and Finale on Norwegian Dances*) | Cello & piano | 1902 | Schott Söhne (undated) |
| *Scotch Strathspey and Reel* (BFMS 28) | (i)  Room-music '20-some (21-some at will)' with 4 men's voices or male chorus | 1901-11 | Schott/Schirmer (1924) |
| *Scotch Strathspey and Reel* (BFMS 37) | (ii)  Piano solo | 1901-37 | Schirmer (1939) |
| *The Sea Wife* (KS 22) | Mixed chorus & brass instruments (or 7 strings, or brass & strings or piano duet or piano or string orchestra) | 1898-1947 | Schott (1948) |
| *Shallow Brown* (SCS 3) | Solo voice(s) and/or unison chorus & piano or clarinet, bassoon, horn or alto | 1910-25 | Schott/Schirmer (1927) |

| Title | Description | Date | Publisher |
|---|---|---|---|
| *Shepherd's Hey* (BFMS 3) | saxophone, euphonium or 2nd horn or 2nd alto saxophone, harmonium, piano, 7 strings. Piccolo, flute, double bassoon, 2 mandolins, 2 mandolas, 2 ukuleles, 4 guitars, and more strings at will.<br>(i) Room-music 12-some (flute, clarinet, horn, concertina, 8 strings) | 1908-11 | Schott (1911) |
| *Shepherd's Hey* (BFMS 4) | (ii) Piano solo | 1908-22 | Schott (1922/Schirmer/ Allan (1939) |
| *Shepherd's Hey* (BFMS 4) | (iii) Piano solo (simplified version) | 1908-37 | Schott/Schirmer (1967) |
| *Shepherd's Hey* (BFMS 16) | (iv) Full orchestra | 1908-13 | Schott (1913) |
| *Shepherd's Hey* (BFMS 21) | (v) Band | 1908-18 | Carl Fischer (1918)/ Schott (?) |
| *Shepherd's Hey* (BFMS 16) | (vi) Two pianos (4 hands) | 1908-47 | Schott (1948) |
| *Sir Eglamore* (BFMS 13 — Schott edition only) | Double mixed chorus, brass, strings, percussion & harps at will | 1904 | Vincent (1904) |
|  |  | rev. 1912-13 | Schott (1913) |
| *Six Dukes went Afishin'* (BFMS 11) | (i) High voice & piano | 1905-12 | Schott (1913) |
| *Six Dukes went Afishin'* (BFMS 11) | (ii) Low voice & piano | 1905-12 | Schott (1913) |
| *Soldier, Soldier* (KS 13) | 6 solo voices & mixed chorus, 'harmonium if needed' | 1907-8 | Schott (1925) |
| *A Song of Autumn* (Adam Lindsay Gordon) | Medium voice & piano | 1899 | Schott (1923) |
| *A Song of Vermeland*<br>(See *La Scandinavie*. The above composition is by 'Ycrep Regniarg') | Mixed 5-part chorus | 1903 | Vincent Music (1904) |

| | | | |
|---|---|---|---|
| *Spoon River* (AFMS 1) | (i) Piano solo | 1919-22 | Schott/Schirmer/Universal Edition (1922) |
| *Spoon River* (AFMS 2) | (ii) Elastic scoring | 1919-29 | Schirmer (1930) |
| *Spoon River* (AFMS 3) | (iii) Two pianos (4 hands) | 1919-29 | Schott/Schirmer (1932) |
| *The Sprig of Thyme* (BFMS 24) | (i) High voice & piano | 1907-20 | Schott/Schirmer/Allan (1921) |
| *The Sprig of Thyme* (BFMS 24) | (ii) Low voice & piano | 1907-20 | Scott/Schirmer/Allan (1921) |
| *Suite on Danish Folk-Songs* | Elastic scoring | Compiled 1926 rev. 1941 | Schirmer (1930) Schirmer (1950) |
| (Including: *The Power of Love* (DFMS 2), *Lord Peter's Stable-Boy* (DFMS 1), *The Nightingale and the Two Sisters* (DFMS 10) *Jutish Medley* (DFMS 9). See separate entries) | | | |
| *The Sussex Mummers' Christmas Carol* (BFMS 2) | (i) Piano solo | 1905-11 | Schott (1911) |
| *The Sussex Mummers' Christmas Carol* (BFMS 17) | (ii) Violin or cello & piano | 1905-11 | Schott (1916)/Schirmer (1917) |
| *There was a Pig went Out to Dig (or Christmas Day in the Morning)* (BFMS 18) | 4-part unaccompanied 'female or children's or both's chorus or high vocal foursome' | 1905-10 | Schott/Schirmer (1915) |
| *Tiger, Tiger* (KS 4& KJBS 9) | Men's chorus, optional tenor solo | 1905 | Schott (1912) |
| *To a Nordic Princess* | (i) Orchestra (organ at will) | 1927-8 | Schirmer (1929/30) |
| *To a Nordic Princess* (short version) | (ii) Piano solo | 1927-8 | Schott/Schirmer (1929) |

| Work | Description | Date | Publisher |
|---|---|---|---|
| *Tribute to Foster* (S. C. Foster & P. Grainger) | Orchestra, piano, soloists, mixed chorus, musical glasses, 2nd piano (& 1st piano) substitute for orchestra | 1913-31 | Schirmer (1932/Oxford University Press (1934) |
| *The Twa Corbies* (Sir Walter Scott) | Voice & 7 strings or piano | 1903-9 | Schirmer (1924) |
| *Two Musical Relics of My Mother* | | | |
| 1) *As Sally Sat A'weeping (British Folk-Song)* | Two pianos (4 hands) | 1905-12 | Schott/Schirmer (1924) |
| 2) *Hermundur Illi (Faeroe Island Dance-Folksong)* | Two pianos (4 hands) | 1905-12 | Schott/Schirmer (1924) |
| *Walking Tune* (RMTB 3) | (i) Wind fivesome | 1900-5 | Schott (1912) |
| *Walking Tune* (RMTB 3) | (ii) Piano solo | 1900-5 | Schott (1912) |
| *The Warriors* | (i) Large orchestra, including 3 pianos & offstage brass | 1913-16 | Schott (1926) |
| *The Warriors* | (ii) 2 pianos (6 hands), offstage brass at will | 1913-22 | Schott/Schirmer (1926) |
| *We have Fed our Seas for a Thousand Years* (KS 2) | 6-part mixed chorus, brass choir, strings at will | 1900-11 | Schott (1911) |
| *Two Welsh Fighting Songs* | | | |
| 1) *The Camp* | 'Big men's' chorus, small mixed chorus, guitars & brass | 1904 | 1 & 2 Vincent Music (1904)/Winthrop Rogers (1922) |
| 2) *The March of the Men of Harlech* | Double mixed chorus & drums | 1904 | |
| *The Widow's Party* (KS 7) | (i) Men's chorus & small or large orchestra or piano duet or massed pianos | 1906-23 | Schott (1923) |

| | | | |
|---|---|---|---|
| *The Widow's Party* (KS 7) | (ii) Men's chorus & band or piano duet or massed pianos | 1906-26 | Schott (1929) |
| *Willow, Willow* (OEPM 1) | (i) Voice & piano | 1902-11 | Schott (1912) |
| *Willow, Willow* (OEPM 1) | (ii) Voice, guitar or harp and 4 muted strings | 1902-11 | Schott (1912) |
| *Ye Banks and Braes* (BFMS 30) | (i) Chorus, single voices, whistlers, harmonium or organ at will | 1901 | Schott (1936)/ Schirmer (1937) |
| *Ye Banks and Braes* (BFMS 31) | (ii) Elastic scoring (school or amateur orchestra) | 1932 | Schott (1936) |
| *Ye Banks and Braes* (BFMS 32) | (iii) Band or wind choirs | c. 1932 | Schott (1937)/ Schirmer (1949) |
| *Youthful Rapture* | (i) Solo cello, violin, piano, harmonium & room-music | 1901-29 | Schott (1930) |
| *Youthful Rapture* | (ii) Cello & piano | 1901 | Schott (1930) |
| *Zanzibar Boat Song* (RMTB 6) | Piano (6 hands) | 1902 | Schott/Schirmer (1923) |

(b) Arrangements of music by other composers

| *Composer* | *Title* | *Instrumentation* | *Date* | *Publication* |
|---|---|---|---|---|
| Addinsell | *Warsaw Concerto* | Two pianos (4 hands) | 1942 | Chappell (1942) |
| Anon | *Alleluia Psallat* (EGM) | Voices with winds or strings or keyboard | c 1943 | Schott/Schirmer (1943) |
| Anon | *Angelus ad Virginem* (EGM) | Voices, optional strings &/or wind or keyboard | c 1943 | Allan/Schott/Schirmer (1943) |

| Composer | Title | Scoring | Date | Publisher |
|---|---|---|---|---|
| Anon | *Beata Viscera* (EGM) | Voices, optional strings &/or wind or keyboard *or* single voice with harp, lute, guitar | c 1943 | Schott/Schirmer (1943) |
| Anon | *Mariounette Douce* (EGM) | Voices, optional strings &/or winds or keyboard | ? | Schott/Schirmer (1950) |
| Anon | *Puellare Gremium* (EGM) | Voices, optional strings &/or winds or keyboard | ? | Schott/Schirmer (1950) |
| Bach, J. S. | *Air (Overture No 3 in D* BWV 1068) | Piano | 1923 | Schirmer (1923) |
| Bach, J. S. | *Blithe Bells* (Free Ramble on Bach's *Schafen Können sicher weiden* from the Cantata BWV 208 *Was mir behagt*) | (i) Elastic scoring (15 or more instruments or band or small orchestra or massed orchestra) | 1930-1 | Schirmer (1932) |
| Bach, J. S. | *Blithe Bells* | (ii) Piano solo—(concert & easy versions) | 1930-1 | Schott/Schirmer (1931) |
| Bach, J. S. | *Blithe Bells* | (iii) Two pianos (4 hands) | 1930-1 | Schott/Schirmer (1932) |
| Bach, J. S. | *Brandenburg Concerto No 3 in G* BWV 1048 | Strings & piano | ? | Schirmer (1930) |
| Bach, J. S. | *Fugue No 18 in A minor* (Book 1, *W. T. Klavier*) BWV 863 | Two pianos (8 hands) or massed pianos | 1929 | Schott/Schirmer (1931) |
| Bach, J. S. | *Toccata in F for Organ* BWV 540 | Three pianos (6 hands) or massed pianos | 1927-38 | Schirmer (1940) |
| Brahms | *Cradle Song Op. 49, No. 4* (FS 1) | Piano solo | 1922 | Schott/Schirmer/Allan 1923 |

| Delius | *Dance Rhapsody No. 1* | Two pianos (4 hands) | 1922 | Universal Edition (1923) |
|---|---|---|---|---|
| Dowland | *Now, O Now I needs must part* (FS 4 (Schott) & FS 6 (Schirmer)) | (i) Piano solo (concert version) | 1935 | Schott/Schirmer (1937) |
| Dowland | *Now, O Now I needs must part* (FS 3 (Schott) & FS 5 (Schirmer)) | (ii) Piano solo (easy version) | 1936 | Schott/Schirmer (1937) |
| Dunstable (attrib.) | *O Rosa Bella* (EGM) | 4 or 6 mixed voices or chorus with instrumental doubling | ? | Schott (1963) |
| Fauré | *Après un Rêve Op. 7 No. 1* (FS 7) | Piano solo | 1939 | Schirmer (1939) |
| Fauré | *Nell Op. 18 No. 1* (FS 3) | Piano solo | 1924 | Schirmer (1925) |
| Ferrabosco, Alfonso II | *Four-note Pavane* (DC 1) | Room-music (strings) | ? | Schirmer (1944) |
| Gardiner | *Prelude, De Profundis* (GV 1) | Piano solo (ed. P.G.) | ? | Schirmer (1923) |
| Gershwin | *Love Walked In* | Piano solo | 1945 | Chappell/Gershwin Pub. Corp. (1946) |
| Gershwin | *The Man I Love* | Concert adaptation for piano solo of Gershwin's own transcription | ? | New World Music Corp. (1944) |
| Gershwin | *Porgy and Bess* | Fantasy for two pianos (4 hands) | ? | Gershwin & Co. (1951) |
| Grainger, Ella | *Love at First Sight* | Unaccompanied women's chorus with soprano soloist (baritone soloist at will) | ? | Schirmer (1946) |
| Grainger, Ella | *Love at First Sight* | Unaccompanied mixed chorus with soprano solo | ? | Schirmer (1946) |

| | | | | |
|---|---|---|---|---|
| Grieg | *Album for Male Chorus Op. 30* | Unaccompanied chorus (ed. P.G.) | ? | Peters (1925) |
| Grieg | *Four Psalms Op. 74* | Baritone solo, mixed voices a capella (ed. P.G.) | ? | Peters (1925) |
| Grieg | *Norwegian Bridal Procession Op. 19 No. 2* | Piano solo (edited and fingered by P.G.) | ? | Theo Presser/Schott (1920) |
| Grieg | *Piano Concerto in A minor Op. 16* | (i) Two piano edition (complete) | 1907-20 | Schirmer/Peters (1920) |
| Grieg | *Piano Concerto in A minor Op. 16* | (ii) Piano transcription of main themes & episodes from 1st movement | 1944 | Schirmer (1945) |
| Handel | *Hornpipe* from *Water Music* (FS 2) | Piano solo | 1922 | Schott/Schirmer (1923) Allan (1926) |
| Jenkins | *Fantasy No. 1 in D* (Five-part) (DC 2) | Room-music ensemble (strings) | ? | Schirmer (1944) |
| Lawes | *Fantasy and Air, No. 1* (six-part) (DC 3) | Room-music (strings) | 1932-44 | Schirmer (1944) |
| Parker, Katherine | *Down Longford Way* | Elastic scoring | 1935 | Boosey & Hawkes (1936) |
| Power | *Sanctus* (EGM) | Voices, optional strings &/or winds or keyboard | ? | Schott/Schirmer (1950) |
| Rachmaninov | *Piano Concerto No. 2 in C minor* | Transcription by P. G. of main themes & episodes from last movement | 1946 | Schirmer (1946) |
| Scarlatti | *Sonata in B minor, L 33* | Strings (retitled by P.G. 'The Quiet Brook' and key-shifted into C minor) | ? | Schirmer (1930) |

| | | | | |
|---|---|---|---|---|
| Schumann | *Piano Concerto in A minor Op. 54* | Transcription of main themes & episodes from 1st movement for solo piano | ? | Schirmer (1947) |
| Scott | *Handelian Rhapsody* | Piano solo (ed. P. Grainger) | ? | Elkin (1909) |
| Stanford | *Four Irish Dances* from *The Complete Petrie Collection of Ancient Irish Music* | | | |
| | a) *A March-Jig (Maguire's Kick)* | Piano solo | ? | J. Fischer & Bro. (1916) |
| | b) *A Slow Dance* | Piano solo | ? | J. Fischer & Bro. (1916) |
| | c) *The Leprechaun's Dance* | Piano solo | ? | J. Fischer & Bro. (1916) |
| | d) *A Reel* | Piano solo | ? | J. Fischer & Bro. (1916) |
| Strauss, Richard | Final duet from *Der Rosenkavalier* Act III retitled by P.G. 'Ramble on the last love-duet in the opera "The Rose-Bearer"' (FS 4 — Schirmer ed. only) | Piano solo | 'begun before 1920 finished 1927' | Fürstner (1928)/ Schirmer (1928) |
| Tchaikovsky | *Flower Waltz* from *Nutcracker Op. 72* | Piano solo paraphrase | 1904 | Forsyth (1905)/ Schott (1916) |
| Tchaikovsky | *Piano Concerto No 1 in B flat minor Op. 23* (FS 8) | Transcription of opening of 1st movement | 1942 | Schirmer (1943) |

APPENDIX B

# Free Music

by PERCY GRAINGER

*December 6, 1938*

Music is an art not yet grown up; its condition is comparable to that stage of Egyptian bas-reliefs when the head and legs were shown in profile while the torso appeared 'front-face' — the stage of development in which the myriad irregular suggestions of nature can only be taken up in regularized or conventionalized forms. With Free Music we enter the phase of technical maturity such as that enjoyed by the Greek sculptures when all aspects and attitudes of the human body could be shown in arrested movement.

Existing conventional music (whether 'classical' or popular) is tied down by set scales, a tyrannical (whether metrical or irregular) rhythmic pulse that holds the whole tonal fabric in a vice-like grasp and a set of harmonic procedures (whether key-bound or atonal) that are merely habits, and certainly do not deserve to be called laws. Many composers have loosened, here and there, the cords that tie music down. Cyril Scott and Duke Ellington indulge in sliding tones: Arthur Fickenscher and others use intervals closer than the half tone; Cyril Scott (following my lead) writes very irregular rhythms that have been echoed, on the European continent, by Stravinsky, Hindemith, and others. Schönberg has liberated us from the tyranny of conventional harmony. But no non-Australian composer has been willing to combine *all* these innovations into a consistent whole that can be called *Free Music*.

It seems to me absurd to live in an age of flying and yet not be able to execute tonal glides and curves — just as absurd as it would be to have to paint a portrait in little squares (as in the case of mosaic) and not be able to use every type of curved lines. If, in the theatre, several actors (on the stage together) had to continually move in a set metrical relation to one another (to be incapable of individualistic, independent movement) we would think it ridiculous; yet this absurd goose-stepping still persists in music. Out in nature we hear all kinds of lovely and touching 'free' (non-harmonic) combinations of tones; yet we are unable to take up these beauties and expressiveness into the art of music because of our archaic notions of harmony.

Personally I have heard free music in my head since I was a boy of eleven or twelve in Auburn, Melbourne. It is my only important contribution to music. My impression is that this world of tonal freedom was suggested to me by wave-movements in the sea that I first observed as a young child at Brighton, Victoria, and Albert Park, Melbourne.

Yet the matter of Free Music is hardly a personal one. If I do not write it someone else certainly will, for it is the goal that all music is clearly heading for now and has been heading for through the centuries. It seems to me the only music logically suitable to a scientific age.

The first time an example of my Free Music was performed on man-played instruments was when Percy Code conducted it (most skilfully and sympathetically) at one of my Melbourne broadcasting lectures for the Australian Broadcasting Commission, in January, 1935. But Free Music demands a non-human performance. Like most true music, it is an emotional, not a cerebral, product and should pass direct from the imagination of the composer to the ear of the listener by way of delicately controlled musical machines. Too long has music been subject to the limitations of the human hand, and subject to the interfering interpretations of a middle-man: the performer. A composer wants to speak to his public direct. Machines (if properly constructed and properly written for) are capable of niceties of emotional expression impossible to a human performer. That is why I write my Free Music for theremins — the most perfect tonal instruments I know. In the original scores each voice (both on the pitch-staves and on the sound-strength staves) is written in its own specially coloured ink, so that the voices are easily distinguishable, one from the other.

APPENDIX C

(From Preface to *Spoon River* by Percy Grainger)

# To Conductors
# and to Those Forming, or in Charge of,
# Amateur Orchestras, High School,
# College and Music School Orchestras
# and Chamber-Music Bodies

### ELASTIC SCORING

My 'elastic scoring' grows naturally out of two roots:

1. That my music tells its story mainly by means of *intervals* and the liveliness of the part-writing, rather than by means of tone-color, and is therefore well fitted to be played by almost any small, large or medium-sized combination of instruments, provided a proper *balance of tone* is kept.

2. That I wish to play my part in the radical experimentation with orchestral and chamber-music blends that seems bound to happen as a result of the ever wider spreading democratization of all forms of music.

As long as a really satisfactory balance of tone is preserved (so that the voices that make up the musical texture are clearly heard, one against the other, in the intended proportions) I do not care whether one of my 'elastically scored' pieces is played by 4 or 40 or 400 players, or any number in between; whether trumpet parts are played on trumpets or soprano saxophones, French horn parts played on French horns or E flat altos or alto saxophones, trombone parts played on trombones or tenor saxophones or C Melody saxophones; whether string parts are played by the instruments prescribed or by mandolins, mandolas, ukeleles, guitars, banjos, balalaikas, etc.; whether harmonium parts are played on harmoniums (reed-organs) or pipe-organs; whether wood-wind instruments take part of whether a harmonium (reed-organ) or 2nd piano part is substituted for them. I do not even care whether the players are skilful or unskilful, as long as they play well enough to sound the right intervals and keep the afore-said tonal balance — as long as they play badly enough to *still enjoy playing* ('Where no pleasure is, there is no profit taken' — *Shakespeare*).

This 'elastic scoring' is naturally fitted to musical conditions in small and out-of-the-way communities and to the needs of amateur orchestras and school, high school, college and music school orchestras everywhere, in that it can accommodate almost any combination of players on almost any instruments. It is intended to encourage music-lovers of all kinds to play together in groups, large or small, and to promote a more hospitable attitude towards inexperienced music-makers. It is intended to play its part in weaning music students away from too much useless, goalless, soulless, selfish, inartistic soloistic technical study, intended to coax them into happier, richer musical fields — for music should be essentially an art of self-forgetful, soul-expanding communistic co-operation in harmony and many-voicedness.

## ORCHESTRAL EXPERIMENTATION

In our age orchestras and orchestral conditions are changing. In a few years an otherwise-put-together orchestra may replace the conventional 'symphony orchestra'. Rather than such a mere replacement of an old medium by a new I, personally, would prefer to see several different kinds of orchestras (included a revised, better balanced, more delicately toned 'symphony' orchestra) thriving side by side in friendly rivalry; none of them final as to make-up and with no hard-and-fast boundaries between them.

We might well look upon the present time as one well suited to bold experimentation with orchestral and chamber-music sound-blends. Let us encourage all music-lovers, particularly those in their teens, to enter orchestras and other music bodies formed partly with the aim of trying new combinations of instruments. In such try-outs let us use copiously all instruments that young people like best — easy to-play, characteristically-toned instruments such as saxophone, piano, harmonium (reed-organ), celesta, dulcitone, xylophone, wooden marimba, glockenspiel, metal marimba, staff bells (shaped like church bells or locomotive bells, having a very metallic, piercing tone), guitar, ukelele, banjo, mandolin, etc.

Let us not snub budding music-lovers because they have chosen instruments unwritten for in 'classical' music! Let us not banish thousands and hundreds of thousands of musically-inclined young people from the boon of orchestral experience simply because their taste runs to instruments (charming instruments, too) which did not happen to have been invented or perfected in Europe a hundred years ago and therefore did not come to form a part of the conventional 'symphony orchestra' as it grew up! Let us remember that at the time of the crystallization of the symphony orchestra most of our most perfect modern instruments (such as the saxophone, the sarrusophone, the harmonium, the modern piano, the modern pipe-organ, the celesta, the dulcitone, the ukelele, the marimbas) did not exist, or were not known in Europe! That, in most cases, sufficiently explains their absence from older symphony orchestrations. But it does not justify their absence from present and future orchestras!

What we need in our composers and in our leaders of musical thought is an attitude like Bach's: he seems to have been willing enough to experiment with all the instruments known to him and to arrange and rearrange all kinds of works for all sorts of combinations of those instruments. It is easy to guess what liberal uses he would have made of the marvelous instruments of to-day.

Let us rid ourselves of esthetic snobbery, priggishness and prejudice when orchestra-building! Let us take full advantage of the great richness of lovely new instruments, using them together with the lovely old instruments sanctioned by 'classical' usage where it proves effective to do so. Let us build better-balanced, clearer-toned, more varied-colored orchestras than ever before. Above all, let us press into orchestral playing as many young music-lovers as possible. Whether they are to become laymen or professionals, they need some experience of musical team-work before they can become *practical* musicians, *real* musicians sensing the inner soul of their art.

In addition to getting to know some of the world's best music the budding musician needs the inspiration of hearing a grand coöperation of myriad sounds surging around him, to which he joins his own individualistic voice. This is the *special experience* of music, without which mere lonely practising to acquire soloistic skill must always remain esthetically barren and unsatisfying.

## ORCHESTRAL USE OF KEYBOARD PLAYERS

Let us use in our orchestras the vast mass of keyboard players (pianists, organists, etc.) that preponderate everywhere in our musical life. Pianists — with their alarming lack of rhythmic neatness, their inability to follow a conductor's beat, their inability to listen while they play — are more in need of some kind of musical team-work (to offset their all too soloistic study activities) than almost any other class of musicians. Use pianists 'massed', in smaller or larger groups, in experimental and study orchestras, letting them play on small, light, cheap, easily-moved upright pianos (where grand pianos are not easily available) and on harmoniums (reed-organs). These instruments are readily found and handled anywhere — in village or city; only laziness prompts a contrary belief! It is my personal experience, in many lands, that serviceable harmoniums (reed-organs) can be found in every community — by advertising in the newspapers, if not otherwise. By this latter means a really good instrument can sometimes be picked up, second-hand, for as low a figure as five dollars. In selecting a harmonium (reed-organ) for orchestral use, be sure that it carries continuous 8 foot, 16 foot and 4 foot stops throughout its full range.

Harmonium (reed-organ) playing gives to piano students the legato-ear and legato-fingers they otherwise usually so sadly lack. Moreover, massed harmoniums (reed-organs) add a glowing, clinging resonance to the orchestral tone, while massed pianos (the more the mellower) provide brilliance, rhythmic snap and clearness of chord-sound. In determining how many pianos and harmoniums (reed-organs) should be used in a given orchestra we must really use our ears, our sense of balance: It is absurd to use only one piano, only one harmonium, in a large orchestra (having 16 first violins, for instance), when common sense listening tells us at once that three or six or eight pianos, and the same number of harmoniums, would be required to keep the proper tonal balance in such a big tone-body!

If I were forced to choose one instrument only for chamber-music — forced to discard all other instruments than the one chosen — I would choose the harmonium (reed-organ) without hesitation; for it seems to me the most sensitively and intimately expressive of all instruments. Its gusty, swelling emotionality resembles so closely the tides of feeling of the human heart. No other chord-giving instrument is so capable of extreme and exquisitely controlled *pianissimo*. It is unique as a refining musical influence, for it tempts the player to tonal subtleties of gradation as does no other instrument. Both in chamber-music and in the orchestra it provides the ideal background to the individualistic voices of the wood-winds. For all these reasons, let us spread the use of this glorious little instrument to ever wider fields.

## ABUSES IN THE PERCUSSION SECTION

One of the stupidest of stupid abuses in the orchestra is the unwarrantable habit of ignoring the composer's intentions with regard to percussion instruments. Conductors who would think twice before they left out 2 horns or a harp called for in a given score think nothing of essaying with 2 percussion players a work needing 4 or 8 percussion players—think nothing of leaving out important passages in glockenspiel, celesta or tubular chimes. I ask myself: Has my orchestral 'Shepherd's Hey' *ever* been performed with the full complement of intended percussion players? If not, then this piece—despite thousands of performances—has never been completely played or heard! This indifference to percussion instruments is the more absurd in the case of amateur and student orchestras; for instruments such as cymbals, bass drum, glockenspiel, xylophone, tubular chimes, dulcitone and celesta are almost the easiest of all instruments to play without special training and are specially well suited to 'breaking in' players to orchestral routine, counting rests, following the beat, etc.

## 'TUNEFUL PERCUSSION' INSTRUMENTS

And what are we to think of the lack of vision, lack of innate musicality, shown by 'high-brow' composers and conductors in their neglect of the exquisite 'tuneful percussion' instruments invented and perfected in America and elsewhere during the last 30 or 40 years—metal and wooden marimbas, staff bells, vibraphones, nabimbas, dulcitone, etc.? Yet these same 'classicists'—who probably consider these mellow and delicate-toned instruments too 'low-brow' to be admitted into the holy precincts of the symphony orchestra—endure without protest the everlasting thumping of kettle-drums (which with brutal monotony wipes out all chord-clearness) in the Haydn-Mozart-Beethoven orchestrations! The truth is that most 'high-brows' are much more 'low-brow' than they themselves suspect!

In this connection it is interesting to note that it is only the most harsh-toned tuneful-percussion instruments (glockenspiel, xylophone, tubular chimes) that have found a place in the symphony orchestra thus far. Can it be that the symphony orchestra prizes stridence of tone *only* in such instruments? If not, why has no place been found for the mellow-toned metal marimba (the continuation downwards of the glockenspiel) and the gentle-toned wooden marimba (the continuation downwards of the xylophone)? Perhaps because their quality of tone is too refined to be heard amidst the harsh sound-jumble of the symphony orchestra? If so, it is high time that we revised our symphony orchestrations in the direction of a delicacy and refinement that can accommodate the subtler creations of modern instrument-building geniuses such as Deagan and others.

To use, orchestrally, a glockenspiel without a metal marimba, a xylophone without a wooden marimba, is just as absurd and incomplete as it would be to use piccolo without flute, violins without lower strings, the two top octaves of the piano without the lower octaves. Let us get rid of this barbarism as soon as we can!

Young people love such colorful, easy-to-play instruments as staff-bells, marimbas, dulcitone, etc. Let us use such tuneful-percussion enthusiasts 'with both hands': every orchestra should sport at least 20 such players; 2 on 1 glockenspiel, 4 on 1 metal marimba, 2 on 1 xylophone, 4 on 1 wooden marimba, 4 or more on 1 staff bells, 2 on 1 tubular chimes, 1 on celesta, 1 on dulcitone. (If the metal and wooden marimbas could be used in twos, threes, fours or fives it would be still better.) Apart from the luscious sounds thus produced—think how many 'low-brow' beginners would be enticed into a knowledge of, and a love for 'high-brow' music by such means? Salvation Army Booth objected to the devil having all the good tunes. I object to jazz and vaudeville having all the best instruments! Let us find a place in high-brow music for the *gentler* instruments—ukelele, guitar, harmonium, saxophone, sarrusophone, marimbas, etc. There is no reason why the symphony orchestra should be given over *exclusively* to loud and strident sounds.

Why do so many of our high-brow composers, our virtuoso conductors, our 'leaders of musical thought' *lag so very far* behind commercial instrument-makers, jazz-musicians and vaudeville artists in musical imagination, refinement and vision? Because they are ignorant or lazy: they do not *know* the wonderful world of tone created by American and other musical instrument-makers or they cannot be bothered adapting it to their own fields. Such ignorance and laziness are dangerous. The public ear, trained to the orchestration refinements of Paul Whiteman, Grofe, jazz and vaudeville music, may get tired of the dulness and coarseness of the sound of the conventional symphony orchestra: it may move on, gently but irresistibly, to better things.

## ORCHESTRAL USE OF SAXOPHONES

If the saxophone (the crowning achievement of Adolphe Sax, that outstanding genius among wind-instrument creators and perfectors) is not the loveliest of all wind-instruments it certainly is *one* of the loveliest—human, voice-like, heart-revealing. It has been used in symphonic music by Bizet, Vincent d'Indy, Richard Strauss and others with lovely results. It has been used in jazz orchestras with excellent effect. Yet it has not yet been taken up into the symphony orchestra. Why not? What are we waiting for? Apart from its glorious orchestral possibilities *as a saxophone*, it is a most useful substitute for trumpet, French horn, bassoon—even for trombone.

The average amateur, school and music school orchestra usually holds artistically unsatisfying rehearsals because of gaping holes in its wood-wind and brass sections. These missing melodies, missing chords, lessen the musical benefits of such rehearsals to those taking part in them. Those in charge of such orchestras should make every effort *never* to rehearse with incomplete texture (with important voices left out). Texture and balance are, musically speaking, much more important than tone-color!

The complete wood-wind parts should always be arranged (an excellent task for the more musical members of the orchestra to tackle) for harmonium (reed-organ) or pipe-organ and played on those instruments if one or more wood-wind players are absent at rehearsal or concert.

All the brass instruments can be replaced or supported by saxophones—always for study rehearsals and often with effect for concerts also. Generally more than one saxophone will be needed to replace each brass instrument with correct balance.

Let it be admitted that there are many passages originally written for French horn that sound better on that instrument than they do on E flat alto or alto saxophone. On the other hand, there are other passages, also originally written for French horn, that happen to sound as well, or better, on E flat alto or alto saxophone as they do on French horn. Let us experiment widely with all such cases, using E flat altos and alto saxophones on French horn parts until we have substituted experience for prejudice.

## HOW TO ACHIEVE TONAL BALANCE IN STRING SECTIONS

In the symphony orchestra of to-day the clearness of the part-writing, the richness of the lower voices of the harmony and the balance of tone are all sacrificed to a cloying, over-sensuous over-weight of violin tone. I know of no good reason for using more violins to a part than violas or 'cellos to a part: I have yet to discover that the higher members of an instrumental family have more difficulty in making themselves heard than the lower members. In performing such a work as Bach's *Brandenburg Concerto No. 3* (for 3 violins, 3 violas, 3 'cellos, 'violone e continuo') with single strings one soon finds that the violas and 'cellos have some difficulty in holding their own, in tonal prominence, with the violins. The top-heaviness of the string section of the symphony orchestra was natural at a time when the melody mostly floated on the top of the musical texture like oil on water — at a time when harmonic expressiveness and subtle many-voicedness were not greatly valued. But our musical tastes are richer, more many-sided, to-day than they were at the time of the up-growing of the symphony orchestra and we now need properly balanced string sections that can do justice to the best many-voiced music of all periods, be it Purcell and Bach or Vaughan Williams and Cyril Scott. Our conductors are too apt to lag behind public taste and the taste of our best composers; our conductors are wedded too closely to the *banal* simplicities of the 18th and 19th centuries; they are too ignorant of the deeper, grander music of the 17th and 20th centuries.

String orchestras and conductors should feed their musical souls on Purcell's sublimely beautiful *Three-, four- and five-part Fantasias for Strings,* recently edited by Peter Warlock and André Mangeot (Curwen edition). This volume should be to string-quartet players and to string orchestras what Bach's 'Well-tempered Clavier' is to pianists.

There is no reason why conductors should put up with such bad tonal balance (top-heaviness) as exists in the string sections of most amateur, school and study orchestras. Suppose your string section consists of 34 violins, 2 violas, 3 'cellos and 1 bass; you can still achieve perfect tonal balance, if you want to. Transcribe the viola part for third violin, either transposing up one octave such notes as lie below the violin range or leaving them out entirely where it seems more desirable to do so. (It is a good musical exercise for orchestral players, especially music students, to transpose and copy their own parts. Being able to read music is not enough; every musician should aim at writing music as freely as he writes his own language.)

Then divide up your violins as follows:

1st violins, 12 players.
2nd violins, 12 players.
3rd violins (substitute for violas), 10 players ⎫
Violas, 2 players                                                    ⎬   12 players on viola part.
                                                                              ⎭
Arrange the 'cello and double-bass parts for piano and have this piano part

played on about 3 or 4 pianos — also on harmoniums, if available. By such means the tonal balance is preserved, though the tone-color is, of course, distorted. But tonal balance is vastly more important than tone-color in most worth-while music. (In this connection consult the 3 viola parts transcribed for 4th, 5th and 6th violins, the 'cello and double-bass parts transcribed for piano 2 in my edition of Bach's *Brandenburg Concerto No. 3*; also my edition for strings of Scarlatti's *'The Quiet Brook'*; both published by G. Schirmer, Inc.)

## LET OUR ORCHESTRAS GROW NATURALLY

The symphony orchestra uses many strings because string players abounded at the time of its formation. That was a good reason. Let us, in forming the orchestras of the present and the future, try using large numbers of the instruments that abound most to-day: the mere fact that they abound (that they are widely liked and therefore draw many beginners into musical habits) should be recommendation enough. If these instruments, under ample experimentation, prove orchestrally ineffective in massed usage, let us then discard such usage. But do not let us discard any instrument, or usage of it, without a fair trial.

*Percy Aldridge Grainger, Dec. 2, 1929*

APPENDIX D

# Discography: Performances by Grainger

The discographer is usually presented with two main ways of laying out his material for classical works. Either it is to be done in alphabetical order by composer or in chronological order by date of recording. With the present discography it is hoped to combine the best of both these worlds. There were seven main recording periods in Grainger's career as a pianist and conductor and these distinct groups are laid out below in chronological order, and within each group the recorded sides are listed in alphabetical order according to composer.

For help in compiling this list I wish to express my gratitude to Gregor Benko of the International Piano Archives in New York, to Brian Rust, doyen of the international fraternity of discographers and Geoff Milne of the Decca Record Company Limited in London.

J.B.

(All 12″ records unless marked with asterisk)

A) *The Gramophone Company and Sister Companies. Recorded and issued in Great Britain only*

| Composer and title | Matrix number | Catalogue number | Recording date |
|---|---|---|---|
| GRIEG | | | |
| *Cadenza only from 1st movt of *Piano Concerto in A minor* Op. 16 (78 rpm) | 8394e | 5570 | 16/5/08 |
| LISZT | | | |
| *Hungarian Rhapsody No. 12* (abridged) (80 rpm) | 2467f | 05503 | 16/5/08 |
| STANFORD | | | |
| *(arr. Grainger) *Irish March-Jig* (77 rpm) | 8393e | 5569 | 16/5/08 |

B) *His Master's Voice. Recorded and Issued in Great Britain only*

| Composer and title | Matrix number | Catalogue number: single-sided | Catalogue number: double-sided | Recording date |
|---|---|---|---|---|
| DEBUSSY | | | | |
| Toccata from *Pour le Piano* (79 rpm) | AI 8034f | 05554 | D 353 | 14/7/14 |
| GRAINGER | | | | |
| *Mock Morris Dances* (79 rpm) | AI 8033f | 05558 | D 353 | 14/7/14 |
| *Shepherd's Hey* (80 rpm) | Ak 18043e | 5581 | E 147 | 14/7/14 |

C) *The Columbia Graphophone Company* (USA) Recorded in the United States and issued in the United States, Great Britain, Europe and Australia

| Composer and title | Matrix and take number | Catalogue number (United States) | Other Issues (a) US set no. (b) Subsequent US number (c) UK number (d) Italian no. (e) Australian no. | Recording Date |
|---|---|---|---|---|
| **BACH** | | | | |
| (arr. Grainger) Blithe Bells | W98750-2 | 68006-D | (a) M-166 | 15/10/31 |
| (Ramble on Sheep may safely graze) | | | | |
| Gigue from 1st Partita    2nd part of: | W98251-1 | 7134-M | (e) 04097 | 9/5/25 |
| (arr. Liszt) Organ Fantasia & Fugue G minor, pt 1. 2nd part of: | | | | |
| As above, pt 2 | W98747-2 | 68005-D | | 13/10/31 |
| As above, pt 3 | W98748-1 | 68005-D | | 15/10/31 |
| | W98749-2 | 68006-D | | 15/10/31 |
| (arr. Liszt) Organ Prelude & Fugue A minor, pt 1 | W98745-1 | 68004-D | (a) M-166 | 13/10/31 |
| As above, pt 2 | W98746-2 | 68004-D | | 13/10/31 |
| As above, pt 3    1st part of: | W98747-2 | 68005-D | | 13/10/31 |
| (arr. Tausig-Busoni-Grainger) Organ Toccata & Fugue | | | | |
| D minor, pt 1 | W98743-1 | 68003-D | | 13/10/31 |
| As above, pt 2 | W98744-2 | 68003-D | | 13/10/31 |
| **BRAHMS** | | | | |
| *(arr. Grainger) Cradle Song | 80487-3 | A-3685 | (b) 2000-M | 2/8/22 |
| *(arr. Grainger) Cradle Song | W144206-5 | 2057-M | (e) 03575 | 15/6/27 |
| Sonata F minor Op. 5, 1st movt, pt 1 | W98217-2 | 67815-D | | 30/1/26 |
| As above, pt 2 | W98218-2 | 67815-D | | 30/1/26 |

| | | | | | |
|---|---|---|---|---|---|
| As above, 2nd movt, pt 1 | | W98219-1 | 67816-D | | 30/1/26 |
| As above, pt 2 | | W98220-2 | 67816-D | | 30/1/26 |
| As above, 3rd movt | | W98221-1 | 67817-D | (a) M-37 | 2/2/26 |
| As above, 4th movt | | W98222-2 | 67817-D | (c) L 1944/5/6/7 | 2/2/26 |
| As above, 5th movt, pt 1 | | W98223-1 | 67818-D | | 2/2/26 |
| As above, pt 2 | | W98224-3 | 67818-D | | 2/2/26 |
| *Waltz A flat Op. 39 No. 15* | 1st part of: | 49749-2 | A-6145 | | 10/2/20 |
| *Waltz A flat Op. 39 No. 15* | 2nd part of: | W98245-1 | 7109-M | (c) L 1805 | 31/3/26 |

## CHOPIN

| | | | | | |
|---|---|---|---|---|---|
| *Etude B minor Op. 25 No. 10* | | W98598-3 | 67605-D | (a) M-116 (d) GQX 10305 | 9/10/28 |
| *Etude C minor Op. 25 No. 12* | 1st part of: | W98245-1 | 7109-M | (c) L 1805 | 31/3/26 |
| *Polonaise A flat Op. 53* | | 49296-2 | A-6027 | (c) L 1352 | 2/1/18 |
| *Prelude A flat Op. 28 No. 17* | | 49441-2 | A-6060 | (c) L 1352 | 7/6/18 |
| *Prelude A flat Op. 28 No. 17* | | W98249-1 | 7109-M | (c) L 1805 | 1/4/26 |
| **Scherzo B flat minor Op. 31 No. 2, pt 1* | | 81582-4 | 30019-D | | 25/2/24 |
| **As above, pt 2* | | 81583-3 | 30019-D | | 25/2/24 |
| *Sonata No. 2 B flat minor Op. 35*, 1st movt pt 1 | | W98593-2 | 67603-D | | 9/10/28 |
| As above, pt 2 & 2nd movt pt 1 | | W98594-1 | 67603-D | | 9/10/28 |
| As above, 2nd movt pt 2 | | W98595-2 | 67604-D | (a) M-116 | 9/10/28 |
| As above, 3rd movt pt 1 | | W98596-2 | 67604-D | (d) GQX 10303/4/5 | 9/10/28 |
| As above, 3rd movt pt 2 & 4th movt | | W98597-2 | 67605-D | | 9/10/28 |
| *Sonata No. 3 B minor Op. 58*, 1st movt pt 1 | | W98177-2 | 67158-D | | 10/6/25 |
| As above, pt 2 | | W98178-1 | 67158-D | | 10/6/25 |
| As above, pt 3 & 2nd movt | | W98179-1 | 67159-D | (a) M-32 | 10/6/25 |
| As above, 3rd movt pt 1 | | W98180-1 | 67159-D | (c) L 1695/6/7 | 11/6/25 |
| As above, pt 2 & 4th movt pt 1 | | W98181-1 | 67160-D | | 11/6/25 |
| As above, 4th movt pt 2 | | W98182-1 | 67160-D | | 11/6/25 |
| *Valse A flat Op. 42* | | 49281-1 | A-6027 | | 3/12/17 |

## DEBUSSY

| Title | | Matrix | Catalog | | Date |
|---|---|---|---|---|---|
| *Golliwog's Cakewalk | | 81323-3 | 30002-D | (b) 2001-M & 183-M | 31/10/23 |
| Clair de Lune | | W98246-1 | 7124-M | (c) L 1892 (e) 04002 | 31/3/26 |
| Toccata from Pour le Piano | | W98248-2 | 7124-M | (c) L 1892 (e) 04002 | 31/3/26 |

## DETT

| Title | | Matrix | Catalog | | Date |
|---|---|---|---|---|---|
| Juba Dance | 2nd part of: | 49749-2 | A-6145 | | 10/2/20 |

## GLUCK

| Title | | Matrix | Catalog | | Date |
|---|---|---|---|---|---|
| *(arr. Brahms) Gavotte | | 81299-2 | 30002-D | (b) 2001-M & 183-M | 29/10/23 |

## GRAINGER

| Title | | Matrix | Catalog | | Date |
|---|---|---|---|---|---|
| *Colonial Song (P. Grainger conducting orchestra with A. Atwater (sop), L. A. Sanchez (ten)), pt 1 | | W145385-3 | 2066-M | | 22/12/27 |
| *As above, pt 2 | | W145386-2 | 2066-M | | 22/12/27 |
| Country Gardens | 1st part of: | 49442-1 | 7001-M | | 7/6/18 |
| Country Gardens | 1st part of: | 49442-? | A6060 | | 7/6/18 |
| *Country Gardens | | W144205-2 | 154-M | (b) 2072-M (c) D 1664 (e) 03620 | 24/5/27 |
| *Gum-suckers March | | 79716-3 | A-3381 | | 7/2/21 |
| Gum-suckers March (with orchestra) | | W498412-7 | 7147-M | (b) 2202-M | 22/11/27 |
| Irish Tune from County Derry (P. Grainger conducting the Kasschau Solo Choir) | | W98171-3 | 7111-M | | 9/5/25 |
| Jutish Medley, pt 1 | | W98613-3 | 50129-D | | 21/1/29 |
| As above, pt 2 | | W98614-3 | 50129-D | | 21/1/29 |
| *Lord Peter's Stable-Boy (piano: P. Grainger, harmonium: R. Leopold with Columbia Symphony Orchestra) | | W145228-6 | 163-M | | 20/12/27 |
| Molly on the Shore | | 49748-2 | A-6145 | | 10/2/20 |
| *Molly on the Shore | | W144246-3 | 2057-M | | 1/6/27 |
| One More Day, My John | 2nd part of: | 49640-1 | A-6128 | (e) 03575 | 17/6/19 |
| One More Day, My John | 2nd part of: | W98358-5 | 7150-M | (e) 04114 | 15/6/27 |

| | | | | |
|---|---|---|---|---|
| The Power of Love (A. Atwater (sop), P. Grainger (harm), R. Leopold (pf) plus 11 instruments) | | W98410-6 | 7147-M | | 20/12/27 |
| Scotch Strathspey and Reel (the Grainger Singers and Players, conducted by Frank Kasschau. P. Grainger & R. Leopold, guitars), pt 1 | | W98175-3 | 7104-M | | 19/5/25 |
| As above, pt 2 | | W98176-3 | 7104-M | | 19/5/25 |
| Shepherd's Hey | 2nd part of: | 49442-1 | 7001-M | | 7/6/18 |
| Shepherd's Hey | 2nd part of: | 49442-? | A-6060 | | 7/6/18 |
| *Shepherd's Hey | | W144204-3 | 154-M | (e) 03620 | 24/5/27 |
| *Shepherd's Hey (P. Grainger conducting Columbia S.O.) | | W145237-4 | 163-M | (b) 2072-M | 25/11/27 |
| *Spoon River | | 80488-3 | A-3685 | (c) D 1664 / (b) 2000-M | 2/8/22 |

**GRIEG**

| | | | | |
|---|---|---|---|---|
| Norwegian Bridal Procession | | 49249-1 | | (c) L 1386 | 19/9/17 |
| Norwegian Bridal Procession | | 49933-8 | A-6217 | (b) 7001-M | 18/2/21 |
| To the Spring | 1st part of: | 49640-1 | A-6128 | | 17/6/19 |
| To the Spring | 1st part of: | W98358-5 | 7150-M | (e) 04114 | 15/6/27 |
| Wedding Day at Troldhaugen | | 49929-3 | A-6192 | | 5/2/21 |
| Wedding Day at Troldhaugen | | W98359-4 | 7150-M | (e) 04114 | 15/6/27 |

**GUION**

| | | | | |
|---|---|---|---|---|
| Sheep and Goat walkin' to pasture | 1st part of: | W98251-1 | 7134-M | (e) 04097 | 1/4/26 |
| *Turkey in the Straw | | 79715-3 | A-3381 | (b) 2002-M | 7/2/21 |

**HANDEL**

| | | | | |
|---|---|---|---|---|
| *(arr. Grainger) Hornpipe from Water Music | | 81588-4 | 30010-D | (b) 2004-M | 27/2/24 |

**LISZT**

| | | | | |
|---|---|---|---|---|
| Hungarian Fantasia (with orchestra), pt 1 | | 49561-3 | A-6115 | (c) L 1368 | 17/12/18 |
| As above, pt 2 | | 49562-3 | A-6115 | (c) L 1368 | 17/12/18 |
| Hungarian Rhapsody No. 2, pt 1 | | 49243-3 | A-6000 | (c) L 1302 | 29/8/17 |
| As above, pt 2 | | 49248-2 | A-6000 | (c) L 1302 | 19/9/17 |

| | | | | |
|---|---|---|---|---|
| Hungarian Rhapsody No. 12, pt 1 | 49750-2 | A-6161 | | 10/2/20 |
| As above, pt 2 | 49751-2 | A-6161 | | 10/2/20 |
| Liebestraum No. 3 | 49999-1 | A-6217 | | 26/11/21 |
| Liebestraum No. 3 | W98357-4 | 7134-M | (e) 04097 | 1/6/27 |
| Polonaise No. 2 E major, pt 1 | 98000-2 | A-6205 | (c) L 1441 | 29/11/21 |
| As above, pt 2 | 98001-3 | A-6205 | (c) L 1441 | 29/11/21 |
| *MACDOWELL* | | | | |
| *To a Water-Lily | 81298-1 | 30006-D | (b) 2003-M | 29/10/23 |
| *SCHARWENKA* | | | | |
| Polish Dance E flat minor Op. 3 No. 1 | 49639-2 | A-6128 | | 17/6/19 |
| *SCHUMANN* | | | | |
| Etudes Symphoniques Op. 13, Theme; Var. 1; Et. 1; Var. 2; Et. 2 | W98507-3 | 67506-D | | 28/5/28 |
| As above, Et. 3; Var. 3; Et. 4; Var. 5; Et. 6 | W98508-1 | 67506-D | | 28/5/28 |
| As above, Var. 6; Et. 7; Var. 7; Et. 8; Et. 9 | W98540-2 | 67507-D | | 28/5/28 |
| As above, Var. 8; Et. 10; Var. 9; Et. 11; Et. 12, pt 1 | W98541-2 | 67507-D | | 28/5/28 |
| As above, Etude 12, pt 2 | W98542-2 | 67508-D | | 28/5/28 |
| Romance F sharp Op. 28 No. 2 | W98543-3 | 67508-D | (a) M-102 | 28/5/28 |
| Sonata G minor Op. 22, 1st movt pt 1 | W98353-3 | 67509-D | | 1/6/27 |
| As above, 1st movt pt 2 & 2nd movt | W98354-3 | 67509-D | | 1/6/27 |
| As above, 3rd movt & 4th movt pt 1 | W98355-2 | 67510-D | | 1/6/27 |
| As above, 4th movt pt 2 | W98356-3 | 67510-D | | 1/6/27 |
| *Warum? Op. 12 No. 3 | 81587-1 | 30010-D | (b) 2004-M | 27/2/24 |
| *SINDING* | | | | |
| *Rustle of Spring | 81324-3 | 30006-D | (b) 2003-M | 31/10/23 |

**STRAUSS, R.**

| | | | | |
|---|---|---|---|---|
| *(arr. Grainger) Ramble on Love (paraphrase of Love Duet from Der Rosenkavalier), pt 1* | W147871-2 | 1898-D | (b) 2137-M (c) DB 28 | 21/1/29 |
| *As above, pt 2* | W147872-3 | 1898-D | (b) 2137-M (c) DB 28 | 21/1/29 |

**TCHAIKOVSKY**

| | | | | |
|---|---|---|---|---|
| (arr. Grainger) Paraphrase of *Flower Waltz* | 49295-5 | A-6192 | (c) L 1386 | 2/1/18 |

Unissued items made at Columbia Studios (in date order) (N.B. Listing is not made of unissued takes from same sessions of issued material)

| | Matrix and take number | Recording date |
|---|---|---|
| *Stanford-Grainger: *Irish Dance No. 1: March-Jig* | 77294-1, -2 | 28/8/17 |
| *Grainger: *Irish Tune from County Derry* | 77295-1, -2 | 28/8/17 |
| *Grainger: *Gum-suckers March* (with 15th Band of Coast Artillery) | 77303-1, -2, -3 | 1/9/17 |
| *Stanford-Grainger: *Irish Dance No. 1: March Jig* | 77294-3, -4, -5 | 31/10/17 |
| *Grainger: *Irish Tune from County Derry* | 77295-3, -4, -5 | 31/10/17 |
| *Grainger: (a) *One More Day, MyJohn* (b) *Shepherd's Hey* | 77605-1, -2 | 3/1/18 |
| *Grieg: *To the Spring* | 77611-1, -2, -3 | 5/1/18 |
| Debussy: *Toccata* from *Pour le Piano* | 49638-1 | 16/6/19 |
| Schubert-Tausig: *Marche Militaire* | 49932-1 | 18/2/21 |
| *(a) Grainger: *Eastern Intermezzo* (b) Handel-Grainger: *Hornpipe* from *Water Music* | 80489-1, -2 | 2/8/22 |
| *(a) Grainger: *Eastern Intermezzo* (b) Handel-Grainger: *Hornpipe* from *Water Music* | 80489-3 | 3/8/22 |
| *Chopin: *Etude A flat* (unidentified) | 80490-1, -2, -3 | 3/8/22 |
| Liszt: *Hungarian Rhapsody No. 15: Rakoczy March* | 98033-1, -2, -3 | 3/8/22 |
| Liszt: *Hungarian Rhapsody No. 15: Rakoczy March* | 98033-4 | 4/8/22 |
| Debussy: *Jardins sous la pluie* from *Estampes* | 98034-1, -2 | 7/8/22 |
| Debussy: *Jardins sous la pluie* from *Estampes* | 98034-3 | 8/8/22 |
| Stanford-Grainger: *Irish Dance No. 4: Reel* | 98035-1, -2, -3 | 8/8/22 |
| Grainger: *Colonial Song* | 98036-1, -2 | 8/8/22 |

Liszt: Liebestraum No. 3      W98247-1, -2    31/3/26
Schumann: Romance F sharp      W98250-1, -2    1/4/26
Grieg: Norwegian Peasant Dance (unidentified)      W98252-1, -2    1/4/26
\*Grainger: Handel in the Strand      W150875-1, -2, -3    14/10/30
\*Grainger: The Hunter in His Career      W150876-1    14/10/30

*Notes*

i) The Columbia Graphophone Company in the United States changed from the acoustic to the Western Electric System of recording in March 1925.

ii) The Columbia Graphophone Company in the United States changed from 80 rpm to 78 rpm recordings during September 1927.

iii) The take number of matrix 49442 is unidentifiable on the author's copy, but is certainly not the same as the one used for issue on 7001-M since the performances are quite different.

iv) Some of the above Columbia records were certainly issued in South America, though no catalogue details have yet come to hand.

D) *Decca Records Inc. (USA)* Recorded and issued in the United States only. All sides 10" (78 rpm) and issued sides produced as Set No. A-586

| Composer and title | | Matrix number | Recording date | Catalogue number |
|---|---|---|---|---|
| DETT | | | | |
| Excerpt from Prelude (Night), 'In the Bottoms' | 2nd part of: | 73059 | 5/9/45 | 24159 |
| Juba Dance | 1st part of: | 73059 | 5/9/45 | 24159 |
| GRAINGER | | | | |
| Country Gardens | 1st part of: | 73071 | 5/9/45 | 24159 |
| Irish Tune from County Derry | | W73055 | 24/9/45 | 24158 |
| Molly on the Shore | | 72821W | 13/4/45 | 24158 |

| | | | | |
|---|---|---|---|---|
| *One More Day, My John* | 2nd part of: | 73071 | 5/9/45 | 24159 |
| **HORN** | | | | |
| (arr. Scott) *Cherry Ripe* | 2nd part of: | W73059 | 24/9/45 | 24160 |
| **SCOTT** | | | | |
| *Danse Nègre* | 1st part of: | W73059 | 24/9/45 | 24160 |
| *Lento* from *Pierrot Pieces* | | 72807 | 4/4/45 | 24160 |

*Unissued items made at Decca Studios* (in date order)

| Composer and title | Matrix number | Recording date |
|---|---|---|
| Gershwin-Grainger: *The Man I Love* | 72665 | 29/12/44 |
| Grieg-Grainger: Concert transcription of main theme from 1st movt of *Concerto in A minor Op. 16* | 72666 | 29/12/44 |
| Grainger: a) *Country Gardens*  b) *One More Day, My John* | 72667 | 29/12/44 |
| Arndt: *Nola* | 72806 | 4/4/45 |
| Cowell: a) *The Aeolian Harp*  b) *The Lilt of the Reel* | 72812W | 4/4/45 |
| Gershwin-Grainger: *The Man I Love* | 72813W | 4/4/45 |
| Gershwin-Grainger: *The Man I Love* | 73613 | 4/4/45 |
| Grieg-Grainger: Concert transcription of main theme from 1st movt of *Concerto in A minor Op. 16* | 72925 | 11/6/45 |
| Gershwin-Grainger: *Love Walked In* | 73156 | 11/6/45 |
| Cowell: a) *The Aeolian Harp*  b) *The Lilt of the Reel* | 73072 | 5/9/45 |

(N.B. The above information was taken from the files of the Decca Record Company Limited in London and Decca Records Inc. in New York. It must be pointed out, however, that there are some radical differences between these details and the entries made in Grainger's own diaries. Grainger was meticulously accurate in his diary entries and in the interests of completeness it was thought best to include them as a separate entry in this list in order that they may be set against the details from the recording companies:—

a) 5/4/45: 'Decca studios. Recorded "The Man I Love".'
b) 13/4/45: 'Decca studios. Recorded "C.G." "One more day" no good.'
c) 11/6/45: 'Recorded at Deccas Grieg 5 times, Danse Negre & Cherry.'
d) 5/9/45: 'Rehearsed all day with F Resta & West Point Band.'
e) 3/10/45: 'Decca, Recorded Turkey, Juba & Prel.'
f) 5/10/45: 'Decca Recorded C Gardens, One more day, 2 Cowells (finished recording).'
g) 24/11/45: 'Practised & recorded "Love walked in" at Decca [. . .]. Heard thru & passed final pressings.'

E) RCA Victor (USA) Recorded in 7th floor ballroom, Manhattan Centre, 311 West 34th Street, New York. Issued in the United States and Great Britain (HMV)

| Composer and title | | Recording date | RCA 12" 33⅓ rpm lp Catalogue number | RCA 7" 45 rpm ep Catalogue number | HMV 7" 45 rpm ep Catalogue number |
|---|---|---|---|---|---|
| **GRAINGER** | | | | | |
| *Country Gardens* | (with Leopold Stokowski | 31/5/50 | LM 1238 | | |
| *Handel In the Strand* | and His Orchestra) | 31/5/50 | LM 1238 | ERA 124 | 7 ER 5046 |
| *Shepherd's Hey* | | 31/5/50 | LM 1238 | | |

*Notes*

a) In *Country Gardens* and *Shepherd's Hey* Grainger appears as an instrumentalist within the orchestra and not as a high-lighted soloist.

b) On the same date as the above recordings were made, Stokowski and His Orchestra recorded: *Molly on the Shore, Mock Morris*, and on 8/11/50 *Irish Tune from County Derry, Early One Morning*, but though Grainger was at the studios he did not play.

c) Two unidentified and unissued items were recorded at the session of 31/5/50.

F) *The Vanguard Recording Society Inc.* (USA) Recorded 25/2/57 with Per Drier and the Aarhus Municipal Orchestra, live performance in the Aarhus 'Scala' hall, Denmark. Scheduled for release in United States but withdrawn shortly before date of issue, though a few copies reached the New York record shops. Catalogue number: VRS 1098 (33⅓ rpm 12").

*GRAINGER*
   *Country Gardens* (solo)
   *Suite on Danish Folk-Songs*

*GRIEG*
   *Piano Concerto in A minor Op. 16*

*STRAUSS, R.*
   *Ramble on Love* (Paraphrase of love duet from *Der Rosenkavalier*) (solo)

G) *Decca Records Inc.* (USA) Recorded and issued in United States only. P. Grainger (pf) with the Goldman Band under Richard Franko Goldman, issued on 12" 33⅓ rpm lp and recorded New York 15/8/57 on matrix number 103078, at Pythian Temple, 135 West 70th Street.

*GRAINGER*
   *Children's March—Over the Hills and Far Away*

APPENDIX E

# Duo-Art Piano Rolls made by Grainger

I wish to express my gratitude to my friend Gerald Stonehill for rescuing me from the inadequacies and obscurities of the Australian Duo-Art cataloguing system and providing me with much necessary information. —J.B.

| Composer and title | Roll number | Issue date |
|---|---|---|
| Bach-Liszt | | |
| Organ Fantasia and Fugue in G minor | 7161 & 7174 | 1927 |
| Bizet-Grainger | | |
| L'Arlésienne Suite | 524 & 525 | 1925 |
| | D-611 & D-613 | |
| Brahms-Grainger | | |
| Cradle Song Op. 49 No. 4 | 6718 & D-1019 | 1923 |
| Chopin | | |
| Etude Op. Posth. No. 2 in A flat | 6548 | 1921 |
| Debussy | | |
| Toccata from Pour le Piano | 6409 | 1921 |
| Delius | | |
| Piano Concerto (2 rolls only of piano transcription of orchestral part) | | |
| | | 1921 |
| | | (unissued) |
| Delius-Grainger | | |
| Brigg Fair (transcription for 2 pianos | | |
| played by Grainger and Ralph Leopold) | 7443 | 1933 |
| North Country Sketches (played by Grainger | | |
| and Ralph Leopold: 2 pianos) | 7190/1 & 2 | 1928 |
| Dett | | |
| Juba Dance (from In the Bottoms) | 6339 | 1920 |
| Fauré-Grainger | | |
| Nell Op. 18 No. 1 | 6931 | 1926 |
| Gardiner | | |
| Humoresque | 6415 | 1921 |
| Grainger | | |
| Children's March: Over the Hills and Far Away | | |
| (played by Grainger and Lotta M. Hough: | | |
| 4 hands, 1 piano) | 6368 | 1920 |

| | | |
|---|---|---|
| *Children's March: Over the Hills and Far Away* | | |
| (2nd piano part only) | 1184 | 1920 |
| *Colonial Song* | 5666 | 1915 |
| *Country Gardens* | 6149 | 1919 |
| *Eastern Intermezzo* | 6997 | 1926 |
| *Eastern Intermezzo* (for 6 hands—4-hand roll) | 1185 | 1926 |
| *Gay but Wistful* | 6072 | 1919 |
| *Gum-suckers March* | 6059 | 1919 |
| *Irish Tune from County Derry* | 5679 | 1915 |
| *Jutish Medley* | 7274 | 1928 |
| *Lullaby* (from *Tribute to Foster*) | 5821 | 1917 |
| *Mock Morris* | 5688 | 1915 |
| *Molly on the Shore* | 6284 | 1920 |
| *One More Day, My John* | 6030 | 1919 |
| *A Reiver's Neck Verse* (song accompaniment | | |
| for tenor or soprano) | 1142 | 1925 |
| *Shepherd's Hey* | 5661 | 1915 |
| *Spoon River* | 6617 | 1923 |
| *Sussex Mummers' Christmas Carol* | 5712 | 1915 |
| *Two Musical Relics of My Mother* | 6760 | 1924 |
|    a) *Hermund the Evil* | | |
|    b) *As Sally sat a-weeping* | | |
| (played by Rose and Percy Grainger) | | |
| *Walking Tune* | 5735 | 1916 |
| *The Warriors* (specially made for the 100th | | |
| anniversary of Denton, Cottier & Daniels, | | |
| Buffalo NY) | | 1927 |
| *Zanzibar Boat Song* | 6824 | 1925 |
| Grieg | | |
| *Ballade in G minor: Variations on a* | | |
| *Norwegian Folk-song Op. 24* | 7437 | 1933 |
| *Concerto in A minor Op. 16* (with orchestral | | |
| accompaniment adapted and added by | | |
| Grainger) | 6475/79/85 | |
| | D-93/95/97 | 1921 |
| *Erotikon Op. 43 No. 5* | 6693 | 1924 |
| *Hochzeitstag auf Troldhaugen Op. 65 No. 6* | 7370 | 1930 |
| *Norwegian Folk-songs Op. 66* | | |
|    a) *Cattle Call* (No. 1) | | |
|    b) *Love Song* (No. 2) | | |
|    c) *In Old Valley* (No. 14) | | |
|    d) *Wedding Song* (No. 10) | | |
|    e) *Gjerdine's Cradle Song* (No. 19) | | |
|    f) *Peasant Dance* (No. 16) | | |
|    g) *Wrapt in Thought I Wander* No. 18) | 7337 | 1930 |
| *To the Spring Op. 43 No. 6* | 6206 | 1920 |
| Grieg-Grainger | | |
| *Peer Gynt Suite Op. 46 No. 1* | | |
|    1) *Morning*    3) *Anitra's Dance* | 6522 | 1922 |

| | | |
|---|---|---|
| 2) *Ase's Death*  4) *In the Hall of the Mountain King* | 6530 | 1922 |
| Guion | | |
| *Sheep and Goat Walkin' to the Pasture* | 7083 | 1927 |
| *Turkey in the Straw* | 6444 | 1921 |
| Handel-Grainger | | |
| *Hornpipe* (from *Water Music*) | 6754 | 1924 |
| Liszt | | |
| *Hungarian Rhapsody No. 12* | 6497 | 1921 |
| *Polonaise No. 2 in E major* | 6668 | 1923 |
| Schumann | | |
| *Etudes Symphoniques Op. 13* Nos 1-8 | 6859 | 1925 |
| Nos 9-12 | 6868 | 1925 |
| *Romance Op. 28 No. 2* | 6384 | 1920 |
| *Sonata No. 2 Op. 22 in G minor* | 7361/2/3 | 1930 |
| Scott | | |
| *Lento Op. 35 No. 1* | 7252 | 1929 |
| *Lotus Land Op. 47 No. 1* | 7217 | 1929 |
| Scott-Grainger/Scott | | |
| *Symphonic Dance No. 1* (played by Grainger and Scott) | 6514 | 1922 |
| Stanford-Grainger | | |
| *Four Irish Dances:* | | |
| a) *March Jig (Maguire's Kick)* (No. 1) | 6572 | 1922 |
| b) *Reel* (No. 4) | 6117 | 1919 |
| c) *Leprechaun's Dance* (No. 3) | 6527 & D-278 | 1922 |
| Strauss, R.-Grainger | | |
| *Till Eulenspiegel's Merry Pranks Op. 28* (for 2 pianos. Played by Grainger and Ralph Leopold) | 7400 | 1932 |
| Tchaikovsky | | |
| *Piano Concerto No. 1 in B flat minor Op. 23* (Solo part only) | C-1087/8/9/90 | 1925 |
| Tchaikovsky-Grainger | | |
| *Nutcracker Suite Op. 71a* | | |
| a) *March* | | |
| b) *Dance of the Candy Fairy* | | |
| c) *Russian Dance—Trepak* | 6798 | 1924 |
| d) *Arab Dance* | | |
| e) *Chinese Dance* | | |
| f) *Dance of the Reed Flutes* | 6810 | 1924 |
| Paraphrase of *Flower Waltz* from *Nutcracker Suite* | 6085 | 1919 |
| *Romeo and Juliet: Fantasy-Overture* (arranged for 4 hands. Played by Grainger and Leopold) | 7351 | 1930 |

APPENDIX F

# Select Discography: Performances of Grainger's Works by Others

This random list reflects its compiler's own taste, and includes the finest performances known to him. Items included in Appendix D are not duplicated in this list for it can be taken for granted that all Grainger's own recordings can be recommended without reservation. Though some of the records in the following list are deleted from the current catalogues and some are even in 78 rpm format, they can be heard with little difficulty in the state archives of recorded sound of most countries. All records are 12" 33⅓ rpm unless otherwise stated.

The last two items came to the author's notice as this work was going to press, and have not been heard by him.

J.B.

W. Forbes (vla): *Arrival Platform Humlet* (unacc)/*Sussex Mummers' Christmas Carol* (with E. de Chaulieu (pf) ). UK: Decca M 540 (10" 78 rpm); Australia: Decca Y 5977 (10" 78 rpm).

B. Harrison (vlc)/Orchestra/M. Sargent: *Youthful Rapture*. UK: HMV C 1929 (12" 78 rpm).

N. Stone (ten)/Oriana Madrigal Society/Kennedy Scott: *Brigg Fair*. UK: HMV E 473 (10" 78 rpm).

Frederick Fennell/Eastman Wind Ensemble: *Lincolnshire Posy*. Included on US: Mercury SR 90173; UK: Mercury AMS 16023.

Frederick Fennell/Eastman Wind Ensemble: *Hill-Song Number 2*. Included on US: SR 90221, SR 90388; UK: Mercury AMS 16078, Fontana 6747177.

Ossip Gabrilowitsch (pf): *Shepherd's Hey*. US: Victor 1095 (10" 78 rpm), included on LM 2824; UK: HMV DA 717 (10" 78 rpm), included on Victor VIC 1210.

I. Partridge (ten)/Elizabethan Singers/L. Halsey: *Brigg Fair*. Included on UK: Argo ZRG 5496.

P. Pears (ten)/B. Britten (pf): *Six Dukes went Afishin'*. UK: HMV DA 2032 (10" 78 rpm), 7EP268 (7" 45 rpm), 7EP7071 (7" 45 rpm).

Philadelphia Wind Quintet: *Walking Tune*. Included on US: Columbia MS 6584.

Benjamin Britten/English Chamber O/soloists and chorus: *Shepherd's Hey*; *Willow Willow*; *I'm Seventeen Come Sunday*; *Bold William Taylor*; *There was a Pig went out to Dig*; *My Robin is to the Greenwood Gone*; *Lord Maxwell's Goodnight*; *Duke of Marlborough Fanfare*; *Let's Dance Gay in Green Meadow*; *Scotch Strathspey and Reel*; *The Pretty Maid milkin' her Cow*; *The Sprig of Thyme*; *Lisbon*; *Shallow Brown*. UK: Decca SXL 6410; US: London CS 6632; Australia: Decca SXL 6410.

Frederick Fennell/Eastman Rochester 'Pops': *Country Gardens*; *Shepherd's Hey*; *Colonial Song*; *Children's March*; *The Immovable Do*; *Mock Morris*; *Handel in the Strand*; *Irish Tune from County Derry*; *Spoon River*; *My Robin is to the Greenwood Gone*; *Molly on the Shore*. US: Mercury SR 90219; UK: Mercury AMS 16060, Wing 18060, World Record Club (WRC) ST 895.

John Hopkins/Sydney SO: *Youthful Suite*; *My Robin is to the Greenwood Gone*; *Mock Morris*; *Irish Tune from County Derry*. Australia: WRC S 4433.

John Hopkins/Sydney SO/soloists and chorus: *Country Gardens*; *Harvest Hymn*; *Under En Bro*; *Over the hills and far away*; *The lonely desert man sees the tents of the happy tribes*; *Colonial Song*; *Duke of Marlborough Fanfare*; *Shallow Brown*; *Handel in the Strand*; *Harvest Hymn*; *La Vallée des Cloches (arr. from Ravel)*; *Scotch Strathspey and Reel*. UK: EMI EMD 5514; Australia: WRC S 5257.

Harry Begian/University of Illinois Symphonic Band: *Over the Hills and Far Away*; *Colonial Song*; *Lads of Wamphray*; *Lincolnshire Posy*; *Ye Banks and Braes O' Bonnie Doon*; *Handel in the Strand*; *Spoon River*; *Hill-Song Number 2*; *Duke of Marlborough Fanfare*; *The Immovable Do*; *Irish Tune from County Derry*; *Shepherd's Hey*; *Country Gardens*; *The Power of Rome and the Christian Heart*. Private recording (2 lp 33⅓ rpm stereo set) available only from University of Illinois or Percy Grainger Library Society USA.

Daniel Adni (pf): *Country Gardens*; Fauré, *Nell*, Op. 18 No. 1, arr. Grainger; *Irish Tune from County Derry*; *Molly on the Shore*; *Nordic Princess*; *Lullaby*; *Over the Hills and Far Away*; *Handel in the Strand*; *Walking Tune*; *Knight and Shepherd's Daughter*; Gershwin, *Love walked in,* arr. Grainger; Gershwin, *The man I love*, arr. Grainger; *Shepherd's Hey*; *Sailors Song*; *Eastern Intermezzo*. UK: EMI HQS — .

Leslie Howard (pf): *Jutish Medley*; *To a Nordic Princess*; *Colonial Song*; *Sussex Mummers' Christmas Carol*; *The Merry King*; *One More Day, My John*; *Country Gardens*; *Shepherd's Hey*; *Harvest Hymn*; *Molly on the Shore*; *Handel in the Strand*; *Knight and Shepherd's Daughter*; *Mock Morris*. Australia: WRC — .

# Index